OXFORD MODERN LANGUAGES
AND LITERATURE MONOGRAPHS

Editorial Committee

A. KAHN   K. M. KOHL

M. L. MCLAUGHLIN   I. W. F. MACLEAN

R. A. G. PEARSON   M. SHERINGHAM   J. THACKER

Landscapes of Desire in the Poetry of Vittorio Sereni

FRANCESCA SOUTHERDEN

OXFORD
UNIVERSITY PRESS

Great Clarendon Street, Oxford OX2 6DP

Oxford University Press is a department of the University of Oxford.
It furthers the University's objective of excellence in research, scholarship,
and education by publishing worldwide in

Oxford New York

Auckland Cape Town Dar es Salaam Hong Kong Karachi
Kuala Lumpur Madrid Melbourne Mexico City Nairobi
New Delhi Shanghai Taipei Toronto

With offices in

Argentina Austria Brazil Chile Czech Republic France Greece
Guatemala Hungary Italy Japan Poland Portugal Singapore
South Korea Switzerland Thailand Turkey Ukraine Vietnam

Oxford is a registered trade mark of Oxford University Press
in the UK and in certain other countries

Published in the United States
by Oxford University Press Inc., New York

© Francesca Southerden 2012

The moral rights of the author have been asserted
Database right Oxford University Press (maker)

First published 2012

All rights reserved. No part of this publication may be reproduced,
stored in a retrieval system, or transmitted, in any form or by any means,
without the prior permission in writing of Oxford University Press,
or as expressly permitted by law, or under terms agreed with the appropriate
reprographics rights organization. Enquiries concerning reproduction
outside the scope of the above should be sent to the Rights Department,
Oxford University Press, at the address above

You must not circulate this book in any other binding or cover
and you must impose the same condition on any acquirer

British Library Cataloguing in Publication Data
Data available

Library of Congress Cataloging in Publication Data
Data available

Typeset by SPI Publisher Services, Pondicherry, India
Printed in Great Britain
on acid-free paper by
MPG Books Group, Bodmin and King's Lynn

ISBN 978–0–19–969845–5

1 3 5 7 9 10 8 6 4 2

For my parents, John and Eliana

Acknowledgements

This book could not have been written without the help and advice of several people. Above all, I would like to thank my former supervisor, Ela Tandello, and Lele Gragnolati for their immense support and encouragement, and especially their friendship. I can only hope that a little of their extraordinary talent as scholars and teachers has rubbed off on me. I am also very grateful to Peter Hainsworth and to Giulio Lepschy for their feedback on my work, and to all my friends and former colleagues in the Oxford Italian Sub-faculty, both past and present, who have provided invaluable criticism and suggestions.

I began work on this project as a doctoral student at Hertford College, Oxford, and I am grateful to the Arts and Humanities Research Council for funding my research in that period. The project developed during my time as a Postdoctoral Researcher at Somerville College, Oxford, to whom I am indebted for its generous support over a number of years, and for providing such a stimulating and friendly environment in which to work. I would also like to express my thanks to my former colleagues at St Anne's College, Oxford, and to everyone in the Department of Italian Studies at Wellesley College, who saw me through the final stages of the preparation of the manuscript and kept me smiling through the cloudy as well as sunny days of research. Many thanks also to Ariane Petit, at Oxford University Press, for her help and advice with getting the manuscript to press.

In Italy, my thanks are due to the staff at the *Biblioteca Comunale* in Luino who helped me during my visit there in 2005, and especially to Barbara Colli, Curator and former Director of the Archivio Vittorio Sereni, who gave her time so generously during my stay. To her I undoubtedly owe my sensibility for all the aspects of the Luinese landscape that influenced Sereni's poetry.

I am also very grateful to Vittorio Sereni's daughters, Silvia and Giovanna Sereni, for the kindness and attentiveness with which they have supported and followed the evolution of my project. Thanks to their generosity in allowing me to reproduce extensive selections from Sereni's poetry and prose, some previously unpublished material also appears here for the first time.

My sincerest thanks also to Marcus Perryman, with whom I collaborated in preparing the translations of Sereni's prose and poetry not included in his and Peter Robinson's *The Selected Poetry and Prose of*

Vittorio Sereni: A Bilingual Edition. His comments were invaluable in helping me to capture in English the depth and intellectual rigour of Sereni's writings on literature.

So many of my friends became essential interlocutors at different stages of the writing process. Amongst them, I would particularly like to thank: Eleanor Parker, with whom I spent long hours discussing the poetics of loss, mourning, and melancholia, fuelled by copious amounts of her homemade brownies; Helen Anderson, who reminded me how important it is to always balance life with laughter; and Hilary Powell, who inspired me with her passion for the Middle Ages and her Olympian discipline in both rowing and research.

Most of all I want to thank my parents, John and Eliana, and my brother Marcus, for their love, kindness, and support through all my endeavours.

Permissions

Grateful acknowledgement is made for permission to reproduce the following copyright material:

The poetry and prose of Vittorio Sereni © Copyright The Estate of Vittorio Sereni. All rights reserved.

Il porto sepolto by Giuseppe Ungaretti, taken from *Vita d'un uomo: tutte le poesie* © Arnaldo Mondadori Editore S.p.A., Milano.

'Oltranzo Oltraggio', from Andrea Zanzotto, *Le poesie e prose scelte* (Milan: Mondadori, 1999) © Copyright Andrea Zanzotto. All rights reserved.

Despite my efforts, some copyright holders had not replied to correspondence at the time this book went to press. If you hold or administer rights for materials published here, please contact the publishers. Any errors or omissions will be corrected in subsequent editions.

Translations

Where available, I have used published translations of poems from the works of Dante, Leopardi, Montale, Petrarch, and Sereni. Thanks for permission to reproduce that material is owed as follows:

Translations of Dante: from *The Inferno* by Dante Alighieri, translated by Robert and Jean Hollander, translation copyright © 2000 by Robert Hollander and Jean Hollander. Used by permission of Doubleday, a division of Random House, Inc.; from *Purgatorio* by Dante Alighieri, translated by Robert and Jean Hollander, translation copyright © 2003 by Robert Hollander and Jean Hollander. Used by permission of Doubleday, a division of Random House, Inc.; from *Paradiso*, by Dante Alighieri, Introduction & Notes by Robert Hollander, translated by Robert and Jean Hollander, translation copyright © 2007 by Robert Hollander and Jean Hollander. Used by permission of Doubleday, a division of Random House, Inc.

Translations of Leopardi, reprinted by permission of the publisher, from Giacomo Leopardi, *The Canti: With a Selection of His Prose*, translated from the Italian by J. G. Nichols, Manchester: Carcanet, Copyright © J. G. Nichols 1994.

Translations of Petrarch, reprinted by permission of the publisher, from *Petrarch's Lyric Poems: The 'Rime sparse' and Other Lyrics*, translated and edited by Robert M. Durling, pp. 36, 86–8, 100, 240–42, 244, 246, 362, 498, Cambridge, Mass.: Harvard University Press, Copyright © 1976 by Robert M. Durling.

Translations of Sereni, reprinted by permission of the publisher, from *The Selected Poetry and Prose of Vittorio Sereni: A Bilingual Edition*, edited and translated by Peter Robinson and Marcus Perryman, Chicago; London: The University of Chicago Press, Copyright © 2006 by The University of Chicago.

All translations of other material are my own, unless otherwise stated.

The cover image of this book was painted by my mother and is inspired by her own reading of Sereni. It captures the fugitive quality of his landscapes of desire perfectly and I want to thank her for the passion and creative spirit with which she approached the project.

Contents

List of Figures	xiii
List of Abbreviations	xiv

Introduction: Assembling the Lyric Universe	1
The place/space of the lyric	1
Infatuations	4
Itineraries	7
Parameters	24

1 *Carte dell'io*: Towards a Definition of Subjectivity in Sereni	31
The preliminaries of theory	31
Forging a new path for the subject: approaches	33
Psychoanalytic subjects	39
Beyond theory	49

2 Replotting the Textual Landscape: The Role of Deixis in *Frontiera* and *Gli strumenti umani*	51
Towards a theory of deixis	52
Deixis in action	65
Beyond deixis	88

3 'L'incerto lembo': Liminal Topographies from Montale to Sereni	90
Sereni and Montale: a visible dialogue	91
Stella variabile: a poetics of the gaze	102
Beyond liminality	126

4 Poetry as Desire-Space: Petrarchan Ascendancies in *Gli strumenti umani* and *Stella variabile*	128
A topographical revision of Petrarch	128
Petrarch: the phantasm of poetry	132
Places in memory: deixis at phantasma and the question of enabling absence	155
Beyond Petrarch	183

5 'Memorie triste', 'passi perduti': The Melancholy
　Journey and the Return to Dante   185
　　Sereni and Dante: an overview   186
　　Rewriting the melancholy journey   210
　　Suspending the poetics of transition: the discourse
　　　of the melancholic   248
　　Beyond Dante   257

Conclusion: 'Sei più in là': The Destination of Poetry,
the Limits of Identity   258

Appendix: Guide to Index of Archive Catalogue, Archivio
Vittorio Sereni, Luino (Varese)   267

Bibliography   268
Index   281
Index of Titles of Poems by Vittorio Sereni   292

List of Figures

3.1. The inverse operations of eye and gaze. 108

3.2. The triangle of geometral vision, adapted with permission of the publisher from Jacques Lacan, *Le Séminaire, Livre XI: Les quatre concepts fondamentaux de la psychanalyse*, ed. by Jacques Alain-Miller © Editions du Seuil, 1973. 108

List of Abbreviations

WORKS BY VITTORIO SERENI

APS   Archivio Vittorio Sereni, Luino (Varese)

References made to archive documents correspond to those used in the Archive's catalogue, based on the system of classification used when the archive was still housed in Sereni's private abode [Archivio Privato della famiglia Sereni] (see Appendix)

DA   *Diario d'Algeria* [*Algerian Diary*]

GA   *Il grande amico: poesie 1935–1981* [*The Great Friend: Poems 1935–1981*]

ID1   *Gli immediati dintorni* [*The Immediate Surroundings*]

ID2   *Gli immediati dintorni: primi e secondi* [*The Immediate Surroundings: First and Second*]

SG   *Sentieri di gloria: note e ragionamenti sulla letteratura* [*Paths of Glory: Notes and Thoughts on Literature*]

SOA   *Senza l'onore delle armi* [*Without the Honour of Arms*]

SU   *Gli strumenti umani* [*The Human Implements*]

SV   *Stella variabile* [*Variable Star*]

TDP   *La tentazione della prosa* [*The Temptation of Prose*]

Un posto   *Un posto di vacanza* [*A Holiday Place*]

OTHER WORKS

RVF   Francesco Petrarca, *Rerum vulgarium fragmenta*

SE   Sigmund Freud, *The Standard Edition of the Complete Psychological Works of Sigmund Freud*

A NOTE ABOUT REFERENCES TO POEMS BY SERENI

References to poems by Sereni are to the *Meridiano* edition of Sereni's poetry, *Poesie*, ed. by Dante Isella, 4th edn (Milan: Mondadori, 2000), unless otherwise stated.

References to Sereni's *Un posto di vacanza* are given in the following form: title, section number, line number(s), page reference to the *Meridiano* edition of Sereni's poetry, e.g. *Un posto* I, 1–2, p. 223.

All emphasis (in italics) in quotations is mine, unless otherwise stated.

Introduction

Assembling the Lyric Universe

'Nel paesaggio italiano collocavo dei ricordi'[1]
(Dino Campana, note to Pariani on his *Arabesco-Olimpia*)

THE PLACE/SPACE OF THE LYRIC

When, in 1957, Vittorio Sereni defined the space of the modern lyric as one progressively estranged from the 'luogo ideale' [ideal place] that had constituted its point of origin, he attested to his place in a poetic landscape that stretched back as far as Dante and Petrarch while pointing forward to the evolving parameters of his own lyric practice:

> Da Leopardi a Pavese la situazione lirica cui la disposizione solitaria dell'-anima offre spunto si va scostando sempre più dal suo elementare, classico schema, da quella specie di *luogo ideale*, antico come la poesia lirica, che dello stato di solitudine faceva il *punto d'equilibrio delle passioni*, il *recupero di esse* nell'*attitudine contemplativa*, la condizione stessa della poesia in quanto *fervido strumento di conoscenza*.[2]
>
> [From Leopardi to Pavese, the lyric situation occasioned by the solitary disposition of the soul distanced itself further and further from its elementary, classical schema, from a sort of *ideal place*, as ancient as lyric poetry itself, which made of the state of solitude the *point of balance between the passions*,

---

[1] [In the Italian landscape, I situated memories.]
[2] Vittorio Sereni, 'Da Apollinaire' ['From Apollinaire'] (1957), in *Gli immediati dintorni primi e secondi* [*The Immediate Surroundings: First and Second*] [*ID2*], ed. Maria Teresa Sereni (Milan: Il Saggiatore, 1983), pp. 59–60. This extract comes from a prose piece which, in the first edition of *Gli immediati dintorni* [*The Immediate Surroundings*] [*ID1*] (Milan: Il Saggiatore, 1962), accompanied Sereni's translation of Guillaume Apollinaire's 'Le Pont Mirabeau' ['Mirabeau Bridge']. The piece was originally conceived as a presentation to accompany a disc produced by La Cetra on the theme of *solitudine* [solitude], recorded in 1957. Amongst the texts chosen by Sereni for the theme, and read by Giorgio Albertazzi, was Apollinaire's poem.

their recovery within a *contemplative attitude*, the very condition of poetry as *a fervent instrument of knowledge*.]

He also measured his distance from any conception of landscape as fulfilment, establishing it rather as the site of a quest, or questioning, that would take it far beyond the more static, Romantic, idea of a world viewed as an extension of the self or as its ideal counterpart.

Sereni's perspective on the panorama of lyric poetry is clear. In its ideal form, the lyric answered to the highest conception of poetry; it was a centralizing and utopian force for a contemplative subject content with gazing on itself and making its solitude the privileged store of its poetic imagination. It was also an idyll, largely self-sustaining, where the 'I'/eye could find place and meaning in a world, more ideal than real, that mirrored its desires perfectly—the locus of a visionary experience that also allowed deep insights into the self, which such contemplation brought (one could think of the quintessential, idyllic pose of Leopardi's 'L'infinito' ['The Infinite'] or Petrarch's 'Chiare, fresche et dolci acque' ['Clear, fresh, sweet waters']).[3]

For Sereni, however, who had by this stage come to view the 'narcissism of the Petrarchan Subject' as a 'veritable original sin of lyric discourse', the landscape of lyric poetry had irrevocably altered.[4] Coinciding with the revolution in his own poetic project that would be constituted by the poems of *Gli strumenti umani* [*The Human Implements*] (henceforth *SU*),

---

[3] Cf. Ll. 4–7 of Leopardi's 'L'infinito', '[...] sedendo e mirando, interminati | spazi di là da quella, e sovrumani | silenzi, e profondissima quiete | io nel pensier mi fingo' [[...] sitting here and gazing, I find that endless | Spaces beyond that hedge, and more-than-human | Silences, and the deepest peace and quiet | Are fashioned in my thought]; and the first strophe of Petrarch's canzone, *RVF* CXXVI, 'Chiare, fresche et dolci acque', in which the poetic 'I' beseeches the landscape (the store or screen of memory) to 'date udïenzia insieme | a le dolenti mie parole extreme' [listen altogether to my sorrowful dying words] (ll. 12–13). Quotations from the *Canti* come from Giacomo Leopardi, *Canti*, ed. by Niccolò Gallo and Cesare Garboli (Turin: Einaudi, 1993), and translations from Giacomo Leopardi, *The Canti: with a Selection of His Prose*, trans. J. G. Nichols (Manchester: Carcanet, 1994). Quotations from Petrarch come from Francesco Petrarca, *Canzoniere*, ed. Gianfranco Contini (Turin: Einaudi, 1992), and translations from *Petrarch's Lyric Poems: the 'Rime sparse' and Other Lyrics*, trans. and ed. Robert M. Durling (Cambridge, Mass.: Harvard University Press, 1976). When referring to Petrarch's text I however use the Latin title, *F[rancisci] P[etrarce] laureati poete rerum vulgarium fragmenta*, which Petrarch gave to his collection of poems in 1368, which better reflects the tension between dispersal and integration in the work as a whole. For a longer discussion of the significance of the title, see Peter Hainsworth, *Petrarch the Poet: An Introduction to the 'Rerum vulgarium fragmenta'* (London: Routledge, 1988), pp. 31–2.

[4] Emmanuela Tandello, 'Between Tradition and Transgression: Amelia Rosselli's Petrarch', in *Petrarch in Britain: Interpreters, Imitators and Translators over 700 years*, ed. Martin McLaughlin and Letizia Panizza with Peter Hainsworth (Oxford: Oxford University Press for the British Academy, 2007), pp. 301–17 (pp. 301–2).

published in 1965, this statement of the loss of the 'luogo ideale' reflects not only Sereni's commitment to charting new territories of poetic subjectivity but also his complex and problematic relationship to the lyric tradition. It was a realization that would carry him far from the place where he had started while instilling in him an intense nostalgia for a poetic moment most desired in its unavailability, which would take him forward by encouraging him to travel ever further back.

For Sereni, knowledge ('conoscenza') can only be the knowledge of loss, 'che la cosa da dire fosse in fondo o un momento o un luogo della propria esperienza *da salvare*' [that what you had to say was, deep down, either a moment or a place in one's experience (existence) *to save*].[5] His landscapes of desire incorporate the aim to recuperate something of the 'ideal space' of the lyric in the present, while moulding it to the very different topography of twentieth-century poetry. The failure of this ideal space to form itself as such, and the different disposition of the poetic 'I' within it, is the material with which this study deals: the very event of subjectivity in language and the poem.

Yet if Sereni resists the autocracy of the lyric 'I' that he has inherited from the Italian poetic tradition, he does not dispense with it completely. This is epitomized in the repeated refrain of the poem by Guillaume Apollinaire, which he quotes alongside his reflections above, in which the poetic subject refuses to take leave: 'Venga la notte suoni l'ora | i giorni vanno io non ancora' [Let night come, let the hour toll | days goes by, I still stay on] ('Il Pont Mirabeau' ['Mirabeau Bridge']). The tenacity of Sereni's own lyric 'I', which endures despite its fragility (its awareness, in a sense, of being *de trop*), provides the creative tension that motivates so much of his poetry, and transforms the space of the lyric into a testing ground for a poetic identity that must reaffirm its right to exist at every turn:

> [Il titolo *La ricerca dell'identità*] non fa che rispondere a un motivo ricorrente nel nostro tempo, tanto da far dire che tutto, oggi, ogni operazione o manifestazione fondata su una volontà espressiva non è altro che ricerca dell'identità. [...] Questa ricerca, almeno nel mio caso, non può fruttare se non riconoscimenti episodici, cioè identificazioni–e autoidentificazioni–parziali e transitorie, è una caccia che non presuppone una preda finale e onni-

---

[5] Vittorio Sereni, 'Il silenzio creativo' ['Creative Silence'] (1962), first publ. in *ID1*, pp. 112–16, now in *ID2*, pp. 74–8 (p. 75); English translation from *The Selected Poetry and Prose of Vittorio Sereni: A Bilingual Edition*, ed. and trans. Peter Robinson and Marcus Perryman (Chicago: University of Chicago Press, 2006) (italics in the original). All translations of Sereni's prose from this edition will be indicated with the short form 'trans. Robinson–Perryman'. All other translations of Sereni's prose are my own.

comprensiva. Vive, se vive, di una contraddizione da cui trapela, a strappi, un originario, vuoi deluso vuoi disatteso vuoi incorrisposto, amore della vita.[6]

[[The title *The Search for Identity*] responds to a recurrent concern in our time, so inescapable nowadays that every piece of work or show founded upon an expressive wish is said to be nothing but a search for identity. [. . .] This search, at least in my case, cannot yield other than sporadic recognitions, that is, partial and transitory identifications—and self-identifications; it is a hunt that doesn't presuppose a final, comprehensive prey. It lives, if it lives, on a contradiction from which filters, on and off, a primary (call it deluded, call it unfulfilled, call it unrequited) love of life.]]

Poetry for Sereni is the product of this contradiction and of a desire that originates in the gap dividing the subject from the promise, or memory, of a primordial state of vitality and completeness, needing to be sought or, at the very best, able to be rediscovered (though only 'a strappi'). It is a journey that does not presuppose any kind of destination but is still motivated by the hope of a return, however disillusioned it may turn out to be. The space of the lyric is also this space of the subject's passage from one partial identification to the other. It is the moment of expectation for a revelation that may be entirely arbitrary in its coming but to which the subject is drawn back again and again in its search for meaning and identity.

INFATUATIONS

Sereni's autobiographical essay, 'Infatuazioni' ['Infatuations'] (1982), which reads almost like a prose poem, is emblematic of this approach. Written just one year before his death, in it he meditates upon the fate of the desiring subject and attests to an infatuation with the landscape of the lyric that has marked his poetry for four decades:

> Qualcuno mi è venuto meno, qualcuno che per me valeva mi respinge, si distoglie, scompare. Allontanandosi allontana, sottrae il paesaggio del quale era stato preannuncio, portatore, segnacolo. Non intende essere più, non ha mai inteso essere alcuna di queste cose e rovesciando su di me il mio stesso disinganno smaschera la mistificazione di cui era oggetto.
>
> Disertato il paesaggio, monco io stesso della parte che dentro me teneva riuniti luogo e persona, se altri li nomina fingo di non aver udito o di avere la testa altrove, svio il discorso. Cancellando in me un viso cancello il paese che

---

[6] Vittorio Sereni, 'Autoritratto' ['Self-Portrait'] (1978), first publ. in *La Rassegna della letteratura italiana* 85, ser. 7.3 (Sept.–Dec. 1981), pp. 427–9, now in *ID2*, pp. 127–32 (pp. 131–2); trans. Robinson–Perryman.

gli era congiunto per affinità inebrianti. Cambio i nomi alle targhe, inverto le insegne, vado in direzione opposta.

Ma è come la montagna di Cézanne: astratta nella sua ripetuta presenza, indicibilmente viva nel suo arioso riproporsi. Il grembo di una medesima vallata mi si apre nuovo e diverso, un già noto pendìo è assolato di futuro.

Solo adesso comprendo che come un viso mi era stato preannuncio, portatore, segnacolo di un paesaggio, così è di questo rispetto ad altro che incomincio a intravedere. Ben oltre il paesaggio.

O almeno mi pare.

Posso tornare sui miei passi, ricominciare di là.[7]

[Someone has gone from me, someone who counted for me is rejecting me, breaking free, disappearing. Distancing himself, he grows distant, withdraws the landscape to which he was prelude, bearer, sign. He no longer intends, never intended to be, any of these things, and, spilling over me my own disenchantment, he unmasks the mystification of which he was the object.

The countryside deserted, me deprived of the part that within me held place and person together, if others mention them I pretend not to have heard or have my mind on other things, I change subject. Cancelling within me a face, I cancel the town it was inseparable from, such were their dizzying affinities. I change the names on road signs, turn the signposts round, take the opposite direction.

But it's like Cézanne's mountain: abstract in its repeated presence, unspeakably alive in its airy persistence. The womb of one self-same valley opens, new and different, a recognized slope is sun-drenched with the future.

Only now do I understand that just as a face was for me the prelude, carrier, sign of a landscape, so is this with respect to something other I start to glimpse. Far beyond the landscape.

Or at least so it seems.

I can retrace my steps, can start again over there.]

Like all infatuations, the mystery of the landscape has begun to wear off, but this has done nothing to lessen its hold on the poet. The 'I' finds itself engaged in a dialogue with the natural world that is problematically one-sided, at the mercy of another, and based upon an act of essential 'disinganno'—a *misrecognition* of what is there. The landscape, and the

---

[7] Vittorio Sereni, 'Infatuazioni' (1982), first publ. in *Sul porto* (Cesenatico), numero unico (1983), p. 32, now in *ID2*, p. 147; trans. Robinson–Perryman. Sereni's implicit interlocutor—designated only as 'qualcuno' [someone]–is thought by Franco Fortini to be the French poet René Char, whom Sereni had translated in the late 1950s and again in the early 1970s and with whom he had a long-standing friendship. However, given its imaginative and phantasmatic qualities and the way it dissipates and recedes from the poet's grasp, that 'someone' stands as a poetic presence above all. On this, see Franco Fortini, 'Oltre il paesaggio', in his *Nuovi saggi italiani* (Milan: Garzanti, 1987), pp. 182–4 (p. 183, n. 1).

fugitive presence that has been its source, have turned out not to be as the subject imagined them, and now refuse to be so, but he still goes back to them at the end. The place where they meet is the scene of a metamorphosis, both negative and positive: from illusion to disillusionment, from absence (blindness) to restoration of vision, and from desire to its frustration to desiring again.

Above all, landscape is the place in which both the subject and its object go through the effects of fading (*venire meno*), (self-)dispossession, and disillusionment. Seeing beyond the landscape initially involves something like the unmasking of the ideal space of the lyric, for Sereni always to be constructed more than discovered (an intimately Petrarchan perspective). The adjective 'monco' ('maimed' or 'truncated'), used to designate the 'I' laid bare along with the idyll, carries the memory of Montale's 'Crisalide' ['Chrysalis'] in *Ossi di seppia* [*Cuttlefish Bones*] (henceforth *Ossi*), which transforms the newly deserted space into a 'limbo squallido delle monche esistenze' [bleak limbo of maimed existences], the source of a 'prodigio fallito' [failed prodigy] that is also the subject.[8] In turn, the main verb of the clause, *fingere*–of clear Leopardian derivation[9]—is no longer the locus of a leap of the imagination toward the infinite but only the sign of a demystification: an act of denial, of turning away, and above all of avoidance or 'evasione'. As such, Sereni's landscape emerges as the site of a confrontation not only with the world in its irreducible otherness but also with the language of poetry itself in its inimitable range and scope.

Yet the tenacity with which the 'I' clings to the genesis of its fall ultimately turns the landscape back into a space of origins and a possible scene of return. At the turn signalled by the 'Ma', the original locus of the vision, just bared for its duplicity and defunct only moments before, is recuperated and recast as a nascent scene that still promises, so to speak, life *after* death. The whole is suffused with a sense of uncertainty, which is

---

[8] Cf. The fourth strophe of Montale's 'Crisalide', 'Così va la certezza d'un momento | con uno sventolio di tende e di alberi | tra le case; ma l'ombra non dissolve | che vi reclama, opaca. M'apparite | allora, come me, nel limbo squallido | delle monche esistenze; e anche la vostra | rinascita è uno sterile segreto, | un prodigio fallito come tutti | quelli che ci fioriscono d'accanto' [So the sureness of a moment passes | in a fluttering of curtains and trees | among the houses; but the opaque | shadow that reclaims you won't dissolve. | Then you seem, like me, to live | in the bleak limbo of maimed existences; | and even your rebirth is a barren secret, | a failed prodigy like all the others | flowered around us.'] All quotations of Montale's poetry are taken from Eugenio Montale, *L'opera in versi*, ed. Rosanna Bettarini and Gianfranco Contini (Milan: Mondadori, 1980), pp. 85–7 (p. 86), unless otherwise stated. All English translations come from *Eugenio Montale: Collected Poems 1920–54*, rev. bilingual edn, trans. and annotated by Jonathan Galassi (New York: Farrar, Straus and Giroux, 2000), unless otherwise stated.

[9] Cf. Leopardi, 'L'infinito', l. 7, 'nel pensier *mi fingo*' [*are fashioned* in *my* thought], but note that the original Italian carries the active sense of a subjective fashioning.

also the uncanny effect produced by the indistinct boundaries between self and Other in this Arcadian reworking of a primal scene. While the underlying landscape remains unchanged by the passage of the 'I' and its object through it, it appears to have an almost tyrannical effect on both (and even, to follow the structural parallel, one of prohibition). There can be no equality between the two orders, only disproportion, which opens up the space of yearning and thus of desire.

There is thus a connection between Sereni's poetics and his geography that exceeds the boundaries of iconography or the aesthetic and goes to the very roots of his identity and self-definition. Understanding this disposition initially involves situating Sereni's development as a poet in the context of the literary and cultural climate in which he began writing, and the personal experiences that shaped his place within those surroundings. From here, it becomes possible to trace the evolution of that same landscape into, and through, Sereni's poetry to the point at which it returns as a poetic version of itself upon the world and the subject writing.

ITINERARIES

Vittorio Sereni was born on 27 July 1913 in Luino, a town situated on the so-called *sponda magra* [scant shore] of Lake Maggiore, in Lombardy, just a few kilometres from the Swiss border. Sereni spent the first twelve years of his life there before moving to Brescia in 1925 (where his father was transferred for work reasons)—a journey of departure that inspired his first foray into creative writing and already suggests the important place that the memory of Luino was to have in his poetic consciousness.[10] Sereni's childhood, in his own words, 'è stata felice, capitolo a sé stante, che non richiede celebrazioni, patrimonio intatto e intangibile' [was happy, a separate chapter, one which doesn't need celebrating, an intact and

---

[10] 'La prima volta che ho preso penna in mano, per scrivere, avevo circa dodici anni e dovevo lasciare il paese dove sono nato: Luino, sul Lago Maggiore. Non ho scritto una poesia malinconica, come ci si potrebbe aspettare data la situazione, ma una poesia scherzosa, una specie di filastrocca di cui ricordo solo due versi' [The first time I took up a pen to write I was about twelve years old and had to leave the town where I was born: Luino, on Lake Maggiore. I didn't write a melancholy poem, as you might expect given the situation, but a playful poem, a kind of nursery rhyme of which I remember only two lines], Vittorio Sereni, *Sulla poesia: conversazione nelle scuole* [*On Poetry: Conversation in Schools*], ed. Giuliana Massani and Bruno Rivalta (Parma: Pratiche, 1981), pp. 41–62 (p. 41). This is the transcript of two interviews Sereni gave at the Scuola Media Inferiore 'G. Pascoli' and Istituto Tecnico Industriale Statale in Parma on 12 Dec. 1979 in front of a student audience, published together with contributions by Bertolucci, Zanzotto, Porta, Conte, and Cucchi.

intangibile legacy];[11] and whilst he did return to Luino at regular periods throughout his adult life, it was less with a sense of pure nostalgia than with the desire to establish, each time, a new identity with the place: 'Si definisce un paese anche collocandolo in una prospettiva diversa, estraniandolo dalla sua quotidianità per poi tornare su questa con sensi rinnovati, arricchiti da scorrerie in territori che solo l'abitudine ci nasconde' [A town can be defined partly by setting it in a different perspective, estranging it from its everyday life and then returning to it with the senses refreshed, enriched by forays into other territories hidden from us only by habit].[12]

Sereni began writing poetry in earnest around 1930, during his time as a student at the Liceo Classico Arnaldo da Brescia, where he excelled in his studies and was introduced to the great works of Italian literature. From here he went to Milan, in 1932, to study at the Università Statale, which was to be the scene for his most important encounters with the literary world and a history of ideas that would have a marked impact upon his poetic identity. He began his course as a student of Law but soon transferred to *Lettere* [the Arts], majoring in *Estetica* [Aesthetics]. During this period Sereni was taught by the philosopher Antonio Banfi and made close friendships with a group of contemporaries, including Gianni Manzi, Antonia Pozzi, Enzo Paci, Remo Cantoni, Giulio Preti, Daria Menicanti, and Giuliano Carta, for whom 'la poesia diventava un segno di riconoscimento' [poetry became a mark of recognition], who importantly shared a literary tradition as well as an education.[13] Their youthful journal, *Corrente*, established by Ernesto Treccani, provided a point of contact and a forum for literary debate that confirmed Milan's place as a centre of cultural and artistic reflection with connections to the rest of Europe.[14]

---

[11] Vittorio Sereni, 'Dovuto a Montale' ['Owed to Montale'] (1983), destined for publication in *La Rotonda, Almanacco Luinese 1983*, 6, p. 163; this essay is included as the Appendix to *ID2*, pp. 159–66 (p. 159).

[12] Vittorio Sereni, 'Negli anni di Luino' ['In the Luino Years'] (1981), in *ID2*, pp. 133–8 (p. 138). This collection of writings on Luino was first published in instalments in *La Rotonda, Almanacco Luinese 1979*, 1 (Luino, Nastro, 1978), pp. 31–9, *La Rotonda, Almanacco Luinese 1981*, 3 (Luino: Nastro, 1980), pp. 33–8, with the title 'Materie prime' ['First Materials'], and *La Rotonda, Almanacco Luinese 1982*, 4 (Luino: Nastro, 1981), pp. 89–90.

[13] Vittorio Sereni, 'Poesia: per chi?' ['Poetry: For Whom?'], *Rinascita* 32.37 (19 Sept. 1975), 21–2 (p. 22).

[14] 'Un punto fisso d'incontro era *Corrente*, la nostra rivista giovanile, fondata da Ernesto Treccani; è stato un modo per affacciarci all'Italia letteraria. Milano a quell'epoca respirava già un'aria europea e noi come città di Europa l'abbiamo vissuta in quegli anni' [A fixed point of contact was *Corrente*, our youthful journal, founded by Ernesto Treccani; it was a way for us to get started with literary Italy. In that period, Milan already had a European air about it and we lived it as a European city in those years], Vittorio Sereni, Interview with Paola Lucarini, *Firme nostre*, Sept. 1982, p. 3.

If, as Laura Barile suggests, Sereni's *liceo* [high school] period in Brescia fostered a knowledge above all of the triad of Giosuè Carducci, Giovanni Pascoli, and Gabriele D'Annunzio, his time at university extended that knowledge to Guido Gozzano (who was the subject of Sereni's *tesi di laurea* [degree thesis], completed in 1936), and to writers of the contemporary period—from Italian poets such as Giuseppe Ungaretti, Eugenio Montale, Umberto Saba, and the Florentine hermetics (Alessandro Parronchi, Piero Bigongiari, Leonardo Sinisgalli) to writers outside Italy who were prominent on the European stage, including T. S. Eliot, Ezra Pound, Guillaume Apollinaire, Paul Valéry, Federico García Lorca, and Boris Pasternak.[15]

The poetry of *Frontiera* [*Frontier*] (1941),[16] written between 1935 and 1941, was the product of this diversity of literary influences, leading to the apparently paradoxical designation of Sereni as, on the one hand, a poet of the late hermetic period, whose compositions retained the rarefied lexicon and atmosphere of the Florentine model, and, on the other, the realist poet of the 'linea lombarda' [Lombard line], of which Sereni was considered by Luciano Anceschi to be the chief exponent.[17]

However, notwithstanding Sinisgalli's presence in Milan from 1932 onwards, and Gatto's and Quasimodo's after 1934, Sereni's relationship to 'ermetismo' [hermeticism], if not to the *ermetici* [hermetics] themselves, remained ambivalent.[18] His comments to Giancarlo Vigorelli in a letter of 1937, in reference to a polemic surrounding the problematic

---

[15] Laura Barile, *Sereni* (Palermo: Palumbo, 1994), pp. 11–24.

[16] Vittorio Sereni, *Frontiera* (Milan: Corrente, 1941); 2nd rev. edn, *Poesie* (Florence: Vallecchi, 1942); 3rd rev. edn, *Frontiera* (Milan: All'Insegna del Pesce d'Oro, 1966).

[17] The concept of a 'linea lombarda' originates with Anceschi, whose anthology of poetry with the same name (Varese: Magenta, 1952) established Sereni as the key figure amongst a group of poets that also included Luciano Erba, Giorgio Orelli, Roberto Rebora, and Nelo Risi.

[18] See Sereni's comments on his relationship to *ermetismo* in several interviews, including the one with Franco Brioschi (1967), in which he states, 'In fondo anche l'ermetismo era ideologico [...] e da questo punto di vista io ero nettamente antiideologico' [At heart, even hermeticism was ideological [...] and from that point of view I was decidedly anti-ideological], *Fogli di letteratura* 4 (1967), pp. 1–3; with Massimo Grillandi (1972), in which he declared his position to be '*a latere, a latere...*' [*to one side, to one side...*], in Massimo Grillandi, *Vittorio Sereni* (Florence: La Nuova Italia, 1972), pp. 1–6; and with Alessandro Fo (1975), 'L'ermetismo fiorentino era un polo di attrazione semiclandestino per estraneità al fascismo [...]. Io in loro, Lombardo, sentivo una specie di misticismo nei confronti direi del fatto poetico stesso' [Florentine hermeticism was a semi-clandestine pole of attraction because of its distance from fascism. [...] As a Lombard, I sensed in them a kind of mysticism about, I'd say, the fact of poetry itself], but Ungaretti, Montale, and Saba 'non si possono dire ermetici' [can't be called hermetics], 'Un'intervista a V.S.', ed. Alessandro Fo, in *Studi per Riccardo Ribuoli* (Rome: Edizioni di storia e letteratura, 1986), pp. 55–75, all cited in Barile, *Sereni*, p. 16.

notion of 'poesia pura' [pure poetry], and a possible antidote to it in the form of a 'ritorno al canto' [return to lyricism], are revealing in this respect:

> Qui ti mando 'Giorno di Natale' per *Frontespizio*, 'Lo scriba' (dovrebbe uscire in *Meridiano*) e 'Nebbia' perché tu ti faccia un'idea un po' meno vaga. La circostanza merita un discorsetto. Riluttavo a mandarti la prima da sola; non volevo che fosse la presentazione di me poeta. Quasimodo dice che è la mia cosa migliore: può darsi, io preferisco non crederci. Il canto, e va bene. Ma qualche volta è troppo comodo e facile. Per questo l'esperienza di un Sinisgalli è interessante anche se non sono accettabili i risultati. E se Sinisgalli è in certo senso, molto lato, un dannunziano, noi si arrischia di diventarlo– per altro verso–non pigliando con la necessaria cautela i presupposti della questione 'canto'.[19]

> [I'm enclosing 'Giorno di Natale' ['Christmas Day'] for *Frontespizio*, 'Lo scriba' ['The Scribe'] (it should be coming out in *Meridiano*) and 'Nebbia' ['Fog'] so that you get a better idea. The occasion merits a brief excursus. I was reluctant to send you the first poem on its own; I didn't want it to be the presentation of myself as a poet. Quasimodo says it's the best thing I've written: I dare say, I prefer not to think so. 'Lyricism' is all very well. But sometimes it falls too readily to hand and is too easy. That's why what someone like Sinisgalli does is interesting even if the results aren't acceptable. And if Sinisgalli is in a sense, the broadest sense, a Dannunzian, we risk becoming one too—in another way–by not treating with due caution the presuppositions of the issue of 'lyricism'.]

These comments suggest not only that Sereni resisted being too rigidly categorized in one way or the other, but also that the language of hermetic poetry itself carried problematic associations for him. As an idiom Sereni inherited from the Italian poetic tradition, which had its roots in the poetry of Petrarch and Leopardi via the mediation of French Symbolism (especially Mallarmé), it was both a natural and an inherited voice, and as such inclusive and exclusive of Sereni's own aspirations for his lyric project.

---

[19] Letter of 25 January 1937 from Sereni to Vigorelli, reproduced in full in Giancarlo Vigorelli, 'Vittorio Sereni', in *Carte d'identità: Il Novecento letterario in 21 ritratti indiscreti* (Milan: Camunia, 1989), pp. 195–214 (pp. 209–10). 'Giorno di Natale' is the poem that will later become 'Compleanno' ['Birthday'] in *Frontiera*. See Vittorio Sereni, *Poesie*, ed. Dante Isella, 4th edn (Milan: Mondadori, 2000), p. 17. All future references will be to this edition of Sereni's poetry, unless otherwise stated, and page numbers will be included in brackets after the text. Translations of Sereni's poetry are taken from *The Selected Poetry and Prose of Vittorio Sereni: A Bilingual Edition*, ed. and trans. Peter Robinson and Marcus Perryman, unless otherwise indicated. 'Lo scriba' was excluded from *Frontiera* on Vigorelli's own suggestion, 'quasimodiante com'era' [as like Quasimodo as it was] (p. 209).

Implicit in *ermetismo* was a particular view of language and poetry, perhaps best embodied by Ungaretti's poem 'Il porto sepolto' ['The Buried Port'],[20] which privileged an originary but inexpressible event of language bordering on silence, out of which poetry (and the poet) emerged as a kind of pure, even divine, miracle.[21] Sereni's poetry, while somewhat rigidly defined on the Lombard model as a 'poesia degli oggetti' [poetry of objects]—in distinction to the 'poesia della parola' [poetry of the word] advocated by the Florentine hermetics (and thus associated with the 'metaphysical' Montale of *Ossi*, more than Ungaretti, for example)—does still bear traces in *Frontiera* of the hermetic legacy: aspects of its voice or idiom if not its precise lexicon.[22] Certainly, Sereni's own unease in the face of some of his more 'hermetic' compositions attests to his awareness of writing within the purview of an elusive and allusive language at odds with his desire to communicate and express something of the world directly. However, as Andrea Zanzotto suggests, this awareness appears to have fostered a period of critical re-evaluation as opposed to an insurmountable obstacle or contradiction to progress:

---

[20] 'Mariano il 29 giugno 1916. Vi arriva il poeta | E poi torna alla luce con i suoi canti | E li disperde | Di questa poesia | Mi resta | Quel nulla | Di inesauribile segreto' [Mariano, 29 June 1916. The poet reaches that place | And then returns to the light with his songs | And scatters them | Of this poem | There remains for me | The barest nothing | Of an inexhaustible secret], in Giuseppe Ungaretti, *Vita d'un uomo: tutte le poesie*, ed. Leone Piccioni (Milan: Mondadori, 1970), p. 23.

[21] The cult of 'purezza' [purity] was a defining characteristic of Florentine hermeticism and largely tempered in Sereni's poetry by his 'voglia di romanzo' [desire for narrative], along Montalian lines. See Vittorio Sereni, 'Ci appassionò alla vita' ['He Gave Us a Passion for Life'] (1975), first publ. in *Epoca* 26.1309 (8 Nov. 1975), pp. 35–8, now in *Sentieri di gloria: note e ragionamenti sulla letteratura* [*Paths of Glory: Notes and Thoughts on Literature*] [*SG*] (Milan: Mondadori, 1996), pp. 86–9 (p. 89), in which he states, of his experience of writing poetry in the 1930s: 'c'era voglia di romanzo in quegli anni [...]. Era il segno sottile e febbricitante di un possibile mutamento nell'ordine esistente. Si insinuava tra le cose attorno a noi ed era Montale, lo sapesse o no, ad alimentarlo. Questo non aveva proprio niente a che fare con l'ermetismo' [There was desire for narrative in those years [...]. It was the subtle and feverish sign of a possible change in the status quo. It crept into the things around us and it was Montale, whether he knew it or not, who fuelled it. This had absolutely nothing to do with hermeticism]. The notion of 'divinity' or 'religiosity' is perhaps strongest in the poetry of Mario Luzi and certainly absent in Sereni. According to Franco Fortini, there was no place in Sereni's early poetry for metaphysical solutions; even in the face of war, he resisted constructing fixed ideologies in which to take shelter. See 'Le poesie italiane di questi anni' (1959), in Franco Fortini, *Saggi italiani* (Milan: Garzanti, 1987), pp. 96–149 (pp. 124–5).

[22] An excellent summary of the breadth of critical studies available on the relationship of Sereni's *Frontiera* to *ermetismo* can be found in Barile, *Sereni*, pp. 75–85. On the poetics of hermeticism, see at least: Francesco Flora, *La poesia ermetica* (Bari: Laterza, 1936); Mario Petrucciani, *La poetica dell'ermetismo italiano* (Turin: Loescher, 1955); Silvio Ramat, *L'ermetismo* (Florence: La Nuova Italia, 1969).

Egli [Sereni] ha accettato in pieno l'intimazione a infrangere la bolla, l'ampolla della partenogenesi, a riesaminare le forme di una propria relativa adesione iniziale al ermetismo e ai suoi canoni, anzi è stato tra i primi a mettersi spontaneamente sulla via di una revisione, ma l'operazione non si è risolta per lui nel negare tali origini, bensì nel discendervi e nell'andare oltre, sotto di esse, nel saggiarne la consistenza bruciandole dall'interno, facendo poi parlare di nuovo le loro ceneri e la loro humus.[23]

[He [Sereni] fully embraced the command to break the bubble–the vial of parthenogenesis—and re-examine the forms of his own initial relative adherence to hermeticism and its rules; indeed he was one of the first to spontaneously set himself on the path toward revision. However, for him that operation was not achieved by negating those origins, but rather by descending into their depths, going through and beyond them, testing their robustness by setting fire to them from the inside and then making their ashes and humus speak again in new ways.]

Indeed, if Sereni resists the hermetic 'culto della parola' [cult of the word], he does not reject the problem of language as such, and already in *Frontiera* the topography of his native Luino is employed to reflect a kind of peripheralism that is at once geographical and poetic, a 'sentimento di frontiera' [feeling of being on the border] that results from the opposition between 'la chiusura antiidillica della vita italiana in quegli anni, d'anteguerra, e la tensione verso [...] un mondo più grande' [the anti-idyllic blockade on life in Italy during those pre-war years, and the tension towards [...] a wider world beyond].[24] As Montale wrote of Sereni's early poetry, 'Il senso lacustre che l'avvolge non consente impennate ma conferma le origini e la serietà di un temperamento. Il giovane poeta esita sulle soglie della poesia in una stagione ingrata che non permette il canto in do maggiore [The lake-like sensibility that envelops it does not allow sudden flares of emotion but confirms the seriousness of a temperament. The young poet wavers on the threshold of poetry during an ungrateful season that does not allow music in a major key].[25] Sereni's language embodies this tension, alternately embracing and resisting the pull of a more hermetic abstractness and high lyric subjectivity, always seeking to reaffirm a connection with the world, particularly the terrestrial. Sereni's descent into, and his going beyond, the space of origins to which Zanzotto alludes is also a sign of this desire for a descent further into the heart of things, a katabasis that importantly coincides with

---

[23] Andrea Zanzotto, '*Gli strumenti umani*' (1967), in *Aure e disincanti nel Novecento letterario* (Milan: Mondadori, 1994), pp. 37–49 (p. 40).
[24] Vittorio Sereni, interview with Ferdinando Camon (1965), in Ferdinando Camon, *Il mestiere di poeta* (Milan: Lerici, 1965), pp. 121–8 (p. 123).
[25] Eugenio Montale, 'Strumenti umani', first publ. in *Corriere della sera*, 24 Oct. 1965, now in *Sulla poesia*, ed. Giorgio Zampa (Milan: Mondadori, 1976), pp. 328–33 (p. 330).

the advent of the Second World War, which will take Sereni far away from the familiar spaces of both his early poetry and his Milanese life, reducing that world to ashes and precipitating the need to rebuild it from the ground up.

In 1940 Sereni married Maria Luisa Bonfanti, whom he had met at university, and began work as a secondary school teacher at the Istituto Magistrale in Modena. However, his departure for North Africa as an infantry officer in the Pistoia Army Division brought this short moment of reprieve to an end. Sereni travelled first to Greece and then to Sicily, where he was captured by the Allied Forces on 24 July 1943. From there he was transferred to North Africa for the remainder of the war, where he spent two years as a prisoner of war in Oran.

Everything Sereni writes about Algeria confirms its importance as a purgatorial space more than one of physical imprisonment *per se*, and as a place of exile it gives shape to what becomes a pathological concern with the marginalization from history and the isolation of the individual, only intensified on Sereni's return to Italy after the war. In the poet's words:

> Già: un male si è insinuato in questi versi. Lo chiamerò male del reticolato, seppure non sia il caso di ricorrere a un termine che vada o venga oltre o da oltre il filo spinato. Posso ora misurare, alla luce di questo complessivo fallimento, tutta la serietà con cui il poeta aveva affidato se stesso ai versi a suo tempo riportati sul foglio murale.[26]
>
> [Quite, a sickness had crept into these verses. I'll call it barbed-wire fever, even if it is inappropriate to use a term that comes from beyond and goes beyond the barbed wire of a prison camp. I can see now, in the light of this overall failure, with what gravity the poet had entrusted himself to the verses he had copied onto the paper from the wall.]

In one way, Sereni's second collection, *Diario d'Algeria* [*Algerian Diary*] (henceforth *DA*),[27] first published in 1947, is a direct outcome of his wartime experiences, yet its genesis tends to complicate its status as a diary of war, and following Ottavio Rossani's designation, I would label it a kind of 'taccuino disorganico' [unsystematized notebook][28] at some distance

---

[26] Vittorio Sereni, 'Male del reticolato' ['Barbed-Wire Fever'] (1945), first publ. in *La Rassegna d'Italia* 1.5 (May 1946), pp. 56–9, now in *ID2*, pp. 16–20 (p. 18); trans. Robinson–Perryman.

[27] Vittorio Sereni, *Diario d'Algeria* (Florence: Vallecchi, 1947). The definitive edition dates to 1965 (Milan: Mondadori, Collezione 'Lo Specchio') and includes some adjustments and revisions with respect to the 1947 version. The third and final edition (Milan: Mondadori, 1979) is identical to the preceding one.

[28] See Sereni's interview with Ottavio Rossani (1982), entitled 'È vero, io rido poco ma so cos'è la gioia' [It's true, I rarely smile, but I know what joy is'], *Il Giornale della Lombardia*, Feb. 1982, p. 22–3 (p. 23).

from the 'bella biografia' [beautiful biography] of Ungaretti's *L'Allegria* [*Joy*].[29] The protracted or dilatory qualities of *DA*, which Barile argues transform it into a 'diario *sui generis*' [diary *sui generis*],[30] are made more evident still when we take into account the structural revisions of the collection that Sereni undertook whilst working on his third collection, *SU*.[31] Despite being, in one sense, very different collections in terms of setting and subject matter, there is undoubtedly a common thread provided by the recursive mode that dominates in Sereni's processing of experience. As with the changes Sereni makes to *Frontiera* in the same period, we are encouraged to see each collection in an organic relationship with the other rather than as an isolated moment of existence:[32]

> Succede persino questo, che di colpo un fatto dell'esistenza, un determinato momento, un fatto davanti al quale vi trovate improvvisamente, getti una luce retrospettiva su quello che era una cosa oscura e lo illumini. [...] C'è tutto un periodo di preparazione, perché quello stimolo, suggestione, ricordo o illuminazione improvvisa viene a noi come una domanda o provocazione dell'esistenza e ci spinge a chiarirla fino in fondo, non per via filosofica, ma per via poetica.[33]
>
> [Even this can happen: that suddenly some part of existence, a certain moment, an event with which you find yourself unexpectedly face to face, throws a retrospective light on something that had been obscure, and illuminates it. [...] There's a whole period of preparation in order that the stimulus, suggestion, memory, or illumination suddenly reaches us as a question or as a provocation of existence and urges us to uncover its deepest meanings, not through philosophy but through poetry.]

The section of *DA* entitled *Il male d'Africa* [*The African Sickness*], which was inserted into the 1965 edition and amalgamates texts written in the 1950s, is perhaps the clearest example of this retroactive mode of writing. However, it is also evident in the title of the first section of *SU*, *Uno sguardo di rimando* [*A Backward Glance*], and in the motif of the 'strumenti umani' themselves which as Sereni stated 'intende [...] significare tutti i mezzi e anche gli espedienti con cui l'uomo, singolo o collettività,

---

[29] 'Questo vecchio libro è un diario. L'autore non ha altra ambizione, e crede che anche i grandi poeti non ne avessero altre, se non quella di lasciare *una sua bella biografia*' [This old book is a diary. Its author has no other ambition, and believes that the great poets had no other either, than to leave behind *a beautiful biography*], Ungaretti, Note to 1931 edn of *L'Allegria*, in *Vita d'un uomo*, pp. 527–8.
[30] Barile, *Sereni*, p. 31.
[31] Vittorio Sereni, *Gli strumenti umani* (Turin: Einaudi, 1965); 2nd rev. edn (Turin: Einaudi, 1975), comprising texts written between 1945 and 1965.
[32] Vittorio Sereni, *Frontiera*, 3rd rev. edn (Milan: All'Insegna del Pesce d'Oro, 1966).
[33] Sereni, *Sulla poesia*, pp. 53–5.

confronta l'ignoto, il mistero, il destino' [aims [...] to represent all of the means and expedients with which man, individually or collectively, confronts the unknown, mystery, destiny].[34] There is therefore a kind of eternal return to the point of capture and imprisonment, as well as a constantly renewed search for liberation from these same troubles, that sees Algeria leave a shadow in Sereni's poetry long after the poet's physical departure from the place.[35] The exiled poetic subject of Sereni's later poetry also undoubtedly has its origins here, in a form of purgatorial existence which establishes a penitential journey in an intimately psychological space—a suspended realm somewhere between the living and the dead that Sereni borrows from Dante, Eliot, and Montale, amongst others, 'Il suo non è un canzoniere né un racconto verseggiato, ma una serie di soliloqui o di appelli o di constatazioni che hanno un tema unico: la prigionia dell'uomo d'oggi e gli spiragli che si aprono in questa prigione' [His is not a *canzoniere* nor a story told in verse, but a series of soliloquies, or appeals, or observations that have a single theme: the imprisonment of contemporary man and the chinks that open up for him in that prison].[36]

On Sereni's return to Milan in 1945, the city's postwar landscape absorbs several of these prison-like features, and the reunion with the forsaken city is a far from harmonious one.[37] Milan is a very different place from the one Sereni left, and he finds it difficult to rediscover a home there.[38] In his later poetry, Milan is often portrayed as a transitory space for a subject ill at ease

---

[34] Sereni, *Sulla poesia*, p. 52

[35] 'Mi ci sono accanito dentro di me per anni, quasi si trattasse di un enigma di cui non venivo a capo, che la memoria riproponeva continuamente e che ammetteva soluzioni disparate e molteplici' [Inside I was seething over them for years. It was almost as if they were a puzzle I couldn't solve—one that memory was constantly reviving, one open to the most various, the greatest number of solutions], Vittorio Sereni, 'L'anno quarantatre' ['The Year '43'] (1963), in *ID2*, pp. 80–8 (p. 81), repr. in *Senza l'onore delle armi* [*Without the Honour of Arms*] [*SOA*] (Milan: All'Insegna del Pesce d'Oro, 1986), pp. 21–32; trans. Robinson–Perryman.

[36] Montale, 'Strumenti umani', pp. 329–30.

[37] See esp. 'Città di notte' ['City at Night'], in *DA*, in which the poet, with outstretched hands, is forced to watch the city (personified as a woman) disappear from view, 'Inquieto nella tradotta | che ti sfiora così lentamente | mi tendo alle tue luci sinistre | nel sospiro degli alberi. || Mentre tu dormi e forse | qualcuno muore nelle alte stanze | e tu giri via con un volto | dietro ogni finestra–tu stessa | un volto, un volto solo | che per sempre si chiude' [Uneasy in the troop train | brushing against you so slowly | I lean to your ominous lights | in the sighing of the trees. || Meanwhile you sleep, and perhaps | someone's dying in the upper rooms | and you turn away with a face | behind each window—yourself | a face, a face only | that forever closes] (p. 60).

[38] '...il rapporto con Milano è ambiguo, ambivalente. Talvolta l'ho odiata. Volevo perfino rompere con 'lei'. Sentivo che non riuscivo a rispondere, non ero in grado di abbracciarla' [... my relationship with Milan is ambiguous, ambivalent. I have sometimes hated the city. I even wanted to break it off with 'her'. I felt unable to respond, I couldn't manage to embrace her], interview with Rossani, p. 23.

with his surroundings, in search of a corner of the city in which he might belong, but often frustrated in that quest. The alien quality of Milan's urban landscapes are set in opposition to the memory of Luino's natural, lakeside, topography and poems in *SU* are roughly divisible into two groups—those that look back, nostalgically, to his native environment, and those that seem trapped in the city, with the subject trying to orient himself to a new world, dominated by industry and an unfamiliar political situation.

In the poem 'Una visita in fabbrica' ['A Factory Visit'], written between 1952 and 1958—when Sereni worked as press officer for the large manufacturer Pirelli—Milan's factory spaces are presented as an infernal realm which can conceivably be made more habitable only by returning to the past, and by rediscovering the city ideals almost entirely lost in the dehumanizing environment of the *miracolo economico* [economic miracle] of the 1950s. In Sereni's eyes, the rebuilding that occurs after the war takes on a surreal quality, almost an uncanniness, so that Milan always possesses a duplicity in the poet's imagination which cannot be made whole:

> [...] Che cos'è
> un ciclo di lavorazione? Un cottimo
> cos'è? Quel fragore. E le macchine, le trafile e calandre,
> questi nomi per me presto di solo suono nel buio della mente,
> rumore che si somma a rumore e presto spavento per me–
> straniero al grande moto e da questo agganciato.
> Eccoli al loro posto quelli che sciamavano là fuori
> qualche momento fa: che sai di loro
> che ne sappiamo tu e io, ignari dell'arte loro...
> Chiusi in un ordine, compassati e svelti,
> relegati a un filo di benessere
> senza perdere un colpo– su tutto implacabile
> e ipnotico il ballo dei pezzi dall'una all'altra sala.
> ('Una visita in fabbrica' II, 8–20, in *SU*, p. 126)

> [[...] What's that?
> A work cycle? Piecework,
> what is it? That uproar. And machines, wire drawers and presses,
> these names soon for me just sound in the mind's dark,
> noise piled on noise and soon fearful for me
> to the great motion foreign and held in its grip.
> Here at their posts are those swarming outside
> a few moments ago; what do you know of them,
> what do we know you and I, of their skill unaware...
> Closed in an order, deliberate and quick,
> condemned to a line of well-being
> not missing a beat–and above all the implacable
> and hypnotic dance of pieces from one room to another.]

'Una visita in fabbrica' is also one of the few poems to come out of a period of creative crisis that Sereni suffered from 1946 to 1954. He himself referred to that crisis as 'un lungo sonno' [a long sleep] from which he could only be awakened by looking outside of the stricter limits of his own production, to the works of others.[39] These included foreign poets he translated such as Guillaume Apollinaire, René Char, and William Carlos Williams, and prose authors he read such as Elio Vittorini, Marcel Proust, and Ernest Hemingway. Writing on his 'silenzio creativo' [creative silence], Sereni stated:

> Programmare una poesia 'figurativa', narrativa, costruttiva, non significa nulla, specie se in opposizione di ipotesi a una poesia 'astratta', lirica, d'illuminazione. Significa qualcosa, nello sviluppo d'un lavoro, avvertire un bisogno di figure, di elementi narrativi, di strutture: ritagliarsi un *milieu* socialmente e storicamente, oltre che geograficamente e topograficamente, identificabile, e in cui trasporre brani e stimoli di vita emotiva individuale, come su un banco di prova delle risorse segrete e ultime di questa, della loro reale vitalità, della loro effettiva capacità di presa.[40]

> [To plan a 'figurative', narrative, constructive poem means nothing, especially if in hypothetical literary opposition to an 'abstract', lyrical poem of illumination. It does mean something, during a work's development, to feel the need for characters, for narrative elements, for structure: find for yourself a milieu that is socially and historically, as well as geographically and even topographically, identifiable. In it you transpose shreds and stimuli of individual emotional life, as if on a test bench for their secret and final resources, their real vitality, their effective capacity to grip.]

The experience of poetic impasse paradoxically leads to a renewed search for identity in a textually composite space and a willingness to embrace more diverse routes towards artistic expression. Taking up the role of editorial director at Mondadori from 1958 onwards, Sereni reconfirmed his commitment to charting new territories on the literary front and was responsible for establishing new series of works including the *Collana della Medusa*, the *Collana 'Il tornasole'*—which showcased the work of young poets such as Zanzotto and Pagliarani—and the *Collana di poesia 'Lo specchio'*. Between 1962 and 1964, and in collaboration with

---

[39] 'Un lungo sonno' was the title of a collection of poems, prose writings, and translations (of poems by William Carlos Williams) for which Sereni was awarded the Libera Stampa Prize in Lugano (Switzerland) in 1956. As a collection, it represents an early nucleus of *SU* as well as some of the fruits of Sereni's reworking and reordering of parts of *DA* and *Frontiera*, with the addition of poems that will be included in the revised versions of both collections in the mid-1960s. 'Un lungo sonno' is preserved in Archivio Vittorio Sereni, APS I 21 (F 21).

[40] Sereni, 'Il silenzio creativo', p. 77, trans. Robinson–Perryman.

Niccolò Gallo, Geno Pampaloni, and Dante Isella, he also founded the journal *Questo e altro* [*This and Other Things*], which sought to interpret literature in light of the wider political and cultural situation of the time, looking at questions of *impegno* [commitment] as well as the possible relationship that art could entertain with industrial and social practices. Sereni felt very strongly that, within contemporary culture, neither absolute creativity nor the demands of sociopolitical reality should be allowed to dominate, but ought rather to engage in dialogue with one another on a common ethical ground:

> Giacché, se uno dei nostri temi dichiarati consiste nella necessità di poter riconoscere alla letteratura e all'arte una creatività inderogabile, una 'tensione', espressiva di valori anche intimamente etici, 'storici', questo non significa per nulla credere nel privilegio del poeta, o attribuirgli una aristocratica o carismatica esenzione dagli impegni del tempo, metterlo al di sopra o al di fuori della 'cultura' di cui si alimenta e che, in ultima analisi, per la sua parte elabora ed istituisce. È se mai il contrario: essendo per noi il lavoro letterario con le sue connaturali possibilità di poesia, sostanzialmente un campo di forze, aperto a esperienze diverse, inserito in un 'tempo' ove non è consentito, pena la loro stessa vanificazione, prevaricare sull'uomo e sulla sua autentica vocazione di vita.[41]

> [Since one of our declared topics is the need to be able to acknowledge that literature and art are inseparable from creativity, a 'tension' that expresses values that are also intimately ethical and 'historical', this does not at all mean that we should believe in the privileged position of poets, or endow them with an aristocratic or charismatic exemption from the commitments of their day and age, placing them above or outside the 'culture' that nourishes them and which, in the end, in their own way they help to develop and institute. If anything it is the opposite: the literary work being for us, with its inborn poetic possibilities, essentially a field of forces, open to diverse experiences, within a 'day and age' in which it is not permitted, without nullifying those possibilities, to prevaricate over human nature or its authentic vocation for living.]

The question of how far Sereni can be considered a committed writer has been the subject of considerable study.[42] It was also a major focus of tension and debate in the poet's friendship with the writer and committed socialist

---

[41] Vittorio Sereni, 'Senza vantaggio?' ['Without Advantage?'], *Questo e altro* 3 (1962), pp. 25–8 (p. 25).
[42] On this topic see Franco Fortini, '*Gli strumenti umani*' and '*Un posto di vacanza*', in *Saggi italiani*, pp. 172–89 and 189–203; Giancarlo Ferretti, 'L'ultima spiaggia di Sereni', in *La letteratura del rifiuto* (Milan: Mursia, 1968), pp. 179–93; Maria Laura Baffoni Licata, *La poesia di Vittorio Sereni: alienazione e impegno* (Ravenna: Longo, 1986); and Remo Pagnanelli, 'Vittorio Sereni nel labirinto della storia', in *Studi critici: poesia e poeti italiani del secondo Novecento*, ed. Daniela Marcheschi (Milan: Mursia, 1991), pp. 44–8.

Franco Fortini, which extended over several decades.[43] As with his relationship to *ermetismo*, Sereni's relationship to the Left was never clear-cut, and his correspondence with Fortini reveals that the postwar years were marked by a severe disillusionment with its political aims, and above all by Sereni's feeling of not sharing the same historical ideologies as the majority of his contemporaries a result of the isolating experience of non-engagement he suffered during the war. Fortini's observations are instructive on this point:

> Storia e politica, cioè le categorie 'sociologiche' che più tardi e poi sempre furono spregiativamente chiamate 'ideologie', furono le forme del sapere interrogate dopo il 1945 da chi aveva vissuto i rivolgimenti del quinquennio precedente. E, come gli esistenzialisti francesi venivano allora spiegando, il tema delle scelte etiche si poneva in diretto rapporto con la storia; e con l'idea medesima di rinnovamento e di rivoluzione. Tutto questo, a chi, come Sereni, veniva da anni di impotenza, di non-partecipazione e di isolamento, dovette sembrare una specie di carnevale ottimistico un po' ridicolo: furono i 'baschi esistenzialmarxisti' di un suo epigramma.[44]

> [History and politics, i.e. the 'sociological' categories that were later on pejoratively called 'ideologies', were the forms of knowledge being questioned after 1945 by those who had lived through the troubles of the previous five years. And, as the French existentialists were then explaining, the theme of ethical choice was one directly related to history and to the idea of renewal and revolution. To someone like Sereni, who had just come out of years of helplessness, non-participation, and isolation, all this must have seemed a kind of optimistic and somewhat ridiculous carnival: the 'existential-marxist berets', precisely, of one of his epigrams.]

This debate with Fortini over *impegno* reaches an apogee in the dialogue that Sereni stages with him in his poem in seven parts, *Un posto di vacanza* [*A Holiday Place*] (henceforth *Un posto*), first published in 1971.[45] Written partly in response to an epigram by his friend, which culminated with the words, 'Rischia l'anima. Strappalo, quel foglio | bianco che tieni in mano' [Risk your soul. Tear it up, that blank | paper you're holding in

---

[43] The correspondence between Sereni and Fortini spanned almost three decades, from 1952 to 1981. Though not published in full, many letters are preserved amongst the archival materials in Luino, APS VI 198 (L 803) [Fortini to Sereni] and APS VII 24 (L 1246) [Sereni to Fortini].

[44] Franco Fortini, 'Ancora per Vittorio Sereni' ['Still for Vittorio Sereni'] (1987), in *Nuovi saggi italiani*, pp. 185–207 (pp. 188–9). The epigram to which Fortini refers is in 'Corso Lodi', in *SU*, p. 150.

[45] *Un posto di vacanza* first appeared in *L'Almanacco dello specchio* 1 (1971) and was then republished in libretto form by Scheiwiller (Milan: All'Insegna del Pesce d'Oro, 1973). It later forms the nucleus (part III) of *SV* with the companion poems 'Niccolò' and 'Fissità' ['Fixity'] (also set in Bocca di Magra). References I make to the poem will be to the latter version, included in the *Meridiano* edition of Sereni's collected poems, *Poesie*, pp. 223–33.

your hand],[46] Sereni's poem answers the injunction, confronting the personal and collective memory of the past, while establishing its own historico-political and moral framework on the basis of an avowed renunciation or reticence.[47]

Simultaneously, Sereni's refusal to adhere to a particular ideology, also poetically speaking, led him to new levels of experimentation with poetic form and a commitment to reshaping the traditionally monologic framework of the lyric to absorb dialogic, prosaic, and narrative elements that could allow this kind of debate to take place inside it, 'sempre in uno spazio e in una situazione locali, in un realismo che rompe la crosta dell'elegia, prova evidente dello scrupolo di lasciar tutto aperto, del timore di evadere dal tessuto della storia in atto' [always in local spaces and situations, in a realism that breaks the crust of elegy, as evident proof of the anxiety of leaving everything open and the fear of escaping from the fabric of history in progress].[48]

Un posto, written over a period of twenty years, becomes a poetic laboratory for just this kind of 'progetto | sempre in divenire sempre | "in fieri" di cui essere parte' [project | ever in becoming, ever | 'in the air' for you to be a part of] (*Un posto* VII, 20–2) and of a selfhood in constant evolution with respect to the world around it. Set in Bocca di Magra, in Liguria, where Sereni spent every summer from 1951, the poem transforms the natural landscape of the holiday space—always already penetrated by elements of social and political reality—into a kind of looking glass in whose depths Sereni recognizes the 'disegno profondo' [deep design] of his entire poetic project (VII, 17). It also changes the idyll from an intimately lyric space of contemplation (of beauty) into the locus

---

[46] Franco Fortini, '*Sereni esile mito…*' (1954), in *L'ospite ingrato* (Bari: De Donato, 1966), p. 18. The passage in question is *Un posto* I, 12–16, 'Venivano spifferi in carta dall'altra riva: *Sereni esile mito | filo di fedeltà non sempre giovinezza è verità |……| Strappalo quel foglio bianco che tieni in mano.| Fogli o carte non c'erano da giocare, era vero. A mani vuote | senza messaggio di risposta tornava dall'altra parte il traghettatore*' [Airs came on card from the far shore: | *Sereni slender myth | thread of faith, youth's not always truth |……| Tear up that blank paper you're holding in your hand*] (p. 223); italics in the original.

[47] Cf. The self-confessed 'mutismo' [mutism] of the poetic subject in *Un posto* (II, 16) and Sereni's comments to Fortini, in a letter dated 8 Sept. 1967, regarding the loquacity of the interlocutors of the Left in distinction to his own silence (in *Un posto* I, 28–33), 'L'intenzione mia era un semplice effetto acustico (come una voce che insista ma intanto va fuori campo = mio intontimento, sbalordimento che recepisce suoni piuttosto che discorsi e significati). Ma già un occhio sospettoso potrebbe vederci invece l'irrisione a una logorrea altrui, parole e non fatti eccetera' [My intention was to create a simple sound effect (like a voice that persists but continues off screen = my stupor, or amazement that apprehends sounds more than discourses or meanings). But a suspicious eye might see in that, instead, a mocking of others' endless chatter, words and not deeds etc.] (APS VII 24 (L 1246)).

[48] Montale, 'Strumenti umani', p. 332.

of an uncertain and questing subjectivity on an epic scale, which must assert its authority and identity within a still-forming—continually interrupted and reinstated—poetic journey to the furthest reaches of language and desire. Concurrently, it establishes a poetic discourse penetrated by a multitude of voices drawn from Sereni's rich literary heritage that found their point of confluence in Bocca di Magra, a channel for re-entering the Montalian universe of *Ossi* and *Le occasioni* [*The Occasions*] in particular, and the postwar haunt of a whole group of intellectuals, several of whom become Sereni's interlocutors in poems from the period (besides Fortini, Vittorini and Giancarlo de Carlo).[49]

In turn, as a microcosm of an increasingly complex conception of poetic space, '[che] incorpora nel suo sviluppo sfiducie e improvvise speranze, dubbi e aperture al suo stesso farsi' [[that] incorporates within its development moments of mistrust and sudden hopes, doubts and openings towards its own creation and becoming],[50] *Un posto* also functions as the bridge between *SU* and Sereni's fourth collection, *Stella variabile* [*Variable Star*] (henceforth *SV*),[51] and is a testament to the increasingly permeable boundaries between poetry and prose that by now characterized his artistic consciousness.[52] Since the publication of *Gli immediati dintorni* [*The Immediate Surroundings*] in 1962, which had collated Sereni's prose writings over almost two decades, the author had embarked upon a long and important 'tentazione della prosa' [temptation to write prose] that would

---

[49] 'Loro sono stati un punto di riferimento, di confronto. Anche con me stesso. Il loro impegno mi ha spinto a capire di più' [They were a point of reference and comparison. Also with myself. Their commitment drove me to understand more], Vittorio Sereni, interview with Anna del Bo Boffino, 'Il terzio occhio del poeta: intervista con Vittorio Sereni erede di Montale' ['The Poet's Third Eye: Interview with Vittorio Sereni, Heir of Montale'], in *Amica*, 28 Sept. 1982, pp. 153–6 (p. 154). Fortini and Vittorini are both mentioned in *Un posto* (pp. 223, 231), Giancarlo de Carlo and his wife, Giuliana, in 'Gli amici' ['The Friends'] (p. 139).

[50] Vittorio Sereni, 'Note' to *Un posto*, accompanying the Scheiwiller edition of the poem, published in 1973, now included in the 'Note' section to Vittorio Sereni, *Un posto di vacanza e altre poesie*, ed. Zeno Birolli (Milan: All'Insegna del Pesce d'Oro, 1994), pp. 44–6 (p. 44).

[51] Vittorio Sereni, *Stella variabile* (Milan: Garzanti, 1981), distributed in 1982. An early version of this collection was made available in 130 copies in 1979, dedicated to Dante Isella, with some significant differences with respect to the later edition. On the genesis of *SV*, see Barile, *Sereni*, p. 67.

[52] 'Produrre figure e narrare storie in poesia come esito di un processo di proliferazione interiore . . . Non abbiamo sempre pensato che ai vertici poesia e narrativa si toccano e che allora, e solo allora, non ha quasi più senso il tenerle distinte?' [To create characters and tell stories in poetry as the result of an inner proliferation . . . Didn't we always think that at the apex poetry and narrative touch, and then, but only then, it makes almost no sense to distinguish between them?], Sereni, 'Il silenzio creativo', p. 77, trans. Robinson–Perryman.

define his creative output until his death in 1983.[53] The essays composing *Gli immediati dintorni* all deal in different ways with the material (events, memories both personal and poetic, reflections on his own work and that of others) that surrounds and shapes the protean terrain of the poetic, and creates a notebook of ideas akin to Giacomo Leopardi's *Zibaldone di pensieri*. As a work, *Gli immediati dintorni* also represents a meeting ground for the many poetic and narrative voices with which Sereni is in dialogue in the arc of his production, rooted in the different places that constitute his personal and intellectual biography.

The authors with whom Sereni has the most intense connection are undoubtedly those with whom he shares a topography, or with whose landscapes he can boast some familiarity: Montale (Liguria and Luino); Petrarch and Char (Vaucluse); Saba and Ungaretti (Milan). Sereni's critical writings demonstrate that he almost always takes the same route into the poetry of others: a preliminary excursus into their native or adopted landscape followed by entry into the domain of their work proper. As Sereni's prose piece 'Un omaggio a Rimbaud' ['Homage to Rimbaud'] (1954) indicates, this instinct is typically bound up with the search for a space against which to measure the self (*misurarsi*), as an antidote to an intrinsically hostile landscape that conceals the horrors of the void (*vuoto*) beneath:

> Le poco parole con cui si sbarazza di questi luoghi, che sono sì e no i miei luoghi (ed è questo *sì e no* che li fa invincibilmente intimi ai miei occhi), ha perpetuato in me la sua presenza da queste parti. I miei mancati studi su Rimbaud hanno trovato a volte un compenso in una specie di sodalizio con lui, bruscamente elargito, bruscamente tolto, fugace; coincidente con le tregue del suo misurarsi, cimentarsi con l'orrore; [...] Penso alle volte che ricorre in lui, misteriosamente, la parola *confort*... La confronto a questa atonìa che ha i colori dell'idillio, *agréable*. Sono portato a pensare che anche in ciò, forse soprattutto in ciò, avrebbe riconosciuto l'orrore, l'orrore del vuoto nella ripetizione, quello con cui non è più possibile misurarsi, cimentarsi.[54]

> [The few words with which he rids himself of these places, which are and aren't places of mine (and it is this *are* and *aren't* which give them an unvanquishable intimacy, to my eyes), have prolonged his presence in me in this area. My neglected studies of Rimbaud have sometimes been

---

[53] *Gli immediati dintorni* [*ID1*] (Milan: Il Saggiatore, 1962), republished posthumously with additional material as *ID2*. *La tentazione della prosa* [*The Temptation of Prose*] [*TDP*] is the title given to another posthumous work, ed. by Giulia Raboni (Milan: Mondadori, 1998), which incorporates *ID2* and *La traversata di Milano* [*Crossing Milan*], a collection of 'poemi in prosa' [prose poems] on Milan which Sereni was still working on when he died.
[54] Vittorio Sereni, 'Un omaggio a Rimbaud' (1954), first publ. in abridged form as 'Sans ombre qu'on est soi-même' ['Without the Shadow We Ourselves Are'], in *Omaggio a Rimbaud, di poeti italiani viventi*, ed. V. Scheiwiller (Milan: All'Insegna del Pesce d'Oro, 1954), pp. 31–2, now in *ID2*, pp. 46–50 (pp. 48–9). Italics in the original.

compensated by a kind of kinship with him, brusquely established, brusquely interrupted, fleeting; coinciding with the moments of respite in his measuring himself against and confronting horror. [...] Sometimes I think the word *comfort* recurs in him, mysteriously... I compare it with the atonicity, with the colours of an idyll, of *agreeable*. I am inclined to think that in this too, perhaps above all in this, he would have recognized horror, the horror of the void through repetition, that void against which it is no longer possible to measure oneself, and which cannot be confronted.]

Reflections of this kind, in the environs of poetry, are thus also a bridge toward more philosophical speculations and acute self-analysis. The 1960s and 1970s intensified Sereni's creative cross-fertilization of poetry and prose, with the publication of other narrative works including 'L'opzione' ['The Option'] (1964), 'Ventisei' [Twenty-Six] (1970), and 'Il sabato tedesco' ['The German Saturday'] (1980). Sereni also revisited his experiences as a prisoner of war in the short story 'La cattura' ['The Capture'] (1963).[55] All were destined to be included in a collection of prose works entitled *La traversata di Milano* [*Crossing Milan*], which Sereni was still working on when he died.[56] During the 1970s, Sereni also composed much of the poetry of *SV* and consolidated his writings on poets and authors as diverse as Eugenio Montale, Jacques Prèvert, Sergio Solmi, Primo Levi, and Guillaume Apollinaire, published collectively as *Letture preliminari* [*Preliminary Readings*] (1973).[57] Finally, he completed his translations of works by Ezra Pound, René Char, William Carlos Williams, and Pierre Corneille, collated in *La musicante di Saint Merry* [*The Musician from Saint Merry*] (1981).[58]

---

[55] All four works are now in *TDP*, pp. 161–89, 190–202, 203–24, and 153–60, from which quotations are taken. They were first published as: 'L'opzione', *Queste e altro* 8 (1964), pp. 33–45; 'Ventisei', *Forum italicum* 4.4 (Dec. 1970), pp. 576–89; *Il sabato tedesco* (Milan: Il Saggiatore, 1980); and 'La cattura', *Pirelli: rivista d'informazione e di tecnica* 16.1 (Feb. 1963), section entitled *Italia 1943*, p. 6. 'La cattura' and 'Ventisei' were subsequently reprinted in *SOA*, pp. 9–20 and 45–63.

[56] Sereni makes clear his intention to publish this collection in the opening letter of a preface to *Graziano: collezione della Galleria d'arte Il Catalogo* (Salerno: Il Catalogo, 1982), p. 9, 'La tentazione della prosa è relativamente recente in me. [...] Nelle intenzioni questo è un capitolo di un libro che vorrei un giorno o l'altro concluso. Strano, ne posseggo già il titolo: *La traversata di Milano*. [...] Forse vi state chiedendo se si tratterà di un romanzo. Non lo vedo come tale. Caso mai come una confessione non proprio esplicita, in parte anticipata nella prosa che vi mando. Si vedrà. O non si vedrà affatto' [The temptation to write prose is relatively new to me. [...] In intention this is the chapter of a book I'd like one day to be finished. Oddly, I already have the title: *Crossing Milan*. [...] Perhaps you are wondering whether it will be a novel. I don't see it that way. More like a not very explicit confession, in part already evident in the piece I'm sending you. We'll see. Or perhaps we won't].

[57] Vittorio Sereni, *Letture preliminari*, ed. Pier Vincenzo Mengaldo et al. (Padua: Liviana, 1973).

[58] Vittorio Sereni, *Il musicante di Saint-Merry e altri versi tradotti* (Turin: Einaudi, 2001).

Common to all these works is Sereni's perception of literature as a supremely interrogative space for the staging of identity. In continuous dialogue with the world, both inside and outside the text, Sereni establishes the site of a poetics in constant evolution and metamorphosis, through which one can map the series of topographic shifts and reconfigurations from one phase of his experience to the next:

> Si ripropone con questo, il carattere dinamico di ogni meditazione sulla poesia: la sua estrema mutevolezza, il suo continuo essere chiamata in causa per scomporsi o ricomporsi, per accogliere o per rifiutare. La vista di un nuovo paesaggio, la lettura d'una pagina che il caso ha aperto un giorno sul tavolo, il suono d'una voce dalla strada bastano a volte per darle una direzione diversa; per costringerla a rivedere tutto quanto da capo.[59]
>
> [Once again this shows the dynamic nature of any meditation on poetry: its extreme changeability, the way it is continuously called into question, deconstructs and reconstructs itself, welcomes or rejects new ideas. The sight of a new landscape, the reading of a page that by chance falls open one day on the table, the sound of a voice from the street, are sometimes enough to give it a different direction; to force it to examine everything over again.]

Sereni's poetic landscape is born from, and continually returns to, this circular itinerary of a subject looking for a place to call its own, also poetically speaking. The journey inevitably transports it back and forward along a line, both familiar and strange, which would (ideally) take it somewhere new: 'come bisogno o ricerca o nostalgia di presenze senza cui quel lavoro non si darebbe o sarebbe bruciato all'origine' [like a need, search, or nostalgia for presences without which that work would not exist or would be reduced to ashes from the start].[60] It is this need, search, or nostalgia for presence(s), always already there from the beginning, which turns Sereni's poetic landscape into a landscape of desire, predicated on an original lack that also provides the impetus to write—to look for, if not to find, an elusive plenitude or fulfilment lying just beyond the point at which poetry would come to be.

PARAMETERS

It is this landscape of desire, and the identity of the 'I' that comes into being through it, that this book sets out to investigate. It argues that a

---

[59] Vittorio Sereni, 'Esperienza della poesia' ['The Experience of Poetry'] (1947), first publ. in *ID1*, pp. 41–6, now in *ID2*, pp. 25–8 (pp. 26–7).
[60] Sereni, 'Poesia: per chi?', p. 22.

major innovation of Sereni's poetry is constituted in the way in which he reworks the boundaries of poetic space to construct a lyric 'I' radically repositioned in the textual universe with respect to its predecessors: an 'I' that is decentred, *in limine*, and struggles to subordinate the world to its point of view. Tracing the evolution of the poetic 'I' from *Frontiera* (1941) to *SV* (1981) becomes a means to reflect upon the changing 'geografie e topografie' [landscapes and places] ('Addio Lugano bella' ['Beautiful Lugano Goodbye'], in *SV*, p. 197) that constitute the lyric landscape, from its origins with Dante and Petrarch through to the twentieth century, and to understand Sereni's unique response to perceiving the limits of that universe and wanting to reshape it on his own terms.

To this extent, what follows is also a study in the construction of literary and cultural memory in the work of a poet who undertakes a particularly active and challenging dialogue with tradition. As Sereni states in his essay 'Saba e l'ispirazione' ['Saba and Inspiration'] (1947) on the question of poetic identity, 'È qui che il problema specifico della poesia si riallaccia al problema più generale della cultura: non di ritrovare *la* tradizione si tratta, ma di stabilire *una* tradizione, qualche punto sicuro di riferimento comune' [It is here that the specific problem of poetry reconnects with the more general problem of culture: it is not a question of rediscovering *the* tradition, but of establishing *a* tradition, some firm and common point of reference].[61] It is in actively establishing a tradition, rather than merely rediscovering what already exists, that Sereni creates a highly original poetics and transforms the traditionally monologic space of the lyric into a discursive arena for a subject looking for some secure space to inhabit beyond the self. Intertextual dialogue allows him to construct a textually composite space that fosters a dynamic and self-questioning relationship between the poetic subject and pre-existing poetic forms. Through it, Sereni revisits and redefines the central constellation of subjectivity, language, and desire that arguably constitutes the very ground of the lyric.

In going beyond the mere identification of Sereni's poetic sources, to an examination of the patterns of desire upon which those sources establish their own discourses, this study proposes a model of intertextuality that is not limited to the analysis of lexical borrowings but deals with the wider question of the structural continuities and differences in the way in which the 'I' is staged in language and the poem. It confirms Sereni's place within a genealogy of poets for whom poetry is regarded as a space of tension

---

[61] Vittorio Sereni, 'Saba e l'ispirazione', first publ. as Appendix to Renato Martinoni, 'Bricchice svizzero-italiane per Vittorio Sereni: Piero Bianconi, il Premio "Libera Stampa" e una collaborazione radiofonica (1947)', *Versants* 16 (1989), pp. 64–6, now in *SG*, pp. 154–8 (p. 157). Italics in the original.

between lack and fulfilment, absence and presence, which originates with Dante and Petrarch, who interrogate that space in different ways, and develops through Leopardi to the modern period.

Sereni recasts that space of tension as one of liminality—a kind of poetic peripheralism or state of 'inbetween-ness' that extends from the identity of his poetic subject to the world of the poem. Within the diminishing domain of the lyric as a 'luogo ideale', geographic exile and poetic expropriation go hand in hand. They engender a perpetual desire for transition and transgression in a subject whose fate, it seems, is to be confined to an 'angolo morto della storia' [dead corner of history], with a restricted view of the outside world, whose wider dimension can only be glimpsed intermittently or through the mediation of an Other (in his early work, a *tu* [you] figure, more or less available to him; in his later work a range of phantasms which are yet more arbitrary in their coming).[62]

The new territory that Sereni's poetic subject inhabits is also that ordained for it by language. The repeated figures of loss, frustration, and immobility that underpin his poetry are above all linguistic. This is the legacy of structuralism and psychoanalysis, but also something which Sereni experiences concretely as a result of the retroactive force that exerts itself on his writing subject and which leads him to pursue a journey in reverse, towards a possession that was once considered available but is not now.

Concentrating on the shifting topography of Sereni's poetic subject, particularly in relation to the universe of its own discourse, the study emphasizes the necessity of reading the text dynamically, with due attention to the mechanisms that contribute to the staging of subjectivity in language. Through a detailed examination of the textual operations that contribute to Sereni's redefinition of the lyric 'I', it seeks to open up new ways of reading the (linguistically articulated) subject of modern poetry, considering the central question of the relationship that the textual 'I' entertains with the experiential self (empirical author) and the implications that this has for our understanding of the internal dynamics of poetic language and literature. Close reading, which has sometimes been a neglected field in scholarship on Sereni and studies of twentieth-century poetry more generally, structures the main body of analysis. Mirroring Sereni's own work, that analysis evolves to captures the increasing complexity of his poetic discourse as it probes deeper into the problematic facets of the self and its text.

---

[62] Sereni, 'L'anno quarantacinque' ['The Year '45] (1965), first publ. in *L'Unità*, 11 Apr. 1963, p. 7, now in *ID2*, pp. 93–101 (p. 99), also in *SOA*, pp. 33–44; trans. Robinson–Perryman.

The protracted genesis of several of Sereni's poems, and their tendency to look back anaphorically to preceding compositions or moments of experience, never wholly transcended, leaves us with the sense that nothing is ever fully concluded. Linear time is constantly undercut by cyclical patterns of return, creating a version of a 'lyric sequence' which, like Petrarch's, exhibits signs of development or evolution but often resists chronology in the traditional sense.[63] For Sereni, poetic memory is always a double construction, which absorbs the recollected fragments of tradition combined with the residues or spectres of his shadow self. For this reason, my study adopts a non-linear structure in order to draw out the continuities and discontinuities between Sereni's earlier and later work, and the importance of his poetic self-reflexivity. The sequence of chapters follows the development of a set of structural tropes (liminality, deixis, a form of exile that is poetic) rather than adhering to a strict chronology. Since Sereni's most radical textual innovations occur in the period corresponding to the genesis of *SU* and *SV* (1950s–1970s), my focus is directed towards the later poetry, while acknowledging that its novelty, in the way that it relocates and redefines the lyric subject, depends also on its dialogue with the earlier work.

The study begins in Chapter 1 with an introduction to the topography of Sereni's lyric subject from the point of view of its genesis as a 'speaking subject' on the Lacanian and Kristevan models, and as a subject of discourse. Here I also establish the parameters of my methodology, which draws upon this psychoanalytic paradigm and combines it with the study of textuality as it relates to Sereni's conception of poetic language. I consider Sereni's place within the arc of twentieth-century poetry and critical theory concerned with redefining what constitutes selfhood in the text, which opens up my argument toward Sereni's innovations in this area and to the syntactical matrix of deixis.

Deixis, as the principal linguistic coordinate of Sereni's lyric universe, is the key figure in shaping his landscape(s) of desire. Chapter 2 argues that Sereni's persistent and almost obsessive use of deictic terms—especially demonstratives ('this' and 'that') and spatio-temporal references coordinated from the point of view of the speaking subject—testifies to their identity as mainstays of the lyric 'I', a degree zero of the poetic landscape that survives (albeit altered) to the very limits of his poetic production.

Fundamentally tied to the relationship between absence and presence that rests at the very heart of lyric poetry and the lyric disposition, deictics

---

[63] I borrow this notion of 'lyric sequence' from Teodolinda Barolini's excellent discussion in 'The Making of a Lyric Sequence: Time and Narrative in Petrarch's *Rerum vulgarium fragmenta*', *MLN* 104.1, Italian Issue (Jan. 1989), pp. 1–38.

are shown to have a 'transformative' power in two senses: as a means to conjure the illusion of the speaking voice (in which the temporal present is privileged) out of written language, and as a way of appropriating an orphic power in poetic language that can create presence out of absence and even bring back the dead. Deictics trace the vicissitudes of the speaking voice and the poetic 'I' trying to establish itself, and a place for itself, in the poem. In a very real way, they correspond to the (desire for the) designation of a space that the 'I' can call its own, and thus possess in language. 'Geografie' and 'topografie' emerge as different configurations of this same linguistic problem: what the 'I' can contain within the bounds of the poem.

In the development of Sereni's poetry from *Frontiera* to *SU*, something shifts in deictic terms to dis-locate and fragment the lyric voice, mirroring the expatriation of the poetic 'I', which finds itself in a poetic landscape that seems increasingly remote and unfamiliar. Exile, traditionally viewed as mere physical displacement, is revealed to be a condition of language and, as such, synonymous with poetry. A great gulf divides the subject from its earlier incarnations, and the problematization of deictic reference itself attests to the growing divorce between desire and reality and the advent of a poetics of loss that keeps returning to the moment of separation from an earlier unity. Deixis in Sereni's poetry is always already an indication of a subject in crisis, one exiled to a liminal space that emphasizes limit over transcendence and increasingly betrays the uncertain ability of language to restore perspective to a subject in decline.

Intertextuality emerges as a key component for the creation of this uncertain textual space, and in Chapter 3 I argue that Sereni models this dimension of desire on Montale's subject *in limine* of *Ossi* and *Le occasioni*. Sereni's reading of Montale's poem 'Il ritorno' ['The Return'] provides a framework within which the intertextual dialogue is set, and I draw a line of continuity between the poets' treatment of liminality as an index of desire, while demonstrating Sereni's increased negativity in this area, with the greater emphasis on absence and the impossibility of transcendence.

SV emerges as the key collection for understanding this dynamic, and I present it as the place where the subject 'falls', out of the realm of perceptual certainty into the elusive fabric of the gaze, viewed in Lacanian fashion as the site of a disappearing act which mirrors the moment of dispossession figured by every act of looking or speaking. The limits of vision manifest in poems by Sereni such as 'Niccolò' and *Un posto* measure the extent of this defeat, which is also poetic, and the visibly reduced qualities of Sereni's topographies vis-à-vis their Montalian counterparts testify to his reconfiguration of liminality away from its mediatory role in regulating access to a higher dimension, towards its more ambiguous status as a place of frustrated movement or limbo.

Chapter 4 takes this notion of desire as lack of movement or frustration, and develops it with respect to the model of the desiring self in Petrarch's *Rerum vulgarium fragmenta*. As I show, this model is intrinsically topographical in being tied to the landscape and to the notion of 'phantasm' which Sereni explores and develops in his essay, 'Petrarca, nella sua finzione la sua verità' ['Petrarch, in His Fiction His Truth'] (1974). The relationship between landscape and the phantasm that Sereni draws upon in shaping his own poetics of desire transports him back to the 'luogo ideale' of the lyric that Petrarch's poetry would represent while acknowledging its inaccessibility for him and the necessity of recuperating Petrarch's landscape of desire–still sustained by the miraculous image or memory of Laura (however fallacious it turns out to be)—as the haunting memory of the subject's own lack.

Sereni's reconfiguration of the idyll, which marks out large parts of *SU* and *SV*, exhibits a number of structural parallels with the universe of the *RVF* and especially with the way in which the Petrarchan 'I' is staged as a product of language and desire. Lexical echoes of Petrarch's text, still identifiable in parts of *Frontiera* and *DA*, cede to Petrarch's deictic legacy for the modern poet, which constitutes the phantasm as a *mise-en-scène* of desire in which the subject is implicated as much as his object. Within this map of desire, the memory of Petrarch is alternately evoked and effaced as Sereni is at one time drawn to, and at another time resists, the pull of the familiar and the impetus to return to the site of an earlier plenitude, now lost. Deixis again mediates in the space between absence and presence and between one universe and the other. Staging a subject at loss, but without the hope of restoration that Petrarch still enjoys, Sereni transforms the poem into the space for cultivating a melancholy desire fixated on psychically prolonging the image of an originally lost object, which is turned into a new goal in itself: a desire never destined to coincide with its object but also unable to give it up or relinquish the attempt.

Chapter 5 extends this discussion to the complementary dialogue that Sereni undertakes with Dante, which reinforces the extent to which the modern poet has become alienated from any concept of poetry as fulfilment or utopia. The melancholy subject of Sereni's later work, into which the memory of Petrarch also feeds, is seen to have its roots in a form of misdirected desire that Sereni models on Dante's *Inferno* and *Purgatorio*.

Sereni returns again and again to the motif of the 'memorie triste' [memories of sin/sorrow] (*Purgatorio* XXXI, 11) and to the topography of Dante's Earthly Paradise to revisit a tension implicit in Dante's encounter with Beatrice that sets a backwards-looking desire against a progressive one, and deals with the dangers of an over-attachment to the past and a fixation on an earthly loss which, because it cannot be fully articulated, cannot be transcended.[64] Sereni, unable to process the loss that his 'memorie triste' refigure in poetry, cannot transform or redeem the self in the same way as Dante, and his own version of Purgatory is reconfigured as limbo, marked by the impossibility of change and the absence of progression. A concrete, historical loss cedes to a more ineffable loss centred on a melancholy fixation with *La Chose*,[65] which, as the *Thing* beyond language, stays buried deep within the self as a silent witness to its fall. Whereas Eden is the place in which Dante stages the double redemption of the subject and his language, earlier exiled from fulfilment, for Sereni it marks the realization of always inhabiting a post-lapsarian universe.

To this extent, Sereni's play of topographic memory, whether it leads him to Montale, Leopardi, Petrarch, or Dante, always stakes its claim with regard to the question of how far poetry can compensate for a primordial lack. The study aims to explore the full implications of this realization and the ways in which, in making that lack a characteristic of the subject more than of its object, Sereni redefines the discourse of desire as he revisits it. It seeks to open up a space in which Sereni can be regarded as a truly original poet who paradoxically fashions himself out of the very stuff of which tradition is made.

If the journey the 'I' makes through its landscape of desire is also the story of its search for a poetic ground in which to root an increasingly deracinated self, Sereni's poetry might just hold the key to fathoming the prevailing but uncertain territory of the modern lyric.[66]

---

[64] Quotations from the *Commedia* are from Dante Alighieri, '*La Commedia*' secondo l'antica vulgata, ed. Giorgio Petrocchi, Società Dantesca Italiana, Edizione Nazionale, 2nd rev. edn, 4 vols (Florence: Le Lettere, 1994). Translations are from Dante Alighieri, *Comedy*, trans. Robert Hollander and Jean Hollander, 3 vols (New York: Doubleday, 2000–2007), unless otherwise stated. While Hollander and Hollander translate 'memorie triste' as 'memories of sin', the Italian 'triste' does also carry associations of the medieval concept of *tristitia*, understood as kind of melancholy malady of the soul. I therefore also include the word 'sorrow' where I discuss this trope in relation to Sereni.

[65] *La Chose*, a term upon which I expand in Ch. 5, is the name Lacan and Kristeva give to the unnameable lost (and perhaps never existing) object at the root of the subject's desire. Their formulation of it can be considered a reinterpretation of Freud's concept of *das Ding* (The Thing) as the most archaic object in the history of the subject's desire, the memory of which motivates all subsequent searches for the original object of satisfaction (the mother's breast).

[66] I take the notion of a 'deracinated self' from Theodore J. Cachey Jr's essay, 'Between Petrarch and Dante: Prolegomenon to a Critical Discourse', in *Petrarch and Dante: Anti-Dantism, Metaphysics, Tradition*, ed. Zygmunt G. Barański and Theodore J. Cachey Jr (Notre Dame, Ind.: University of Notre Dame Press, 2009), pp. 3–49 (p. 13).

1

Carte dell'io

Towards a definition of subjectivity in Sereni

> È scorsa un'ala rude, t'ha sfiorato le mani,
> ma invano: la tua carta non è questa.
> (Eugenio Montale, 'Brina sui vetri[...]')[1]

THE PRELIMINARIES OF THEORY

In plotting the space that subjectivity occupies in Sereni's concept of the lyric, the 'carte' of my title incorporates the double meaning of papers and maps. I borrow it in part from Sereni's 'Un sogno' ['A Dream'], in *SU*, in which the poet's encounter with a faceless figure prompts a debate about identity, 'Me lo impediva uno senza volto, una figura plumbea. | "*Le carte*" ingiunse. "Quali carte" risposi' [A leaden body without face blocked my way. | '*Papers*', he ordered, 'what papers?', I answered] (p. 159), and in part from Fulvio Papi's study of *Un posto di vacanza* [*A Holiday Place*], in which he writes of Sereni's poem:

> Là è e permane la ragione di poesie 'surplace', che restano segni di poesie, tracce di possibilità incompiute, *carte di un io* che si perde nella vanità di chiamate, avvertimenti, speranze che vengono dal profondo degli anni e s'incorporano nella geografia dei luoghi, secondo, ormai sospette, migrazioni di immagini e animismi privati del mondo.[2]

> [It is there we find the reason for poems 'that get stuck', that exist only as signs of poems, or traces of unrealized possibilities, *the maps of an 'I'* who loses himself in the vanity of calls, premonitions, or hopes, which come from the depths of the years and incorporate themselves into the geography of

---

[1] [A harsh wing passed, and grazed your hands, | to no avail: it's not your card], 'Frost on the Windowpanes'.
[2] Fulvio Papi, 'La non-poetica di Vittorio Sereni', in *La parola incantata e altri saggi di filosofia dell'arte* (Milan: Guerini, 1992), pp. 83–185 (p. 168).

places, through already suspect migrations of images and private animisms of the world.]

As 'Un sogno' reveals, Sereni's identity card is his poetry—'i *pochi* fogli che erano i miei beni' [the *few* papers; my worldly goods]—something reduced, even deficient, that still incorporates something essential of the self which cannot rest until its meaning is found, 'La rissa | dura ancora, a mio disdoro' [the fight | still goes on, to my dishonor] ('Un sogno', ll. 21–2). From a dream to a place where the subject finds himself lacking: this is the pattern that repeats itself from the earliest poetic incarnations of the 'I' in *Frontiera* right through to *SV*. As Papi suggests, the potential hollowness of words and poetry provides the problematic material out of which the self is made: the vanishing poetic topography that is held by the memory of the poem itself—a ghost map of aborted attempts to write, or to understand.

Studies that have treated the question of *l'autobiografismo sereniano* [Sereni's tendency towards autobiography] have not fully explored the ambiguities inherent in this staging of the self through writing, though Sereni's poetry invites, if not openly demands, a more complex understanding of the relationship between author and text. This is not to discount the value of biographical scholarship, which has occupied a prominent place in Sereni studies and provides an important point of reference for reading his poetry, which is undoubtedly committed to expressing the world and the subject's place in it.[3] However, it is important to recognize that the historical identity of the writing subject is just one facet of a much wider poetic existence in which the history of the poem, and of poetry itself, continuously interacts with a more immediate existential dimension.

This shifts the centre of the subject from the world to language, or, if you like, from an understanding of the lyric 'I' as a unified, monologic self that is the measure of its universe (and in a transparent relationship to it) to its identity as a subject of discourse, with which the world interacts (without being equal to it), and which also decentres it. This more dynamic conception of the poetic subject emerges alongside some key developments in literary and psychoanalytic theory and criticism, and the

---

[3] On *l'autobiografismo sereniano* see e.g. Remo Pagnanelli, *La ripetizione dell'esistere: lettura dell'opera poetica di Vittorio Sereni* (Milan: All'Insegna del Pesce D'Oro, 1980), and Giovanna Cordibella, 'La tensione autobiografica nella poesia di Vittorio Sereni: il caso di *Un posto di vacanza*', in *Autobiografie in versi: sei poeti allo specchio*, ed. Marco A. Bazzocchi (Bologna: Pendragon, 2002), pp. 67–85. Studies of Sereni's poetry taking a more chronological or biographical approach include Massimo Grillandi, *Vittorio Sereni* (Florence: La Nuova Italia, 1972); Francesco Paolo Memmo, *Vittorio Sereni* (Milan: Mursia, 1973); and Maria Laura Baffoni Licata, *La poesia di Vittorio Sereni: alienazione e impegno* (Ravenna: Longo, 1986).

present chapter seeks to contextualize the evolution of the Serenian 'I' within these boundaries, introducing the theoretical framework within which the linguistic and psychological complexity of the Serenian subject can be explored and understood.

FORGING A NEW PATH FOR THE SUBJECT: APPROACHES

As Elizabeth Wright declares in her study, *Speaking Desires can be Dangerous: The Poetics of the Unconscious*:

> Desire works in the very structure of language. [...] Psychoanalysis has a particular theory about why language is literary all the time, a particular way of accounting for the irrepressible figurality of language as it betrays the operations of desire and fantasy: the fact that language is inescapably figural makes equally for the stuff of literature, criticism and psychoanalysis.[4]

I also propose to present language—specifically poetic language—as the key to comprehending Sereni's poetic subject and his poetic identity. Psychoanalysis will provide one path to understanding and poetry another, each meeting in the linguistic space that mediates between the two, which in Sereni's case finds its clearest expression in deixis and the experience of liminality that ensues. While Sereni does not take his language from the Symbolist tradition, he does seem to have an awareness of the innate figurality of the poetic word: its resting along the cusp of being and non-being, its working by displacement and substitution, and its status as a mere simulacrum both of the 'I' who speaks and of the Other it would seek to represent.

To this extent, my analysis draws on some core ideas from critical theory, especially psychoanalysis and psycholinguistics, and recent studies of the poetic text that have sought to highlight the complexity of the question of identity in the lyric poem. This development follows a broader evolution in the epistemology of the poetic subject and an awareness of the textual strategies that poets use to bring it into being.[5] As Patricia Parker notes, the term 'lyric persona' emerged as a major part of the critical vocabulary only following the advent of New Criticism, which posited it as distinct from the notion of 'poet' (the empirical subject/experiential

---

[4] Elizabeth Wright, *Speaking Desires Can be Dangerous: The Poetics of the Unconscious* (Cambridge: Polity Press, 1999), p. 3. See also her comment, on p. 13, that 'Freud's repeated linguistic discovery throughout his work' was 'that desire cannot name itself except by substitution'.

[5] On this, see Paul Jay, *Being in the Text: Self-Representation from Wordsworth to Roland Barthes* (Ithaca, NY: Cornell University Press, 1984).

self) or, at most, interacting with it, often in problematic ways. The relationship between subjectivity and the lyric voice has remained an important matter of critical debate in studies of the poetic text, with increasing acknowledgement of the necessity of paying attention to the internal dynamics of poetic language itself and especially the 'conditions permitting the subject of lyric to speak'.[6]

Recently, emphasis has been on the 'displacing operations' of the modern (especially twentieth-century) lyric and its de-centring effects on the subject when viewed against the traditional, centralizing ones of Romantic poetry, in which each 'stanza' of the poem was still a room, complete in itself.[7] However we look at it, poetry is on some level a 'self-contained world where reality is verbal reality', and even if this world interacts with a notion of the world on the outside, there is something in the text that belongs to a realm we can only think of as poetic.[8] The 'I' partakes of both realities, and in Sereni's poetry, especially in its heavy reliance on deixis, the 'I' is always negotiating the poetic space between word and event, voice, and being, which Paul de Man has spoken of as the 'undecidability' of the relationship between fiction and autobiography, or the 'impossibility of closure and of totalization' when dealing with self-hood in the text.[9] As Paul Jay comments, revisiting de Man's thesis in 'Autobiography as De-Facement':

> The subject of an autobiographical work is by nature supposed to be factual, but, as the subject of a poem, it is also already figurative. [...] This is why the scene of writing becomes for the poem both locus and theatre, a site where the language of imagination struggles with the perception of fact, where neither can alone resolve the poet's dilemmas, and where those dilemmas deepen as history and present purpose fold into each other.[10]

Following Rimbaud's famous statement, 'Je est un autre' [I is another], the textual 'I' is recognized as 'always partly a fictive other'.[11] In the transition from the nineteenth to the twentieth centuries, doubt is cast

---

[6] See Patricia Parker, 'Introduction', in *Lyric Poetry: Beyond New Criticism*, ed. Chaviva Hošek and Patricia Parker (Ithaca, NY: Cornell University Press, 1985), pp. 11–28 (p. 25).
[7] For a good discussion of this, see Northop Frye, 'Approaching the Lyric', in *Lyric Poetry: Beyond New Criticism*, ed. Hošek and Parker, pp. 31–7.
[8] Ibid. 34.
[9] Paul de Man, 'Autobiography as De-Facement', *MLN* 94.5, Comparative Literature (Dec. 1979), pp. 919–30 (pp. 921, 922).
[10] Jay, *Being in the Text*, p. 91.
[11] Arthur Rimbaud, 'Lettre à Paul Demeny du 15 mai 1871', in *Lettres du Voyant*, ed. Gérald Schaeffer (Geneva: Minard, 1975), pp. 133–44 (p. 135). See also Jay, *Being in the Text*, p. 117.

upon the unity and consistency of the autobiographical or psychological subject, now viewed as subject to fragmentation, multiplicity, and temporal dispersion, and also to language itself, in which discourse and identity can be problematically discontinuous. Above all, doubt arises as to whether any individual can restore or recover the whole of itself in or through writing a text.[12]

In scholarship on Italian poetry, this has led to some major revisionary studies also on the early lyric, including those on the Petrarchan subject and the Leopardian 'I'. In the 1980s, Antonio Prete and Aldo Valentini both sought to underline Leopardi's modernity in this area, with Prete having recourse to Freud to explain the presence of 'questo fantasma che nel contempo è una pulsione, e che di lí ad alcuni decenni la psicoanalisi avrebbe sottratto definitivamente allo statuto cosciente e compatto dell'io, per leggerlo nella tumultuosa e frantumata economia dell'inconscio' [this phantasm, which is at the same time a drive, which a few decades later psychoanalysis would definitively remove from the conscious and firm dominion of the 'I', and locate instead in the tumultuous and fragmented economy of the unconscious].[13] Both studies have a bearing on my analysis of the Serenian subject, which similarly foregrounds the dynamic properties of the textual 'I' and the necessity of viewing it in a dialectic with, rather than in a transparent relationship to, the writing self.

These facets of lyric subjectivity are in turn discussed and developed in the context of twentieth-century Italian poetry by Enrico Testa, whose work on Sereni and other poets of the 1960s demonstrates how the self-reflexivity of the writing process was both intensified and rendered problematic by the fall of the poetic fourth wall and the subject's exile to 'una regione testuale [...] posta al di fuori dei canonici confini della poesia diaristica e confessionale' [a textual region [...] situated outside of the canonical boundaries of diaristic and confessional poetry].[14] In turn, this reflected a wider literary and cultural phenomenon that saw poetic practices changing to accommodate a new vision of the world founded upon increasing uncertainty in the face of social and economic change. For Sereni, this coincided with the intensification of a poetic and linguistic crisis which had already begun to make itself felt in the 1940s and 1950s, when all unity and harmony with the world was lost. If, following Gilberto Lonardi, we can see this as evidence of a 'cadenza leopardiana' [Leopardian

---

[12] See ibid. 176.
[13] Antonio Prete, *Il pensiero poetante: saggio su Leopardi* (Milan: Feltrinelli, 1980), p. 23; Alvaro Valentini, *Leopardi: l'io poetante* (Rome: Bulzoni, 1983).
[14] Enrico Testa, 'Introduction' to *Dopo la lirica: poeti italiani 1960–2000* (Turin: Einaudi, 2005), pp. v–xxx (p. xii).

cadence] in Sereni's work, then it is revealing of the contradictions at the heart of Sereni's project that his redefinition of the poetic subject should be made in the context of a return to an earlier model of lyric subjectivity *par excellence*, rather than a rejection of it:

> Si è comunque alzata di molto la soglia di ammissione al fare poesia, con Sereni. Questa ammissione si fonda su fini e criteri ormai molto concentrati sul soggetto. Se il fine può ridursi a un'autoterapia sempre ricominciata, il criterio è pressappoco quello della verità e unicità delle cose da testimoniare o da dire. Detto leopardianamente, la poesia può trovare un'ultima stretta via d'uscita come testimonianza dell''avventura storica' dell'io, della problematica unicità-verità di un'esistenza.[15]

> [With Sereni, the threshold of admission to writing poetry has been raised considerably. By now, that admission is founded on ends and criteria highly concentrated upon the subject. If the end amounts to a personal therapy always begun anew, the criterion is roughly that of the truth and uniqueness of the things to bear witness to or to say. Put in Leopardian terms, poetry can find a last, narrow escape route as the account of the 'historical adventures' of the 'I': the problematic truth and uniqueness of an existence.]

Unlike the more experimentalist practitioners of the Gruppo 63, Sereni sought a less extreme solution to the problems facing lyric poetry, attempting to rejuvenate the genre from within rather than breaking with it altogether.[16] As Laura Neri notes in her study of Sereni, like Andrea Zanzotto and Giovanni Giudici, he never abandons or rejects the 'I' completely. Rather, his poetry comes into being as a way of exploring the relationship between the 'I' and the world, and the extent to which that 'I' can still be represented in, or sustained by, language:

> L'io [...] appare sempre una forma rappresentabile. Se la poesia è una modalità privilegiata attraverso cui si vive un'esperienza, l'io è [...] lo strumento essenziale di conoscenza, il veicolo necessario affinché si stabilisca

---

[15] Gilberto Lonardi, 'Introduction' to Vittorio Sereni, *Il grande amico: poesie 1935–1981* [*The Great Friend: Poems 1935–1981*] [*GA*], ed. Gilberto Lonardi and Luca Lenzini (Milan: Rizzoli, 1990), pp. 5–25 (pp. 7–8).

[16] The Gruppo 63 was a group of neo-avant-garde poets and writers, formed in Palermo in 1963. While it never had a manifesto, its exponents were joined by their formal experimentalism and their desire to take Italian literature in a new direction, away from the neo-realist practices of the 1950s. Its high aesthetic values and its preference for complex literary codes meant, however, that it was criticized for creating works that were overly cerebral and too distanced from reality. An anthology of poems by *I Novissimi* was published in 1961, bringing together the works of Pagliarani, Balestrini, Giuliani, Porta, and Sanguineti, who in their different ways proposed an extreme abolition of subjectivity, aiming for a complete renewal of language. For a discussion of Sereni's relationship to *I Novissimi*, see Laura Neri, *Vittorio Sereni, Andrea Zanzotto, Giovanni Giudici: un'indagine retorica* (Bergamo: Bergamo University Press, 2001), pp. 17–18.

il rapporto con il mondo e con le cose. In questo senso, l'ambito della tradizione appare ancora praticabile.[17]

[The 'I' [...] always appears as a form that can be represented. If poetry is the privileged modality through which an experience is lived, the 'I' [...] is the essential instrument of knowledge, the necessary vehicle for the establishment of a relationship with the world and with things. In this sense, the domain of tradition still appears practicable.]

Like Leopardi, Sereni retains a certain nostalgia for a time when unity with the world was possible, also poetically and linguistically speaking, and he looks to poetry for ratification, if not resolution, of the more conflicting aspects of his existence. More than merely practicable, the dialogue with tradition is the space in which Sereni's poetic subject finds the way to its specific existence, and its own unique radicalism. It defines what Sergio Solmi would term a 'paradossale classicità' [paradoxical classicism], in which the lyric disposition endures but can only be constructed from the remains of the lyric itself: a creative stance that is both conservative and revolutionary at the same time.[18]

The source of this revolutionary dimension lies in language which each poet of the *terza generazione* [third generation] moulds to his own ends, from Andrea Zanzotto's concerns with the inauthenticity of existing linguistic materials to Giorgio Caproni's theatrical approach to staging his subject.[19] Sereni's approach is both less consciously literary than Zanzotto's and more intrinsically lyrical than Caproni's, although like them he has an awareness of the diminishing force and ground of the poetic word and the necessity of looking beyond the dominant Symbolist and Petrarchan modes of discourse that had largely defined the direction of lyric poetry up to that point:

> Cosí la definitiva soluzione della questione della lingua e la conquista, per la poesia, di un codice espressivo coincidente con l'italiano nella sua organica totalità, vanno di pari passo con l'acuirsi del senso dell'inadeguatezza dello

---

[17] Ibid. 18.
[18] 'La paradossale classicità, o meglio volontà classica, di Eliot e degli altri scrittori [...] consiste soprattutto in una suggestione di disperata salvezza, nello sforzo di non lasciarsi sommergere dal flusso incalzante, e in pari tempo di dominarlo, comprendendolo nelle sue segrete ragioni' [The paradoxical classicism or, better, classical will, of Eliot and other writers [...] consists above all in an atmosphere of despairing salvation, in the effort not to allow themselves to be overwhelmed by the insistent flux, and at the same time to dominate it, grasping its hidden causes], Sergio Solmi, 'Volontà classica del Novecento' (1946), in *La letteratura italiana contemporanea*, ed. Giovanni Pacchiano, 2 vols (Milan: Adelphi, 1992–8), II (= *Opere di Sergio Solmi*, III), pp. 511–19 (pp. 516–17).
[19] For a good introduction to the poetics of *La terza generazione*, see Anna Dolfi, *Terza generazione: ermetismo e oltre* (Rome: Bulzoni, 1997).

strumento linguistico a far fronte all'esperienza di un reale che appare, ad un tempo, irriconoscibile nel suo repentino mutamento e immodificabile nella sua evoluzione.[20]

[In this sense, the definitive solution to the language question, and poetry's attainment of an expressive code that coincides with Italian in its organic totality, go hand in hand with the heightening of the sense of inadequacy of the linguistic medium to face the experience of a reality that seems at once unknowable in its sudden mutability and unmodifiable in its evolution.]

Language and the world in disharmony with one another; a loss of faith in the power of poetry to completely embody reality or the self in their incessant, mutual, yet discrete, unfolding; the absence of any transparent relationship between the subject and his own discourse: these are the coordinates within which Sereni establishes the parameters of his poetic quest. Simultaneously, the 'I' renounces any hope of rediscovering meaning in the text and recuperates the poetic/writing experience as one of trauma. As Sereni writes in 'I versi' ['The Lines'] (in *SU*):

> Si fanno versi per scrollare un peso
> e passare al seguente. Ma c'è sempre
> qualche peso di troppo, non c'è mai
> alcun verso che basti
> se domani tu stesso te ne scordi.
> ('I versi', ll. 12–16, p. 149)

> [Lines are made to shrug off a burden
> and move on to the next one. But there's always
> some burden too many, there's never
> any line that's enough
> if tomorrow you yourself forget it.]

It is from these observations that I posit the view that in Sereni we are dealing with what is primarily a textual or linguistic subjectivity, whose identity depends upon its mode of expression and whose language inflects a persistent desire to bring that subject (back) to completion. Whether dealing with the genesis of the self, desire, or the poem, there is an ambivalence or doubleness at the moment in which the subject would be constituted as whole or meaningful. This brings Sereni's conception of identity close to some of the tenets of psychoanalysis, particularly in its post-structuralist dimensions.

---

[20] Enrico Testa, *Dopo la lirica: poeti italiani 1960–2000* (Turin: Einaudi, 2005), p. xii.

PSYCHOANALYTIC SUBJECTS

While not the dominant mode of criticism on Sereni, studies of his poetry within the framework of psychoanalysis have provided useful insights in this area, albeit almost solely with reference to Sigmund Freud. Stefano Agosti, for example, takes a Leopardian formulation ('Del fingere poetando un sogno' [Of depicting a dream in poetry], 1820) as his starting point to consider the relevance of Freud's theory of the interpretation of dreams for understanding what he terms a '*vera e propria stilistica e addirittura* [...] *una vera e propria grammatica della "rappresentazione"*' [*consummate style and even* [...] *grammar of 'representation'*] in Sereni's work, in which 'rappresentazione' would refer to the phase of dream that Freud terms the latent, as opposed to manifest, dream-contents. Agosti argues that this coincides with elements of Sereni's text— for example, his extensive use of ellipsis, of present participles with the functions of nouns, and oxymora—that imply a contiguity or non-differentiation of traditionally distinct elements. The confusion of subject and object, and especially the perceptual uncertainty that often strikes the subject of Sereni's poems, often depicted on the border between waking and sleeping, can be explained in these terms. Most relevant to the present discussion is Agosti's identification of the significance of Sereni's repeated designation of the border or limit as specifying the locus of an 'other' scene that is '[lo] *spazio in cui si attua la rappresentazione*' [[the] *space in which the representation takes effect*]—the place in which the true centre of the subject's being is stationed, which the unconscious would represent but is as such unreachable in its original guise.[21]

Both Remo Pagnanelli and Alessandro Di Bernardi also read aspects of Sereni through Freud, from the compulsion to repeat to the vagaries of Eros.[22] Di Bernardi's study of regression and the return of the repressed in

---

[21] Stefano Agosti, 'Interpretazione della poesia di Sereni', in *La poesia di Vittorio Sereni: atti del convegno*, ed. Stefano Agosti et al. (Milan: Librex, 1985), pp. 33–46 (p. 42) (italics in the original).
[22] Remo Pagnanelli, 'L'altra scena: "Lavori in corso" di Sereni', in *Studi critici: poesia e poeti italiani del secondo Novecento*, ed. Daniela Marcheschi (Milan: Mursia, 1991), pp. 56–65. Pagnanelli interprets the phantasms that populate Sereni's poetry as the presence of something like the Freudian 'uncanny': 'disegnano alla perfezione la natura del classico perturbante freudiano che invece di vestire i panni del *mostruoso* o del *lontano* è qualcosa che si agita dentro il grumo nucleare della famiglia, nel primo stadio della costituzione della personalità' [they perfectly outline the nature of the classic Freudian uncanny, which rather than taking the form of something *monstrous* or *distant*, stirs in the very nucleus of the family, during the first stage of the constitution of personality], p. 62 (italics in the original); Alessandro Di Bernardi, *Gli specchi multipli di Vittorio Sereni: 'Un posto di vacanza' e la crisi italiana degli anni Sessanta* (Palermo: S. F. Flaccovio, 1978).

Sereni's *Un posto* bridges Freudian and Jungian psychoanalysis. He interprets the poetic and linguistic crisis that affected Sereni in the 1950s as a sign of uncertainty as to the kind of subject of which Sereni could conceive in poetic terms, when forced to dissociate himself from the 'frustrazione narcisistica' [narcissistic frustration] associated with the more traditionally compact and monologic lyric 'I' which only broke the surface of reality, and to embrace a situation in which the 'I' 'sfugge continuamente a se stesso in una contrapposizione senza sintesi, giuocando una drammatica ed incerta partita che ora lo porta ai confini della dissoluzione, ora a quelli della totalità e della pienezza esistenziale' [continually eludes itself in a juxtaposition without synthesis, playing a dramatic and uncertain game that at one moment takes it to the very edges of dissolution, and at another towards those of totality and existential fullness].[23]

This tension is one upon which Zanzotto also elaborates in his study of *SU*, but he relates it instead to the guilt ('colpa') that Sereni feels in the face of the poetic act itself, defined as: '[la] ripetizione all'infinito di una presenza propria della poesia autoprospettantesi come unicità iniziale-edenica (e di là, con discutibile estrapolazione, come autosufficienza)' [[the] endless repetition of a presence characteristic of a poetry that projects itself as an original-Edenic unity (and beyond, with debatable inference, as self-sufficiency)]. Breaking with this Edenic guilt or original sin constitutes the event of trauma that ultimately coincides with the act of writing itself, for Sereni, 'rivolto all'anima e nascente da essa, da "quello che diciamo anima e non è che una *fitta* di rimorso" [...] destinato proprio per questo ad avviare di maschera in smascheramento, di illusione mitopoietica in trauma disillusorio' [directed toward the soul and born from it, from 'what we call the soul and is nothing but a pang of remorse' [...] destined precisely for this reason to turn from mask into unmasking, from mytho-poietic illusion into traumatic disenchantment]: an ulterior moment of disillusionment and a second fall.[24]

These studies already hint at the complexity of the discourse of desire that underpins Sereni's poetic project and the necessity of considering desire in all its facets, including those of language and the poem. This takes us beyond the Freudian conception of desire predominantly as Eros to the Lacanian and Kristevan formulation of desire in language.

---

[23] Pagnanelli, 'L'altra scena: "Lavori in corso" di Sereni', pp. 94–5.
[24] Zanzotto, '*Gli strumenti umani*', in *Aure e disincanti nel Novecento letterario* (Milan: Mondadori, 1994), p. 39.

Desire, or the topography of the subject after Freud

If Freud's revolution was the discovery of the unconscious, his primary legacy for Jacques Lacan and Julia Kristeva was that of the de-centred subject. Whether one took Freud's earlier topology of unconscious, conscious, and pre-conscious or his revised topology of id, ego, and superego, one had to accept that the subject was irrevocably split and part of itself was permanently barred from consciousness.[25] This constituted a 'topography' of the subject (the word is Freud's) that foregrounded the boundaries between the different elements, viewed as constantly shifting and easily invaded by their neighbouring territory.[26]

Yet if Freud's theory and praxis ultimately emphasized that the goal for the subject was to reach a viable, if elusive, synthesis, Lacan, after him, stressed instead the foreclosure of that possibility. In 'L'instance de la lettre dans l'inconscient ou la raison depuis Freud' ['The Agency of the Letter in the Unconscious or Reason since Freud'], Lacan states that the post-Freudian subject is not only dislocated and divided at the level of psychology but, more problematically still, split between different levels of discourse—conscious and unconscious, self-reflexive and intersubjective—which leaves it incomplete and in a state of perpetual (linguistic) alienation:

> Il ne s'agit pas de savoir si je parle de moi de façon conforme à ce que je suis, mais si, quand j'en parle, je suis le même que celui dont je parle. [...] Ce jeu signifiant de la métonymie et de la métaphore, jusque et y compris sa pointe active qui clavette mon désir sur un refus du signifiant ou sur *un manque de l'être* et noue mon sort à la question de mon destin, ce jeu se joue, jusqu'à ce que la partie soit levée, dans son inexorable finesse, là où je ne suis pas parce que je ne peux pas m'y situer.[27]
>
> [It is not a question of knowing whether I speak of myself in a way that conforms to what I am, but rather of knowing whether I am the same of which I speak. [...] This signifying game between metonymy and

---

[25] Freud's revised topology was introduced in 1923 in 'The Ego and the Id', in *The Standard Edition of the Complete Psychological Works of Sigmund Freud* [*SE*], ed. James Strachey, 24 vols (London: Hogarth Press, 1953–74), vol. XIX (1961), pp. 3–66.

[26] See esp. part II of his essay 'The Unconscious' (1915), which carries the heading 'Various Meanings of "the Unconscious": The Topographical Point of View', in *SE*, vol. XIV (1957), pp. 161–215 (pp. 172–6).

[27] Jacques Lacan, 'L'instance de la lettre dans l'inconscient ou la raison depuis Freud', in *Écrits I (Nouvelle édition, texte intégral)* (Paris: Éditions du Seuil, 1999 [1966]), pp. 490–526 (pp. 514–15); available in English in *Écrits: A Selection*, trans. Alan Sheridan (London: Routledge, 1977), from which translations of *Écrits* are taken, unless otherwise stated.

metaphor, up to and including the active edge that splits my desire between a refusal of the signifier and *a lack of being*, and links my fate to the question of my destiny, this game, in all its inexorable subtlety, is played until the match is called, there where I am not, because I cannot situate myself there.]

The speaking subject thus always begins from a point of loss and exile in language and is always already a subject of desire. In Kristeva's words: 'Notre don de parler, de nous situer dans le temps pour un autre, ne saurait exister qu'au-delà d'un abîme' [Our gift of speech, of situating ourselves in time for another, could exist nowhere except beyond an abyss].[28] This is not just a matter with which modern, psychoanalytic theory has concerned itself. As is well known, St Augustine's theory of language and language acquisition posits the birth of desire with the birth of language (the discrete word),[29] and Leopardi, in the nineteenth century, also seems to suggest that as soon as the child learns to speak and utters the name of an object, that object has already entered memory; it is already lost:

> E le più antiche reminiscenze sono in noi le più vive e durevoli. Ma elle cominciano giusto da quel punto dove il fanciullo ha già acquistato un linguaggio sufficiente, ovvero da *quelle prime idee che noi concepimmo unitamente ai loro segni*, e che noi potemmo fissare colle parole.[30]
>
> [The most ancient recollections are the most alive and enduring in us. Yet they originate precisely from that point at which the child has acquired a sufficient language; or better *from those first ideas that we conceived together with their signs* and could still fix in words.]

Speaking thus entails a loss for the subject as well as a gain, a balance which has shifted progressively towards the former with the development

---

[28] Julia Kristeva, *Soleil noir: dépression et mélancolie* (Paris: Gallimard, 1987), p. 54. Available in English as Julia Kristeva, *Black Sun: Depression and Melancholia*, trans. Leon S. Roudiez (New York: Columbia University Press, 1989), from which translations are taken.

[29] See e.g. Saint Augustine, *Confessions*, trans. Henry Chadwick (Oxford: Oxford University Press, 1992), vol. IV, x (15), pp. 61-2, 'So when things rise and emerge into existence, the faster they grow to be, the quicker they rush toward non-being. This is the law limiting their being. So much have you given them, namely to be parts of things which do not all have their being at the same moment, but by passing away and by successiveness, they all form the whole of which they are parts. That is the way our speech is constructed by sounds which are significant. What we say would be incomplete if one word did not cease to exist when it has sounded its constituent parts, so that it can be succeeded by another.' On Augustine's theory of language and desire, see also Elena Lombardi, 'Augustine: The Syntax of the Word', in *The Syntax of Desire: Language and Love in Augustine, the Modistae, Dante* (Toronto: University of Toronto Press, 2007), pp. 22-76.

[30] See Giacomo Leopardi, *Zib.* 1103, on the relationship between memory and language, in *Zibaldone*, ed. Lucio Felici (Rome: Grandi Tascabili Economici Newton, 1997), p. 256.

of modern (especially post-structuralist) theorizations of the relationship between subjectivity, language, and desire. As Elena Lombardi writes:

> With Lacan, lack, 'la manque à être,' is turned into an irremediable loss, not referring to any initial plenitude but indeed to initial nonexistence, or to the mere phantasmatic existence of both meaning and the object of desire. At the same time, however, desire is formulated as an omnipotent, all-driving force, which, crucially, excludes fulfilment.[31]

In other words, the object is absent, and what the 'I' pursues in language is only a ghost, or the sign of its disappearance. Desire emerges out of the gap dividing need from demand, and the subject, which exists only insofar as it desires, is located in the space between lack and fulfilment, merely endlessly deferred from one figuration to the next along the signifying chain but finding its home nowhere, since no single object (what Lacan terms the *objet 'a'*) can satisfy it or replace the originally lost object (*objet 'A'*) that motivates its search.[32]

Looking to linguistics, and to a distinction which Émile Benveniste makes between the *sujet de l'énonciation* [speaking subject] and the *sujet de l'énoncé* [subject of the statement], it follows that the latter can never contain the former in its entirety, but is merely a shadow of what existed moments before, which can only be retrospectively recuperated as such.[33] Lacan sees this epitomized in expletives of the 'ne' variety, in statements such as 'je crains qu'il *ne* vienne' [I'm afraid he'll come] in which that one word testifies to a disjunction between the overt message of the statement and the underlying motivations of the subject (of the

---

[31] Lombardi, *The Syntax of Desire*, p. 195.
[32] On desire as the gap between need and demand, see Lacan, 'La direction de la cure et les principes de son pouvoir' ['The Direction of Treatment and the Principles of Power'], in *Écrits II (Nouvelle édition, texte intégral)* (Paris: Éditions du Seuil, 1999 [1966]), pp. 62–123 (pp. 104–5), and Malcolm Bowie's commentary of the passage in *Lacan* (London: Fontana, 1991), pp. 136–7. On the identity of 'objet *a*' as the object of desire *par excellence*, see Lacan, 'Remarque sur le rapport de Daniel Lagache: "Psychanalyse et structure de la personnalité"', in *Écrits II*, pp. 124–62 (p. 159).
[33] 'La forme *je* n'a d'existence linguistique que dans l'acte de parole qui la profère. Il y a donc, dans ce procès, une double instance conjuguée: instance de *je* comme référent, et instance de discours contenant *je*, comme référé. La définition peut alors être précisée ainsi: *je* est l' "individu qui énonce la présente instance de discours contenant l'instance linguistique *je*"' [The form of *I* has no linguistic existence except in the act of speaking in which it is uttered. There is thus a combined double instance in this process: the instance of *I* as referent and the instance of discourse containing 'I' as the referee. The definition can now be stated precisely as: *I* is 'the individual who utters the present instance of discourse containing the linguistic instance *I*'], Émile Benveniste, 'La nature des pronoms' ['The Nature of Pronouns'], in *Problèmes de linguistique générale* (Paris: Gallimard, 1966), pp. 251–7 (p. 252). Translations are taken from Émile Benveniste, *Problems in General Linguistics*, trans. Mary Elizabeth Meek (Coral Gables, Fla.: University of Miami Press, 1971).

unconscious).[34] The 'ne' is precisely that which foregrounds the subject who is speaking whilst confirming its disunity and transitoriness, its being-for-death: 'le moment d'un fading ou éclipse du sujet, étroitement lié à la *Spaltung* ou refente qu'il subit de sa subordination au signifiant' [the moment of a 'fading' or eclipse of the subject that is closely bound up with the *Spaltung* or splitting that it suffers from its subordination to the signifier].[35]

The distinction between these two entities becomes important in relation to Sereni, since the fleetingness of the appearance of the true subject—the *sujet de l'énonciation*—and its propensity for continual fading is something he highlights in his grammatical and lexical choices. The poem 'Paura seconda' ['Second Fear'] demonstrates its effects, showing Sereni's unique ability to foreground areas of ambiguity traditionally effaced by the lyric text—in this case the potential for dissociation of the writing subject from his written self:

'Paura seconda'

Niente ha di spavento
la voce che chiama *me*
proprio *me*
dalla strada sotto casa
in un'ora di notte: 5
è un breve risveglio di vento,
una pioggia fuggiasca.
Nel dire il *mio* nome non enumera
i *miei* torti, non *mi* rinfaccia il passato.
Con dolcezza (Vittorio,   10
Vittorio) *mi* disarma, arma
contro *me* stesso *me*.
(In *SV*, p. 252)

['Second Fear']

There's nothing terrifying
about the voice that beckons *me*
actually *me*
from the street below *my* home
at some hour of night: 5
it's a wind's brief wakening,

---

[34] See Jacques Lacan, '*Das Ding (II)*', in *Le séminaire de Jacques Lacan. Livre VII: L'éthique de la psychanalyse, 1959–1960*, text established by Jacques-Alain Miller (Paris: Éditions du Seuil, 1986), pp. 71–86 (p. 79); available in English in *The Ethics of Psychoanalysis, 1959–1960: The Seminar of Jacques Lacan, Book VII*, ed. Jacques-Alain Miller, trans. Dennis Porter (London: Routledge, 2008).

[35] Lacan, 'Subversion du sujet et dialectique du désir dans l'inconscient freudien' ['The Subversion of the Subject and the Dialectic of Desire in the Unconscious'], in *Écrits II*, pp. 273–308 (p. 296).

a fleeting shower.
In speaking *my* name it doesn't list
my misdeeds, rebuke *me* for my past.
With tenderness (Vittorio,   10
Vittorio) it disarms *me*, is arming
me myself against *me*.]

The pronouns 'me' and 'mi', and the first person possessive adjectives 'mio' and 'miei', occur eight times in the space of twelve lines. Yet language (specifically speech) is still presented as a highly ambiguous source of identification for a subject divided from himself and unable to square the circle of his identity. The unthreatening quality of the voice, its proximity to nature, and its sweetness all contrast dramatically with its startling effects on the subject, the last three lines of the poem encapsulating the final linguistic trick that dissolves and reinstates the subject in the space of a moment. That the final confirmation of disunity is also the strongest affirmation of the subject's presence—'me' appearing twice in the same line and emphasized by the intermediate 'stesso' which paradoxically strengthens the sameness of the two halves—is indicative of Sereni's attitude elsewhere: only if the subject is under threat, only if he is not alone, does he have confirmation that he exists.

As in 'I versi', there is no linguistic liberation here, merely an intimately poetic version of 'suicide' which sees Sereni revisit and rewrite Pier della Vigna's 'ingiusto fece me contra me giusto' [made me, though just, against myself, unjust] (*Inferno* XIII, 72) in the third person, 'arma | contro me stesso me', in which words themselves have the agency rather than the subject.[36] There is no closure or finality, merely the interminable circle of the present action, which brings Sereni close to Maurice Blanchot's concept of the misguided writer who is always destined, in Lacanian fashion, to look for himself where he cannot be and to be where he does not think to look:

Écrire, c'est se faire l'écho de ce qui ne peut cesser de parler [...]. J'apporte à cette parole incessante la décision, l'autorité de mon silence propre. Je rends *sensible*, par ma médiation silencieuse, l'affirmation ininterrompue, le murmure géant sur lequel le langage en s'ouvrant devient image, profondeur parlante, indistincte plénitude qui est vide. Ce silence a sa source dans l'effacement auquel qui écrit est invité.[37]

---

[36] 'L'animo mio, per disdegnoso gusto, | credendo col morir fuggir disdegno, | *ingiusto fece me contra me giusto*' [My mind, in scornful temper, | hoping by dying to escape from scorn, | made me, though just, against myself, unjust], *Inf.* XIII, 70–2.

[37] Maurice Blanchot, *L'espace littéraire* (Paris: Gallimard, 1955), pp. 21–2. The English translation is taken from Maurice Blanchot, *The Space of Literature*, trans. Ann Smock (Lincoln: University of Nebraska Press, 1982) (italics in the original).

[To write is to make oneself the echo of what cannot cease speaking [...].
I bring to this incessant speech the decisiveness, the authority of my own
silence. I make *perceptible*, by my silent meditation, the uninterrupted
affirmation, the giant murmuring upon which language opens and thus
becomes image, becomes imaginary, becomes a speaking depth, an indistinct
plenitude which is empty. This silence has its source in the effacement
towards which the writer is drawn.]

'Un'angoscia limbale':[38] subjectivity in process

The presence of a subject in Sereni's poetry that is alternately created and effaced in the act of writing, and which straddles the interior and exterior dimensions of poetic space, brings us in turn into dialogue with Julia Kristeva's theory of poetic language. The highly original ways in which Sereni constructs his poetic subject within the parameters of his textual universe gain clarification and meaning when viewed as evidence of a 'sujet en procès' [subject in process/on trial].[39] For Kristeva, this is the poetic subject *par excellence*, modelled on the speaking and desiring subject of Lacanian psychoanalysis and reinterpreted in light of the specifically textual issues that surround the question of identity in poetry.

Kristeva's 'sujet en procès' is one caught up in the process of 'signifiance' which rivals, disrupts, and counteracts the 'signification' of normal, rational discourse. Its presence is always indicative of a rupture—an interrogation or transgression of the syntactic position (what Kristeva calls the 'thetic')—which is simultaneously a contesting of 'la *position* d'un ego, comme seule et unique contrainte constitutive de tout acte linguistique' [[the] *positing* [of] an ego as the single, unique constraint

---

[38] [Limbic anxiety].

[39] 'Décentrant l'*ego* transcendantal, le coupant et l'ouvrant à une dialectique dans laquelle son entendement syntaxique et catégoriel n'est que le moment liminaire du procès, lui-même toujours agi par le rapport à l'autre que domine la pulsion de mort et sa réitération productrice du 'signifiant': tel nous apparaît ce sujet dans le langage' [We view the subject in language as decentering the transcendental ego, cutting through it, and opening it up to a dialectic in which its syntactic and categorical understanding is merely the liminary moment of the process, which is itself always acted upon by the relation to the other dominated by the death drive and its productive reiteration of the 'signifier'], Julia Kristeva, *La révolution du langage poétique. L'avant-garde à la fin du xixe siècle: Lautréamont et Mallarmé* (Paris: Éditions du Seuil, 1974), p. 30. English translations are taken from Julia Kristeva, *Revolution in Poetic Language*, trans. Margaret Waller (New York: Columbia University Press, 1984). See also 'Le sujet en procès', in Julia Kristeva, *Polylogue* (Paris: Éditions du Seuil, 1977), pp. 55–106.

which is constitutive of all linguistic acts].[40] Dividing the subject between symbolic and semiotic processes, 'poetic language' leaves the 'I' exposed to heterogeneous forces that pull it in two directions simultaneously, and end its desire for unity:[41]

> Nous distinguerons le sémiotique (les pulsions et leurs articulations) du domaine de la signification, qui est toujours celui d'une proposition d'un jugement; c'est à dire un domaine de *positions*. Cette positionnalité, que la phénoménologie husserlienne orchestre à travers les concepts de *doxa*, de *position* et de *thèse*, se structure comme une coupure dans le procès de la signifiance, instaurant l'*identification* du sujet et de ses objets comme conditions de la propositionnalité.[42]

> [We shall distinguish the semiotic (drives and their articulations) from the realm of signification, which is always that of a proposition or judgement, in other words, a realm of *positions*. This positionality, which Husserlian phenomenology orchestrates through concepts of *doxa*, *position*, and *thesis*, is structured as a break in the signifying process, establishing the *identification* of the subject and its object as preconditions of propositionality.]

These concepts prove useful in analysing Sereni's poetry, since the positionality of his poetic subject is often put in doubt or disrupted, resulting in it being able to achieve only a partial identification with objects and with itself, which leaves it in a perpetual state of incompleteness and (thus of) desire. In the transition from Sereni's first collection, *Frontiera*, to his fourth, *SV*, monologue gradually comes to be replaced by dialogue and the linguistic hegemony of the 'I' by a more heterogeneous and intersubjective discourse reality. It is rare in his work to find any entity that permits a stable definition, and his subject resists articulation on its own terms, so that we are often faced with successive incarnations from poem to poem and collection to collection rather than any over-reaching

---

[40] Kristeva, *La révolution du langage poétique*, p. 31.
[41] The semiotic realm is formed by the collection of drives and energy discharges that were intrinsic to an early stage of the subject's development in its orientation and connection with the mother's body. Like Freud's instinctual drives, which incorporate the death drive, these semiotic forces are simultaneously assimilative and destructive and threaten to draw the subject back towards a state of nothingness or non-being. The symbolic forces would seek to counteract this by reinstating a more centralized position for the subject, a position of 'thesis' that Kristeva aligns with the transcendental ego of Husserlian phenomenology, able to put into parenthesis all that is heterogeneous to the subject, under the illusion of conscious control. For a detailed discussion of these ideas, see ibid. ch. 1, 'Sémiotique et symbolique' ['The Semiotic and the Symbolic'], pp. 17–100.
[42] Kristeva, *La révolution du langage poétique*, p. 41 (italics in the original). The key contradiction rests, as Kristeva explains, in the active pushing away of objects as they come to be substituted by the sign, so that possession on one level corresponds to dispossession on the other.

sense of unity or identity: different configurations, precisely, of the subject's changing relationship to the universe of its own discourse.

Thus while my focus will be more on the linguistic displacement of the subject than on the specific conflict between semiotic and symbolic, it is helpful to consider the parallels that emerge between the divided and heterogeneous nature of Kristeva's 'subject in process' and Sereni's disunified subject, exiled in language, which sits awkwardly in the realm of its own making. Above all, Kristeva's theory of the speaking and desiring subject can shed light upon the presence of a threshold subject in Sereni's universe, always already divided between two (linguistic) realities, or between the memory of an earlier (linguistic) fullness and the recognition of its loss in the present:

> O voce ora abolita, già divisa, o anima bilingue
> *tra* vibrante avvenire e tempo dissipato
> o spenta musica *già* torreggiante e triste.
> (*Una visita in fabbrica* [*A Factory Visit*] I, 19–21, p. 125)
>
> [O voice now banned, already split, O two-tongued spirit
> *between* vibrant days-to-come and wasted time,
> O silenced music, towering and sad *already*.]

'Tra [...] già'—these are the key coordinates of Sereni's poem, which suspend the subject in a textually indeterminate space between past, present, and future, between time lost and time to be regained, and lead every object to be defined by its imminent, or already complete, annihilation. This condition of liminality is, for Sereni, an intimately poetic version of exile which leads to the poet suffering from what, following Stefano Agosti's study of Montale's poem 'Sul lago d'Orta' ['On Lake Orta'], we can term 'un'angoscia limbale'—the result, precisely, of inhabiting a place that is also a no-place because it cannot be embraced on its own terms but only through its difference with the spaces that border it:

> Il 'limbo' è, etimologicamente, un 'lembo': il lembo di un luogo *e* dell'altro. È il punto di raccordo, di sutura di due margini, di due orli, dell'orlo di due luoghi diversi ed estremi. 'Angoscia *limbale*' sarà allora l'equivalente di un'angoscia del *'tra'*, di un'angoscia dell'intervallo, o, come è detto qui a tutte lettere, dell'*intermezzo* (v.15): angoscia del Non-luogo, angoscia dell'essere TRA due luoghi, di non trovarsi in nessuno.[43]
>
> ['Limbo' is etymologically a 'border': the border between one place *and* the other. It is the joint or suture of two margins, two edges, or of the edge of two different and extreme places. '*Limbic* anxiety' is therefore the equivalent of an anxiety of the '*between*', of the interval, or as it is said here in so many

---

[43] Stefano Agosti, 'Il testo della poesia: "Sul lago d'Orta"', in *Cinque analisi: il testo della poesia* (Milan: Feltrinelli, 1982), pp. 69–87 (p. 78) (italics in the original).

words, of the *interlude* (v. 15): the anxiety of a No-place, of being BETWEEN two places, of finding oneself in neither.]

Sereni's progressive attenuation of the domain of his lyric subject, and its increasing absence of a fixed identity, derives from just such a positional anxiety. Returning to Sereni's designation of the lyric as a 'luogo ideale', we can say that he *is* a lyric poet in essence, to the extent that he never renounces the place of the lyric even when it has ceased to function in an ideal way, but he does radically alter its parameters. The always implicit threat of disintegration of his poetic landscape correlates with an uncertainty with regard to his own poetic identity and, as Barile suggests, this constitutes Sereni's own version of a 'soggetto "debole"' ['weak' subject], reminiscent of Vattimo's:

> La poesia di Sereni si svolge sempre al confine, argine, foce [...]. Chi sta sul limite 'svela la sua perenne attrazione alle ragioni dell'opposto', ed è dunque il suo uno stato di indicibilità, della perdita della totalità, dell'ingresso in una nuova dimensione di soggetto 'debole' [...].
>
> La sua è una poesia senza canto, senza il conforto della tensione metrica (vedi Caproni) o delle grandi forme, la possibilità della regressione all'infanzia. Il personaggio di Sereni sbanda, subisce rimorsi e dileggio senza una maschera o un compenso alla incompletezza dell'io.[44]
>
> [Sereni's poetry always takes place at the border, bank, or river mouth [...]. Whoever rests on the edge 'reveals his perennial attraction for the law of opposites', and his state is consequently one of undecidability, the loss of totality, and the entry into a new dimension of the 'weak' subject [...].
>
> Sereni's is a poetry without lyricism, without the security of metrical tension (see Caproni), grand poetic forms, or the possibility of regression to childhood. As a character, Sereni swerves off course, suffers remorse and derision, without a mask or any kind of compensation for the incompleteness of the 'I'.]

BEYOND THEORY

My exploration of the ways in which Sereni establishes his poetic subject, and redefines lyric discourse, thus begins from this point. As will become

---

[44] Barile, *Sereni*, p. 115. 'Pensiero debole' or 'weak thought' is a notion conceived by the philosopher Gianni Vattimo (b. 1936) in the 1980s to explain the crisis of reason which was prevalent in philosophical and literary thought of the 1970s. With this notion, Vattimo proposes a break away from logocentric philosophies and absolute doctrines of power in order to embrace a more relativist and multiplist view of the world which takes into account differences and contradictions in distinction to more unified models of thought. See *Il pensiero debole*, ed. Gianni Vattimo and Pier Aldo Rovatti (Milan: Feltrinelli, 1983).

evident, regression in his case indeed has little to do with the longing to return to childhood, and pivots instead upon a nostalgia that is intimately poetic, which leads him back to places in his own poetry and the poetry of others—a phase in his poetic infancy, more than his actual one. In turn, the semiotic residues of Kristeva's theory are evident in Sereni less in a cult of the maternal and more in a form of poetic memory that sees the poet return to sites of a primordial contact with nature and with other, feminine, presences often recuperated only very fragmentarily in his own poetic universe.

As Lonardi notes, 'l'assenza di una forma-canzoniere comporta l'estraneità—in una poesia che pure gioca in modo straordinario alcune delle sue carte sul dialogato—l'estraneità a un dialogo continuo, fondante, ontologico col Femminile' [the absence of a canzoniere form implies the distance from a continuous, foundational, and ontological dialogue with the Feminine, in a poetry that still stakes—in remarkable ways—some of its key strategies upon dialogue];[45] In Sereni's poetry, landscape effectively replaces the Other as the locus of desire, or becomes so completely bound up with it as to be indistinguishable. This makes his object of desire both broader in scope and less secure than the traditional lyric object. The comfort which, according to Barile, is denied Sereni in the absence of metrical tensions, or the support of illustrious or substantial poetic forms, is sought, often unsuccessfully, in the boundaries of poetic space. Taking Sereni far beyond the traditional limits of lyric practice, his configuration of his textual landscape opens up uncharted territories of lyric subjectivity that it will be his poetry's particular course to navigate, 'Se l'idea di poesia che ogni poeta porta con sé fosse raffigurabile in uno specchio, noi vedremmo quello specchio assumere di volta in volta tutti i colori possibili, riflettere non un'immagine ma una battaglia di immagini' [If the idea of poetry that each poet carries with him could be represented in a mirror, we would see that mirror take on over time all the colours of the rainbow, reflect not one image but a series of conflicting images].[46] The following chapters each explore a different facet of Sereni's poetic subject as it confronts the changing contours of its figural existence.

---

[45] Sereni, *GA*, p. 16.
[46] Sereni, 'Esperienza della poesia' ['The Experience of Poetry'] (1947), first publ. in *Gli immediate dintorni* [*The Immediate Surroundings*] (Milan: Il Saggiatore, 1962) [*ID1*], pp. 41–6, now in *Gli immediati dintorni: primi e secondi* [*The Immediate Surroundings: First and Second*] ed. Maria Teresa Sereni (Milan: Il Saggiatore, 1983) [*ID2*], pp. 25–8 (pp. 26–7).

2
Replotting the Textual Landscape

The Role of Deixis in Frontiera *and* Gli strumenti umani

> Dovrò cambiare geografie e topografie.
> Non vuole saperne,
> mi rinnega in effigie, rifiuta
> lo specchio di me (di noi) che le tendo.
>
> (Vittorio Sereni, 'Addio Lugano bella')[1]

When, in his *Zibaldone*, Leopardi wrote that 'tempo e spazio non sono in sostanza altro che idee, anzi nomi' [time and space are in essence nothing but ideas, or, better, names], he could almost have been speaking about the language of deixis in the lyric poem.[2] His words certainly prefigure Sereni's own awareness of the ideal role which deictics—as markers of subjective experience—can have within the poetic universe, from spatio-temporal coordinates creating worlds out of words, to personal pronouns and demonstratives designating figures, more ideal than real, that inhabit the realms of poetic space. Where deictics appear in Sereni's poetry—and they remain one of its constituent features—we are transported to the very heart of the lyric universe, and to a concern with the power of poetry to give voice and meaning to a speaking subject posited as its origin.

As such, the realm of deictic reference coincides with the most problematic and original aspects of Sereni's lyric universe: the obsessive concern with situating the self in space and time; the relationship to the Other (object of desire); and the locality or illocality of that Other within the domain of the poem (desiring field). As the epigraph to this chapter from 'Addio Lugano bella' [Beautiful Lugano Goodbye'] (in *SV*) reveals, Sereni's later poetry is marked by disorientation and uncertainty, with landscape—here personified as a woman—refusing the poet's mirror or, better, refusing

---

[1] [I'll have to change landscapes and places. | She doesn't want to know, | denies me in effigy | refuses, the mirror of me (of us) I offer] ('Beautiful Lugano Goodbye').

[2] Leopardi, *Zib.* 4233, in *Zibaldone*, ed. Lucio Felici (Rome: Grandi Tascabili Economici Newton, 1997), p. 873.

to act as the poet's mirror. He reaches out to her but his appeal is denied, the phrase 'in effigie' [in effigy] indicating that it is the reflected (poetic) image itself which has become distorted, or her (their) perception of it. The specular relationship which has aided the poetic 'I' in the past, going right back to *Frontiera*, is failing, and Sereni must therefore pursue new modes for its representation, new 'geografie e topografie' [landscapes and places], which go beyond pre-established frameworks of lyric discourse.[3]

Looking at the changing role of deictic reference from *Frontiera* to *SU* in fact allows us to map a profound revolution occurring at the level of poetic space and lyric subjectivity. The comparison between the two collections with regard to the deictic strategies Sereni employs is a particularly fruitful one, since the later poetry explicitly establishes itself as a retrospective on the earlier work. Sereni consciously revisits and re-tropes the landscapes of the past (both geographic and poetic) in a backward turn that is the mark of his later poetry, as well as a sign of his commitment to redefining the coordinates of the lyric 'I' in line with his changing view of the world. It is these changing features of Sereni's textual landscape that this chapter sets out to investigate.

TOWARDS A THEORY OF DEIXIS

Deixis, a word from classical Greek grammar, designates as a whole the elements of language that have the function of pointing or indicating, whether to the presence of the speaker or to his/her location relative to his/her surroundings. These functions have acquired central importance in linguistic and literary theory, especially in the work of Karl Bühler in the 1930s and Émile Benveniste in the 1950s and 1960s. It was Benveniste who underlined the unique status of the 'pronoun' 'I', which does not stand in for a noun, but rather signals the source of the 'speech act', in other words the speaking subject (*sujet de l'énonciation*), not the subject of the sentence (*sujet de l'énoncé*), who establishes the egocentric perspective at the root of language.[4] Deictics 'sont les indicateurs [...] qui organisent les

---

[3] On the deictic reorientation that takes place in Sereni's *SV*, see Niva Lorenzini, 'Nuove configurazioni del paesaggio testuale', in *La poesia italiana del Novecento: modi e tecniche*, ed. Marco A. Bazzocchi (Bologna: Pendragon, 2003), pp. 213–29 (pp. 214–16).

[4] 'C'est pourtant un fait à la fois original et fondamental que ces formes "pronominales" ne renvoient pas à la "réalité" ni à des positions "objectives" dans l'espace ou dans le temps mais à l'énonciation, chaque fois unique, qui les contient, et réfléchissent ainsi leur propre emploi' [Yet it is a fact, both original and fundamental that these 'pronominal' forms do not refer to 'reality' or to 'objective' positions in space or time but to the utterance, unique each time, that contains them, and thus they reflect their proper use'], Émile Benveniste, 'La

Replotting the Textual Landscape 53

relations spatiales et temporales autour d'un 'sujet' pris come repère [...] c'est à dire sous la dépendance du *je* qui s'y énonce' [are the indicators [...] which organize the spatial and temporal relationships around the 'subject' taken as referent [...] that is, in dependence upon the *I* which is proclaimed in the discourse].[5] They are consequently an existential as well as a linguistic index, which foregrounds the present instance of discourse through which the speaking subject gains life, announcing itself.[6]

From here derives the complementary designation of deictics as 'empty signs' ('signes vides') of discourse, or 'shifters' ('embrayeurs'),[7] made 'full' only as each speaker appropriates them in turn, and their complementary poetic function, which Enrico Testa terms 'enunciativa (o meglio che *simula* l'enunciazione)' [enunciative (or better that simulates the enunciative act)]:

> L'azione dei deittici è volta ad instaurare una situazione enunciativa, a determinare un universo di discorso, che vuol far intravedere dietro la figura, irrimediabilmente lontana e passata, di chi scrive (di chi ha scritto) quella, illusoriamente presente, di chi parla. L'interagire e il vicendevole richiamarsi di queste *personae* danno luogo ad una diplopia, ad uno sfalsamento dei piani, in cui s'avanza ciò che pare star dietro al testo (il dire) e arretra quanto ne costituisce—fisicamente e percettivamente—la superficie (il detto).[8]

> [Deictics are there to establish an enunciative situation, to determine a universe of discourse, which allows us to glimpse behind the irremediably distant and past figure of the one who writes (who has written), that, illusorily present, of the one who speaks. The interaction and mutual recall of these *personae* give rise to a form of double vision, a staggering of levels in which what lies behind the text (the act of speaking) comes to the fore, and what constitutes its surface (what is said), physically and perceptively speaking, falls into the background.]

nature des pronoms', in *Problèmes de linguistique générale* (Paris: Gallimard, 1966), p. 254. I am indebted to Giulio Lepschy for his help with this formulation.

[5] Émile Benveniste, 'De la subjectivité dans le langage' ['Subjectivity in Language'], in *Problèmes de linguistique générale*, pp. 258–66 (p. 262).

[6] 'L'essentiel est donc la relation entre l'indicateur (de personne, de temps, de lieu, d'objet montré, etc.) et la *présente* instance de discours' [The essential thing, then, is the relation between the indicator (of person, time, place, object shown, etc.) and the *present* instance of discourse], Benveniste, 'La nature des pronoms', p. 254 (italics in the original).

[7] On the designation of deictics as 'signes "vides"' ['empty' signs], see ibid. 254; on deictics as 'embrayeurs' [shifters], see Roman Jakobson, 'Les embrayeurs, les catégories verbales et le verbe russe', in *Essais de linguistique générale* (Paris: Minuit, 1963), pp. 176–96 (p. 179); in English as 'Shifters and Verbal Categories', in Roman Jakobson, *On Language*, ed. Linda R. Waugh and Monique Monville Burston (Cambridge, Mass.: Harvard University Press, 1990), pp. 386–92.

[8] Enrico Testa, '*Sur la corde de la voix*: funzione della deissi nel testo poetico', in *Linguistica, pragmatica e testo letterario*, ed. Umberto Rapallo (Genova: Il Melangolo, 1996), pp. 113–46 (p. 120) (italics in the original).

In this way, deictics create a bridge between the linguistic and extralinguistic domains, the world of the text and the (possible) world on the outside. In poetry of course, that 'world' may be projected by the utterance more than described, in the same way that the speaking subject, as the originating locus of the poetic voice, is essentially constructed *post factum* from the written word but is presented as its foundation or source. That which was nothing moments before assumes a form that radiates out from the subjective heart of the utterance, and language (*langue*—at the disposal of all speakers) is transformed into discourse (*parole*—appropriated uniquely by each individual speaker in turn).[9] In turn, this discourse reality, to which the speaking 'I' also belongs, opens language up beyond itself while simultaneously attesting to the fact that the boundaries of that world are dependent upon the speaker's own limits: his/her situation in time and space. As Jean François Lyotard states of deictics in *Discours, Figure*:

> L'intérêt, l'énigme de ces mots [...] c'est précisément qu'il s'ouvrent le langage sur une expérience que le langage ne peut pas stocker dans son inventaire, puisqu'elle est celle d'un *hic et nunc*, d'un *ego*, c'est-à-dire précisément de la certitude sensible [...]. Avec ces 'indicateurs' le langage est comme percé de trous par où le regard peut se glisser, l'œil voir au dehors et s'y ancrer, mais cet 'au dehors' renvoie lui-même à l'intimité première du corps et de son espace (et de son temps).[10]
>
> [The interest, the enigma of these words [...] is precisely that they open language onto an experience that language cannot stock in its inventory because it is the experience of a *hic et nunc*, of an *ego*, i.e. precisely that of sense-certainty [...]. With these 'shifters' it is as though language is pierced by holes through which the gaze can insinuate itself, the eye see outside and anchor itself there, but that 'outside' itself refers to the primary intimacy of the body and of its space (and time).]

Deictics are thus figures of speech in a more urgent sense than merely that of a rhetorical use of language, or even the evocation of the spoken over the written word. They actually engender being in the text. It is these features of deixis that have made it one of the mainstays of lyric poetry, and its egocentrism a key facet of the traditional lyric universe with which Sereni engages. As 'il segno (*lo stigma*) di una naturale disposizione lirica'

---

[9] On the notions of *langue* and *parole*, see Ferdinand de Saussure, 'Linguistique de langue et linguistique de parole', in *Cours de linguistique générale* (Paris: Payot, 1972), pp. 36–9.
[10] Jean François Lyotard, *Discours, Figure* (Paris: Klincksieck, 1971), p. 39 (italics in the original). 'Sense-certainty' is a Hegelian concept discussed in his *Phenomenology of Spirit* as a concrete 'Thisness' which brings the subject face to face with the object-world through consciousness.

[the sign (*the stigma*) of a natural lyric disposition], deixis is regarded by Sereni as a powerful but problematic heritage.[11] Initially embraced as a sign of the 'I''s ability to subordinate the natural world to its point of view, it is later resisted as the mark of a kind of poetic tyranny that sits uneasily with Sereni's desire to encompass a more heterogeneous view of the world.

As Keith Green has argued, poets (especially lyric poets) often employ deictic reference to mobilize a 'powerful deictic centre', to install the 'I' at the very centre of its universe where it can exercise experiencing and observing modes simultaneously: a version of poetic anthropocentrism that would imply easy possession of both space and language. This 'deictic centre' is dependent upon the *origo* or 'centre of utterance', against which the extensions of time, space, and subjectivity are measured.[12] Its anchoring effects are reinforced through the appositional quality of the space it determines—the fact that 'here' is opposed to 'there', 'this' to 'that', 'I' to 'non-I'—and its ability to reinforce the separateness of the 'I' from the objects around it. Discussing the philosophical implications which deixis has for 'self-designation', Paul Ricoeur highlights its identity as the extension of a subject wishing to establish itself as fixed, stable and locatable, designating the 'regione deittica' [deictic region] that the 'I' can bring under its jurisdiction:

> Il en est de même du 'ici': il s'oppose au 'là-bas', comme étant le lieu où je me tiens corporellement; ce lieu absolu a le même caractère de limite du monde que l'*ego* de l'énonciation; [...] absolument parlant, 'ici', en tant que lieu où je me tiens, est le point zéro par rapport auquel tous les lieux deviennent proches ou lointains.[13]

---

[11] Matteo Boero, 'La grana della voce: ritmo e intonazione negli *Strumenti umani*', *Stilistica e metrica italiana* 6 (2006), pp. 177–98 (pp. 184–5).

[12] On this notion of *origo*, see Keith Green, 'Deixis and the Poetic Persona', *Language and Literature* 1.1 (1992), pp. 121–34 (p. 122). The term was originally used by Karl Bühler in *Sprachtheorie: die Darstellungsfunktion der Sprache* (Jena: Fischer, 1934), available in English as *Theory of Language: The Representational Function of Language*, trans. Donald Fraser Goodwin (Amsterdam: Benjamins, 1990).

[13] Paul Ricoeur, *Soi-même comme un autre* (Paris: Éditions du Seuil, 1990), p. 70 (italics in the original). The English translation is from Paul Ricoeur, *Oneself as Another*, trans. Kathleen Blamey (Chicago: University of Chicago Press, 1992), p. 53. I take the notion of 'regione deittica' from the *Grande grammatica italiana della consultazione*, ed. Lorenzo Renzi et al., 3 vols (Bologna: Il Mulino, 1995), vol. III, ch. 6, 'La deissi', pp. 261–375 (p. 270), defined as 'la porzione di spazio che il parlante assume come direttamente collegata con il luogo in cui si trova. Atteggiamenti soggettivi e fattori extralinguistici determinano l'estensione della regione deittica rilevante, assegnando un valore relativo a termini quali "vicino" e "lontano"' [the portion of space that the speaker appropriates as directly linked to the place in which he finds himself. Subjective attitudes and extralinguistic factors determine the extension of the deictic region in question, giving a relative value to terms like 'near' and 'far'].

[The same thing is true with respect to 'here': it is opposed to 'there' as the place in which I am situated corporally. This absolute place has the same limit-of-the-world character as the *ego* of the utterance. [...] absolutely speaking, 'here', as the place where I am, is the zero point in relation to which all other places become near or far.]

The centripetal force that forms around the more unified and monologic 'I' of *Frontiera* is a mark of this disposition, but also indicates its limits. As an intimately relational space, the deictic field necessarily also highlights the interdependency of the 'I' on a range of objects that occupy the space outside the self and from which, for Sereni, any true dialogue with the world must begin.[14] So demonstratives, which designate the position of an object or referent relative to the *origo*, can be linked positively ('questo' [this]) or negatively ('quello' [that]) to the 'I', in the same way that 'qui' or 'qua' [here] imply proximity to the speaking 'I', and 'lì' or 'là' [there], distance. Looking at Sereni's poetry in detail, it also becomes possible to draw more nuanced conclusions about the value of these deictics as markers of the desiring field. For example, 'quello' will tend to coincide with temporal distancing, or the otherness of the desired object, while 'questo' is generally charged with a sense of ownership of the present. However, these functions can be complicated by the intercession of memory or the imagination, which have the potential to reverse the terms where the desired object is being recovered from the past.

An example from *Frontiera* provides an indication of the complexity of this mechanism. In the poem 'Diana', centred upon the recuperation of a dead female figure, all the efforts of the 'I' go into creating a situation in which the return of that lost Other might be possible. The repetition of the deictic 'qui' (ll. 15, 24), as the space which the 'I' occupies, and to which he would have the *tu* [you] return, marks the deictic centre of the poem, but its location shifts in such a way as to render it ambivalent. Initially, it coincides with a space on the outside that is the scene (and event) of Diana's return: where he recognizes her gait and where her name is spoken, conjuring her back to life, 'Ronza un'orchestra in sordina; | all'aria che *qui* ne sobbalza | ravviso il tuo ondulato passare, | s'addolce nella sera il fiero nome | se qualcuno lo mormora | sulla tua traccia' [Muted, an orchestra hums; | *here* with the bouncy air | I recognize your

---

[14] 'Io in poesia sono per le "cose"; non mi piace dire "io", preferisco dire: "loro". [...] Con tutti i pericoli che ne derivano; notazioni, magari impressionismi, non risolti; "loro" ma soltanto "loro" senza che ci sia dentro "io"' [In poetry I'm for 'things', I don't like saying 'I', I prefer to say 'they'. [...] With all the dangers that derive from it; notations, doubtless an unresolved form of impressionism; 'they' just 'they', without an 'I' inside them], Vittorio Sereni, letter to Giancarlo Vigorelli, 25 Jan. 1937, reproduced in Dante Isella, *Giornale di 'Frontiera'* (Milan: Archinto, 1991), pp. 33–5 (p. 34).

swaying walk | the proud name sweetens in the evening | should somebody murmur it across your wake] (ll. 14–19, in *Frontiera*, p. 23). However, by the end of the poem, all that returns 'here' is a melancholy nostalgia for her song; an elegiac lamentation of her death. The 'qui' shifts its coordinates entirely to bare its true nature as *internal* to the 'I': 'e il canto che avevi, amica, sulla sera | *torna* a dolere *qui dentro*, | alita sulla memoria | a rimproverarti la morte' [and the song you had in the evening | *returns* to ache *within here*, | breathes on the memory | to reprove you for dying] (ll. 23–6). In deictic terms, the power of poetry is enough to breathe life into a dead image, yet it also revives the painful memory of a loss that it would seek to exorcise but cannot. Perceptually, 'qui' marks the spot in which past and present are bridged, but it cannot fully elide the awareness of the underlying absence at its heart, leaving the 'I' bereft a second time.

Similarly, a hierarchy is often implied in Sereni's poetry between 'qui/lì' and 'qua/là'. The former pair normally suggest that the space designated by the deictics has been pinpointed and circumscribed (though may also be fixed or limited in some way); the latter do not offer such a firm coordination of boundaries but perhaps allow a freer enjoyment of space. In addition, 'qui/lì' often coincide with an exact, though often limited, frame of visual perception, 'qua/là' with a more open gaze or perspective, not necessarily so much within the subject's control. Leopardi's 'L'infinito' ['The Infinite'], perhaps the primary point of reference in Sereni's deictic quest, provides the 'luogo ideale' [ideal place] of these facets of deixis, combining as it does the poles of extreme visual prescription and foreclosure, and intense imaginative and imaginary 'wandering' (*errare*). The latter is potentially disconcerting and even dangerous for an 'I' that almost loses itself in the experience, but poetically speaking the goal: infinite enjoyment of a linguistically dilated space. Just a few lines from the poem will suffice to indicate their deictic power:

> Sempre caro mi fu quest'ermo colle,
> e questa siepe, che *da tanta parte*
> *dell'ultimo orizzonte lo sguardo esclude.*
> [...]
>
> *Così tra questa*
> *immensità* s'annega il pensier mio:
> e il *naufragar* m'è dolce in *questo mare.*
> (ll. 1–3, 13–15)
>
> [I always did value this lonely hill,
> And this hedgerow also, *where so wide a stretch*
> *Of the extreme horizon's out of sight.*

[...] And so
In this immensity my thought is drowned:
And I enjoy *my sinking* in *this sea*.]

As Antonio Prete puts it, 'ciò che è escluso diventa l'oggetto della vera appropriazione' [that which is excluded becomes the object of the true act of appropriation].[15] The landscape (both interior and exterior) is transformed by the power of the gaze to invert the initial hierarchy of inclusion and exclusion, metamorphosing the extraneous stance of the 'I'/eye (on '*this* hill', blocked by '*this* hedgerow') into one of inclusion (in '*this* immensity' and '*this* sea'). Concurrently, a space that did not exist before can be brought into the bounds of the poem and opened up to infinite exploration.

As Leopardi states in the *Zibaldone*, 'il nulla è necessariamente luogo' [nothingness is necessarily a place], 'dove è nulla *quivi* è spazio' [where nothing is, *there* is space]: spaces can be born out of nothingness; nothingness is still a space.[16] As in 'L'infinito', as soon as the subject situates itself in relation to that 'nulla', its identity as a 'place' is already certain: it becomes a here ('*quivi*'), becomes a space to be inhabited. Citing Heidegger, we can say that the language of deixis here harnesses the miracle of poetic language as such:

> A space is something that has been made room for, something that is cleared and freed, namely within a boundary, Greek *peras*. A boundary is not that at which something stops but, as the Greeks recognised, the boundary is that from which something *begins its presencing*. [...] Accordingly, spaces receive their being from locations and not from 'space'.[17]

Discussing Leopardi's use of deixis in 'L'infinito', Margaret Brose underscores its 'conversional power',[18] that is to say the transformation of language into discourse but, more fundamentally, its presencing force within the poem, which is 'the product of the linguistic capacities of the speaker', 'The indefinite (*sempre*) and the past (*fu*), both axial to the Leopardian sublime, are transfigured in a spatial and temporal presence

---

[15] Prete, 'Lo scacco del pensiero: per un'esegesi dell'infinito', in *Il pensiero poetante: saggio su Leopardi* (Milan: Feltrinelli, 1980), pp. 48–62 (p. 51).
[16] Leopardi, *Zib.* 4233, p. 873.
[17] Martin Heidegger, *Poetry, Language, Thought*, trans. Albert Hofstadter (New York: Perennial Classics, 2001), p. 152 (italics in the original). The most rewarding sections are 'Building, Dwelling, Thinking', pp. 143–59, and '...Poetically Man Dwells...', pp. 209–27, a study of the meaning of that phrase drawn from a poem by Hölderlin.
[18] Cf. Benveniste, 'La nature des pronoms', p. 254, in which he states of deictics: 'Leur rôle est de fournir l'instrument d'une conversion, qu'on peut appeler *la conversion de langage en discours*' [Their role is to provide the instrument of a conversion that one could call *the conversion of language into discourse*].

(*questo*) which otherwise would have been an affective absence. This metaleptic leap depends upon Leopardi's careful control of deixis'.[19]

For Leopardi, the manipulation of the deictic realm (the reversal of past and present, far and near, 'quello' and 'questo') is thus the key to (re)discovering the infinite. Deictics allow the present of the poem (uninhabitable in all other respects) to become the propitious site of this figurative act, or poetics of the 'sublime', in which an underlying lack can be transformed into a kind of (linguistic) possession of the self and space (which come together in Leopardi's self-generating landscape, 'nel pensier mi fingo'). What is at stake is nothing less than 'the substitution of an absent plenitude for a present void',[20] something that because it is destined to be lost can be celebrated for its transience and momentary fullness—an operation that defines the lyric as such in its Leopardian and Petrarchan extensions.

'L'infinito' consequently stands to Sereni's deictic enterprise as its ideal and elusive goal. It represents the conversional power of deixis that he would seek to harness and the maximum of lyric (imaginative) extension that, by paradoxically limiting the 'real', permits the 'I' to play lord and master in the landscape, maintaining an ideal balance between desire (future, possible), memory (Edenic past, recoverable), and the poem (present, 'miraculous').

Sereni's own border spaces, especially in *Frontiera*, also often located on the boundary with 'nothingness', would similarly seek to harbour the power that deictics have to create a space for the 'I' to inhabit and for something to 'begin its presencing'. 'Locations' in his own poetry, and that of others, always carry this deictic charge for him, as his words in 'Dovuto a Montale' ['Owed to Montale'] make clear:

> La mia attenzione si faceva più precisa non appena mi si prospettavano aspetti, oggetti d'uso, strumenti, ambienti tra i quali io stesso vivevo o avrei potuto vivere: urbani o extraurbani, familiari o remoti non importava, purché *avvertiti presenti, inseriti nella natura, raggiungibili in qualche punto del mondo a portata di sensi*.[21]
>
> [My attention became more acute at the appearance of aspects, objects, implements, and environments among which I myself lived or could have lived: urban or suburban, familiar or remote, it didn't matter, as long as they were *felt as present, within nature, accessible in some part of the world within reach of the senses*.]

---

[19] Margaret Brose, 'Leopardi's "L'infinito" and the Language of the Romantic Sublime', *Poetics Today* 4.1 (1983), pp. 47–71 (pp. 61–5).
[20] Ibid. 64, 60.
[21] Sereni, 'Dovuto a Montale' (1983), included as Appendix to *Gli immediati dintorni: primi e secondi*, ed. Maria Teresa Sereni (Milan: Il Saggiatore, 1983) [*ID2*], pp. 159–66 (pp. 160–1).

These qualities of presence and naturalness go hand in hand with the discovery of a space that can be reached and encoded through sense experience, which Sereni terms elsewhere in the same essay, 'un luogo deputato' [a chosen place] (p. 160). Deictics are the hallmarks of a creative project that constantly strives to transform landscape, in the sense of a natural scene or vista (the object of the gaze), into a topographically charged space that the subject would seek to delineate and map, not just contemplate.

Not by chance, Sereni's 'luogo deputato' is Luino, where this level of possession was once possible or construed as possible. All future topographies are in a sense mapped against his first and it is here that we must seek the roots of a deictic disposition that survives (albeit altered) to the very limits of his poetic production.

Horizons of experience: setting parameters on deixis

As the title of Sereni's first collection suggests, there is a frontier or boundary in play that defines the parameters of poetic space—a limit against which the 'I' measures itself and a line which divides one dimension of reality from another. Often this limit is perceptual, measured by either the gaze of the 'I', or its ear. The selective topography upon which *Frontiera* is based transposes the poet's native Luino into recurring elemental images of water (lake), wind, and fog, to construct a constant and symbolic backdrop within which the 'I' situates its quest. These figures of the landscape are also the imaginative nucleus of a series of poetic tropes that extend from a Leopardian-like sublime 'naufragar [...] dolce in questo mare' [sweet [...] sinking in this sea], to one of imminent, Orphic loss. The distance (boundary or horizon) dividing the two dimensions of experience may be small, but it remains intact. The 'I' enjoys—perhaps for the last time—a sense of familiarity with its surroundings, and the conviction of being in the presence of something if not actually complete, then at least bordering on plenitude or the promise of fulfilment, 'E pure con labile passo | c'incamminiamo su cinerei prati | per strade che rasentano l'Eliso' [Yet still with traceless steps | we're setting out over ashen fields | through streets that border Elysium] ('Strada di Zenna' ['Zenna Road'], ll. 5–7, in *Frontiera*, pp. 33–4 (p. 33)).

It is deictic reference that helps to communicate the still intact nature of the world and the subject who inhabits it. When considering the quality and extension of the lyric voice that emerges in *Frontiera*, 'Incontro' ['Encounter'] represents a significant case. Taking the lyric encounter as its subject, the poem exhibits the hallmarks of an 'egocentrismo lirico' [lyric egocentrism] while hinting at the diminishing hold of its domain, staging a speaking subject that is both centralized and fading, but still able to posit itself at the heart of the lyric:

> Come un rosaio,
> un vortice d'ombra e di vampe
> *che mi fioriva d'intorno*
> sulla strada cancellata dal sole
> a mezzogiorno.
> (In *Frontiera*, p. 10)
>
> [Like a rose garden,
> a whorl of shadow and blazes
> *that blossomed around me*
> on the road cancelled out by the sun
> at midday.]

The suggestion is that the 'I' is very much at the centre of the vision, where the encounter takes place, but the imperfect tense betrays the fact that it can only happen (or has happened) in memory. Typically, the locus of the encounter no longer seems to exist outside of the memory or utterance (it may be solely poetic). It is temporally and spatially removed from the ostensible place from which the 'I' speaks, just as the object of the encounter is elliptically absent, described only in terms of attributes, not identity ('come'...). Yet through a staggering of levels akin to that of which Testa speaks, subject and (absent) object are made to coincide in the poem, as the 'I' declares itself centrally located both with respect to the vision and the poem itself, the middle-placed line 'che *mi* fioriva *d'intorno*' performing both roles. It is significant in this respect that whilst the poem opens towards an absent vortex—the disappearing road that has been cancelled out by the sun—it still presents the encounter as having taken place in a kind of garden space, of which the subject is the measure, rather than the other way round.

The notion of the poem as garden is in fact heralded by the title of the first section of *Frontiera*, *Concerto in giardino* [*Garden Concert*], from which 'Incontro' comes. It stands as a topos for the circumscribed space in which the encounter with the Other would take place as well as the fragile construct on which that intimately lyric encounter depends, already under threat from the outside, which the poet acknowledges as so. In depicting the shifting boundaries of that space and its ultimate obliteration ('cancellata'), Sereni shows how the walls, though still firmly in place, are beginning to move outward or inward, expanding towards a disconcerting proliferation or contracting to imprison the 'I' within.

In *Frontiera*, Sereni's horizon is established between the 'I' as the *origo* of the deictic field and the furthest point that it can reach in perceptual terms, beyond which it has no immediate control but within whose boundaries it enjoys a certain perceptual and semantic power. The 'I', or eye, seeks to limit and synthesize its space as it defines it, and the subject at its centre is inevitably static since it must suspend movement elsewhere in order to ensure that the three coordinates of the *origo*—the 'I', the 'here', and the 'now'—remain in place. It seeks to affirm its absolute presence and control on three planes at once: existential, spatial, and temporal.

Furthermore, as 'Incontro' demonstrates, linguistic (self-)possession goes hand in hand with deictic capability, and *Frontiera* as a whole functions as a repeated attempt to possess objects in language, harnessing a visionary potential that opens up in the relationship established at the horizon, which is also the line that mediates in the poetic space between word and thing. In this dimension, *Frontiera*'s topography is strongly reminiscent of the Montalian landscape of the *Ossi*, in which there is a strong memory of the time in which 'si vestivano di nomi | le cose' [things were dressed in names] and 'il nostro mondo aveva un centro' [our world had a centre] ('Fine dell'infanzia' ['End of Childhood']).[22] In other words, the recollection of a landscape in which the Logos is still intact, or where the 'I' feels it has control of its language. Again, deixis contributes to maintaining a centralized perspective, and the specular relationship at the basis of such a 'limit-of-the-world' practice (I am again quoting Ricoeur) leads us to explore the proximity of deixis to what Kristeva terms the thetic operations of language, by which the speaking subject asserts itself at the core of the linguistic universe at the same moment it enters into the world of objects and articulated discourse.

Deixis and the thetic

These primary facets of deixis can be explained in the legacy that it takes from the mirror stage. In the *Écrits*, Lacan asserts that at the mirror stage, for the child caught up in the lure of spatial identification, 'l'image spéculaire semble être le seuil du monde visible' [the mirror-image would appear to be the threshold of the visible world].[23] This operation is a prototype for the subject's relationship to the world of objects that will extend throughout life, even after the mirror stage has ended and the subject is forced to confront its disunity and alienation. Revisiting Lacan's

---

[22] Montale, *L'opera in versi*, ed. Rosanna Bettarini and Gianfranco Contini (Turin: Einaudi, 1980), pp. 65–7 (p. 66).
[23] Jacques Lacan, 'Le stade du miroir comme formateur de la fonction du Je telle qu'elle nous est révélée dans l'expérience psychanalytique' ['The Mirror Stage as Formative of the Function of the *I* as Revealed in Psychoanalytic Experience'], in *Écrits I* (Paris: Éditions du Seuil, 1966), pp. 92–9 (p. 94).

work on this stage of the subject's development, Kristeva adds that 'la position du moi imagé induit la position de l'objet lui aussi séparé et signifiable' [positing the imaged ego leads to the positing of the object, which is, likewise, separate and signifiable], which coincides with the birth of voice (the child's first holophrastic utterances) and begins the thetic processes that will ultimately determine the separation of the subject from its objects of perception, which it sets up as external to itself and thus describable.[24]

The prototype of this activity is to be found in the fort-da (disappearance-return) dialectic of the child's game outlined by Freud in 'Beyond the Pleasure Principle', which both Lacan and Kristeva draw upon in their theories. This sees the child learning to cope with his mother being alternately present and absent to him by throwing away and retrieving a toy that stands in for her, rehearsing the act of 'negation' (*Verneinung*) that constitutes the very foundation of language as such.[25] According to Kristeva, this thetic division is consolidated with castration and coincides with the child's consent to enter the social order, or symbolic, and its appropriation of syntactic rules (the mastery of the distinction subject-predicate). This gives the newly born subject the illusion of control and possession of its language while installing a dependency on the ego of the utterance, which must retain the appearance of stability and control in order to maintain intact a series of stable and controlled objects.

Kristeva, like Ricoeur, emphasizes the anchoring qualities of this process and relates the ego of denotation to the transcendental ego of phenomenology which 'juge ou parle' [judges or speaks] and in so doing, is able to put into parenthesis all that is heterogeneous to the

---

[24] Julia Kristeva, 'Le miroir et la castration posant le sujet absent du signifiant' ['The Mirror and Castration Positing the Subject as Absent from the Signifier'], in *La révolution du langage poétique. L'avant-garde à la fin du xixe siècle: Lautréamont et Mallarmé* (Paris: Éditions du Seuil, 1974), pp. 43–9 (p. 44).

[25] Sigmund Freud, 'Beyond the Pleasure Principle' (1920), in *The Standard Edition of the Complete Psychological Works of Sigmund Freud* [*SE*], ed. James Strachey, 24 vols (London: Hogarth Press, 1953–74), vol. XVIII (1955), pp. 7–64. According to Kristeva, the loss of the desired object (first and foremost the Mother) is effectively denied by the subject at the point of entry into language, as he/she consents to recover that object as sign: 'Les signes sont arbitraires parce que le langage s'amorce par une *dénégation (Verneinung)* de la perte [...]. "J'ai perdu un objet indispensable qui se trouve être, en dernière instance, ma mère", semble dire l'être parlant. "Mais non, je l'ai retrouvée dans les signes, ou plutôt parce que j'accepte de la perdre, je ne l'ai pas perdue (voici la dénégation), je peux te récupérer dans le langage "' [Signs are arbitrary because language starts with a *negation (Verneinung)* of loss [...]. 'I have lost an essential object that happens to be, in the final analysis my mother', is what the speaking being seems to be saying. 'But no, I have found her again in signs, or rather since I consent to lose her I have not lost her (that is the negation), I can recover her in language'], *Soleil noir: dépression et mélancolie* (Paris: Gallimard, 1987), p. 55 (italics in the original).

subject.[26] This preserves the illusion of unity for a subject that is seen as always 'present and waiting'—seeming to pre-exist and to transcend any individual instance of discourse—and never once loses sight of an object that is always already distinct from it.

As Kristeva also suggests, this predicative act upon which all language, and the very birth of linguistic subjectivity, rests has an intimately deictic value.[27] The 'nommant' [naming] and 'synthétisant' [synthesizing] functions of the thetic are reinforced each time deixis comes into play to bolster the position of the speaking 'I', in the same way that the universe of the traditional lyric poem takes shape around the *origo* of the speaking voice. Not by chance have deictics become the cornerstone of Western literature:

> Il qui e il là: non avevamo anticipato che la rivoluzione si misura sui deittici? Proprio là dove la manifestazione sembrava un'innocuità grammaticale? La fissazione nel dentro e lo sprofondamento nel fuori, distantissimo e irraggiungibile. Appartenenza e disappartenenza. Contiguità con l'essere (mondo degli oggetti) e sua illusione.[28]

> ['Here' and 'there': had we not anticipated that the revolution would be measured in terms of deictics? Precisely where their appearance seemed a grammatical innocuity?: A fixation on the inside versus a sinking into the outside, infinitely distant and unreachable; belonging and not belonging; the contiguity with being (the world of objects) and its illusion.]

Sereni's own revolution with regard to the lyric subject similarly resides in his use of deictic reference. In the transition from *Frontiera* to *SU*, we move from inclusion to exclusion, from belonging to not belonging, and from the dream of contiguity with objects to the revelation of their otherness. Concurrently, the poetic subject is exiled to a space outside of the happier domain it once enjoyed. Mapping the route Sereni takes from one lyric 'place' to the other reveals that the event of dispossession is linguistic or poetic even more than physical, and topographically speaking we move

---

[26] Derived from her study of Husserl, this theory is outlined by Kristeva in *La révolution du langage poétique*, pp. 30–7 (pp. 30–1).

[27] 'Toute prédication comporte une valeur "profonde" qui est sa valeur locative-déictique. [...] Par ailleurs, la valeur "profonde" locative et déictique a été constatée dans l'analyse des constructions existentielles aussi bien que possessives, dérivant synchroniquement et diachroniquement de constructions locatives.' [Every predication carries a 'deep' value which is its locative-deictic value. [...] Moreover, the 'deep' locative and deictic value has been noted in the analysis of existential constructions as well as in the case of possessives, deriving synchronically and diachronically from locative constructions], Kristeva, *Polylogue* (Paris: Éditions du Seuil, 1977), p. 330.

[28] Giorgio Bertone, 'Paesaggi primi: il monte', in *Lo sguardo escluso: l'idea del paesaggio nella letteratura occidentale* (Novara: Interlinea, 2000), pp. 97–147 (pp. 132–3). Significantly for this study, Bertone's point of reference in making this statement is Petrarch. For Bertone, Petrarch's modernity resides precisely in his conception of landscape as founded on absence more than presence (see p. 142, n. 22).

from familiarity to strangeness, and identity to difference, something which the following selection of poems from each collection foregrounds.

DEIXIS IN ACTION

Frontiera, or the limits of spatial identification

'Inverno', the poem with which *Frontiera* opens and, deictically speaking, the gateway into Sereni's vision of the lyric, immediately establishes the poetic boundary with which the collection as a whole will concern itself:

'Inverno'

....
ma se ti volgi e guardi
nubi nel grigio
esprimono le fonti dietro te,
le montagne nel ghiaccio s'inazzurrano.
Opaca un'onda mormorò   5
chiamandoti: ma ferma—ora
nel ghiaccio s'increspò
poi che ti volgi
e guardi
la svelata bellezza dell'inverno.   10

Armoniosi aspetti sorgono
in fissità, nel gelo: ed hai
un gesto vago
come di fronte a chi ti sorridesse
di sotto un lago di calma,   15
mentre ulula il tuo battello lontano
laggiù, dove s'addensano le nebbie.
                                        (p. 7)

['Winter']

....
but if you turn and watch
fountains behind you exhale
clouds against the gray,
mountains in the ice turn blue.
Opaque, a wave murmured   5
calling you: but stilled—now
in the ice it rippled
just as you turn
and watch
the beauty of winter unveiled.   10

> Harmonious features rise
> in fixity, in the freeze: and you
> make the vaguest gesture
> as if to someone who'd smile at you
> from beneath a lake of calm 15
> while your distant boat laments
> down [t]here, where the fogs grow dense.]

Originally entitled 'Lontananze' ['Distances'], 'Inverno' is also a poem in which Sereni is openly in dialogue with the deictic legacy of his lyric predecessor, Leopardi. It revisits some of the key poetic coordinates of 'L'infinito', particularly in the way that Sereni configures the boundaries of perceptual and imaginative space. However, it also complicates them with the interference of the Virgilian echo, which turns the backward look into a pose of Orphic loss and introduces an interlocutor who appears to be both present at the scene and absent. Like Leopardi's poem, 'Inverno' is constructed on the tension between a constricted gaze and the potential to see that opens up beyond it, which meet in the 'gesto vago', the latter being an adjective of clear Leopardian derivation. Yet in Sereni's poem, the relationship between this 'vaghezza' [indefiniteness] and its counterpoint of 'fissità'—the frozenness of a lifeless image—is not clear-cut, and one comes to be contaminated by the other. This ultimately renders the scene at odds with the Leopardian idyll, even though it retains elements of it.

From the opening ellipsis through to the close of the poem, the central interaction established between the three core elements—*l'io* ['I'], the *tu* [you] figure, and the world or nature—is almost entirely dependent upon the spatio-temporal coordinates and personal pronouns which frame the poem and set the parameters of the encounter. The poet never explicitly says 'I', and yet there is a clearly defined *origo* or deictic centre, which gravitates around a central controlling consciousness. The 'I' is everywhere present, if only momentarily locatable in the shifters which define his position, either as coextensive with their frame of reference—so, for example, the 'ora' in line 6 is his 'now', the one which he determines—or as being at the opposite pole: in line 17, he must be 'quassù' [up here] to designate the *tu* as 'laggiù' [down there].

To this extent, the 'I' very much functions as the pivot of the vision and the poem, both played on a dialectic of near/far and high/low. However, the landscape can only be perceived (revealed, 'svelata') by looking back, which is a perspective that also changes it. This metamorphosing, backward gaze sees the landscape transform to become more beautiful but also more menacing as the surface gives way to a descent into the depths (not coincidentally, cast as a kind of underworld). The poet can manipulate time and space but only to the extent that he freezes them. There is a strong intimation of verticality and creative energy at the centre of the poem ('armoniosi aspetti *sorgono* in *fissità*'), but eventually this cedes to the downward pull from below. Space is always already double, a property of the landscape that deixis foregrounds.

Deictics also help us to map the 'I''s relationship to the *tu* figure and the world, as well as to define his own substance as a persona. As the deictic phrase 'dietro te' in line 3 shows, the *tu* figure acts as point of orientation for the 'I' in deictic terms, and he reads every aspect of the landscape in relation to her. Opening up the space behind her, he draws her into dialogue with him, and seeks to bring her into line with his own perceptions: to encourage her to 'turn and look' and to see what he sees. This is the first intimation of a perceptual hierarchy that extends through the poem, symptomatic of the poet's desire to bring a set of disparate elements into line. The repetition of 'nel' in lines 2, 4, 7 and 12 shows how Sereni tries to do this by limiting perspective to a series of very precise locations, installing a freeze-frame that is both perceptual and linguistic.

As the epitome of the *origo* or subjective time (which is also the time of the poem), the deictic 'ora' is consequently the most important word of the first strophe since it acts as a hinge for the entire episode and marks the turning point at which the *volgersi* and *guardare* of the *tu* figure are made inevitable: the 'svelata bellezza dell'inverno' *will* be revealed to her (ll. 1, 10). In turn, this leads to the 'poi che' of line 8 displacing the more tentative conditional clause of line 1. The adjective 'svelata' completes the effect, implying that the beauty has been pre-disclosed to the 'I' who is then in a position to direct the *tu* figure to partake of that same revelation. Up to this point, the perceptual and ordering faculties of the subject cannot therefore be stressed enough. Not only is he able to identify the key ingredients for his idyll, but he also manages to install the necessary visual angle for the role of seer to be transferred to the *tu* figure.

But the turn signalled by the 'poi che' is also a more ambiguous one, which indicates both the passage of time and the moment of loss concomitant with the intimately Orphic gesture of turning and looking that radically alters the landscape, fixing it. As suggested above, its frozenness is at once a moment of perceptual stillness that would allow access to it, and a sign of a more ambivalent stasis: that of a frozen image being caught or held captive while something else dissipates from view ('mentre ulula il tuo battello..., l. 16'). The opaque 'onda' that calls to the *tu* figure represents the locus of the transformation and this doubleness because it is already changed or changing as the 'I' turns to look at it: the moving voice replaced by a still and silent image. In a real sense, the landscape is thus all *behind* the 'I', in striking contrast to the stance of the poetic subject in Leopardi's 'L'infinito', although Sereni's desire is similarly directed toward harnessing and prolonging the beauty implicit in this moment of (imaginative) suspension.

In the second strophe, something shifts again. The effects of the deictics become more ambiguous, as well as more wide-ranging. On the one hand the preciseness of perspective is maintained, on the other it seems to slide towards a more Leopardian-type 'vaghezza', worked through a juxtaposition of proximity and distance, movement and stasis. These contrary motions are epitomized in the final lines of the poem in which an ill-defined, potentially expansive space in the distance ('lontano | laggiù') is offset, and brought up short, by the poet's being able to identify a precise location within it, the place in which the fog thickens (ll. 16–17). There is more than a hint of Orphic negativity again here, with the 'nebbie' conjuring up the mists of oblivion which carried Eurydice back to the underworld, away from Orpheus' outstretched hands. Yet like Montale in 'La casa dei doganieri', Sereni manages to hold on to a thread of something (memory, perhaps), keeping the *tu* figure just about within reach, precisely in 'qualche punto del mondo a portata di sensi' [some part of the world within reach of the senses] ('Dovuto a Montale', p. 161).[29]

The *tu* figure is itself a point of contention and an intimately double figure. The self-sufficient quality of the experience described leaves room for the possibility that the dialectic between the 'I' and the 'you', which drives the poem, may be merely projected or self-referential, with the *tu* as a *tu interno* [internal you]. What Sereni would seek to preserve, and what threatens to slip away from him, in this case would be the poetic moment itself—the heightened moment of experience—which is already behind him at the start of the poem, and which recedes further into the distance the closer he gets to the end. Whether the *tu* is a true female other, or merely a facet of the self, the poet's desiring pursuit is directed towards its capture, and deixis provides the measure of his success. His goal is the synthesis of the disparate elements that make up the experience and the fulfilment of his desire to make nature complicit in his approach. One reading of the *tu* figure thus reinforces the other, with the poet playing on the Orphic uncertainty as to whether he is Orpheus watching Eurydice descending into the mists or Eurydice herself.

---

[29] 'Tu non ricordi; altro tempo frastorna | la tua memoria; un filo s'addipana. || Ne tengo ancora un capo; ma s'allontana | la casa' [You don't recall; other times | assail your memory; a thread gets wound || I hold one end still; but the house recedes], Eugenio Montale, 'La casa dei doganieri' ['The House of the Customs Men'], ll. 10–13, in *Le occasioni*, in *L'opera in versi*, p. 161.

This uncertainty is compounded in the second strophe, in which true deictics (coextensive with the present instance of discourse) momentarily cede their place to their phantasmatic counterparts, just as the landscape transforms again, from harmonious fixity to something less tangible. The phantasmatic dimension of 'Inverno' is introduced with the appearance of the 'gesto vago' (l. 13), which prompts the visual detour into the hypothetical imaginary heralded by the poetic simile, 'come *di fronte* a *chi* ti sorridesse | *di sotto* un lago di calma' (ll. 14–15)—played upon an alternative imaginative landscape, more or less aligned with where the 'I' presently resides—which displaces the more secure frame with which the second strophe opens. These '"fantasmi" deittici' [deictic 'phantasms'], whose terminology I borrow from Maria Antonietta Grignani, displace the 'I' from its place opposite the *tu* figure with the intercession of the unnamed, third person 'chi' surfacing ambiguously from below.[30] It is also no coincidence that this usurping of the 'I''s position by another also implies the attenuation of his gaze, or rather its splitting between the sense of proximity implied by the 'hai | un gesto vago'—as though he is looking at her face to face—and the 'mentre ulula il tuo battello *lontano* | *laggiù*', as though she is barely perceptible and almost certainly fading.

In this latter phrase, the possessive adjective 'tuo' and adverbial deictic 'laggiù' rest at opposite ends of the spectrum deictically speaking (one implying closeness, the other distance), and yet Sereni brings them together, implying that things are not so straightforward. Either the 'tuo' has a predominantly physical meaning (she is 'down there', on the boat) which testifies to her absence 'quassù'—this is dialogue become monologue—or the poet uses it instead to suggest how she too sees her boat disappearing into the mists below but remains on the near side, with him. If she can share a certain complicity in this looking, then he retains part of her and

---

[30] 'L'apparato verbale sfrutta allo scopo gli indicatori di spazio e tempo, dove *laggiù* | *dal mare* significa anche lontananza nel tempo e *oggi* o *qui in Wall Street* sono "fantasmi" deittici della compresenza tra il soggetto che non viene esplicitamente allo scoperto e le materializzazioni del passato' [To that end, the verbal apparatus exploits the spatial and temporal indicators in which *down there* | *from the sea* also signifies distance in time, and *today* or *here in Wall Street* are deictic 'phantasms' dependent on the co-presence of the subject—who does not explicitly allow himself to be discovered—and the materializations of the past], Maria Antonietta Grignani, '"Lavori in corso": addetti e dintorni', in *La poesia di Vittorio Sereni: atti del convegno*, ed. Stefano Agosti et al. (Milan: Librex, 1985), pp. 119–34 (p. 130). Grignani is discussing Part III of Sereni's 'Works in Progress' and in particular the section which reads, 'Inopportuno futile intempestivo | lo spiritello di cui sopra. || Scatta e lo annienta un altro | battente diversa ala da laggiù | dal mare se mare è quel grigio | d'inesistenza attorno a Ellis Island' [Inopportune futile untimely | the imp of the above. || Another leaps up and annuls him | beating a different wing down there | from the sea if the sea it is that gray | of nonexistence round Ellis Island].

the conversation which was the source of their interaction in the first place can continue.[31]

In this reading, by pinpointing those albeit immaterial 'nebbie' within his visual field, the 'I' would manage to maintain a point of orientation in deictic terms, to establish a Leopardian 'ultimo orizzonte' [extreme horizon] ('L'infinito, l. 3) that reinstalls the 'I' at the *origo* of the deictic field in a favourable position 'quassù' which the *tu* figure might just share. By focusing paradoxically on where the fog thickens to conceal her boat from view, the poet manages to keep these entities in range, albeit at the very edges of his visual and auditory horizon. The boat cannot perhaps be seen but it can still be read as present, since its sound reaches them 'up here', and it is this which ultimately enables him to bridge the distance which has opened up between himself and the *tu* figure, and between them and the world, and to finally contain her within the boundaries of that space, and between the borders of the text.

This dialectic between the 'I' and the 'you' that 'Inverno' establishes as the founding situation of Sereni's lyric landscape underscores much of *Frontiera*, in which it is both developed and altered by the play of extension between the two terms. A comparison of 'Inverno' with 'In me il tuo ricordo' demonstrates this point, revealing how the development of desire resides in the capacity of the 'I' to control the coordinates of its poetic landscape:

'In me il tuo ricordo'

In me il tuo ricordo è un fruscìo
solo di velocipedi che vanno
quietamente *là dove* l'altezza
del meriggio discende
al più fiammante vespero   5
tra cancelli e case
e sospirosi declivi
di finestre riaperte sull'estate.
Solo, *di me*, distante
dura un lamento di treni,   10
d'anime che se ne vanno.

E *là* leggera *te ne vai* sul vento,
ti perdi nella sera.

(p. 39)

---

[31] For a discussion of how deixis intends to foster a complicity between the 'I' and its interlocutor, see Michel Collot, 'La dimension du déictique', in *La poésie moderne et la structure d'horizon* (Paris: Presses Universitaires de France, 1989), pp. 187–208.

['Your Memory in Me']

Your memory *in me* is a solitary
whirring of pedal-bikes that go
peaceably *where* the height
of noon descends
to the more blazing sunset   5
amongst gates and houses
and wistful inclines
of windows reopened onto summer.
What's left *of me*, only
a faraway wail of steam trains lingers   10
of souls that are departing.
And light on the wind *there you leave,
lose yourself* in the evening.]

'In me il tuo ricordo' is reminiscent of a poem by Montale, 'Ripenso il tuo sorriso' ['I think back on your smile'] (*Ossi*, p. 30). However, it reverses the central dynamic of the Montalian model, since it moves not from perceptual and metaphysical uncertainty—'non saprei dire, o lontano, | se dal tuo volto [...]' [I can't say, distant one, | whether your look [...]], to perceptual and emotional security ('Ma questo posso dirti, che la tua pensata effigie [...]' [But I can say this: that your contemplated image [...]])—but from possession to dispossession, and inclusion to exclusion. As in 'Inverno', there is a definite endeavour by the poet to establish a frame in which to contain the *tu* figure—or rather the memory of her: 'il tuo ricordo'. However, from the precise locus with which the poem opens ('in me'), and the positive sense of containment it seems to offer, the poem takes on an expansiveness which threatens to move it beyond the control of the subject.

We can chart this progression through a series of juxtapositions. For example, the 'solo' of line 2, which implies the desire for a descriptive totality, is instantly qualified by the 'velocipedi' in the plural which leads on to the relative clause that negates the sense of the 'solo' yet further. Similarly, the 'fruscìo' itself is cancelled out by the 'quietamente', as though the two halves of the picture do not add up. This is consolidated by the fact that what precedes the 'che' (l. 2) is much shorter than what follows, the effect being that of an entire world tumbling out from a central, localized point. This detracts from the idea of contained-ness and leads to a real visual detour, a roving 'I' or 'eye' that tries hard to maintain a fixed point of observation ('là dove') but is ultimately unable to prevent a sliding down, through, and out of the frame he creates.

Not only does this process seem to divide *l'io* from the *tu* figure, but it importantly divides him from himself, so that he no longer knows where he is and where he is looking from. The juxtaposition of the 'di me' and the 'distante' (l. 9) testifies to this ambiguity, making it unclear as to whether he has himself travelled on the tortuous route that her memory has taken, and has now arrived at some distance from where he began—part of him remaining on that other bank[32]—or whether he is essentially in the same place but no longer feels totally self-coincident, no longer entirely inside himself. It is significant in this respect that the 'solo' aspect of the 'ricordo' should be repeated in reference to the 'I', this time referring to 'all that is left' rather than to 'all that is', and there is also a transference of the pluralized aspect of the 'tuo ricordo' to the 'I' himself, so that a tension persists.

Indeed, from this point onwards it is as though the only memory he has left is of himself—as though all he has left to remember *is* himself—which shifts the semantic field entirely and installs the divide between the 'I' and the 'you', made visible in the typographic space between the first and second parts of the poem. The passage from 'Solo' to 'se ne vanno' (ll. 2–11) instigates a double figure of loss for which the two terms of reference—the two sides of the mirror—are none other than the 'I' and the 'me'. This eclipses the 'you' altogether: she is on the outside of the frame. This effect is compounded in the last two lines of the poem in which there is a very strong sense indeed of the *tu* figure inhabiting an entirely different world altogether, in which the 'I' has no place.

The deictic 'là leggera' (l. 13) is therefore less of a spatial coordinate—'là' ('there') is a somewhat vague indicator of her position, since all we can say is that it is not 'here'—than a semantic one, implying that what divides them is a difference of substance, as though their paths were not destined to cross. The use of the reflexive 'ti perdi' in the final line, meaning that she loses herself, entirely excludes the 'I' from the action; he rests very much at the margins, an observer to the action, but with no real connection to it.

There is thus the sense that in order to find a middle space which can be a positive transfer of terms, the frame needs to be a contrastive one. Only an oppositional framework seems able to create the necessary tension, which—however prone to rupture or imbalance it may be—preserves the possibility of an interaction, not possible when the 'I' is himself on both sides of the frame, which ends up tautologous in the extreme: the 'solo di me' idea. This would also appear to be the limit of the narcissistic identification associated with the lyric 'I', which may be able to install a totality but only at the expense of excluding everything that is heterogeneous to it, as in this poem in the fact that the *tu* is seen only in relation to

---

[32] This looks forward to the 'altra riva' motif at the heart of Sereni's *Un posto*.

him—as his memory of her. The poet needs at least to maintain the illusion that the world or the *tu* figure come to confront him from the outside—have a certain independence of thought and action—otherwise the experience of writing can only end in tautology or solitude, 'io solo' [I alone].

In *Frontiera*, we thus find the paradox of a centralized lyric 'I' offset by a series of 'other' terms which it consciously tries to bring under control via the imposition of a perceptual frame. The 'I', in keeping with phenomenological thinking, would seek to 'intend' its objects, retaining a certain measured ability to 'see' ('voir et juger') that would make meaningful its interaction with the object world and impose a certain naturalistic causality, as though the world pre-exists the text but is just at that moment being made meaningful in confrontation with the subject.[33] Deictics foreground this moment as the event of poetry itself, always already bound up with the realms of memory and the imagination.

It is ultimately this which enables us to read the *Frontiera* of the title as a poetic kind of horizon, rather like the 'siepe' [hedgerow] of Leopardi's 'L'infinito', which marks a dividing line between what is perceptually possible (visible, definable) and what is invisible (merely imagined). This gives deictics a supreme poetic function which Testa calls 'astanziale':

> I deittici vengono nello iato tra *manque* e presenza immaginaria. Adempiono ad una funzione che, in mancanza di meglio potremmo chiamare *astanziale*: permettono di cogliere, nel luogo dell'assenza, i tratti ostensivi dell'oggetto di desiderio, di individuare le tracce della sua sparizione, di raffigurarlo, ossessivo fugace silenzioso, nell'*hic et nunc* del testo, di costruire un suo fragile simulacro.[34]

> [The deictics appear in the gap between lack and imaginary presence. They perform a function that, in the absence of a better term, we can call *that of the onlooker*: they allow us to grasp, in the place of absence, the ostensible traits of the object of desire, to individuate the traces of its disappearance, and

---

[33] The terminology is once again Kristeva's: 'Comme l'explicite d'ailleurs Husserl, ce sens et son ego ont une assise réelle dans le *voir* et dans le *juger*. Intervenants à différents niveaux de la réflexion phénoménologique, le *voir* et le *juger* se trouvent être solidaires pour poser l'ego transcendant qui posera l'intention et l'intuition transcendantales. Dans et par la *représentation*—nous dirons le signe—, et le *jugement*—nous dirons la syntaxe—, s'articule un *ego posé*, pour pouvoir, de cette position, doter de sens un espace posé comme préalable à son avènement' [Moreover, as Husserl demonstrates, this meaning and its Ego have a real basis in *seeing* and *judging*. Although they intervene at different levels in phenomenological reflection, *seeing* and *judging* prove to be at one in positing the transcending Ego, which will posit transcendental intention and intuition. A *posited* Ego is articulated in and by *representation* (which we shall call the sign) and *judgement* (what we shall call syntax) so that, on the basis of this position it can endow with meaning a space posited as previous to its advent], *La révolution du langage poétique*, p. 34 (italics in the original).
[34] Testa, '*Sur la corde de la voix*', p. 129 (italics in the original).

represent it, obsessive, fleeting and silent as it is, in the *here and now* of the text, to construct a fragile simulacrum of it.]

The 'I' can make visible what is invisible, and what is absent, present, or—as is more common in Sereni's case—seeks to capture objects on the moment of their departure as they threaten to slip beyond the frame. Poetry, especially deictic poetry, is born as a project of recuperation.

Significantly for the present study, the intimations of loss and absence that the 'I' seeks to counter deictically in this way become more pronounced as Sereni's poetry develops, and the intensification of loss is mirrored by a concomitant strengthening of nostalgia for the diminishing force of the imagination—nostalgia for an 'ottica idillica' [idyllic optic] in a truly Leopardian sense. The deictic field is redefined in line with this evolution, and I will now explore, with reference to *SU*, the implications of this reconfiguration of the textual landscape away from a perceptually amenable space towards a more hostile linguistic environment.

Gli strumenti umani: deixis and displacement

Sereni's third collection, *SU*, provides several interesting points of comparison with his first. Firstly, he tries to incorporate the same deictic strategies that have served him in the past but finds that they do not hold. Secondly, familiar topographies, when they do resurface, no longer provide a secure footing, and any neat distinction between subject and object breaks down. Thirdly, this calls into question any system based upon their reliability, including the lyric 'I' in relation to its surroundings. As a result, the increasingly uninhabitable nature of space in *SU* is both an expression of the poet's disorientation in a dramatically altered social and political environment (the machine age and industrial boom of the 1950s) and a sign of the extraneous qualities of his poetic subject—its inability to inhabit its textual realm as it had done before.

While the poet tries to maintain a dialectic between himself and the Other, revisiting the appositional structures at the basis of many poems in *Frontiera*, the distinction becomes untenable, as the terms of the subject/object dichotomy become interchangeable within the field of discourse, which is precisely the stage on which the drama of *SU* is played out. Here the 'funzione enunciativa' [enunciative role] and 'funzione astanziale' [onlooker role] of deixis overlap, lending speech the often hallucinatory qualities of dream, and dream the linguistic structures of dialogue. As the 'I' encounters its many interlocutors, it is also called upon to take up a position linguistically and morally speaking.

The increase in dialogic elements in *SU*, and the ever more unreal and dream-like quality of the encounters with the Other and the self, go hand in hand with Sereni's redefinition of his poetic subject and its relocation to a textually indeterminate space understood as a field or threshold of desire. If deictics have the power to manipulate the space between what exists, has existed, or ceased to exist, and what may exist again in the poem, their identity in Sereni's *SU* is rooted firmly in creating a temporal bridge between past and present, which is also the space between the memory of possession and the dream of recovery or, more negatively, between the hope of redemption and the reality of loss.

The 'sguardo' [gaze] which established the perceptual frame of *Frontiera* and defined its own particular landscape comes to be contaminated by the interpolations of speech. This does not give the 'I' the same level of ownership or control of the poetic space of which it is part, and tends to divide it between the two levels of discourse (*l'énonciation* and *l'énoncé*):

> Mentre il dire rivela la certezza della non piena dicibilità e perfino di una indecifrabilità del reale, la poesia corteggia l'istanza del discorso, tende all'allocuzione e perfino all'urlo, proverbiale risvolto del silenzio quando chiama come voce nel deserto.[35]
>
> [While speaking reveals the certainty of not being able to articulate anything fully and even declares the indecipherable nature of the real, poetry courts the instance of discourse, tends towards exhortation and even shouting, the proverbial connotations of silence as it calls out like a voice in the desert.]

Any possibility of arriving at full speech, as a means of accessing the world in its entirety, is lost, and the poetic voice that survives is both less effective and more urgent, with the 'I' crying out with desperation like a voice in the desert. Deictics mediate in this space between vocal plea and absent response, living up to their designation as 'empty signs' that, poetically speaking, betray their foundations in nothingness and in something as insubstantial and transitory as the voice. This underlying negativity of language, which according to Giorgio Agamben is the very foundation of discourse, is something which deixis in Sereni's *SU* foregrounds and suspends the 'I' between the event of its appearance on the scene—in the landscape, inside the poem—and its inevitable fading out of both.[36]

---

[35] Maria Antonietta Grignani, 'Derive dell'identità', in *La costanza della ragione: soggetto, oggetto e testualità nella poesia del Novecento* (Novara: Interlinea, 2002), pp. 89–107 (p. 97).
[36] See Giorgio Agamben's discussion of shifters and their relationship to what he calls the 'metaphysics of language', in *Language and Death: The Place of Negativity*, trans. Karen E. Pinkus and Michael Hardt (Minneapolis: University of Minnesota Press, 1991). 'Pronouns and other indicators of the utterance, before they indicate real objects, indicate precisely *that language takes place*. In this way, still prior to the world of meanings, they permit the reference to the very *event of language*, the only context in which something can

Describing the texture of Sereni's language in *SU*, Zanzotto attests to this designation of a textually indeterminate, and ultimately unlocatable, space in Sereni's later poetry, which would embody the fugitive nature of the world and the self—a linguistic black hole that is both enticing and threatening:

> Il molto non detto che sta attorno ad ogni suo componimento [...] vibra e si fa percepire nel detto, che ha insieme la secca violenza dell'immediato, del tangibile e lo sfumato e persino la dolcezza di un *non-luogo*. Ciò attesta una situazione psichica, mentale e poi formale che tenderebbe a rendere *incollocabile* tutto il vissuto e ogni spazio nel momento in cui si annuncia come *incollocabile* essa stessa.[37]

> [The much that remains unsaid around every composition [...] vibrates and allows itself to be perceived in what is said, which has both the blunt violence of immediacy—of the tangible—and the vanishing quality, even the sweetness, of a *no-place*. This is evidence of a psychic situation, that is at first psychological and then formal in nature, which tends to render *unlocatable* all of lived experience, and every space, in the moment in which it announces itself to be similarly *unlocatable*.]

This space is at once the space of the poem, of language, and of the subject's own psyche. The short poem 'Un ritorno', from *SU*, indicates the shortfall that now defines them and the distance that divides them from the ideal place of the lyric, which has opened up in Sereni's poetic landscape since *Frontiera*:

'Un ritorno'

Sul lago le vele facevano un bianco e compatto poema
ma pari più non gli era il mio respiro
e non era più un lago ma un attonito
specchio di me una lacuna del cuore.

(p. 108)

['A Return'

On the lake the sails made a white and compact poem
but my breath was no longer equal to it
and it was no longer a lake but an astonished
mirror of me a lacuna of the heart.]

Like other poems in which the poetic subject explicitly declares itself in dialogue with the landscapes of the past, 'Un ritorno' is a supreme example

---

only be signified' (p. 25). However, in being tied to the 'voice', which 'must necessarily be removed for in order for meaningful discourse to take place [...] that which articulates the human voice in language is a pure negativity' (p. 35).

[37] Andrea Zanzotto, 'Per Vittorio Sereni', in *Aure e disincanti nel Novecento letterario* (Milan: Mondadori, 1994), pp. 50–3 (p. 50).

of what John Lyons, in *Semantics*, terms 'textual deixis'.[38] Immediately identifiable in the titles of poems such as '*Ancora* sulla strada di Zenna' ['On the Zenna Road *Again*'] and '*Ancora* sulla strada di Creva' ['On the Creva Road *Again*'], which recall near-eponymous poems from *Frontiera*, textual deixis is an inherently anaphoric and backward-looking mode of discourse which indicates the extent to which Sereni's use of deixis, and his language more generally, has become self-reflexive.

In writing 'Un ritorno', Sereni is returning not only to Luino (the 'lake-place') but also to his earlier poetry (the 'bianco e compatto poema' of *Frontiera*)—an entire field of reference with which he is no longer in kilter ('ma *pari più non gli era* il mio respiro'). Paradoxically, this intimately poetic space continues to act as a mirror, yet the poet must recognize it as a flawed or hollow one, since the image which the world now reflects back to him is not the *imago* of the mirror stage (a neat unity based on a *méconnaissance*), but rather a disunified and fragmentary image.[39] That which was initially designated as external or Other (i.e the 'lago', posited at some distance from the subject) is revealed merely to be a facet of the self. More importantly, it installs the subject in a space that is characterized by absence, 'una *lacuna* del cuore'.

We are also given the impression that whereas the lake of *Frontiera* was a real geographical location above and beyond its metaphorical import (which partly determined its status as a kind of foothold for the subject), it has now become a purely phantasmatic entity, an interiorized landscape. Here we have a model for the most common landscapes of *SU* centred on dream and memory, and the lake is both the surface in which the 'I' finds itself reflected and the source of alienation—the adjective 'attonito' able to qualify either the personified mirror, or the 'I' itself. Overall, the poem testifies to the way in which the other term—here, the 'lago'—has become increasingly unreliable and elusive, too closely bound up with the interior life of the subject, for it to lend him the ratification or comfort he seeks from it.

As 'Un ritorno' suggests, this experience of displacement penetrates to the very heart of selfhood, and the subject of *SU* is exiled linguistically as much as physically as a result of deixis and the dispossession of space that it implies. Discourse is fragmented or liable to dissolve as soon as there is an

---

[38] In *Semantics*, Lyons identifies five types of deixis as follows: temporal, spatial, personal, textual, and social. See John Lyons, 'Deixis, Space, and Time', in *Semantics*, 2 vols (Cambridge: Cambridge University Press, 1977), vol. II, pp. 636–724. In Sereni's poetry, making such rigid categorizations is largely impossible, since spatial and temporal deixis tend to overlap and, as Lyons theorizes, often fuse with personal deixis.

[39] Lacan, 'Le stade du miroir comme formateur de la fonction du Je telle qu'elle nous est révélée dans l'expérience psychanalytique', in *Écrits I* (Paris: Éditions du Seuil, 1966), pp. 92–9 ['The Mirror Stage'], pp. 94–8.

incongruity between the self-affirming aspirations of deixis and the disorienting nature of its effects. Nowhere is this more evident than in poems in which Sereni definitively breaks with the compact, monologic voice of *Frontiera* to favour a dialogic mode which opens the subject up to the vagaries of speech and the uncertainty of a textual realm inhabited by a range of alter egos more or less identifiable with the individual who says 'I'. 'Appuntamento a ora insolita' is a case in point:

'Appuntamento a ora insolita'

La città—mi dico—dove l'ombra
quasi più deliziosa è della luce
come sfavilla tutta nuova al mattino...
'... asciuga il temporale di stanotte'—ride
la mia gioia tornata *accanto a me* 5
dopo un breve distacco.
'Asciuga al sole le sue contraddizioni'
—torvo, già sul punto di cedere, ribatto.
Ma la forma l'immagine il sembiante
—d'angelo avrei detto in altri tempi— 10
risorto *accanto a me* nella vetrina:
'Caro—mi dileggia apertamente—caro,
con *quella faccia di vacanza*. E pensi
alla città socialista?'.
Ha vinto. E già mi sciolgo: 'Non 15
arriverò a vederla' le rispondo.
            (Non saremo
più insieme, dovrei dire). 'Ma è giusto,
fai bene a non badarmi se dico *queste cose*,
se le dico per odio di qualcuno
o rabbia per qualcosa. Ma credi all'altra 20
cosa che si fa strada in me di tanto in tanto
che in sé le altre include e le fa splendide,
rara come *questa mattina di settembre*...
giusto di te tra me e me parlavo:
della gioia'.
            Mi prende sottobraccio. 25
'Non è vero che è rara,—mi correggo—c'è,
la si porta come una ferita
per le strade abbaglianti. È
quest'ora di settembre in me repressa
per tutto un anno, è la volpe rubata che il ragazzo 30
celava sotto i panni e il fianco gli straziava,
un'arma che si reca con abuso, fuori
dal breve sogno di una vacanza.

                              Potrei
con questa uccidere, con la sola gioia... '.
Ma dove sei, dove ti sei mai persa?
'È a questo che penso se qualcuno
mi parla di rivoluzione'
dico alla vetrina ritornata deserta.
                    (In *SU*, pp. 140–41)

['Appointment at an Unusual Hour'

The city—I'm saying—where shade
is all but exquisite as light,
how it sparkles brand new in the morning...
'...dries out last night's storm'—laughs my
joy, *beside me* once more
after a short estrangement.
'Dries out its contradictions in the sun'
—sour, as good as resigned, I come back.
But the shape, image, resemblance
—an angel I'd have said in other times—
reborn *beside me* in the windowpane:
'Dear'—she openly taunts me—'dear,
with *that holiday look* of yours.
You're thinking of the socialist city?'
She wins. And already breaking down:
'No, I won't get to see it,' I reply.
                    (We won't be
together any more, I should say.) 'But it's fair,
you're right not to mind me if I say such things,
if I say them from hating somebody
or angered by something. But *that other thing*
now and then making its way in me,
that includes the others and makes them shine,
believe in it, rare as *this September morning*...
I was fairly talking to myself of you:
of joy.'
                    She takes my arm.
'Not true it's rare,'—correcting myself—'it is,
you bear it like a wound
through dazzling streets. It's *this time
in September* repressed in me all year,
it's that fox the boy stole
and hid in his clothes and it ripped his thigh,
a gun you carry recklessly, beyond
the brief dream of a holiday.

I could
kill *with this*, with joy alone...'
But where are you, where have you gone?   35
'*This* is what I think of if someone
talks to me of revolution,'
I'm saying to the window empty once more.]

    This poem allows us to understand the extent to which the circumstances of the lyric encounter have changed since 'Incontro', analysed earlier from *Frontiera*. Like several other poems in *SU*, 'Appuntamento a ora insolita' immediately makes us aware of a dialogic context with the inclusion of the verb 'dirsi', but Sereni takes the figure of the double beyond that of merely talking to oneself. There is a great deal of shifting between roles, with both the 'I' and the 'she' (the female Other in the poem) taking up the positions of 'I' and 'you' alternately, complicated by the fact that this Other may just be a facet of the self externalized.

    This initial plurality is extended to the remainder of the exchange, which alternates between the predominant use of reflexive verbs in the first person every time that the 'I' 'speaks'—which is also to speak to himself, as well as to the 'other of himself', e.g. 'mi dico', 'mi correggo', 'mi sciolgo'— and a more objective, third person narration which intercedes and counterbalances the subjective code. Although a kind of symmetry is suggested by the binary, mirror-like nature of the encounter, a close reading of the text leaves us rather with a feeling of disorientation and it becomes increasingly difficult to keep track of who is speaking to whom.

    This is most evident in the section of the poem which runs from lines 17 to 24 that juxtaposes a brief snippet of internal monologue, in which the 'I' feels he ought to say something but keeps quiet, with a passage of direct speech whose ownership is unclear. In keeping with the 'botta e risposta' [repartee] framework of the encounter as a whole, it seems likely that the statement is uttered by the third person 'forma', 'immagine', or 'sembiante' who may or may not be equivalent to the 'gioia' who first speaks (or, more accurately, laughs) in line 4. If it is the phantasm speaking, we may well ask how we reconcile its being able to designate 'gioia' in the second person if that is what it is itself. Ultimately we must confront the possibility that it is the 'I' of line 1 that is speaking to maintain the original dialectic or, better still, that the original dialectic has been lost, to be replaced by a second, third, even fourth one as each new instance of discourse takes place and the 'I' and his interlocutor fight for control of the stage.

    Their antagonism is further offset by the parallelism, and sense of community, implied in the 'mi prende sottobraccio' and the repeated sequence, 'accanto a me... accanto a me', which may, however, refer to different entities each time. It seems significant that the reflected image remains essentially indefinable except for its location 'in the window' and 'beside me'. The deictic 'accanto' (l. 11) is of central importance in this last phrase, since when juxtaposed with the other spatial locator, 'nella vetrina', it projects the 'I' (already double) into the double space of the mirror. He is apparently on both sides of the mirror, just as he is on both sides of what is said.

The exchange of persona that seems to take place between lines 17 and 24 can be traced out in the grammatical and syntactical tension surrounding the abstract notion of 'gioia' itself. A constant presence in the poem, its reappearances in the field of discourse testify to its being a knot of resistance—precisely what keeps the conversation between the two (or more) personae of the poet going, but which also prevents a unity between the two sides. Within the semantic frame of the poem, 'joy' thus epitomizes the figure of the double or multiple. At one time labelled as '*l'altra | cosa* che si fa strada in me' (ll. 20–1), it cedes its status as an abstract entity (or 'third person') to its more concrete incarnation as the *tu* figure, paradoxically when designated as most elusive: '*rara* come questa mattina di settembre... | giusto *di te* tra me e me parlavo: *della gioia*' (ll. 22–4). Finally, its physical and symbolic values are joined in the metaphoric statement in lines 30–3, 'è la volpe rubata che il ragazzo | celava sotto i panni e il fianco gli straziava, | un'arma che si reca con abuso, fuori | dal breve sogno di una vacanza'.

As Luca Lenzini points out in his commentary on the poem in *GA*, 'con abuso' here carries the meaning of 'illicitly', suggesting that happiness in the present is always experienced at best as clandestine, and at worst as unsustainable.[40] Like poetry, the 'gioia' of the poem belongs to an order which lies outside the rigid schemes of existence, and deictic reference is used to chart the alternate appearance and disappearance which it makes above the level of the bar.[41] Deictics mark out the interplay of surface level versus depth, which applies equally well to the 'I''s levels of consciousness (inner and outer psychology) and to the confrontation of the different orders.

The transitions between levels are marked out by the use of the deictic 'questo' and the deictic encoding of time in particular. Traditionally 'questo' is used to indicate the proximity of what it designates to the

---

[40] Lenzini, 'Commento', in *Il grande amico: poesie 1935–1981*, ed. Gilberto Lonardi and Luca Lenzini (Milan: Rizzoli, 1990) [*GA*], pp. 189–272 (p. 227).
[41] Here, I am thinking in particular of the bar that Lacan, following Saussure, posits between Signifier and signified, representing the sovereignty of the former over the latter in the Symbolic order and the asymptomatic relationship between the two.

speaking subject. Yet by having more than one subject utter the same word, Sereni manipulates and divides the deictic field to convey the divisions internal and external to the subject which his language in the poem foregrounds. All this is further complicated by the fact that the dialogue is, as we have already seen, constructed on the basis of a specular relationship—a mirroring—but one which is antagonistic in nature, so that proximity to one subject of discourse implies distance from another. Line 18 is a good example of this, since the deictic phrase 'queste cose' is used anaphorically to recall what has already been said, but does so to reinforce the sense of the 'I''s present exclusion from that particular reality. Lenzini explains: 'v.18 *queste cose*: si riferisce a quanto detto prima, cioè a una sfera di discorso propriamente politica che l'io avverte come falsa o comunque estranea (proprio in qualità di poeta), e di cui si può appropriare, con senso di colpa, solo sull'onda di reazioni emotive (vv.19–20)' [l. 18, *these things*: refers to what was said before, i.e. to a strictly political sphere of discourse that the 'I' perceives as false or else extraneous (precisely in his role as a poet), and which one can take possession of, with a sense of guilt, only on the wave of an emotional reaction (ll. 19–20)].[42]

The shift in the deictic field in lines 23 and 29 similarly works to reinforce the differences, rather than similarities, between the 'I' and his alter ego, and consolidates the sense of the unsustainable nature of joy in the present. In line 23, 'gioia' is described as 'rara come questa mattina di settembre'; it is *'l'altra cosa* che si fa strada in me [...] che in sé le *altre* include e le fa splendide'. The emphasis is on the present moment, whose rareness is compared to that of 'gioia' but which is set apart from the experience of 'gioia' itself that rests in a Montalian 'altra orbita' [other orbit], mythicized in its ability to subsume everything to it when it comes, but gaining value only from the infrequency of its coming—like the 'angelo' that it was 'in altri tempi', it remains elusive now. It is in a sense the road not taken, or the road presently unavailable to the subject.

Yet from line 26 onwards the 'I' works to counter this statement, refining the distinction between the two orders of experience ('la mattina di settembre' and 'la gioia') in a way which suggests that the difference between the two 'characters' of the poem is above all one of perspective, 'Non è vero che è rara,—*mi correggo*—c'è, | la si porta come una ferita | per le strade abbaglianti'. A double shift occurs to transform the 'strada' from a metaphorical entity into the literal road the speaker walks along and 'gioia', which was largely a positive force only negative in its unavailability,

---

[42] Lenzini, *GA*, p. 227.

becomes a more ambiguous entity still, somewhat less rare but somewhat more devastating in its effects. As the speaker now tells us, joy, '*È quest'ora di settembre in me repressa | per tutto un anno*'—the hour of September itself, repressed internally by the subject 'fuori dal breve sogno di una vacanza'. Like the 'breve sogno' at the basis of the *RVF*, which Petrarch aligns in his opening sonnet with all mortal things, Sereni's own dream in this poem draws out a tension between the permanent and the fleeting, and between the individual and the social order:

> et del mio vaneggiar vergogna è 'l frutto,
> e 'l pentersi, e 'l conoscer chiaramente
> che quanto piace al mondo è breve sogno.
> (*RVF* I, 12–14)

[and of my raving, shame is the fruit, and repentance, and the clear knowledge that whatever pleases in the world is but a dream.]

As it is subsumed by the subject as something internal, 'gioia' thus becomes, paradoxically, a real and formidable weapon and leads to a strong affirmation of a future power, 'Potrei | *con questa* uccidere, *con la sola gioia*'. This time, the demonstrative 'questa' is paired with 'la *sola* gioia', indicating how it has now become the figure of a totality, an absolute and ultimate catalyst to the powers of resistance. Yet in reaching this totality, speech essentially burns itself out and ends on what is effectively a tautology, 'con questa... con la sola gioia', since this line takes us back full-circle to the beginning of the poem in which 'gioia' first made her appearance.

The final four lines of the poem take place outside of the main frame of action, with the 'Ma dove sei, dove ti sei mai persa?' apparently referring to the disappearance of both the poet's interlocutor and 'gioia' herself. What results is a kind of flattening out of discourse by which the 'I' suddenly seems to regain his compact unity but only at the expense of communication (which is increasingly the only way in which he has proof that he exists). So whilst the last phrase the poet utters somehow manages to tie up all the loose ends, subsuming the great heterogeneous dialogue of the previous pages into the compact and contained 'È *a questo* che penso se qualcuno | mi parla di rivoluzione', it seems that he has lost more than just the image in the window, he has lost part of himself, recreated linguistically in the 'dico' of the final line which is minus the 'mi' of line 1.

As in Leopardi's 'Aspasia', the poem with which Sereni is in dialogue here,[43] deictics can thus take on an 'elegiac colouring' in light of the poet's

---

[43] See Leopardi, 'Aspasia', in *Canti,* ed. Niccolò Gallo and Cesare Garboli (Turin: Einaudi, 1993), pp. 233–8, in which the 'sembiante' [image/phantasm] of Aspasia similarly returns to the poet's mind as a mysterious and fleeting vision on the screen of the landscape.

struggle to reach out to an Other who finally presents itself as irretrievable, something which permeates the language of *SU*, and its topography.[44] The frustrations of the speaking subject mirror in turn the foreclosure of an experience—its premature end or fleetingness.

An intense figuration of this process is to be found in 'Il muro', a poem that revisits—geographically and poetically—the quintessential border space of *Frontiera*, still singled out as the site of a possible event or epiphany but now viewed as unremarkable (since nothing really happens there, and all space seems equal):

'Il muro'

Sono
quasi in sogno a Luino
lungo il muro dei morti.
Qua i nostri volti ardevano nell'ombra
nella luce rosa che sulle nove di sera   5
piovevano gli alberi a giugno?
Certo chi muore... ma *questi* che vivono
invece: giocano in notturna, sei
contro sei, *quelli* del Porto
e delle Verbanesi nuova gioventù.   10
Io da loro distolto
sento l'animazione delle foglie
e in *questa* farsi strada la bufera.
Scagliano polvere e fronde scagliano ira
quelli di là dal muro—   15
e tra essi il più caro.
          'Papà—faccio per difendermi
puerilmente—papà...'.
Non c'è molto da opporgli, il tuffo
di carità il soprassalto in me quando leggo
di fioriture in pieno inverno sulle alture   20
che lo cerchiano *là* nel suo gelo al fondo,
se gli porto notizie delle sue cose,
se le sento tarlarsi (la duplice
la subdola fedeltà delle cose:
capaci di resistere oltre una vita d'uomo   25
e poi si sfaldano trasognandoci anni o momenti dopo)
su qualche mensola
in via Scarlatti 27 a Milano.

---

[44] It is Patrick Boyde who speaks of deictics taking on an 'elegiac force' in Leopardi's poetry, specifically in relation to 'Aspasia', in which 'that', as designating the ideal Aspasia of the mind, is initially preferred to 'this', real one and 'then shown to be less enduring': '"Ecfrasi ed ecceità" in Leopardi's *Canti*', *Italian Studies* 43 (1988), pp. 2–20 (pp. 13–14).

Dice che è carità pelosa, di presagio
del mio prossimo ghiaccio, me lo dice come in gloria   30
rasserenandosi rasserenandomi
mentre riapro gli occhi e lui si ritira ridendo
—e ancora folleggiano *quei* ragazzi animosi contro bufera e notte—
lo dice con polvere e foglie da tutto il muro
che una sera d'estate è una sera d'estate   35
e adesso avrà più senso
il canto degli ubriachi dalla parte di Creva.

(In *SU*, pp. 179–80)

['The Wall']

I am
almost in a dream in Luino
along the wall of the dead.
Here our faces glowed in the shade,
in the rosy light the trees rained   5
near nine of an evening in June?
Whoever dies of course... but *these* the living
on the other hand: play nightly,
six a side, the younger generation
of Porto or the Verbanesi.   10
Turned from them, I sense
the animation of the leaves
and in the storm making headway.
They cast dust and leafage, cast anger
those on the wall's far side—   15
and among them my most dear.
                       'Papa'—in childish
self-defence—'papa...'
I've not much to resist him, the pang
of love, the start in me when I read
of flowerings in the winter's depth   20
on upland surrounding him in frost *down there*,
if I bring him news of his things,
if I feel them worm-eaten (the two-faced
insidious fidelity of things:
able to outlast a man's life   25
and then crumble astonishing us years or moments after)
upon some shelf
in 27 Via Scarlatti, Milan.

He says it's self-interested love, foreseeing
I'll soon be frozen, tells me as if in glory   30
reassuring himself, reassuring me
while I reopen my eyes and he draws away laughing
—and *those* spirited lads still fooling against the storm and night—

> with dust and leaves the length of the wall he says
> that a summer's evening is a summer's evening 35
> and there will be more sense now
> to the song of the drunks around Creva.]

The deictic regions in the poem, determined by the series of spatio-temporal references, have a particular role in designating the liminal realm that pertains to the relationship between the dead (father) and the living (son). In fact, the whole first stanza is played upon the opposition between 'questi', referring to the living, and 'quelli' the dead, a division established only to be transgressed, first by the movement of the leaves that heralds the storm and evokes the concomitant animation of the dead, then with the (regressive, childlike) discourse addressed by the poet to his dead father, which stands as his only defence against their (his) anger. The 'I' sits uneasily between the two domains, belonging entirely to neither. He is not wholly aligned with the living since he is 'da loro distolto' (l.11), but neither can he fully embrace the realm of the dead, since if he is along the wall he never crosses it, and despite his proximity to his dead father and the brief 'conversation' they share, their encounter is largely based on a misunderstanding, or at the very least a failure to comprehend one another.

The uncanny nature of the experience (which in Freudian terms could indicate the return of the repressed, as something both familiar and unfamiliar at the same time) is matched by the uncanny nature of space centred on the undefined and indefinable 'qua' (l. 4) which bridges memory and perception, dream and waking, life and death.[45] Not as circumscribed as the alternative deictic 'qui' would have been, this 'qua' has boundaries that are fluid and shifting, which indicates the temporal and spatial uncertainty that underlies the encounter (again dramatically different from the 'Incontro' of *Frontiera*) and the more troubling doubt (note the question mark in line 6) as to whether the 'I' is in the right place at all. Framed by verbs in the present ('Sono') and imperfect ('ardevano') tense, this 'here' properly suspends the 'I' between the 'here and now' of the wall as it appears in dream and the 'here and then' of how it may have appeared in memory when 'i nostri volti ardevano nell'ombra'—when father and son were on the same side, so to speak.

---

[45] In his essay, 'Das Unheimliche' ['The Uncanny'] (1919), Freud describes the uncanny as 'in reality nothing new or alien, but something which is familiar and old-established in the mind and which has become alienated from it only through the process of repression'. It is 'something which ought to have remained hidden but has come to light', an experience common 'in the relation to [...] the return of the dead, and to spirits and ghosts': 'The Uncanny', in *SE* XVII (1957), pp. 219–56 (p. 241).

Geographically, too, the wall maps a spatial and temporal boundary which spreads in memory from Luino all the way to Sereni's paternal home in Via Scarlatti in Milan. The things ('cose') that occupy the central section of the poem are the linking thread between one world and the next but also carry the same temporal doubleness, 'la *duplice* | la subdola fedeltà' (l. 23–4), which conceals a potential for disintegration, as though at any moment ('anni o momenti dopo'), they will become unravelled and all that they represent with them. Their real value is in the 'trasognandoci'—the causing us to daydream—where the real communication can perhaps take place (as here, in dream). Indeed, the 'tra' [between] of the 'trasognandoci' could provide a *mise en abyme* for the whole poem which we could say comes into being between two dreams: between the 'I''s dream of death and his father's dream of life and the living.

There can be contact between the two but no synthesis. Apart from the vocative address to 'papà' at line 17, the remainder of the 'dialogue' between father and son is communicated first through the 'I''s internal monologue, then through reported speech, so that the father remains in the third person—Benveniste's 'non-person' of discourse—so that he never becomes a 'you', never allowing a truly reciprocal communication to take place.[46] This lends weight to the feeling that the father exists mainly as an extension of the 'I', an alter ego that would be a premature figuration of an essentially posthumous self, permitting the 'I' a moment of deep reflection on his own 'prossimo ghiaccio' (l. 30).

There is more than a hint of menace in his father's words and in the derision that accompanies them, but not much understanding. The 'I' bathes in the reflected glory of his father for a moment, as their emotions are tightly mirrored ('rasserenandosi rasserenandomi', l. 31) but by the next line it is as though his father has already left, receding beyond the wall and returning to his humic foundation in dust and leaves. His words just linger on the horizon as it continues to recede, until we are back in the present frame of reference, looking with the 'I' into the future, but a future that is strikingly similar to the past: 'lo dice con polvere e foglie *da tutto il muro* | che una sera d'estate è una sera d'estate | e adesso avrà più senso | il canto degli ubriachi della parte di Creva' (ll. 34–7).

There is more than an echo here of the meeting between the poet and his dead father in Montale's 'Voce giunta con le folaghe' ['Voice That Came with the Coots'] (in *La bufera e altro* [*The Storm, etc.*]; henceforth *La bufera*), which is similarly phantasmagoric in setting and also stages a kind of encounter manqué, in which the 'I' never fully fathoms the

---

[46] See Benveniste, 'La nature des pronoms', pp. 255–6.

meaning of his father's life, and his father cannot make him understand his dread of being forgotten by the living. The situation of the poetic subject in lines 45–50 of Montale's poem, 'Il vento del giorno | confonde l'ombra viva e l'altra ancora | riluttante in un mezzo che respinge | le mie mani, e il respiro che mi si rompe | nel punto dilatato, nella fossa | che circonda lo scatto del ricordo' [The wind of day | melds the living shadow | and the other, still reluctant one | in an amalgam that repels my hands, | and the breath breaks out of me at the swelling point, | in the moat that surrounds the release of memory], find a correlative in 'Il muro'. Along the uncertain boundary of the wall, the Serenian 'I' similarly finds itself a living shadow, and his spring of memory is also surrounded by a pit or grave that threatens to swallow them both as it expands (*dilatare*) outward. Yet in Sereni's poem there is no intermediary, Clizian[47] presence to mediate between the living and the dead and no hope of a higher meaning beyond.

Not coincidentally, Sereni's poem ends on a tautology, a semantic impasse that is also the insurmountable distance dividing the living from the dead and a sign that, by the end, the wall has become more formidable and impenetrable than ever, extending its boundaries even further than before ('*da tutto* il muro'). No 'varco' [passageway] opens up, and there is no hole in the wall through which the 'I' can enter the other realm, or his father leave it. The poem ends with a kind of non-answer from a non-question, with the subject's child-like but affectionate imploration, 'papà [...] papà' being met only by the disengaged voice that speaks, distantly, of other things. The final meaning that the poem discloses is only another enigma whose answer still lies with the dead.

BEYOND DEIXIS

Whereas in *Frontiera*, any ratification for the subject comes through a shared visual perspective, in *SU* this only seems possible if the poet can find an *entente* between the two parties involved in the enunciative act: the 'I' and his interlocutor, the word and the thing. In turn, the transformation in the role and power of deictics from Sereni's earlier to his later poetry mirrors a key temporal shift at the level of the poetry itself: from a predominant reliance on the present to a much heavier reliance on the past and the necessity of turning back.

---

[47] Clizia is the senhal Montale gives to the figure of his beloved, beginning from *Le occasioni*. She is often characterized in that collection, and *La bufera e altro*, as a salvific presence, nonetheless inseparable from the metaphysical uncertainty and existential anxiety that characterize the Montalian poetic subject.

Deictically speaking, *SU* as a whole thus finds its overreaching sense of purpose in the opening lines of 'Via Scarlatti' (p. 103): 'Con non altro che te | è il colloquio' [with none other than you | is the word], in which the *tu* is the phantasm of poetry as much as a true Other. The dialogue or audience the poet seeks is increasingly hard to come by, and even if he finds the formula of his existence, he cannot guarantee that he can make it work *in situ*, or more properly *in camera*, when put on trial by the very same interlocutors he seeks as remedy for his own shortcomings.

It is significant in this respect that 'Via Scarlatti' should end with the poet still waiting for the dialogue to happen. The deictic 'qui' of the last line of the poem ('E *qui* ti aspetto' [And *here* for you I wait]) is less a physical coordinate than a kind of poetic location which, although potentially all-encompassing, is also characterized by a certain incompleteness—this is where he will be waiting forever. What seems to be contained in that 'qui' is all of the poet's self and all that cannot progress until the *tu* figure can be found. It is properly the meeting point of his (absolute) presence and her (absolute) absence, properly a kind of fixation on a missing or absent object.

It is from this awareness that the study of Sereni's later poetry must proceed, from the notion of a subject caught between a backwards look that leads nowhere and an impetus towards speaking that ends in silence. The interactions of speech and gaze that deixis brings together in the realm of poetic space open up an understanding of how Sereni's lyric subject is articulated, and the coordination of space that deictics imply embodies not only a perceptual orientation but also a process of self-definition, which extends to the very heart of language and to the very centre of the subject's speech.

As they occupy a liminal status in language and the poem, between emptiness and fullness, nonexistence and the possibility of being, deictics become markers of a threshold experience in a more concrete sense too. They express the poet's condition as desirer and his reworking of a major poetic topos by which the dialogue *in absentia* which underscores so much of lyric discourse can ideally, though not without difficulty, be transformed into a dialogue *in praesentia*. From *Frontiera* to *SU* and beyond, deixis is a syntactical matrix that constantly resituates the 'I' at the point at which it would gain access to this ideal space of the lyric, while radically altering the possibilities that the 'I' has to embrace it or to make the leap from one dimension into the other.

3

'L'incerto lembo'

Liminal Topographies from Montale to Sereni[1]

> Oh l'orizzonte in fuga, dove s'accende
> rara la luce della petroliera!
> Il varco è qui?
>
> (Montale, 'La casa dei doganieri')[2]

This chapter explores the role of liminality—understood as the condition of being caught between two opposing orders or realities, or in desiring terms between possibility and frustration—in shaping the poetic landscapes of Sereni's fourth collection, *Stellla variabile* (*SV*), in its dialogue with the Montalian heritage. It begins from the intertextual relationship that Sereni establishes with Montale in his 1977 essay, 'Il ritorno' ['The Return'], to identify the locus of a threshold subjectivity that rests in a topographically liminal space, which is also the space of desire and the poem. I argue that the primary trope of liminality—'l'incerto lembo' [the uncertain margin]—through which Montale's 'Il ritorno' (in *Le occasioni*) is articulated constitutes the structural legacy that Sereni reworks to great effect in a series of poetic topographies that lead him back to the intimately Montalian landscape of Bocca di Magra in Liguria (familiar also to him), while transforming it in line with his own perceptions and experiences, and essentially recasting it on the basis of an increased doubt and negativity.

As discussed in the preceding chapter, poetic space is the place in which the perceptual and linguistic faculties of the subject intertwine to define his status vis-à-vis the object world, and deictic reference provides the measure of this domain. On the one hand, deictics offer the poetic subject the possibility of eliding the distance or lack dividing him from his desired object; on the other, they bare the insubstantiality of the intermediary (poetic) image that would seek to compensate for the underlying loss. In

---

[1] 'Incerto lembo' is a trope I borrow from Montale's 'Il ritorno' ['The Return']. It is best translated here as 'uncertain margin', though Jonathan Galassi renders it as 'fudged edge' in its original context in his translation of the poem.

[2] [Oh the vanishing horizon line, | where the tanker's light shines faint! | Is the channel here?], 'The House of the Customs Men'.

revisiting the Montalian trope of 'l'incerto lembo', and on the model of what is known in Lacanian terms as the 'scopic drive' (the dimension of desire that relates to vision), Sereni's deictics are shown to actually mark the spot at which a double gaze is elicited that would both conceal and reveal the subject's fallenness in this area.

Poems in *SV* that deal with the limits of vision, such as 'Niccolò' and 'Fissità' [Fixity], testify to this process and to the foreclosure of the 'I''s journey towards possession. In turn, Sereni is led to rework the already ambivalent loci of Montale's poetic universe, in which the desire for transcendence is constantly present if not always achieved, as a place of frustrated desire, which occludes fulfilment. To this extent, prominent space will be given to an analysis of Sereni's *Un posto*, which, as well as being the nucleus around which *SV* is built, also represents the poet's most sustained reflection on the discourse of desire in these terms. Montale emerges as the voice, or better the gaze, underpinning Sereni's undertaking in this area, and the chapter as a whole charts the metamorphosis of the Montalian universe of *Ossi* and *Le occasioni* into Sereni's *SV*, to offer a comparative reading of poems that through the motif of perceptual uncertainty engender a liminal zone in subjectivity, language, and desire.

SERENI AND MONTALE: A VISIBLE DIALOGUE

Sereni's writings on Montale span over four decades.[3] While Sereni tends to privilege *Le occasioni* in his writings on his Ligurian predecessor, he always views the collection organically, as having grown out of the earlier

---

[3] Vittorio Sereni, 'In margine alle *Occasioni*', first publ. in *Tempo* 4.62 (1 Aug. 1940), p. 45, now in *SG*, pp. 56–60; 'Ognuno riconosce i suoi' ['Each Recognizes His Own'], *Letteratura* 30.79–81, n.s. 13 (Jan.–June 1966), pp. 305–10; '"Satura" di Eugenio Montale' ['Eugenio Montale's *Satura*'], *L'Approdo letterario* 17.53 (1971), pp. 107–16. This is the text of the transmission 'Piccolo Pianeta letterario', aired on *Terzo Programma Radiofonico*, with contributions by M. Corti, S. Solmi, S. Spender, Sereni, and an interview with Montale. Sereni's contribution is on pp. 110–12; 'Ci appassionò alla vita' ['He Got Us Excited about Life'], first publ. in *Epoca* 26.1309 (8 Nov. 1975), pp. 35–8, now in *SG*, pp. 86–9; 'Intervento' ['Contribution'], in *Incontro con Eugenio Montale* [*Conversation with Eugenio Montale*] on the occasion of Montale's award of the Nobel Prize, in the series *Testimonianze radiotelevisive*, ed. Servizio Stampa and the Public Relations Office of *Radio Televisione della Svizzera Italiana* (Bellinzona: Istituto grafico Casagrande, 1976), pp. 29–32, under the title 'Sereni'. The original broadcast took place on 28 Oct. 1975, directed by S. M. Fares, with the participation of E. Montale, P. Bernasconi, A. Soldini, G. Orelli, G. Ferrata, and M. Forti; 'Il ritorno' (1977), first publ. in *Letture montaliane*, ed. Comune di Genova in celebration of Montale's 80th birthday (Genova: Bozzi, 1977), now in *SG*, pp. 147–53; 'Il nostro debito verso Montale' ['Our Debt Towards Montale'], in *La poesia di Eugenio Montale: Atti del Convegno Internazionale (Milano 12/13/14 settembre, Genova 15 settembre 1982)* (Milan: Librex, 1983), pp. 37–9; 'Dovuto a Montale' ['Owed to

poetic landscape of *Ossi*. At the beginning of 'In margine alle *Occasioni*' [In the Margins of *The Occasions*] (1973), for example, Sereni declares that neither book should be viewed in isolation, and ends by reaffirming the significance of Montale's poetry in its totality, rooted in the poet's commitment to 'rivelare [...] tutte le risorse di poesia che il nostro mondo moderno racchiude' [reveal [...] all the resources of poetry that our modern world contains], and never shying away from the challenge of translating even the material world ('il nostro mondo fisico') into language.[4] From *Ossi* to *Le occasioni* and beyond, Montale's poetry, Sereni suggests, exists in the liminal space between normal (everyday) perception and its transformation into poetic language and event. It is 'spesso, *un limite incantato* entro cui le cose possono veramente esistere' [often, *an enchanted borderspace* within whose bounds things can truly exist].[5] This enchanted space—which is paradoxically also a place of confinement ('limite')—coincides with the advent of poetry and the possible existence of another world beyond the physical. Both realities remain to be tested, but the origins and scope of liminality are already implicit in this process of becoming.

This intertextual dynamic, in which, in reading Montale, Sereni also reads himself, finds its apex in two of Sereni's later essays on the Ligurian poet—'Il ritorno' (1977) and 'Dovuto a Montale' ['Owed to Montale'] (1983)—both particularly concerned with the temporal relationship between past and present. In each case, Sereni casts the journey into Montale's poetry specifically as a return (to a place earlier relinquished), and thus a memory, one which becomes interlaced with a series of poetic memories to which that returning landscape gives rise.[6]

'Il ritorno' is the clearest example of this, focusing as it does on Montale's eponymous poem of 1940, set in Bocca di Magra, the place where Sereni returned almost every summer between 1951 and 1971 and which was the inspiration for his 'poesia in sette parti' [poem in seven parts], *Un posto*, written during that twenty-year period.[7] Looking at Sereni's writings on Bocca di Magra, included in a special anthology of poems that take that 'luogo deputato' [chosen place] as their setting, we

---

Montale'] (1983), first publ. in *La Rotonda* 6 (Almanacco Luinese per il 1984, Luino: Nastro, 1983), pp. 6–12, now included as Appendix to *ID2*, pp. 159–66.

[4] Sereni, 'In margine alle *Occasioni*', p. 60.
[5] Ibid.
[6] In 'Il ritorno', the landscape in question is Bocca di Magra; in 'Dovuto a Montale', Luino.
[7] Although *Un posto* is often referred to as a 'poemetto', Sereni preferred the label 'poesia in sette parti'; see the interview with Domenico Porzio, 'In viaggio verso me' ['Journeying toward myself'], *Panorama*, 22 Mar. 1982, pp. 117–21 (p. 117).

can appreciate the extent to which, geographically speaking (but not only), Bocca di Magra functions as a bridge into the world of Montale's *Ossi* and *Le occasioni* and represents for Sereni the space of liminality *par excellence*, 'Lo stesso passaggio da una riva all'altra del fiume sembrava comportare una decisione importante, significativa; e anche più, un rituale, un sortilegio, quasi si trattasse del *trapasso da un mondo a un mondo diverso* [The same passage from one bank to the other seemed to bring with it an important, a significant, decision; and more than that a ritual, a sorcery, almost as if what was at stake was *the passage from one world into another*].[8]

The 'altra riva' [other bank] motif, which also resonates with Dantesque associations, turns out to be decisive for Sereni's *Un posto*.[9] The question of the poet's ability or inability to make the passage from one shore to the other, and from one world into the next (*trapassare*), becomes the ultimate dilemma driving the poem and the greatest test for desire when that farther shore moves out of reach. In the space that separates the physical from the metaphysical, and self-conscious, rational action ('decisione') from witchcraft or black magic ('sortilegio'), liminality emerges as the uncertain status of a subject negotiating a journey of desire. For Sereni, this journey of desire inevitably finds its origins in Montale.

Montale: the origins of liminality

Those origins can be traced back to the opening poem from Montale's *Ossi*, '*Godi se il vento...*' [*Be happy if the wind...*]. This threshold proem, *in limine* [on the threshold], establishes the particular coordinates of space with which the collection as a whole will concern itself and to which Sereni will be drawn back time and again.[10] The poetic 'I' is depicted, via deixis, as being situated in '*questo lembo | di terra solitario*' [*this solitary strip of land*], '*di qua dall'erto muro*' [*over* [more specifically, *on this side of*] *the sheer wall*] ('*Godi*', p. 5), which creates a dividing line between the 'here' and the 'there' that is destined to recur throughout *Ossi*

---

[8] Vittorio Sereni, 'Tra fiume e mare' ['Betwixt River and Sea'] (1976), in *Un posto di vacanza e altre poesie*, ed. Zeno Birolli (Milan: All'Insegna del Pesce d'Oro, 1994), pp. 57–67 (p. 62).
[9] See e.g. Charon's words in *Inf.* III, 85–7, 'Non isperate mai veder lo cielo: | i' vegno per menarvi a l'altra riva | ne le tenebre etterne, in caldo e 'n gelo' [Give up all hope of ever seeing Heaven. | I come to take you to the other shore | into eternal darkness, into heat and chill], and the description of Matelda in *Purg.* XXVIII, 67–9, 'Ella ridea da l'altra riva dritta, | trattando più color con le sue mani, | che l'alta terra sanza seme gitta' [Straightening up, she smiled from the other shore, | arranging in her hands the many colors | that grow, unplanted, on that high terrain], as well as my reflections on this topic in Ch. 5.
[10] *In limine* is the title of the first section of *Ossi*, which includes just one poem, '*Godi se il vento...*'.

as a correlative of the poet's position in a place or phase of liminality, on the one hand hemmed in by some kind of limit or boundary, on the other, on the threshold of something beyond or Other.

Conceiving of liminality as a phase, Rossella Riccobono emphasizes the way in which movement through and within that phase is centred upon 'images of direction and changes of direction'.[11] This is a point that Margaret Brose also develops in relation to what she calls the 'line' in *Ossi*, represented by wall, coastline, or horizon:

> Montale's *line* marks the point of interface of two domains, spatial in the first instance, metaphysical in the second. But it is less a boundary to be crossed than a condition to be inhabited. It is a threshold to be sure, but it is also a situation which provides the occasion for the experience of liminality itself, the experience of being in *varco*, in passage, in movement.[12]

The 'lembo' of '*Godi*' is just one such line, from which the lyric subject at the heart of Montale's poem draws its specific identity and the poem its status as the locus of a transformation, typically for Montale entrusted to the *tu* [you] figure who alone could flee, altering the status quo, '*tu balza fuori, fuggi!* | *Va, per te l'ho pregato,—ora la sete* | *mi sarà lieve, meno acre la ruggine...*' [*burst through, break free!* | *Go, I've prayed for this for you—now my thirst* | *will be easy, my rancour less bitter...*] (ll. 16–18). The 'I', defined by the act of passive renunciation which, however, frees the Other, is witness to an event in which he is both implicated and excluded. The double locus of memory and desire, which turns the poem from orchard into reliquary into crucible, establishes the terms of liminality: the scene of the subject's dual perception of his wish, and the Other's fulfilment of it. In Rebecca West's words:

> Rather than expressing the fullness of a center or concentrating on completely realized spaces either physical or psychological in nature, the poet instead turns to those areas of thought, experience and expression that can be designated as marginal. [...] The poetic voice's emergence into expression is as tenuous as the images that seek to fix and capture the location of observed or intuited occurrences, emotions, and objects.[13]

---

[11] Rossella Riccobono, 'The Question of Liminality and the Dissolution of Spatio-temporal Dimensions in Montale's Poetry: "Sul limite", "Vasca" and "Carnevale di Gerti"', *The Italianist* 17 (1997), pp. 74–98 (pp. 77, 78).

[12] Margaret Brose, 'The Spirit of the Sign: Oppositional Structures in Montale's *Ossi di seppia*', *Stanford Italian Review* 4 (1984), pp. 147–75 (p. 154) (italics in the original).

[13] Rebecca West, *Eugenio Montale: Poet on the Edge* (Cambridge, Mass.: Harvard University Press, 1981), pp. 9, 22.

It is this locus of marginality—in thought, language, and the apprehension of reality—that Sereni chooses to revisit and recast on his own terms in his dialogue with the Montalian heritage.

'Il ritorno': Montale's return to *Ossi di seppia*, Sereni's return to Montale

It is significant in this respect that the 'lembo' of *In limine* should recur in a later poem by Montale entitled 'Il ritorno' (1940), in *Le occasioni*, which not only represents a return for the poet to the landscape and poetics of *Ossi* but is also chosen as the subject of Sereni's eponymous essay of 1977. Like Sereni, I begin by quoting the poem in full:

>   *Bocca di Magra*
> *Ecco* bruma e libeccio sulle dune
> sabbiose che lingueggiano
> e là celato dall'*incerto lembo*
> o alzato dal va-e-vieni delle spume
> il barcaiolo Duilio che traversa 5
> in lotta sui suoi remi; *ecco* il pimento
> dei pini che più terso
> si dilata tra pioppi e saliceti,
> e pompe a vento battere le pale
> e il viottolo che segue l'onde dentro 10
> la fiumana terrosa
> funghire velenoso d'ovuli; *ecco*
> ancora quelle scale
> a chiocciola, slabbrate, che s'avvitano
> *fin oltre* la veranda 15
> in un gelo policromo d'ogive,
> *eccole* che t'ascoltano, le nostre vecchie scale,
> e vibrano al ronzìo
> allora che dal cofano tu ridésti leggera
> voce di sarabanda 20
> o quando Erinni fredde ventano angui
> d'inferno e sulle rive una bufera
> di strida s'allontana; ed *ecco* il sole
> che chiude la sua corsa, che s'offusca
> ai margini del canto—*ecco* il tuo morso 25
> oscuro di tarantola: son pronto.
>   (In *Le occasioni*, p. 178)

>   [*Bocca di Magra*
> *Here's* mist and wild wind on the sandy,
> flickering dunes, and there,

hidden by *the foam's fudged edge*
or lifted on its rise and fall,
Duilio the boatman at the crossing 5
battling his oars;
here's the sharper turpentine of the pines
rising through poplar and willow,
and windmills flailing their arms
and the path that follows 10
the waves into the muddy stream
mushrooming poison ovula;
and *here are* the timeworn spiral stairs
that climb to the veranda
in a multicoloured 15
ice of arches;
here they are listening, our old stairs,
ahum with the buzz,
now you've revived the saraband's soft voice
out of your treasure chest 20
or when cold Furies vent their hell-snakes
and a storm of screams moves off
along the shore;
and *here's* the sun
ending his run and dying out 25
at the song's edges—*here's* your black
tarantula bite: I'm ready.]

 The recasting of the first 'lembo' of *In limine* in a frame of uncertainty testifies both to its importance as a recurring trope of liminality and to its shifting location with respect to the subject, who now perceives it at some distance rather than situating himself within its bounds. No longer grounded in the earth, this 'lembo' follows the undulating course of the surface of the waves and is thus 'incerto': perceptually blurred or shifting as well as indistinct (Jonathan Galassi translates it as 'fudged'). As in '*Godi*', the 'lembo' also designates a memory-space, or better, the place in which vision and memory flow seamlessly in and out of one another, pivoting upon the temporal doubleness of the place itself, the return to which is made explicit only in lines 13–14, 'ecco | *ancora quelle* scale'.

 Thus, while the landscape would still mark the locus of an event, again explicitly bound up with the identity of an Other, the *tu* figure emerges late (much later than '*Godi*'), and the ghostly scene—initially devoid of her—is later transformed by her presence only to the extent that it becomes more infernal and menacing. If, as is now generally accepted, 'Il ritorno' is part of the Arletta cycle of poems in Montale's work, this Other is to be construed as dead more than lost, a perception that colours the poem in its entirety and impacts also upon the status of the 'I' who does finally gain life, but only through a gesture of death, 'ecco il tuo morso | oscuro di tarantola: son pronto' (l. 26–7).[14] Conjured through a complex interplay of memory, scene, and gaze, the encounter between the 'I' and its object is once again essentially shrouded in a '*morto | viluppo di memorie*' [*dead web | of memories*] ('*Godi*', ll. 3–4), and the power of the poem lies in being able to resurrect a series of images from the dead and project them into the future. As Sereni writes, attesting to the force associated with liminality in the poem:

> Il suo movimento passa dall'aperto al chiuso e da questo torna all'aperto in un'alternanza di infiltrazioni e sortite, di percezione del particolare e di slargo sulla veduta d'assieme, dilatando lo spazio in uno spazio diverso, ondulante, imprecisabile, il dato temporale in atemporalità non per questo meno brulicante di presenze e assenze (altrove: *ed io non so chi va e chi resta*), ma soprattutto densa di attesa.[15]
>
> [Its movement passes from outdoors to indoors and then returns to the open in alternating infiltrations and sorties, the perception of the particular to a widening out in a vision of the whole, expanding space into a different space—undulating and indefinable—and the temporal event into an atemporality that is nevertheless no less swarming with presences and absences (elsewhere: *and I don't know who's going and who'll stay*), but above all dense with expectation.]

To this extent, Montale's 'Il ritorno' establishes for Sereni the coordinates of a (poetic) space in which the perceptual limits of the subject function as an index of desire. They spell either the opening up or foreclosure of a space in which, or at which, the encounter with the (lost) Other would take place. As Sereni suggests, the particularity of

---

[14] Although there is still some disagreement, the 'Arletta cycle' is generally considered to begin with '*Godi se il vento*', which opens the *Ossi*, and is developed in that collection in 'Vento e bandiere' [Wind and Flags], '*Fuscello teso dal muro...*' [*Twig that juts from the wall...*], 'Il canneto rispunta i suoi cimelli' ['The canebrake sends its little shoots'], 'Casa sul mare' [House by the Sea], 'I morti' [The Dead], 'Delta', and 'Incontro' [Encounter]; in *Le occasioni*, it incorporates '*Il balcone*' ['*The Balcony*'], 'Accelerato' ['Local Train'], 'La casa dei doganieri' ['The House of the Customs Men'], 'Bassa Marea' ['Low Tide'], 'Stanze' ['Stanzas'], 'Punta del Mesco', 'Il ritorno', and 'Eastbourne' (though, as Emmanuela Tandello notes, critics are divided on the last); in *La bufera*: 'Due nel crepuscolo' ['Two in Twilight'] and '"Ezekiel saw the wheel..."'. Arletta is also present in several poems in the later work, including some in *Diario del '71 e del '72*, *Quaderno di quattro anni*, and *Altri versi*. On the 'Arletta cycle', see Emmanuela Tandello, 'Fanciulle morte: Arletta, Silvia, Euridice', in *Amelia Rosselli: La fanciulla e l'infinito* (Rome: Donzelli, 2007), pp. 85–95; and Éanna Ó Ceallacháin, 'Arletta', in *Eugenio Montale: The Poetry of the Later Years* (Oxford: Legenda, 2001), pp. 19–24. See also Maria Antonietta Grignani, *Prologhi ed epiloghi: sulla poesia di Eugenio Montale; con una prosa inedita* (Ravenna: Longo, 1987), pp. 24–5.

[15] Sereni, 'Il ritorno', p. 151.

perspective that Montale's poem creates thus results from the permeability of space and time, and from their mutual withdrawal into an almost purely phantasmatic realm that would however signify, in its uncertain, indeterminable boundaries and 'atemporality', the promise of something outside or beyond the rigid schemes of existence.

Characteristically for Montale, and Sereni after him, this uncertain margin between perception and memory is also the deictic realm that, as discussed in the previous chapter, marks the place where possession and dispossession, absence and presence, collapse into each other. As Sereni perceives, the force of the poem (its 'quadro magico' [magic frame], 'Il ritorno', p. 153) largely derives from the role of the deictic 'ecco's through which the poetic gaze is constructed and the personae of the poem conjured into presence. The 'flickering' ('lingueggiano') quality of the landscape is both the gateway to this magical dimension and the presentiment of closure—the fact that, as Sereni states, when the desired moment of illumination or epiphany is about to take place, 'la poesia à già tutta consumata in quella preparazione' [the poem is already completely consumed in that preparation] so that the true event of the poem remains on the outside, or both inside and outside at the same time (p. 151).

Each 'ecco' thus functions as a temporal bridge which also reveals the gap that has opened up in time between the original vision and its re-evocation in memory. Typically these 'ecco's—as deictics which foreground the present frame over the past, and perceptual immediateness over the potentially fading images of memory—mark the dividing line between what is there, not there, or merely imagined by the subject to be there. As Sereni perceptively argues, confirming his deictic sensibility:

> I segnali, le percussioni, i trasalimenti di quegli *ecco* culminanti in un 'eccomi' testualmente non profferito ma risultante dalla convergenza degli effetti (*son pronto*) preparano lo schermo sul quale s'accamperà quello che una volta avrebbe chiamato 'il miracolo' e che ora è piuttosto la folgorazione, illuminazione, epifania (altrove: *il quadro dove tra poco romperai*). ('Il ritorno', p. 151)
>
> [The signals, the percussion instruments, the startling of those *here*s culminating in a 'here I am' not textually proffered but resulting from the *convergence* of the effects (*I'm ready*), prepare the screen on which will appear what once he would have called 'the miracle' and now is more like a flash, an illumination, an epiphany (elsewhere: *the frame from which you'll soon erupt*).]

These 'ecco's are thus the key to producing an act of perceptual convergence that could potentially spell also the reconciliation of desire and its object—both subject and object equally implicated in the image that will come forth upon the screen and constitute the miraculous event of the poem, which reaches its height only in the last line in which the colon, which links as well as divides the two figures, represents the most (least) that the poet can achieve.

As Montale's poem reveals, and Sereni's commentary confirms, 'l'incerto lembo' thus refers to a number of dimensions of experience simultaneously:

(i) *The topographic point* at which the waters of the river and the sea confront each other, which strikes Sereni for its visual force, and its realism–a space conceived as a meeting point between two fields that border each other but may never cross:

> Poi *l'incerto lembo*. Stando in riva al fiume a Bocca di Magra lembo e incertezza si percepiscono a vista, nel concreto, specie se una libecciata vuole il mare battagliante alla foce contro la forza inversa e univoca del fiume; e la momentanea vittoria, il prevalere del mare, è segnata dallo scorrimento delle *spume* al di qua del punto in cui le acque più che mescolarsi e fondersi, come di solito, si affrontano. ('Il ritorno', pp. 148–9)

> [Then *the uncertain margin*. On the banks of the river at Bocca di Magra, margin and uncertainty are perceived together, concretely, especially if a southwesterly wind pits the battling sea at the estuary against the opposite and univocal force of the river; and the momentary victory, the prevailing of the sea, is shown by the flow of the *sea foam* on the near side of the point at which the waters, rather than mixing and blending with one another, as is usually the case, clash.]

(ii) *The locus of desire*, which, within the scheme of the poem, is designated as the place in which perception and memory overlap, peopled on the one hand by the phantasms of lost objects or those that have vanished (which Sereni terms 'L'inventario di esseri, aspetti e cose scomparsi o mutati' [The inventory of beings, aspects, or things, either lost or changed], 'Il ritorno', p. 149) and, on the other, by the constant return of the dying or black sun, which cancels itself out more than sets—each echo of it in the voice, 'ai margini del canto' [at the song's edges], recalling the 'trauma' of successive returns to the place, and successive losses: 'Al punto da trasporsi *sulle rive* perdendosi in *bufera di strida*, in *sole che chiude la sua corsa, che s'offusca*— oppure, in qualche modo suscitandoli?' [To the point of transposing itself *along the shore* losing itself in a *storm of screams*, in *the sun ending his run and dying out*—or, in some way generating them?] (p. 152).

(iii) *The poetic realm* that comes to occupy the space between them—the uncertain space in which the encounter with the *tu* figure would take place, which is the edge (both verge and limit) of the poem itself, since 'canto' can mean both song and poem. This is the space to which the 'I' is confined by the 'trauma' of the experience (the designation is Sereni's), in expectation of 'il morso oscuro | di tarantola', which 'esplode puntualmente nel cuore dell'estasi rivelandone il fondo ancipite' [invariably explodes at the heart of the moment of ecstasy, revealing its ancipital basis] ('Il ritorno', p. 151). Between visibility and invisibility, the poetic subject, like the boatman Duilio, is seen and not seen at the same time. The textual space after the final colon is also the liminal place in language and the poem to which the 'I' is summoned and removed by the writing process. Significantly, within an Arletta poem, this final incarnation of an 'incerto lembo' would also specify, in a deictically charged moment, the revelation of life into death and vice versa.

(iv) *The 'old stairs' ('vecchie scale')* that are the site at which the traumatic event is staged, which as Sereni notes potentially mark 'una "contaminazione" di memorie' [a 'contamination' of memories] ('Il ritorno', p. 149), appearing in one location (Bocca di Magra) but being transposed from another (Monterosso, in the *Cinque terre*).[16] There is a doubt as to whether the poet really remembers things as they were.[17]

(v) *The self-reflexivity* of the poem that prompts Sereni to make a comparison between Montale and Petrarch, and between Montale and Proust.[18] Quoting the end of Proust's *Du coté de chez Swann* [*Swann's Way*], he cites a passage which bridges the dimensions of space and time ands stands as a *mise en abyme* of his own poetic project:

> Les lieux que nous avons connus n'appartiennent pas qu'au monde de l'espace où nous les situons pour plus de facilité. Ils n'étaient qu'une mince tranche au milieu d'impressions contiguës qui formaient notre vie d'alors; le souvenir

---

[16] 'Verso quale *veranda*, rischiarate da quali *ogive*, in quale casa? [...] Non è che siano stato demolite o siano franate con gli anni, sono state incorporate in nuove costruzioni. [...] Mi resta un dubbio. Non sarà un trapianto dalle Cinque Terre, da Monterosso, una "contaminazione" di memorie diverse, diversamente datate?— Può darsi, può darsi—dice, eludendo, Montale' [Toward what *veranda*, made clear by what *ogives*, in which house? [...] It is not that they have been demolished or have collapsed with age, they have been incorporated into new building developments. [...] A doubt remains in my mind. Mightn't they have been transplanted from the Cinque Terre, from Monterosso: a case of 'contamination' from different memories, differently dated?—Perhaps, perhaps—says Montale, evading the question] ('Il ritorno', p. 149). On this point, see Laura Barile, 'Una luce mai vista: Bocca di Magra e *Un posto di vacanza* di Vittorio Sereni', *Lettere italiane* 51.3 (July–Sept. 1999), 384-404, in which she discusses the possibility that the return figured by the poem includes the memory of Montale's first trip to Lunigiana 16 years earlier, in the summer of 1924 (pp. 397–8).

[17] Cf. The line Sereni quotes from 'Accelerato' in the same essay: 'Fu così, rispondi?' [like this, you say?], 'Il ritorno', p. 150.

[18] Quoting the *congedo* of Petrarch's *RVF* CXXVI, and comparing it to Montale's own poem, Sereni writes, 'Speculare a questo sta il rapporto con l'anonimo che vive sul posto e non sul posto quel testo resuscitandolo in sé, anzitutto per via emotiva, nella propria storia' [Mirroring this is the relationship with the anonymous individual who, lives that text there and not there, reviving it in himself, above all emotionally, within his own history] ('Il ritorno', p. 150).

d'une certaine image n'est que le regret d'un certain instant, et les maisons, les routes, les avenues sont fugitives, hélas, comme les années.[19]

[The places we have known do not belong only to the world of space on which we map them for our own convenience. They were only a thin slice, held between the contiguous impressions that composed our life at that time; the memory of a particular image is but regret for a particular moment; and houses, roads, avenues are as fugitive, alas, as the years.]

Sereni, like Proust, perceives the landscape as fugitive: as a 'luogo del rimpianto' [place of regret] shaped by the transience of lost moments. 'L'incerto lembo' is also a metaphor for this: the ambiguity of the subject's perception of the concealed loss or lack that lies behind or beyond the image of something it treasures. The Orphic gesture implicit in this operation, which we have already identified operating as early as Sereni's 'Inverno' [Winter] (in *Frontiera*), is thus fully developed in the dialogue with Montale, marking a poetic point of non-return for the Serenian subject that is synonymous with the stance of the Montalian subject in another poem designating a perceptual doubleness or ambivalence, 'Forse un mattino andando' [Maybe one morning, walking]:

> [...] rivolgendomi, vedrò compirsi il miracolo:
> il nulla alle mie spalle, il vuoto dietro
> di me, con un terrore di ubriaco.
>
> Poi, come s'uno schermo, s'accamperanno di gitto
> alberi case colli per l'inganno consueto.
> Ma sarà troppo tardi; ed io me n'andrò zitto
> tra gli uomini che non si voltano, col mio segreto.
> (ll. 2–8, in *Ossi*, p. 40)
>
> [[...]I'll turn, and see the miracle occur:
> nothing at my back, the void
> behind me, with a drunkard's terror.
> Then, as if on a screen, trees houses hills
> will suddenly collect for the usual illusion.
> But it will be too late: and I'll walk on silent
> among the men who don't look back, with my secret.]

That 'terrore' is the subject's natural response to his perception of the hole beneath things, which poetry both bares and counters. The interval dividing the revelation of nothingness from the return to customary

---

[19] Marcel Proust, *Du côté de chez Swann*, in *À la recherche du temps perdu*, ed. Jean-Yves Tavié (Paris: Gallimard, 1999), p. 542. English translations of Proust are taken from *In Search of Lost Time*, trans. C. K. Scott Moncrieff and Terence Kilmartin, rev. D. J. Enright, 6 vols (London: Chatto & Windus, 1992).

blindness and mis-seeing—marked by the typographic space between lines 4 and 6—is poetry's own domain of liminality. The burden that the poetic subject carries silently is still revealed by the language of his text. While the writing 'I' declares itself as posthumous to a fall that, within the bounds of the poem, is yet to take place, the poem itself is always *between* the two states—between the fall and the expectation of it.

In parallel to 'Forse un mattino', Montale's 'Il ritorno' culminates, as Sereni states, in a feeling of 'spaesamento' [disorientation], a sense of 'inappartenenza che tuttavia apre varchi a un avvento' [non-belonging, which still opens up paths toward a moment of becoming], which is the lasting sign of '[un]'elaborazione fantastica compiuta dall'intervento poetico sulle cose' [[an] imaginary elaboration accomplished by the poetic intervention into things] ('Il ritorno', p. 153). This is the double gaze afforded the poet on the material of his text and its transformation into language, but also the disconcerting revelation of poetry's otherness.

In poetic terms, the double gaze that Montale's poem foregrounds for Sereni thus incorporates both the awareness of having reached a perceptual limit and the possible opening up of a space beyond. When it comes to the vicissitudes of desire and desiring, the crux of the matter lies in the subject's ability or inability to control or manipulate that other realm (to move into, or out of, the unknown) and to negotiate the dual guise of liminality itself, which hangs between the promise of change or passage and the elusiveness of the same. As we have seen in 'Il ritorno', 'L'incerto lembo' can represent either the playground of memory and the imagination, or the point at which they come unstuck. For Sereni, both dimensions are plausible but only the latter surfaces where the subject falls. In his later work, liminal topographies mark the place where this fallenness can be perceived (it is, in fact, the very nucleus of perception) and where a failure to move beyond partiality, or to possess objects fully, increasingly spells the eternalization of desire as lack.

STELLA VARIABILE: A POETICS OF THE GAZE

In 'La non-poetica di Vittorio Sereni' ['The Non-poetics of Vittorio Sereni'], Fulvio Papi finds evidence of 'una patologia dello sguardo' [pathology of the gaze] underlying Sereni's poetic experiences in *SV*.[20] Specifically in relation to the poem 'Fissità', which casts the subject in a

---

[20] Fulvio Papi, 'La non-poetica di vittorio Sereni, in *La parola incantata e altri saggi di filosofia dell'arte* (Milan: Guerini, 1992), pp. 83–185 (p. 155).

search for a totality of vision which seems unavailable,[21] he comments on Sereni's propensity for upturning the natural order of things, with the 'I' finding himself in a world which lacks firm coordinates, having to react to maintain a perspective, however flawed or problematic it may be:

> Fissare significa rovesciare nella sfera della superficie visibile quello che era l'unità dell'oggetto della memoria, cambiare approccio al mondo: trovare nella fascinazione di un realismo senza relazioni la ragione della propria stasi, identificare il presente con una immagine senza vicenda, trovarsi involontariamente nella foresta degli eventi oggettivi che seguono attraverso la loro oggettività e l'alone della loro oggettività, la differenza dal se stesso.[22]
>
> [To fix [one's gaze] means upturning at the level of what is visible that which was the unity of the object of memory, changing one's approach to the world: finding in the fascination of an unconnected realism the reasons for one's stasis, identifying the present with an eventless image, finding oneself involuntarily in the forest of objective events that follow, through their objectivity and the halo of their objectivity, the difference from oneself.]

Sereni certainly seems to have had a fascination or fixation with the notion of the gaze, evident not only in its numerous appearances in his poetry but also in what he says of it in his prose writings, in which his observations on how the gaze functions in the field of desire suggest that its value as a poetic topos incorporates a libidinal dimension too. In the short story *L'opzione* [*The Option*], for example, Sereni's protagonist speaks of having suffered from a 'feticismo dello sguardo fin da [...] ragazzo' [fetish about glances since I was a boy] which binds him to a double gaze in desire that finds completion and fulfilment only when both sides partake equally in the visual game, 'tanto da ritenere impossibile, e più che impossibile ingiusto, che uno sguardo, l'impegno di uno sguardo, non sia ripagato da uno sguardo di ritorno' [such that I consider it impossible, worse, unjust that a glance, the commitment of a glance, should not be repaid with a returning glance].[23]

It is here that we find the roots of that search for reciprocity at the level of vision which comes to characterize large parts of *SU* and *SV* and which explains in part Sereni's attraction to liminal spaces where exchanges of

---

[21] 'Da me a quell'ombra in bilico tra fiume e mare, | solo una striscia di esistenza | in controluce dalla foce. | Quell'uomo. | Rammenda reti, ritinteggia uno scafo. | Cose che io non so fare. Nominarle appena. | Da me a lui nient'altro: una fissità. | Ogni eccedenza andata altrove. O spenta' [From me to that shadow poised between river and sea | only a strip of existence | against the light from the estuary. | That man. | He's mending nets, repainting a boat. | Things I don't know how to do. Can barely name. | From me to him nothing more: a fixity. | All excess gone elsewhere. Or exhausted] (p. 236).

[22] Papi, pp. 155–6.

[23] Sereni, 'L'opzione', p. 164, trans. Robinson–Perryman.

this nature tend to occur—on the boundary of the Montalian wall of 'Il muro' ['The Wall'] (p. 170), or at the border with the 'garrulo schermo di bambini' [chattering barrier of children] of 'L'equivoco' ['The Misapprehension'] (p. 112).[24] The importance of the gaze as an index of desire is something reiterated in much of what Sereni writes in relation to Montale, especially when he talks about the overlay of perceptions and memories which can occur in poetic zones of experience of this kind, where stratified layers of conscious and unconscious thoughts operate to conjure up several angles of vision on the same object simultaneously. Meditating on a glance exchanged with a girl on a bicycle, Sereni reflects in 'Dovuto a Montale':

> Quello sguardo reciproco era il guizzo con cui si saluta una novità?
> Ripensandoci qualche ora più tardi m'immaginai che la ragazza avesse sorriso e che avessi sorriso a mia volta. Ma senza malizia o lusinga di qualunque genere da entrambe le parti, non quello che si potrebbe supporre. Piuttosto uno sguardo d'intesa. A che cosa? A un tutto o a un nonnulla che stava oltre le rispettive persone? Finii con assimilare il piccolo fatto all'episodio della vetrina illuminata.[25]
>
> [Was that look back and forth between us the flash with which one greets something new?
> Thinking about it a few hours later I imagined that the girl had smiled and that I had smiled back. But without malice or flattery of any kind on either side, not what you might suppose. Rather, a look of understanding. About what? About everything or nothing which lay beyond the respective individuals? I ended up connecting the little event with the episode of the lit shop window.]

The episode of the shop window to which Sereni refers is the one which he recounts in the first part of 'Dovuto a Montale', in which a sudden illumination cast into the blackness from a pharmacy window prompts a meditation on the auspiciousness of the chiaroscuro for the revelation of a hidden dimension. The intimation of something beyond or other is summed up by Sereni in the line from Montale's 'Eastbourne', 'Anche tu lo sapevi, luce-in-tenebra' [And you knew it, light-in-shadow], which 'avvertirà certo la sproporzione tra la luce che esso [quel verso] suscita e la vetrina illuminata' [will undoubtedly alert us to the disproportion between

---

[24] The 'wall' of 'Il muro' recalls the 'rovente muro' [blistering [...] wall] and 'muraglia | che ha in cima cocci aguzzi di bottiglia' [wall | with broken bottle shards imbedded in the top] of Montale's 'Meriggiare pallido e assorto' ['Sit the noon out, pale and lost in thought'] which Sereni quotes in 'Dovuto a Montale' (p. 163). The 'garrulo schermo di bambini' recalls the 'schermo' of 'Forse un mattino andando' as well as the 'ragazzi' [boys] of 'I limoni' ['The Lemons'] and 'fanciulli' [children] of '*Caffè a Rapallo*' ['Café at Rapallo'] and 'Flussi' [Flux] (all in *Ossi*).

[25] Sereni, 'Dovuto a Montale', p. 162.

the light generated [by that verse] and the lit shop window].[26] Here words, images, and landscape come together in a kind of miraculous way, in which the memory of the poem is enough to transform his perception of the scene, and vice versa. Something is set in motion by the reflection that exceeds the boundaries of normal perception, and it is that particular zone which Sereni seeks to recreate in his own poetry. The 'sguardo' [gaze] proposes the 'sfida' [challenge] that constitutes the landscape of desire as such:[27]

> Ogni tanto qualcuno mi rimprovera di guardare fisso, in modo quasi indecente, le donne. Sarà. [...] Ma lo sguardo immesso in altre esistenze che si schiudono all'immaginazione non distingue tra uomini e donne. Caso mai sta qui l'indecenza, nell'intrusione che immagina e immaginando prolunga situazioni, inventa atmosfere, suppone vicende, infine ne è parte, o tenta. Accetto che mi si dia del *voyeur*, che non è ancora veggente ma non già più guardone.[28]
>
> [Occasionally I am reproached for staring unwaveringly—almost indecently—at women. It may be so. [...] But the gaze that enters other existences as they offer themselves to the imagination makes no distinction between men and women. Maybe that's where the indecency lies: in the imaginative intrusion which, through the process of imagining, draws out situations, invents atmospheres, conjures events, eventually becomes part of them, or tries to. It's fair to call me a *voyeur*: a little short of being a seer but some distance away from being a peeping Tom.]

Rooting his own conception of identity in desire, and in the elusive fabric of the gaze, Sereni confines his subject to a liminal phase of experience. The 'I' characteristically rests somewhere in between the mythical status of seer, who can penetrate the mystery of things, and the more ambivalent peeping Tom, who looks just for the sake of looking, and Sereni's poetry as a whole comes into being in the distance which opens up between the two poles.

A comparison of *SV* with *Frontiera* makes evident the extent to which, by the late 1970s, the gaze in Sereni's poetry has undergone a redefinition in the development of his poetics, especially regarding the status of the

---

[26] Ibid. 160.
[27] On this notion of 'sguardo' as proposing a 'sfida', see also Sereni's comments in ibid. 159 that '[...] vivevo uno di quei momenti di completezza di piena fusione tra sé e il mondo sensibile, grazie e di fronte ai quali lo spirito desiderante si appaga di se stesso, rifiuta i contorni, sdegna ogni soccorso specie di parole, dissuaso com'è dal cimentarsi nella sfida che lo sguardo gli propone' [[...] I was living one of those moments of completeness, of perfect fusion between the self and the apprehended world, faced with and by virtue of which the desiring spirit seeks no gratification beyond itself, refuses outlines, disdains all help especially from words, dissuaded as it is from rising to the challenge thrown down to it by the gaze].
[28] Sereni, 'Il sabato tedesco', p. 212.

poetic subject. As was discussed in the preceding chapter, the 'I' of *Frontiera*, though not unchallenged, is depicted as having a relatively centralized role in the field of perception, frequently able to subordinate the world to its point of view. By the time we reach *SV*, however, the 'I' has a much more peripheral role in the field of perception. The determinate role has been ceded to objects, which usurp the poet's powers of looking (and speaking) in a complete reversal of the traditional order of perception. Any search for reciprocity at the level of vision has to adapt to the changing coordinates of the desiring field, and liminality is revealed to be just another symptom of a mismatch between the subject's aims in this area and his achievements.

Visualizing the scopic field: Sereni's 'variable star'

The most explicit sign that we have moved beyond simple perception to a more complex semantic field is Sereni's choice of the title *Stella variabile* for his fourth collection as a whole. As he explains in an interview given to *Amica* in 1982, variable stars are not only those which vary in intensity of light but also those which are alternately visible or invisible to us depending on their relationship to other celestial bodies:

> In astronomia, si conoscono le stelle variabili. L'ho scoperto così: una sera accendo la TV e sento parlare di stelle variabili, e mi son detto, ecco è questa la cosa che io cercavo di esprimere. Detto in parole molto povere, queste stelle variano nell'intensità della loro luce, o addirittura scompaiono nel cielo, a seconda della posizione rispetto alla Terra. Su questo tema della variabilità, della contraddizione, delle cose come ti appaiono e del loro rovescio, si è formato tutto il libro.[29]

> [Variable stars are known from astronomy. I heard about it like this: one evening I turn on the TV and I hear someone talking about these variable stars, and I say to myself: there, that's what I was trying to express. Put simply, these stars vary in the intensity of their light or even disappear from the sky, according to their position in relation to the Earth. The whole book took shape around this theme of variability, contradiction, the way things appear to you and their reverse.]

We can draw two main conclusions from what Sereni says of visual experience here, which help to clarify the way in which he brings the 'incerto lembo' of Montalian derivation into his own poetic landscape. First, Sereni stresses the importance of where one is positioned within the visual field. Like those stars that are alternately visible and invisible,

---

[29] Interview with Anna del Bo Boffino, 'Il terzo occhio del poeta: Vittorio Sereni l'erede di Montale', *Amica*, 28 Sept. 1982, p. 156.

present and absent in the sky, depending on where they fall in relation to the earth, there is the sense that for every object that comes to the fore in the field of vision, another recedes or falls into shadow. Sereni is thus putting the emphasis on what is excluded by any one visual relation, as well as what is included between the 'I' and it.

Secondly, destined as we are to see from only one point at a time, and from a single perspective, something is always destined to elude us. The view of things merely as they 'appear' to us ('come ci appaiono') is in some sense insufficient since it does not account for the other dimension beyond—'il rovescio delle cose', how things are in themselves. In opening up the boundaries of visual experience, it is precisely this seeing from the other side which Sereni seeks to bring into play in *SV*. Yet the contradiction which elicits the enquiry cannot be easily put aside and, if anything, is intensified by every attempt the subject makes to see himself from the outside, putting himself under the gaze of objects.

At this point it is pertinent to consider the value of Lacan's theory of desire and the scopic drive for our understanding of what is at stake in the visual dimension of Sereni's poetry. In Book XI of his *Séminaire*, entitled *Les quatre concepts fondamentaux de la psychanalyse* [*The Four Fundamentals of Psychoanalysis*] (1964), Lacan dedicates over forty pages to his exposition of the scopic drive, which he posits as an example of the contradiction and tension at the heart of desire that sees perceptual experience playing a central role in the constitution of subjectivity, especially vis-à-vis the object world.

Lacan's theory rests on the belief that there is a disjunction at the level of the subject's perceptions, which divides him between two modes of looking that are represented by an opposition between the 'eye' and the 'gaze', 'l'œil et le regard'.[30] Showing how both are in play in vision even when the subject is not aware of it, Lacan seeks to reaffirm the split nature of the subject and its ex-centricity to itself, which lie at the heart of his conception of subjectivity. Moreover, in labelling this activity a 'drive' he means it less in the purely libidinal sense it had for Freud, and more in what it teaches us of the subject's reality as a subject of desire—prey to a set of unconscious motivations which define it in a hugely important way even in this part of its life in which it has the illusion of being very much in control.

---

[30] 'La schize de l'œil et le regard' ['The Split between the Eye and the Gaze'] is section VI of the second topic of the *Séminaire*, entitled 'Du regard comme objet petit *a*' ['Of the Gaze as *Objet petit a*']. My theoretical exposition groups ideas taken from sections VI and VII ('L'anamorphose' ['Anamorphosis']). Jacques Lacan, *Séminaire XI: les quatre concepts de la psychanalyse* (Paris: Éditions du Seuil, 1973), pp. 79–91 and 92–104 respectively. English translations are from *The Four Fundamental Concepts of Psychoanalysis*, ed. Jacques-Alain Miller, trans. Alan Sheridan (Harmondsworth: Penguin, 1979).

108   'L'incerto lembo'

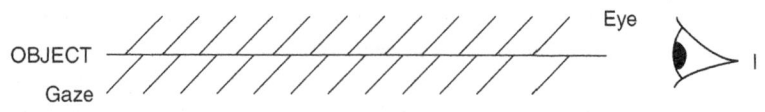

Fig. 3.1. The inverse operations of eye and gaze.

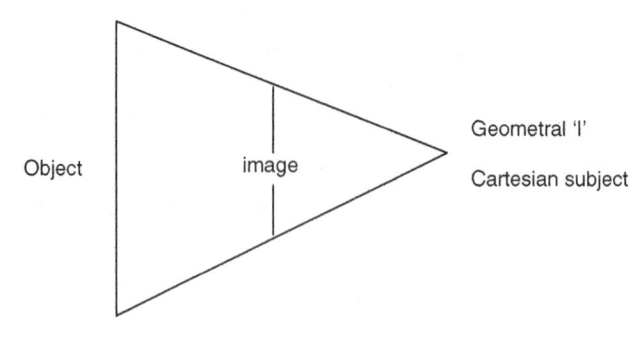

Fig. 3.2. The triangle of geometral vision, adapted with permission of the publisher from Jacques Lacan, *Le Séminaire, Livre XI: Les quatre concepts fondamentaux de la psychanalyse*, ed. by Jacques Alain-Miller © Editions du Seuil, 1973.

To try and explain what Lacan means when he talks about a dialectic between eye and gaze, and to relate it back to Sereni's own conception of vision, it is helpful to begin from Fig. 3.1, which demonstrates the 'double view' upon the object implied by the inverse operations of eye and gaze.

In the top half of the figure we find something akin to Sereni's conception of 'le cose come ti appaiono': the workings of the conscious mind which are represented by the eye. Lacan aligns this mode of vision with the ego, since he wishes to emphasize how it comes into being to bolster the image the subject has of itself, to draw objects to it and make them like it, or like it wants them to be, i.e. fixed, stable, and locatable. This ultimately makes the eye into an organ of what Lacan calls the Imaginary order of experience which finds its roots in the mirror stage and in a kind of primary narcissism which, Lacan says, is founded on a fundamental moment of 'méconnaissance' [mis-seeing] since it situates the agency of that looking in a fictional direction, within the realm of illusion.[31] The eye is involved in instigating a dimension of vision which Lacan terms 'geometral', since it functions to install a naturalness of vision and an unproblematic relationship between the subject and its object(s) of perception. It is a neat method, but not, as Fig. 3.2 shows, an entirely

---

[31] Cf. Lacan, 'Le stade du miroir' ['The Mirror Stage'], p. 98.

truthful one, which functions by establishing a triangular arrangement between the image captured by the eye, the object understood as its origin (and thus as located somewhere behind it), and the subject (what Lacan terms the 'Geometral "I"', consequently understood as the Cartesian subject, since it is apparently in control of the situation).

As a result, the subject perceives the image interposed between the 'I' and the object as 'real', as a sign that the object is out there for the taking, and that it is essentially offering itself up to the subject for its possession. Lacan explains:

> Bien plus, les phénoménologies ont pu articuler avec précision, et de la façon la plus confondante, qu'il est tout à fait clair que je vois *au-dehors*, que la perception n'est pas en moi, qu'elle est sur les objets qu'elle appréhende. Et pourtant, je saisis le monde dans une perception qui semble relever de l'immanence du *je me vois me voir*. Le privilège du sujet paraît s'établir ici de cette relation réflexive bipolaire, qui fait que, dès lors que je perçois, mes représentations m'appartiennent.[32]

> [Furthermore, the phenomenologists have succeeded in articulating with precision, and in the most disconcerting way, that it is quite clear that I see *outside*, that perception is not in me, that it is on the objects that it apprehends. And yet I apprehend the world in a perception that seems to concern the immanence of the *I see myself seeing myself*. The privilege of the subject seems to be established here from that bipolar reflexive relation by which, as soon as I perceive, my representations belong to me.]

However, as Lacan clarifies, this can only be half the story, since it does not account for the subject's reality in the Symbolic order of experience—the realm of lack and interdiction—where the true centre of the subject's being is stationed. This is the place in which it is subordinated to the pull of desire and is prey to a whole set of unconscious impulses manifest in visual terms in the action of the gaze. This is the truest form of vision available to the subject, but also that which threatens to upturn everything the subject knows, or thinks he knows, about himself and about the world existing 'out there':

> Schématisons tout de suite ce que nous voulons dire. Dès que ce regard, le sujet essaie de s'y accommoder, il devient cet objet punctiforme, ce point d'être évanouissant, avec lequel le sujet confond sa propre défaillance. Aussi, de tous les objets dans lesquels le sujet peut reconnaître la dépendance où il est dans le registre du désir, le regard se spécifie comme insaisissable. C'est pour cela qu'il est, plus que tout autre objet, méconnu, et c'est peut-être pour cette raison aussi que le sujet trouve si heureusement à symboliser son propre

---

[32] Ibid. 94 (italics in the original).

trait évanouissant et punctiforme dans l'illusion de la conscience de *se voir se voir*, où s'élide le regard.[33]

[Let us schematize at once what we mean. From the moment that this gaze appears, the subject tries to adapt himself to it, he becomes that punctiform object, that point of vanishing being with which the subject confuses his own failure. Furthermore, of all the objects in which the subject may recognize his dependence in the register of desire, the gaze is specified as unapprehensible. That is why it is, more than any other object, misunderstood (*méconnu*), and it is perhaps for this reason, too, that the subject manages, fortunately, to symbolize his own vanishing and punctiform bar (*trait*) in the illusion of the consciousness of *seeing oneself see oneself*, in which the gaze is elided.]

This is where the bottom half of Fig. 3.1 comes into play, which represents something like the underside of the perceptual field Sereni calls 'il rovescio delle cose', or the beyond and between of Montale's 'l'incerto lembo' in 'Il ritorno'. Here the gaze acts in the most dramatic of ways to upturn the security of the geometral perspective and effectively to dispossess the eye at the Symbolic level of the object it thinks it is possessing at the Imaginary level. Whereas the eye makes us think that we have found what we are looking for, the gaze testifies to the fact that this is not the case. It comes into being precisely as a function of lack, since the truly desired object—the (m)Other—is inevitably barred to us in the Symbolic, literally beyond where we can ever seek to reach, represent, or look at her.

For Lacan, there is no pure looking, since everything is mediated and overwritten by the sign which, as Sereni states in *Un posto* VI, 20–1, 'non è | la cosa ma la imita soltanto' [is not | the thing but imitates it only] (p. 232). The disjunctive patterning of Fig. 3.1 is thus also a metaphor for the slippage occurring in linguistic terms between signifier and signified, which stops short our desire for possession and unity at that level too. It is this which finally makes geometral vision into a fundamental act of mis-seeing, since it reveals the triangle of Fig. 3.2 to be a purely psychological construct and not, as the 'I' likes to think, something discovered innately 'out there'.

Once the subject is faced with the reality of the scopic drive, he has to accept that the image is not in fact that which opens up the path towards the object but rather what turns him away from it, to prevent him seeing what is really there, beyond appearances. In a further twist, what the image conceals is not even the object itself but more negatively still the fact that the object is not there in the first place: it conceals the hole left by the object being pushed to the outside. This is what the gaze bares in its ability

---

[33] *Les quatres concepts*, p. 97 (italics in the original).

to penetrate beyond the surface of appearances and if it can be said to have its home anywhere this can only be in the space between two objects, or between the illusion of the object's presence and its actual absence:

> N'est-il pas clair que le regard n'intervient ici que pour autant que ce n'est pas le sujet néantisant, corrélatif du monde de l'objectivité, qui s'y sent surpris, mais le sujet se soutenant dans une fonction du désir?
> N'est-ce pas justement parce que le désir s'instaure ici dans le domaine de la voyure, que nous pouvons l'escamoter?[34]
>
> [Is it not clear that the gaze intervenes here only in as much as it is not the annihilating subject, correlative of the world of objectivity, who feels himself surprised, but the subject sustaining himself in a function of desire?
> Is it not precisely because desire is established here in the domain of seeing that we can make it vanish?]

Lacan thus attests to the doubleness of vision as an index of desire, and to the identity of the gaze as the place in which the truth of desire is bared beyond illusion. If vision is normally the field of experience in which the subject seeks to deny the reality of desire as lack, making the hole in the world disappear and the illusion of possession possible, the gaze uncovers what Malcolm Bowie terms the ordinarily 'unperceivable "fallenness" of the subject': the place in which it loses not only its object but also any consistency of self.[35]

Sereni's notion of the contradiction at the heart of vision should thus be understood precisely in this mismatch between what the eye seeks from the world and what is actually given it in return (from the side of objects). It too deals with the disparity between what geometral vision offers the subject in terms of self-certainty and autonomy and what the gaze in turn takes away. Sereni's landscapes embody the very tensions implicit in this relationship, and can thus be considered as poetic versions of the scopic experience; in other words, landscapes of desire.

'Arsenio' and 'Niccolò': towards a topography of liminality

Several of the liminal topographies through which the poetic 'I' of *SV* articulates itself rest upon this functioning of the gaze, which operates to foreground the appearance/disappearance, presence/absence dialectic also at the basis of many of Montale's poetic landscapes, especially in *Ossi*. 'Niccolò', a companion poem to *Un posto*, which is included alongside it in part III of *SV*, shows how Sereni configures tensions in space and sight

---

[34] Ibid. 98.
[35] Malcolm Bowie, *Lacan* (London: Fontana, 1991), p. 172.

to reflect tensions at the basis of the desiring relationship, here between the poet and his dead friend, Niccolò Gallo, to whom the poem is addressed. In turn, the landscape of Sereni's poem, which takes the Virgilian-like 'ripae ulterioris' as its scene of action, can be seen to rework similar liminal topographies in Montale's 'Arsenio', 'Marezzo' ['Moiré'], and 'Fine dell'infanzia' ['End of Childhood'], to turn it into a multiple Montalian intertext:[36]

'Niccolò'

Quattro settembre, muore
oggi un mio caro e con lui cortesia
una volta di più e questa *forse* per sempre.
Ero con altri un'ultima volta in mare
stupefatto che su tanti spettri chiari *non posasse*   5
a pieno cielo *una nuvola immensa*,
definitiva, *ma solo* un vago di vapori
si ponesse tra noi, pulviscolo
lasciato indietro dall'estate
(dovunque, si sentiva, in terra e in mare *era là*   10
affaticato a raggiungerci, a rompere
lo sbiancante diaframma).
Non servirà cercarti sulle spiagge ulteriori
lungo tutta la costiera spingendoci a quella
detta dei Morti per sapere *che non verrai*.   15
                          Adesso
che di te si svuota il mondo e il *tu*
falsovero dei poeti si ricolma di te
adesso so chi mancava nell'alone amaranto
che cosa e chi disertava le acque   20
di un dieci giorni fa
già in sospetto di settembre. Sospesa ogni ricerca,
i nomi si ritirano dietro le cose
e *dicono no dicono no* gli oleandri
mossi dal venticello.   25
E poi rieccoci
alla sfera del celeste, ma non è
la solita endiadi di *cielo e mare*?
Resta dunque con me, qui ti piace,
e ascoltami, come sai.   30
            (*SV*, pp. 234–5)

---

[36] Virgil, *Aeneid* VI, 314, in *Eclogues, Georgics, Aeneid I–VI*, trans. H. Rushton Fairclough (Cambridge, Mass.: Harvard University Press, 1974), p. 528.

'L'incerto lembo'

[Fourth of September, today
one dear to me dies and with him courtesy
one more time and this *perhaps* forever.
I was with others a last time in the sea
astonished that over so many clear ghostings 5
a vast, definitive cloud wouldn't settle
over all the sky, *but just* a blur of vapor
put itself between us, powder
left behind from the summer
(*there he was*, we felt, everywhere on earth [and sea 10
straining to reach us, to break
the whitening diaphragm).
No use searching for you on further beaches
all along the coast pressing on the one
called the Dead's to know *you won't come*. 15
                      So now
the world empties of you and the poets'
false-true *you* replenishes with you
now I know who was missing in the amaranth halo
what and who deserted the waters 20
of some ten days ago
already with hints of September. All search abandoned,
the names withdraw behind things,
and *say no, they say no*, the oleanders
stirred by the breeze. 25
                   And then we're back
to the sphere of the heavens, but isn't it
the usual hendiadys of *sky and sea*?
So stay with me, you like it here,
and heed me, you know how.] 30

'Arsenio'
[...]
È il segno di un'altra orbita: tu seguilo.
Discendi all'*orizzonte* che sovrasta
una tromba di piombo, alta sui gorghi,
più d'essi vagabonda: *salso nembo* 15
vorticante, soffiato dal ribelle
elemento alle *nubi*; fa che il passo
su la ghiaia ti schricchioli e t'inciampi
il viluppo dell'alghe: quell'istante
è *forse*, molto atteso, che ti scampi 20
dal finire il tuo viaggio, anello d'una
catena, immoto andare, oh troppo noto

                    delirio, Arsenio, d'immobilità...
                [...]
                Discendi in mezzo al buio che precipita
                e muta il mezzogiorno in una notte   35
                di globi accesi, dondolanti a riva, —
                e fuori, *dove un'ombra sola tiene
                mare e cielo*, dai gozzi sparsi palpita
                l'acetilene—
                            finché goccia trepido
                il cielo, fuma il suolo che s'abbevera,   40
                tutto d'accanto ti sciaborda, sbattono
                le tende molli, *un frùscio immenso* rade
                la terra, giù s'afflosciano stridendo
                le lanterne di carta sulle strade.
                [...]
                                    (*Ossi*, pp. 81–2)
                [*Sign of another orbit*: follow it.
                Descend to the *horizon*, overhung
                by a lead stormcloud high above the riptide
                and more erratic: *a salty,*   15
                roiling maelstrom, blown
                from the rebellious element up to *the clouds*;
                let your step rasp on the gravel
                and the tangled seaweed trip you:
                this *may be* the long-awaited moment when you [escape   20
                from finishing your journey, link in a chain,
                stalled motion, oh too familiar
                frenzy, Arsenio, of immobility...
                [...]
                Go down into the falling dark
                that makes the noon into a night   35
                of lit globes, swaying by the shore—
                and out there, where a *single shadow*
                covers sea and sky, acetilene
                torches throb on the scattered dories—
                                            till the apprehensive sky
                starts spattering, the earth smokes as it drinks,   40
                everything around you overflows,
                drenched awnings flap, *an enormous rustling*
                grazes the earth, the shrieking paper lanterns
                so soggy in the streets.
                [...]]

Like Montale's 'Marezzo', Sereni's poem articulates a double perspective that opens up as one world (life, in decline) ends, and another (death, in the ascendant) begins, and where the depths of existence are seen as though 'sformato da una lente' [deformed by a lens] ('Marezzo', l. 16, p. 88, my translation). However, more like 'Arsenio', the ghostly dialogue between Sereni and Niccolò that takes place at the shoreline is cast as an imploration to the Other, whose uncertain status between living and dead, being and seeming (note the common use of 'forse', l. 3, 'Niccolò'; l. 20, 'Arsenio') vitiates the force of the encounter, or rather transforms it into a play of desire in which the 'I' projects its own lack onto its interlocutor in the hope that together they can surpass it. However, 'the visionary moment doesn't hold', as movement collapses in all three poems into immobility and the poetic voice surrenders to the pull of the undertow so that desire ultimately rests in a kind of suspension.[37]

The textual echo that we find of lines 22–5 of 'Niccolò' in Sereni's 'Dovuto a Montale' suggest that the dialogue with Montale is situated precisely at that point of liminality in the landscape (both real and poetic) at which something would happen, or cease to happen, or take effect:

> Per un periodo successivo anche più lungo si fecero sempre più rari i segnali che mi giungevano dal luogo, magari in forma di aneddoti legati alla singolarità ora esilarante ora grottesca di episodi offerti dalla cronaca. *Perduto ogni incanto, dissoluto ogni alone, ogni ricordo rimosso.* Un capitolo chiuso?[38]
>
> [For an even longer period afterwards, the signals that reached me from that place became rarer and rarer, sometimes in the form of anecdotes associated with the peculiarity—at times exhilarating, at other times grotesque—of events in the news. *All enchantment lost, every halo dissolved, every memory repressed.* A closed chapter?]

Even though, or perhaps because, the landscape empties out or something is lost from it, Sereni cannot help but return to it. Typically, the zones of liminality in 'Niccolò' bridge the perceptual and linguistic domains simultaneously, situated between the double loci of vision and memory. 'Lo sbiancante diaframma' (l. 12) is another version of 'l'incerto lembo', which carries the intimation of something more but simultaneously withdraws the certainty of reaching it. The presence of the poet's dead friend is felt in the beyond but he is prevented from crossing into the world of the living, so leaving the 'I' bereft for a second time. The very substance (mist) which originally gave shape to his phantasm ultimately fails to surrender up its object, and the 'diaphragm' lives up to its name, acting both as a point of

---

[37] Jonathan Galassi, commentary to 'Marezzo', in Montale, *Collected Poems*, p. 474. The ending of Sereni's 'Niccolò' reiterates the double statement of immobility in 'Marezzo', l. 27, 'ora resta così [. . .]' [stay this way now [. . .]] and ll. 61–2, 'Ah qui restiamo, non siamo diversi. | Immobili così' [Ah, let's stay here, we're unchanged. | Motionless this way].

[38] Sereni, 'Dovuto a Montale', p. 165.

transference ('dià', from the Greek meaning 'across') and as a barrier (from 'phragmýnai', meaning 'to obstruct'). As the poet's gaze is drawn to the site of a disappearing act, he fixates on an area of the landscape which seems to counter and to reaffirm a loss at the same time, recalling the 'vuoto risonante di lamenti | soffocati' [an emptiness | that echoes muffled cries] of 'Arsenio' (ll. 49–50) which draws its poetic force and identity from the presence of an absence, and the fullness of its requiem.

Knowing that Niccolò will never again come to this place gives retrospective shape and value to the memorial phantasm associated with his final appearance in the scene ten days earlier (ll. 16–21). In turn, this gives rise to the poetic phantasm which will remain long after his definitive disappearance from the world, encapsulated in 'quel fatale, contagiante *tu*' [that fatal, infectious *you*] also of Montalian derivation (ll. 17–18).[39] Yet, in 'Niccolò', Sereni's repeated emphasis on lack (in the verbs *svuotare, mancare, disertare* [to empty, to lack, to desert]) tends to foreground the passage from existence to nonexistence, rather than securing the lost object's poetic afterlife, and by line 22 every active search has ceased. This leads to the foreclosure of perspective heralded by the withdrawal of words behind things, and the rebuke that the poet suffers at the hand of the oleanders, which reverses the sublimating power of the 'parola' [word] with which 'Arsenio' closes, which seems to endure despite its threatened dissolution amid 'la cenere degli astri' [the ashes of the stars] (l. 59). Instead, Sereni's declaration that 'I nomi si ritirano dietro le cose' literally strips things of language, and words of their predicative power, as he inverts the phrase 'si vestivano di nomi | le cose' [things were dressed in names] from Montale's 'Fine dell'infanzia'. Where Montale, in 'Fine', rues the loss of a primordial state which, while unavailable now, still constitutes an enduring myth of presence, Sereni emphasizes instead the present (and future) emptiness of language, and the retreat of the sign behind objects, which remain impenetrable in their wordless reality. If Montale's 'Fine' is ultimately a poem about origins, celebrating the Edenic time when 'eravamo nell'età illusa' [it was the time of illusion, l. 79], Sereni's own gesture of commemoration—here of the dead 'Niccolò'—marks instead the definitive passing ('Ero con altri *un'ultima volta*', l. 4) of the privileged moment of priority, towards the uncertainty of the present on which the poem ends, characteristically for Sereni, with a question and a supplication, as yet untested and unanswered.

For a moment in 'Niccolò', transcendence seems possible, if not actually achieved, as the deictic 'eccoci' (l. 27) declares. It embodies the poetic

---

[39] Sereni, 'Dovuto a Montale', 162.

and linguistic gesture that transports the poetic 'I' and its object to the 'sfera del celeste', but also brings the realization that the 'heavenly sphere' may be nothing more than a terrestrial *trompe l'œil*: merely the reflection of the sky on the water, another version of a horizon that blocks out the wider view. Once again Sereni incorporates a double gaze into his poem that the final index of liminality—'la solita endiadi di cielo e mare' (l. 28)—represents, which replays the uncertainty of a poetic space that can bring something of the other world into its bounds but cannot necessarily guarantee access to it.

The line that joins sea and sky is also what separates them. What is familiar ('solita') is also nothing new, located in a *time before* more than a *time after*. As a 'hendiadys' (a figure of speech representing 'one through two'), the last horizon of the poem, which can never be got beyond, collapses into itself, and memory (fixed but unchanging) provides the final resting place for a poetic subject who, if he cannot rise to meet the other in the realm beyond, would prefer to keep the dead other with him: '*Resta dunque con me, qui ti piace,* | *e ascoltami come sai*' (ll. 29–30).

The mythical space of Bocca di Magra, to which Sereni returns in this poem and several others in *SV*, thus gains value from its being a site of loss, and of (a failed) mourning, as much as of (poetic) restitution.[40] As soon as the poet's gaze penetrates beyond the surface of appearances, he is faced with the threat of the unknown which quickly has him running for cover until, in *Un posto*, we find him holed up amongst the 'ripe', recoiling from the water's edge and unable to take flight:

Mai così—*si disse rintanandosi*
tra le ripe lo scriba—mai stato
così tautologico il lavoro, ma neppure mai
ostico tanto tra tante meraviglie.
Guardò lo scafo allontanarsi tra due ali di fresco,
sfucinare nell'alto—e già era fuori di vista, nel turchino
rapsodico dattilico fantasticante
perpetuandosi nell'indistinto di altre estati.
[...]
(*Un posto* IV, 1–8, p. 228)

[Never quite so—*the scribe taking shelter*
between the banks told himself—never been
quite so tautological, the work, nor ever *so*

---

[40] The poems from *SV* set in Bocca di Magra include, besides 'Niccolò' and *Un posto*, 'Fissità', 'La malattia dell'olmo' ['The Disease of the Elm'], 'In salita' ['Uphill'], 'Il poggio' ['The Knoll'] and 'Autostrada della Cisa'; In *SU*: 'Gli squali' ['The Sharks'], 'Di passaggio' ['Passing'], 'Gli amici' ['The Friends'], and 'La spiaggia' ['The Beach'].

troublesome among so many splendours.
Between two wings of freshness he watched the launch diminish,
forging off into high seas—and already out of sight in the turquoise,
rhapsodic dactylic daydreaming
prolonging itself in the haze of other summers.]

Unable to fully embrace the world of his poem, or to relinquish it, the writing subject gazes upon poetry in all its elusive glory, powerless to move, and thus witness to his own insufficiencies. The liminal status of the subject in relation to his text and the liminality of his perceptual position mirror one another almost to the letter. Speech, as unbreachable monologue, turns inwards just as the eye records the vanishing of its object ('lo scafo': the only available instrument of transcendence, more physical than spiritual) and the endless dissipation of the image beyond all circumscribable space.

The double nature of space in *Un posto di vacanza*

Sereni thus recognizes that there are 'tante meraviglie' to be had, if only he could see them. Instead, he perceives only the difficulty of the activity and the inevitability of the paralysis which forces him to watch as things disappear from view. Objects can continue to exist without the poet being able to look at them ('*perpetuandosi* nell'indistinto di altre estati'), but once they pass beyond, they cease to have any meaning for him. *Un posto* as a whole charts the double dispossession that such moments imply, and engenders as its prime poetic ground the anamorphic perspective of a subject forced to confront the absence at the heart of things and of the self.

A poem in seven parts, *Un posto* was first published in *L'Almanacco dello specchio* 1 (1971), and was then reprinted in libretto form by Scheiwiller (Milan: All'Insegna del Pesce d'Oro, 1973), accompanied by a long note by the author. In the preface to the 1973 edition of the poem, Sereni remarks that it should be viewed as 'un episodio a sé stante' [a self-contained episode] within the context of his poetic production, and also emphasizes its metapoetic dimension, 'forse perché si porta dietro e addirittura incorpora nel suo sviluppo sfiducie e improvvise speranze, dubbi e aperture rispetto al suo stesso farsi?' [perhaps because it brings with it, and even incorporates within its own development, moments of mistrust and sudden hopes, doubts and openings towards its own creation and becoming?].[41]

---

[41] These comments are both cited in the 'Note' section of *Un posto di vacanza e altre poesie*, p. 44.

The protracted genesis of the poem over a period of roughly twenty years (c.1951–71) is evident in the texture of its language, and particularly in the interweaving of temporal and spatial coordinates which bring the past right into the frame of the present and give it a composite form. Laura Barile remarks on the ongoing dialogue between the circumstances of the poet's chronological existence in the period and the sustained gaze on the place in the poem's title, which is actually made up of a series of returns, a set of multiple realities laid one on top of the other, 'Un testo, questo è il progetto, che riproduca il lungo approfondimento della cosa e delle sue metamorfosi nella costanza dello sguardo, la *durée* con tutte le sue scorie, incrostazioni, delusioni, mutamenti di persone e cose, passi falsi' [The project is this: a text that reproduces the long elaboration of the thing and its metamorphoses under the constancy of the gaze, the *durée* with all its debris, deposits, transformations of people and things, false steps].[42]

The poem thus draws together, in a wide arc, a whole set of fragmentary experiences which are shaped by the poet's consciousness from the point of view of the present frame: his visit out of season, on a winter's day in 1971, which transforms the familiar encounter into something new and unexpected. It is this first shift in perspective that provides the intimation of something other, which lies just beyond the natural order of things and is reinforced through a series of perceptual encounters which mark out the boundaries between one dimension and the next. The multidimensionality of space is recreated topographically, too, in the liminal geography of Bocca di Magra which Sereni foregrounds in the poem's opening lines:

> Un giorno a più livelli, d'alta marea
> —o nella sola sfera del celeste.
> Un giorno concavo che *è* prima di esistere
> sul rovescio dell'estate la chiave dell'estate.
> Di sole spoglie estive ma trionfali.
> Così scompaiono giorno e chiave
> nel fiotto come di fosforo
> della cosa che sprofonda in mare. [...]
>   (*Un posto* I, 1–8, p. 223; italics in the original)
>
> [A day at various levels, of high tide
> —or in the sphere of the blue.
> A concave day that *is* before existing
> on the reverse side of summer, summer's key.
> Of spoils only, summer's but triumphal.
> This way daylight and key disappear

---

[42] Laura Barile, 'Alcuni materiali per "Un posto di vacanza"', in *Un posto di vacanza e altre poesie*, pp. 95–109 (p. 98).

> in the flare like phosphorus
> of the thing going down in the sea.]

Sereni's setting of a surface-level representation against profundity—the depths concealed beneath the sea, the sinking object which leaves its phosphorescent trace on the crest of the waves—establishes the parameters of the visual field and already hints at the fact that it is the underside of perception which interests him most: the space of objects. In this passage he transforms the very order of the seasons by way of a parabola which joins the height of winter with the base of summer, 'Sul rovescio dell'estate. | Nei giorni di sole di un dicembre' [On the reverse of summer. | In one December's sunlit days] (*Un posto* VII, 25–6). In writing the poem, Sereni seeks to draw the disparate temporal and spatial dimensions into line—to contain them in a single all-encompassing perspective—, which, to use a visual metaphor, might represent something like the canvas of a cubist painting, which posits in a total picture a series of different angles on the same object.

Composed of just over 300 lines of verse, *Un posto* contains more than twenty overt references to seeing and looking. Sereni is particularly fond of compound verb forms that work to reaffirm the oppositional structures at play in the field of vision. These include for example: '*pre*vedere' [to *fore*see], '*tra*guardare' [to aim; lit. look *across/through*], and '*sog*guardare' [to peer/peek; lit. to look *with diminished force*], often employed by the poet to embody his own confused perceptions in distinction to the clarity afforded to objects. These compound verbs also suggest that the poet must work hard to maintain a steady line of vision, and they often reflect his being passivized—almost literally cornered—by the gaze of objects which tend to solicit a look which the poet must counter, or to which he must react:

> [...] Di là dagli oleandri,
> mio riparo dalla vista del mare,
> là è la provocazione e la sfida—
> un natante col suo eloquio
> congetturante:
> confabula dietro uno scoglio sale di giri vortica via
> triturando lo spazio in un celeste d'altura
> con suoni di officina monologa dialoga a distanza—
> (*Un posto* II, 46-53, p. 226)
> [Beyond oleanders,
> my shelter from the vision of the sea,
> there's the provocation and the challenge—
> a craft with its speculative
> manner of speaking:

confabulates behind a rock, revs up, spins away
dicing space in a deep-sea blue
with workshop sounds, soliloquizes, converses from a distance—]

This passage is strongly reminiscent of the opening of Montale's 'Il ritorno' and the perception of an 'incerto lembo' that elicits the call of desire. The 'oleandri', which as we have seen resurface in 'Niccolò', also constitute the particular provocation and challenge for the subject here, concealing as well as revealing the vision of the craft with its alluring speech/language ('eloquio'), which draws the subject into dialogue with a space that only becomes more elusive and fragmented. The poetic 'I''s location 'tra fiume e mare' [betwixt river and sea], signalled at the beginning of Part I, quickly transforms into the locus not only of a confrontation but also of a battle, as the subject struggles to assert his place in a mobile and heterogeneous object-field, wrestling not only with himself but also with the matter of his creation, the repeated refrain of the poem being 'Non scriverò questa storia' [I'll not write this story].[43] This renders Sereni's version of the liminal both more fraught and less conceptually defined than Montale's. In the absence of a *tu* figure to whom to entrust the project of transcendence denied the 'I', the subject itself withdraws and the gap separating desire from its goal becomes greater still.

As the passage above shows, the subject's status is at best passive and at worst forcibly disengaged until, in part V of the poem, he is nothing but 'il superstite voyeur' [the surviving voyeur] (V, 22), paradoxically in excess of, as well as inadequate to, the demands of the scopic duel through which the game of desire is played. All the poem's references to vision punctuate the different stages of the poet's interaction with the field of objects, and suggest that looking, for the poet at least, is never a straightforward activity but rather one that is fraught with danger and potential misdirection.

The poetic subject is essentially misplaced from the start, displaced from the superior perspective he would seek to occupy by those objects who inhabit the 'other bank' ('l'altra riva') towards which his own desiring gaze is directed and constantly returned to the 'here' ('qui'), understood as partial and incomplete. The disjunctive bipolarity which defines the scopic field is thus recreated on several levels at once in Sereni's poem, from the physical distance that separates his desire from its goal to the incommensurability between one order of experience and the other. The other bank, as the locus of an all-seeing eye, may indeed hold the key to

---

[43] This phrase from *Un posto* appears for the first time in I, 27 (p. 224) and is repeated in II, 11, 'Non scriverò questa storia—mi ripeto | se mai una storia c'era da raccontare' (p. 225).

achieving a totality of vision, but it is one from which the poet is excluded, and its establishment as a kind of mythical space of pre-thetic unity and wholeness is the result, precisely, of its being unavailable and thus retrospectively valued as an infinite object of desire and desire's impossible destination:

> Chissà che *di lì traguardando* non si allacci nome a cosa
> ... (la poesia sul posto di vacanza).
> Invece torna a tentarmi in tanti anni quella voce
> (era un disco) *di là, dall'altra riva*. Nelle sere di polvere e sete
> quasi la si toccava, gola offerta alla ferita d'amore
> sulle acque. *Non scriverò questa storia.*
> [...]
>
> (*Un posto* I, 22–7, p. 224)
>
> [Who knows *if on arrival over there* name's not conjoined to thing
> ... (the poem on the holiday place).
> Instead the voice returns to tempt me many years
> (a record, it was) *from over there, the far shore*. Dusty, thirsty evenings
> you almost touched it, throat offered to the wound of love
> upon the waters. *I'll not write this story.*]

This failure is compounded at the level of intersubjective experience, since the objects responsible for instigating the (poetic) lure do not offer a happy end to desire. The 'sguardo di rimando' [return glance] which the poet hopes to solicit from them, by projecting his eye over to the other side, is not borne out. Objects—personified through the poem in Sereni's extensive use of prosopopoeia—flatly refuse to be captured by the subject in this way, and proceed to capture him instead. In turn, since, in trying to establish a meaningful relationship with objects on the visual plane, the poet is simultaneously seeking to draw them into a dialogue, the absence of reciprocity at the level of vision translates into a corresponding series of moments of failed communication. This renders Sereni's version of liminality inherently metapoetic.

This phenomenon is most clearly enacted in two episodes in Part II of *Un posto* in which there is a marked interweaving of the voice and the gaze (the defining characteristic of prosopopoeia in the poem). The first recounts the poet's encounter with the 'rive' [banks], an intimately Montalian location here brought to life as the antagonistic entity resisting the 'I''s attempts at engagement:

> [...]
> Non scriverò questa storia—mi ripeto, se mai
> una storia c'era da raccontare.
>
> *Sentire*

cosa ne dicono le rive
(*la sfilata delle rive*
   le rive
    come proposte fraterne:
ma mi avevano previsto sono mute non inventano niente per me) 15
Pare non ci sia altro: il mio mutismo è il loro.
[...]
       (*Un posto* II, 11–16, p. 225)
[I'll not write this story, I repeat myself, if
there ever was a story to be telling.
 Listen
to what the banks have to say
(*the banks' parade*
   the banks
    like fraternal propositions:
but they were expecting me, are mute, invent nothing for me). 15
It seems there's nothing else: my muteness is theirs.]

 In perceptual terms and beyond, what the 'rive' contest is precisely that 'belong-to-me' aspect of representation that Lacan posits at the heart of the geometral dimension. Although the 'I' initially reads the 'sfilata delle rive' as an invitation to converse, and as evidence of a potential visual and linguistic engagement, he finally has to accept that the show is not for him and that those fraternal propositions he sees existing will not actually be borne out. This instance of prosopopoeia is thus only ever hypothetical, and whilst there is the potential for the 'rive' to speak, the dialogue remains unrealized or is merely imagined by the writing subject to be about to take place, '*Sentire* | cosa ne dicono le rive...'.
 The crucial moment in desiring terms occurs at the turn in line 15, which indicates how the 'rive' have literally silenced themselves as they see the poet coming, which overturns the visual hierarchy established up to that point. Typically, Sereni suffers this silence of objects both as a kind of rejection and as a result of a lack in himself, so that one failure to communicate mirrors the other, 'Pare non ci sia altro: il *mio* mutismo è il *loro*'. What the poet is finally left with as a result of this experience is thus not even the 'rive' themselves, but only the awareness of his own loneliness. Visual activity has been entirely overrun by an all-encompassing 'mutismo', and the self is stuck with itself in a kind of endless tautology (the dialogue, that may only have been imagined to begin with, is now lost forever). The poet is forced to accept that the world is not in fact how it appears to him, but something quite different, independent of his own desires. In very Lacanian fashion, the eye must accept that it has been

misdirected, since all that the poet has found is loss and absence where plenitude and solidarity were promised.

The poet suffers a similar act of perceptual and linguistic dispossession in another episode, recounted a few lines on:

> Sul risucchio sul nero scorrimento
> altre si accendono *sulla riva di là*   25
> —lampade o lampioni—anche più inaspettate,
> luci umane evocate di colpo—da che mani
> su quali terrazze?—*Le suppongo* segni convenuti
> non so più quando o con chi
> per nuove presenze o ritorni.   30
> —Facciamo che da anni t'aspettassi—
> da un codice disperso è la mia controparola.
> Non passerà la barriera di tenebra e di vento.
> Non passerà il richiamo già increspato d'inverno
> a un introvabile
>   traghettatore.   35
> Così lontane immotivate immobili
> *di là da* questo acheronte
> non provano nulla non chiamano me
> né altri quelle luci.
> [...]
>   (*Un posto* II, 24–39, p. 226)

> [On the undercurrent, on the flowing blackness
> others come alight *on the bank over there*   25
> —lanterns or street lamps—yet more unexpected,
> at a stroke human lights called forth —by which hands,
> on what balconies?—*I imagine them* as signals agreed,
> don't know when or with whom anymore
> for new presences or returns.   30
> —Let's say I awaited you for years—
> my countersign's from a lost code.
> It won't pass the barrier of shadows and wind.
> It won't pass the call already wrinkled by winter
> to an unfindable
>   ferryman.   35
> So distant, unmotivated, motionless
> *over there from* this Acheron
> they don't prove a thing, don't call me
> or call others, those lights.]

In the first two lines of the passage the poet tries hard to pinpoint the others ('altre') in his visual field, focusing on their apparently precise physical location (note the repetition of 'sul', ll. 24–5). However, the limiting of perspective that secures the first focal point is almost immediately undone when the 'lampade o lampioni'—and the poet does not know which they are—break onto the scene unexpectedly. They are, he tells us, 'anche più inaspettate' (l. 26), the element of surprise forcing a readjustment of perspective which is also a response to the anxiety caused by the 'I' being unable to identify them securely.

The passage from 'Le suppongo' to 'ritorni' (ll. 28–30) sees the poet trying to install a second geometral frame after the first has failed, and the imaginary quality of the vision is emphasized by the purely hypothetical nature of the statement—its truth cannot be verified. Paradoxically, the conferral of the label of 'signs' onto these entities, which the poet hopes might give them meaning, is actually what condemns him not to understand them, since if they are part of a language (or a coded landscape) then it is one he no longer possesses the tools to read or decipher. As he himself admits his 'controparola' is 'da un codice *disperso*' (l. 32), powerless to overcome the barriers which take root in the middle distance.

His eye is thus stopped short of its desired target and there is a foreshortening of perspective, a literal myopia, which pushes those lights into the distance, beyond the subject's focal point and outside of the intersubjective arena (which is also the field of speech). This is reflected at the poetic level in the fact that the lights move in the space of just a few lines from being '*sulla* riva *di là*' ('over there', l. 25) to a position '*di là da* questo acheronte' (intangibly, but unquestionably, beyond, l. 37). So long as the speaking and desiring subject cannot cross 'this river', the other side is closed off to him for good, and he is confined more than ever to a truly infernal, limbo-like, middle space which ends all hope of progression.

Perceptual uncertainty in *Un posto* thus tends to manifest itself also as linguistic failure, particularly aphasia, and it is ultimately impossible to extricate the subject's cognitive abilities from his perceptual position in the scopic field.[44] Once again it is Sereni's use of deixis that brings these facets of his landscape together in one grammatical dimension. As we have seen, moments of semantic indirection, in which the poet loses control of his 'materia' [material], are communicated through his interactions with objects and with a landscape that is constantly shifting its contours in line with the subjective dimension of desire.

---

[44] For an extended analysis of the significance of aphasia in Sereni's *Un posto*, see my '"*Per-tras-versioni*" *dantesche*: Post-Paradisiacal Constellations in the Poetry of Vittorio Sereni and Andrea Zanzotto', in *Metamorphosing Dante: Appropriations, Manipulations and Rewritings in the Twentieth and Twenty-First Centuries*, ed. Manuele Gragnolati, Fabio Camilletti, and Fabian Lampart (Vienna: Turia + Kant, 2010), pp. 153–74.

Increasingly, rather than uncover a parabolic unity commensurate with summer and winter, the poet is forced to confront the distance opening up between the subjective and objective worlds, as the objects become impenetrable to the eye and closed in upon themselves. The image that the 'I' then attempts to interpose between them is left to hover uneasily between the two domains, unable to provide the bridge between them upon which geometral vision, and the thetic division, rest.

This is an idea which finds a strong correlation with Proustian notions of perception, which brings us back full circle to the complex interaction of scene and gaze in *À la recherche du temps perdu*, to which Sereni was drawn in meditating upon Montale's 'Il ritorno'. The two episodes just analysed from *Un posto* recall the predicament of Proust's protagonist, Marcel, as he fights to preserve intact the image he has created in his mind of the mythical Madame de Guermantes even as he is forced to confront the many mis-matches between that image of her and reality, 'Sur cette image toute récente, inchangeable, j'essayais d'appliquer l'idée: "C'est Mme de Guermantes" sans parvenir qu'à la faire manœuvrer en face de l'image, comme deux disques séparés par un intervalle' [I was endeavouring to apply [...] to this fresh and unchanging image, the idea: "It's Mme de Guermantes"; but I succeeded only in making the idea pass between me and the image, as though they were two discs moving in separate planes with a space between.][45] As we have seen, that interval in perception—which reveals itself to be unbridgeable, even in the poem— leads to the Serenian 'I' becoming fixated with the beyond from the point of view of the between: the chief coordinates of his landscape of desire. The subject tries desperately to retrieve its object, always already lost or other than the subject imagines it to be, but finds that it is destined to remain on the other side of the wall.

BEYOND LIMINALITY

Sereni's *Un posto* is thus paradigmatic of the way in which, in his reappropriation of the Montalian trope of 'l'incerto lembo', he extends liminality from the perceptual plane, through metaphysical space, to the very heart of the subject–object relationship. Intimately related to the dialectic of desire, as manifest in the scopic drive between the eye and the gaze, the 'line' with which Sereni is concerned in *SV* encompasses not only the parameters of the visual field but also, more importantly, the

---

[45] Proust, *Du Côte de chez Swann: Première partie*, 'Combray, II', in *À la recherche*, p. 145.

domain in which the speaking (and writing) subject is made to confront, and constantly redefine, its relationship to the world it creates and which creates it.

Sereni is attracted to the liminal topographies of Montalian poems such as 'Il ritorno' and 'Arsenio' because boundary spaces of the kind he later recreates in *Un posto* and 'Niccolò' are understood to be the primary zones, poetically speaking, for the revelation of a higher dimension. Yet, as is often the case in Montale too, the poetic subject comes to inhabit the liminal condition that should only be a phase in the journey to transcendence, which condemns him to a frozen or suspended existence on the near side of the line he would really seek to cross.

Liminality emerges as the tangible expression of a desire which, on the Lacanian model, is 'oblique and evanescent', exists 'in a gap, at a tangent, as a residue', and from which there is no escape.[46] In Sereni's poetry in particular, the subject's inability to transcend his more limited condition is communicated above all in terms of a crisis of perception, so that his gaze no longer settles neatly on the things it apprehends but rather hovers in an intermediate zone, which also represents the gulf between language and the objects it seeks to describe. Ultimately the gaze, as an index of desire, bares the reality of desire as lack and not fulfilment. In poetic terms, since it occupies a liminal space between the visible and the invisible, it foregrounds the ambiguity of the object of desire, which may be purely imagined by the subject to exist or have existed. This turns landscapes like Bocca di Magra into topographies of desire and Sereni's poetry into a 'desire-space'.[47] It opens the way to the phantasm which poetry itself, as a particular configuration of the Imaginary order of the subject's experience, might represent. This leads Sereni back to the conception of the lyric as a 'luogo *ideale*', from which he is progressively exiled, and to the memory of Petrarch's *RVF*.

---

[46] Bowie, *Lacan*, p. 139.
[47] Ibid. 138.

4

Poetry as Desire-Space

Petrarchan Ascendancies in Gli strumenti umani *and* Stella variabile

'Il ricordo è poesia, e la poesia non è se non ricordo'
(Giovanni Pascoli, Preface to *Primi poemetti*)[1]

This chapter returns to Sereni's designation of the foundational site of the lyric as a 'luogo ideale' [ideal place] (interchangeable for him with a Petrarchan notion of poetry, as we shall see) in order to show how the relationship between landscape and desire, so central to the dialogue with Montale, finds an ulterior point of origin in the universe of the *RVF*. It considers how, in *SU* and *SV* in particular, Sereni reworks the poetic locus of the Petrarchan idyll to incorporate the memory of Petrarch's text at the same time as marking his estrangement from it, and his impossibility of fully embracing the model of the lyric that Petrarch's poetry would represent.

As Sereni's writings on Petrarch reveal, that model is explicitly linked for him to the identity of poetry as phantasm—the space of a *mise en scène* of desire, in which the subject is implicated as much as his object, and which finds its most intense expression in Petrarch's repeated figurations of the *locus amoenus*, as both recollected space of the imagination and memory, and its representation in the poem. Showing how the two dimensions meet in the realm of deixis at phantasma common to both poets' work, in which landscape and phantasm become indistinguishable, I argue that Sereni revisits this intimately lyric space and reshapes it on his own terms.

A TOPOGRAPHICAL REVISION OF PETRARCH

It is significant that Sereni should have chosen to approach his own dialogue on Petrarch through landscape, and in the broader context of a

[1] [Memory is poetry, and poetry is nothing if not memory.]

meditation on the identity of poetry. His essay 'Petrarca, nella sua finzione la sua verità' ['Petrarch, in His Fiction His Truth'] opens with a topographical description of the river Sorgue, in Vaucluse, which is mediated in an important way by Sereni's reading and translation of the French poet René Char. Both Sereni's article on Petrarch and his translation of Char's *Retour amont* [*Return Upstream*] date to 1974.[2] Writing in 'Il mio lavoro su Char' ['My Work on Char'] (1977) about the importance of landscape as a way into Char's poetry, and revealing the extent of his topographic sensibility, Sereni states:

> Un paesaggio illimitato e in buona parte inesplorato mi stava davanti e non potevo che inoltrarmici per gradi. Portato *per vecchia inclinazione* a cercare oggetti, luoghi e volti prima di ogni altra cosa anche in un libro di versi, *ho tentato da principio gli aditi a me più accessibili*. Mi sono attaccato anzitutto a un paesaggio fisico, geografico e topografico, lo stesso in cui René Char vive, si muove, e lavora: il Vaucluse.[3]

[A boundless and largely unexplored landscape lay before me and I could only inch forward into it. *Inclined, as usual,* to look for objects, places, and faces before anything else, even in a book of poems, *from the beginning I sought to enter via what was most accessible to me.* I attached myself above all to a physical landscape, at once geographical and topographical, the same one in which René Char lives, moves, and works: Vaucluse.]

Thus, the seemingly limitless world of Char's poetry, still unfamiliar to Sereni in its unbounded qualities, became accessible during that period through the memory of something, or *someone* else, that was known to him. This orienting, if somewhat archaic force—which dovetails with the phantasmatic presence that underlies Sereni's later meditation on

---

[2] 'Petrarca, nella sua finzione la sua verità' is the definitive title of a lecture on Petrarch that Sereni gave in Lugano on 7 May 1974, Pavia (14 May 1975), Gargnano (13 July 1975), Modena (2 Apr. 1980), and Milan (3 Sept. 1980). The text was first published as an article (in abridged form) with the title 'Sì dolce è del mio amaro la radice' ['So Sweet is the Root of My Bitterness'], *Corriere del Ticino*, 22 June 1974, pp. 36–7, then as 'Amati Laura come io ti amo' ['Love Yourself, Laura, as I Love You'], *Il Giorno*, 14 July 1974, pp. 11–12. The original text (unabridged) appeared first in AA. VV. *Francesco Petrarca nel VI centenario della morte* (Bologna: Massimiliano Boni, 1976), pp. 69–78. It was then published in libretto form as *Petrarca, nella sua finzione la sua verità* (Vicenza: Neri Pozza, 1983) and, most recently, was included amongst Sereni's collected essays on literature in *SG*, pp. 127–46, from which quotations are taken. Sereni's translation of Char's *Retour amont, Ritorno sopramonte*, was published in 1974 by Mondadori. As Francesca D'Alessandro notes in her study of Sereni's intertextuality with Petrarch, the date is important, as it is the period in which Sereni is working on poems that will be included in *SV*, and those destined for the revised edition of *SU*, published in 1975. See Francesca D'Alessandro, 'Il dialogo con i classici', in *L'opera poetica di Vittorio Sereni* (Milan: Vita e Pensiero, 2001), pp. 163–210 (pp. 174–5).

[3] Vittorio Sereni, 'Il mio lavoro su Char', in *Premio Città di Monselice per una traduzione letteraria*, ed. l'Amministrazione Comunale (Monselice, 1977), pp. xxv–xxviii (p. xxvii).

landscape in 'Infatuazioni' ['Infatuations'] (discussed earlier)—can only be Petrarch.[4] The 'vecchia inclinazione' that has Sereni searching for 'oggetti, luoghi e volti'—a landscape that is in a sense known and familiar—is arguably an allegory for the distinctive nature of his 'Petrarchism': a bridge from one poetic world into another, and the world itself (here Vaucluse) as it comes to be '(ri)creato intorno ad un unico abitante' [(re)created around a single inhabitant].[5]

A more detailed analysis of 'Petrarca, nella sua finzione' takes this analogy between landscape, poetry, and subjectivity a step further. As just stated, Sereni begins by focusing on the font of the river Sorgue, '[il] luogo deputato per eccellenza della poesia del Petrarca' [[the] chosen place *par excellence* of Petrarch's poetry] (p. 127). However, a certain anxiety of influence is immediately in evidence since, having stated the centrality of that place to the Petrarchan imagination, he distances himself from it. This has not been 'un pellegrinaggio petrarchesco' [a Petrarchan pilgrimage] (p. 127), as we might think, but a journey into Char's poetry, or rather Sereni's translation of Char.

The short prose poem by Char, 'Tracé sur le gouffre' ['Traced on the Abyss'], provides Sereni with the customary screen-mirror through which he views himself and, by extension, here also the Petrarchan element of himself. As he turns Char's poem from one originally addressed to a 'you' figure (arguably monologue parading as dialogue)[6] into one that incorporates a 'he' (monologic in the extreme), he paradoxically both intensifies and dissolves the distance between himself and Petrarch, redefining the terms of the traditional lyric coupling 'io–'tu' (already distorted in Char's text) while opening up a space for the phantasm of Petrarch himself, as desiring subject, to appear in the landscape:

---

[4] As noted in my introduction, the phantasmatic interlocutor of Sereni's later meditation on memory and landscape, 'Infatuazioni', is likely to be Char, providing a meaningful symmetry with the passage under discussion here. On Sereni's relationship to Char see Elisa Donzelli's recent study, *Come lenta cometa: traduzione e amicizia poetica nel carteggio tra Sereni e Char* (Turin: Aragno, 2009), and René Char/Vittorio Sereni, *Due rive ci vogliono: quarantasette traduzioni inedite*, ed. Elisa Donzelli (Rome: Donzelli, 2010).

[5] Giorgio Bertone, 'Gli occhi di Laura, i passi di Francesco', in *Lo sguardo escluso: l'idea del paesaggio nella letteratura occidentale* (Novara: Interlinea, 2000), pp. 95–147 (p. 116).

[6] Cf. Emmanuela Tandello's comment on Zanzotto's identification of the essence of Petrarch's linguistic legacy for twentieth-century poetry in 'its power of resistance, its refusal to succumb to each failed attempt at dialogue, its determination to reaffirm the inevitable "non-answer" [...] that the poetic voice, *forced into monologue*, unavoidably has to confront today, as it did then': 'Between Tradition and Transgression: Amelia Rosselli's Petrarch', in *Petrarch in Britain: Interpreters, Imitators and Translators over 700 years*, ed. Martin McLaughlin and Letizia Panizza with Peter Hainsworth (Oxford: Oxford University Press for the British Academy, 2007), pp. 301–17 (p. 302).

Questo 'vous', questo 'lui' implicito alla mia versione è senz'altro il Petrarca. Ma può essere riferito, insieme, a tutt'altra persona: a uno che oppresso da una sua pena occulta, da un suo male dissimulato e stento, *passa per gli stessi luoghi in cui il Petrarca celava, o piuttosto nutriva, un male analogo, una pena similare*; e come il Petrarca, per una mercé concessagli da una sua dote interiore, da una sua eccellenza intellettuale o altro, converte quella pena, quel male, in grazia e in valore. *Per un trapasso istantaneo viene identificato in quell'acqua verde, in quella strada che solca i detriti dell'inesistenza, della morte, diviene il Petrarca stesso.* (pp. 128–9)

[Undoubtedly, this 'you', this 'he', implicit in my version, is Petrarch. But it may also refer to someone else entirely: someone who, weighed down by a concealed pain, by a barely dissimulated suffering, *passes through the very places in which Petrarch concealed, or rather nourished, a similar pain and suffering*; and like Petrarch, by an act of mercy granted him by an inner gift—his powerful intellect or something else—transforms that pain and suffering into grace and valour. *Through an instantaneous passing he becomes identifiable in that green water, in that road that furrows the detritus of non-existence, of death, becoming Petrarch himself.*]

Through Sereni's reconfiguration of the original Charian abyss on his own terms, Petrarch finds a way into a landscape which, initially at least, seems remote from the *RVF*, and does so through a pronoun ('lui'), a persona, or a syntactic trace in language. Sereni suggests that the third-person presence in his poem is and is not Petrarch, just as his decision to versify, and thus essentially to lyricize, Char's *poème en prose* is a gesture towards acknowledging Petrarch's ghost in the poem, but also exorcises it, since that act of versification is some way from being an expression of pure lyricism in a traditionally Petrarchan sense.

Instead, if Petrarch is there, he is so only as a kind of lyric hybrid (mirroring Sereni's own version of the poem)—the double figure who finds himself at one moment 'tracciato sul baratro' [traced on the abyss], in the 'piaga chimerica di Valchiusa' [chimeric wound of Vaucluse] (a wounded and phantasmatic landscape that is his own soul) and, at another, the 'fiore ondulato d'un insonne segreto' [undulating flower of a sleepless secret], which would represent the possibility of recovering something miraculous or idyllic beneath or beyond the landscape of trauma and loss. As Sereni's words imply, that double space is the very place of conversion or transcendence, of 'un trapasso istantaneo' that allows Petrarch, through poetry, to transform his experience of pain and suffering into one of 'grazia e valore'. Yet, if it allows the subject to move beyond the self and its theatre of lament, it maybe only does so to put him further along (and so not to liberate him from) 'quella strada che solca i detriti dell'inesistenza, della morte'. Petrarch is the figure who bridges the *locus amoenus* and the *locus horridus*, self and Other, who traverses death and possibly emerges on the other side, but simultaneously provides a firm point of reference in an otherwise disturbing scene. As impure and fragmentary as the memory of the Petrarchan landscape becomes, something of it survives in the 'acqua verde' that transforms the emptiness of the abyss, only populated by the self's shadow, into '*anche* una strada' [*also* a road]: the possibility of a path to something more.[7]

Consequently, the world that Petrarch's poetry represents carries a powerful intimation of another (an Other) order. However, access to it occurs laterally, rather than directly, through an intermediate (here Charian) screen, which simultaneously tempers its domain. Already this suggests that there is something natural in Sereni's relationship to Petrarch as well as a knot of resistance that limits his sphere of influence: a form of poetic memory rooted to landscape, of which, as D'Alessandro has commented, Sereni 'ne ha fatto una serie di luoghi nell'animo' [made a series of places in his mind], but which simultaneously houses a kind of horror of repetition or fixation, in the inability to relinquish or liberate oneself from them.[8]

PETRARCH: THE PHANTASM OF POETRY

When asked to further elucidate his relationship to Petrarch in 'Petrarca e i poeti d'oggi: problemi e illuminazioni' [Petrarch and the Poets of Today: Problems and Illuminations] (1974), Sereni responded: 'Più che un discorso fatto qui sui due piedi, globale e attuale, più che una risposta al quesito mi è facile ricollegarmi alle mie reazioni nel tempo e alla memoria che conservo di lontane letture' [Rather than improvise a reply here and now and, rather than respond to the issue as it has been put, I find it easy to go back to my responses over time and to the memory I have of what I read long ago].[9] For Sereni, Petrarch's idiom cements itself through memory. It is a language of memory, or the language that memory speaks:

> Se poi interrogo la mia memoria, ecco risbucare certi versi divenuti luoghi comuni della sensibilità individuale tanto da parere insostituibili, o meglio irrinunciabili... Certe aperture, certe chiuse: restano annidate

---

[7] Both these phrases derive from Sereni's translation of Char's poem, 'Tracciato sul baratro'.

[8] D'Alessandro, 'Il dialogo con i classici', p. 179.

[9] 'Petrarca e i poeti d'oggi: problemi e illuminazioni', *L'Approdo letterario*, 20.66 (1974), pp. 93–100 (p. 94). This is the transcript of a radio debate aired on 10 May 1974 on RAI Tre, in which Sereni participated with Maria Corti, Antonio Porta, and Andrea Zanzotto.

nell'inconscio, uno non se ne libera più. (Quando si dice memorabile, non è questo che si dice?). (p. 94)

[If, furthermore, I search my memory, certain lines of poetry pop up again, those that have become such common places of the individual sensibility that they seem irreplaceable or, better, impossible to give up... Certain openings, certain endings: they remain tangled in the unconscious, you can't free yourself of them (when we say something is memorable, isn't it this we mean?)]

The topography of Petrarch's text thus extends well into the poet's unconscious, where it fixes itself like strata in rock, able to draw the subject back to it at any point. More ambiguously, Sereni's words cast the memorability of the medieval author as a kind of compulsion to remember or repeat whose persistence grants a sense of belonging and continuity with the past, but is also synonymous with a kind of tyranny ('irrinunciabili [...] uno non se ne libera più'). As we shall see, this is also the force of the lyric that Petrarch's universe represents, 'sia che si tratti del ritorno alla primavera [...] sia che una voce divenga anima nel paesaggio notturno [...] sia che un'esistenza si riconosca e si dichiari ormai avviato non senza sollievo alla propria fase declinante' [whether it deals with the return to spring [...] a voice that becomes a spirit in the night landscape [...] or an existence that acknowledges and declares, not without relief, that it has embarked on its declining phase]: a fixation on a landscape infused with a sense of finitude that is the mark of the self's mortality, but which poetry expressly struggles and strives against and ideally redeems.[10]

It is the strength of (and the poet's identification with) these Petrarchan 'commonplaces', for which there is no substitute lyrically speaking, that provides a clue to understanding the way in which the memory of Petrarch survives, though not necessarily harmoniously, right into the later phase of Sereni's production where we might not expect to find him. While a strong case can, and has, been made for an authoritative Petrarchan presence underlying Sereni's first two collections, his apparent absence from the later work has tended to tantalize critics, particularly since, like the panther of the *volgare illustre* [illustrious vernacular] in Dante's *De vulgari eloquentia*, his scent appears to be left everywhere, but he is nowhere to be seen.[11]

The apparent remoteness of the Petrarchan landscape in *SU* and *SV* is particularly evident since Sereni largely favours the dialogic and narrative

---

[10] 'Petrarca, nella sua finzione', p. 130. The ellipses correspond to where Sereni quotes from Petrarch's *RVF* CCCX, 1–4; *RVF* CCCXI, 1–5, and *RVF* CCCXV, 1–3, respectively.

[11] 'redolentem ubique et necubi apparentem', *De vulgari eloquentia* I, xvi, 1, quoted from Dante Alighieri, *De vulgari eloquentia*, ed. and trans. Steven Botterill (Cambridge: Cambridge University Press, 1996), pp. 38–9.

strand of discourse, which emerges in his work in the 1950s and 1960s, over the more traditionally monologic voice still in play in *Frontiera*, and to an extent *DA*. However, it never disappears completely: while the more memorable topoi tend to be drawn from the Dantean heritage—including the dialogue with the dead, and the infernal realm in which those encounters take place—they are consistently mediated (contaminated) by the phantasm of Petrarch. This is particularly true where the discourse of desire incorporates a strong dimension of self-reflexivity, which sees the 'ombre' [shades] emerge less as figurations of an Other than as fragments of a divided self, or where the *locus horridus* still carries the distant memory of a *locus amoenus*, which leads back to the *RVF*. The overtly Dantean text 'Intervista a un suicida' [Interview with a Suicide] is a case in point:

> L'anima, quello che diciamo l'anima e non è
> che *una fitta di rimorso*
> *lenta deplorazione sull'ombra dell'addio*
> mi rimbrottò dall'argine.
> [...]
> *Decresceva alla vista, spariva per l'eterno.*
> Era l'eterno stesso
> [...]
> ma non se ne curano, *la sanno lunga*
> *le acque falsamente ora limpide* tra questi
> oggi diritti regolari argini,
>   lo spazio
> si copre di case popolari, di un altro
> segregato squallore *dentro le forme del vuoto.*
> [...]
>   ('Intervista a un suicida', ll. 1–4, 43–4, 52–6,
>   in *SU*, pp. 163–5)

> [The soul, what we call the soul and is nothing
> but *a pang of remorse,*
> *slow reproof on the shadow of farewell,*
> upbraided me from the banks.
> [...]
> *He shrank from view, disappeared for eternity.*
> It was eternity itself
> [...]
> but indifferently, *the waters know*
> well enough, falsely limpid now *between these*
> regular embankments today so straight,
>   the space
> is covered with cheap housing, with another
> fenced-off squalor *in the form of nothingness.*]

Stefano Dal Bianco, in his study of Petrarch's influence on Sereni, identifies four major points of contact between the two authors, which I believe actually find their point of confluence in this poem: (i) an innate sense of guilt or shame for something done or not done, often associated with the poetic act itself; (ii) the theme of the journey or passage, paradoxically a sign in both of the essential immovability of the subject and its fixation to certain coveted sites of experience and/or memory; (iii) 'dialogic' situations, in which the interlocutor is the alter ego of the speaking 'I' more than a true Other; (iv) the emergence of a series of phantasmatic presences which populate the landscape of both poetic universes in similar ways. Highlighting the 'povertà di riferimenti [diretti]' [scarcity of [direct] references] to the text of Petrarch's *RVF*, but demonstrating the richness and suggestiveness of its *loci* (geographic and poetic) for Sereni, Dal Bianco ultimately argues for a psychological or existential link between the two poets in which the apparent suppression (repression?) of Petrarch at the formal level is mainly a sign of 'la nota avversione di Sereni [...] per tutte le manifestazioni di una forma data a priori, di una gabbia precostituita di contenuti a piacere' [Sereni's notorious aversion...towards all expressions of a predetermined form or a pre-established cage of contents to choose from at will].[12]

This brings us to Petrarch's emblematic status as the poet representing, more generally, Sereni's (uneasy) relationship to the lyric tradition and the burden of an inherited idiom, which he can neither wholly resist nor fully embrace. Sereni's writings on the medieval author imply that the memory of Petrarch always carries this weight of tradition, and unlike in his relationship with Montale, the problematic associations of the word 'lyric' itself. Commenting, in 'Petrarca, nella sua finzione la sua verità', on the genesis of the lyric tradition, and his relationship to it, Sereni meditates on the following question:

> Petrarca, la poesia del Petrarca, agisce ancora o non agisce più in noi? C'è stato un momento, o piuttosto un periodo, nel nostro secolo italiano in cui ogni possibile nozione di poesia si restringeva nei termini della poesia lirica, anzi della lirica senz'altro. Quei termini sono oggi in disuso. La parola stessa, lirica, è usata malvolentieri, con riluttanza. La nostra gioventù—parlo di una parte della mia generazione letteraria e senza alcun riferimento alla cosiddetta poesia pura—se pensava alla poesia pensava anzitutto a Leopardi, ma dietro Leopardi evocava il Petrarca. Petrarca era *la* poesia, ne rappresentava l'essenza o, come si diceva una volta, la quintessenza. E Dante? E Ariosto? Prego non

---

[12] Stefano Dal Bianco, 'Vittorio Sereni: Petrarca come forma interna', in *Un'altra storia: Petrarca nel Novecento italiano. Atti del Convegno di Roma, 4–6 ottobre 2001*, ed. Andrea Cortellessa (Rome: Bulzoni, 2004), pp. 185–99 (p. 188).

equivocare. Non è che fossero proposti o negletti: erano, semplicemente, altro. Operavano su altri territori. Il terreno sul quale pareva ancora possibile, per noi, operare era quello di Leopardi: dunque di Petrarca. (p. 144, italics in the original)

[Petrarch, Petrarch's poetry, does it still act upon us, or not? There was a moment, or rather a period, in our century in Italy in which every possible notion of poetry restricted itself to the terms of lyric poetry, in fact the lyric pure and simple. Those terms are now no longer in use. The word lyric itself is used grudgingly, with reluctance. The youth of today—and I'm speaking about a part of my literary generation and without reference to so-called pure poetry—if they thought of poetry they thought above all of Leopardi, but behind Leopardi they saw Petrarch. Petrarch *was* poetry, he represented its essence or, as we used to say, its quintessence. And what about Dante? And Ariosto? Make no mistake. It's not that they were put forward or neglected: they were simply something else. They operated in different territories. The ground upon which it still seemed possible for us to work was Leopardi's, that is to say: Petrarch's.]

Sereni thus roots Petrarch's quintessence in a poetic ground essentially tied to the past and to his early poetic experiences, now superseded (though not definitively, as we know from his meditations on the endurance of Petrarch's memory elsewhere in the same essay). What is significant is that in looking back, poetry is said to have been experienced at the time as an event of contraction and closure ('si *restringeva*'), insofar as it was contained (constrained) by the notion of lyric, a clearly delineated territory that was defined above all by what it excluded, and especially in its difference/distance from Dante. Leopardi was the prime mover of that universe, but only to the degree that his poetry evoked Petrarch; in other words, we encounter a Leopardi reduced to a Petrarchan synthesis.

That aligning of Petrarch with the notions of reduction, exclusion, and essentialization is an important one, and in fact extends beyond merely the consideration of the territory that he occupies in relation to Dante (and Leopardi) in the field of literary and cultural memory. In terms of Sereni's poetry, it has a direct bearing upon the nature of the intertextual heritage, and especially upon (i) the way in which Petrarch's influence on Sereni has traditionally been viewed, and (ii) the possibility of arriving at a deeper understanding of the space that Petrarch, as lyric archetype (albeit one mediated *through* Leopardi) occupies in Sereni's universe, particularly in his later work.

Dante Isella's study 'La lingua poetica di Vittorio Sereni' ['Vittorio Sereni's Poetic Language'] is paradigmatic in this respect. Defining the verbal fabric of *Frontiera* and *DA* in terms of its reductiveness, Isella draws the following analogy between Petrarch and Sereni:

Resta però il fatto che proprio questa esigenza di chiudere in contorni fermi la propria inquietudine esistenziale determina un'individuazione rigorosamente riduttiva dei *realia* e dei materiali adibiti a nominarli. Sicché, sia pure per eterogenesi dei fini, il risultato, in *Frontiera* e nel *Diario* del '47, è una lingua poetica diversa, ma non meno aristocraticamente selettiva di quella degli adepti dell'orfismo fiorentino. Non volendo, a scanso di equivoci, chiamarla ermetica, si potrebbe dirla 'petrarchesca', se è lecito nominare dal Petrarca, per analogia, qualsiasi processo di decantazione della complessità del reale per estrarne delle levigate essenze primarie, tali da riassumere in sé, sublimandolo, l'intero universo.[13]

[The fact remains, however, that this desire to enclose his existential anxiety within firm boundaries leads to a rigorously reductive individuation of reality and the materials used to name it. Consequently, and notwithstanding the difference in the end result, what we end up with in *Frontiera* and in the 1947 edition of *Diario d'Algeria* is a poetic language that is different from, but no less aristocratically selective than, that of the Florentine orphic poets. Not wanting to risk misunderstanding by labelling it 'hermetic', we could call it 'Petrarchesque', if it is legitimate to give Petrarch's name, by analogy, to every process of distilling reality that extracts its polished, primary essences and incorporates, through sublimation, the whole of the universe.]

The most significant trait of this poetic selectivity is thus, paradoxically, its desire to embrace through a part ('[la] *decantazione* della complessità del reale') the whole ('l'*intero* universo'). Petrarch's (and by extension, Sereni's) use of a 'vocabolario chiuso' is a means to appropriate a sense of inclusivity and possession, to the very extent that it fixes and reduces. The sublime or sublimating space of the lyric is none other than this space of tension between part and whole, and between exclusion and appropriation: the very traits of deixis analysed in Chapter 2 and in fact the key to recuperating a space for Petrarch in Sereni's work beyond *Frontiera* and *DA*, and beyond the traditional identification of Petrarch (merely) with the notion of 'poesia pura' [pure poetry] in hermetic terms.

As Sereni's states in 'Petrarca e i poeti d'oggi', Petrarch stands in his lexicon for a concept of poetry seen (again in opposition to Dante) as distinct from 'lo sguardo in senso realistico' [the gaze in a realistic sense], i.e. Petrarch as a concept of poetry *tout court*, or what Maria Corti terms in the same discussion 'poesia' [poetry] as '"altro" dalla realtà' [other than reality].[14] However, whereas for Corti this notion of Petrarchan poetry as 'other than' or 'the other of' reality finds its prime modern exemplum in

---

[13] Dante Isella, 'La lingua poetica di Sereni', in *La poesia di Vittorio Sereni: atti del convegno*, ed. Stefano Agosti et al. (Milan: Librex, 1985), pp. 21–32 (p. 25).
[14] Sereni, in 'Petrarca e i poeti d'oggi', p. 94; Maria Corti, ibid. 93.

the abstract poetry of hermeticism, which drew on Petrarch's symbology and his 'strutture formali, metriche, ritmiche, foniche' [formal, metrical, rhythmic and phonic structures] in order to arrive at a form of absolute expression, for Sereni it figures more as the power of Petrarch's language vis-à-vis 'altri poteri (terreni, temporali)' [other (worldly, temporal) powers], i.e. its power to create an alternative world order and a different constellation of reality.[15] As we shall see, this power is explicitly aligned for Sereni with the strength of Petrarch's deictic legacy—not so much a lexical heritage, as a linguistic and syntactic one, rooted at a deeper level within the notion of poetic discourse.

Thus, while Isella's predominantly philological approach limits his sphere of investigation to Petrarch's presence in *Frontiera* and *DA*, I would suggest that the model of the lyric to which he refers, as opposed to its extant lexical features, exceeds those boundaries, especially where the discourse of desire is concerned. This is particularly true when we consider its similarities with Sereni's own conception of the lyric as a 'luogo ideale', which in 'Petrarca, nella sua finzione' he explicitly aligns with Petrarch, and which incorporates this impetus towards essentiality and containment at the level of language as much as topography *per se*. Revisiting the well-known Continian distinction between Petrarch's *monolinguismo* [monolingualism] and Dante's *plurilinguismo* [plurilingualism], Sereni reflects upon the different qualities of the poetic landscape that the works of the two medieval authors embody, and the corresponding traits of their language:

> Si pensi a come vive la fisicità del mondo sensibile, a come si leva e respira il paesaggio in Dante e a come si fissa una volta per tutte nel Petrarca. In Dante accompagna una vicenda specifica di questo o quel paesaggio [...] È *quel* luogo, *quell'*ora, *quella* circostanza; guizza e si irradia in un discorso che porta altrove [...] Oppure fa supporto a un concetto, riempie di sé una similitudine, la fa concreta e visibile [...]. In Petrarca è luogo ideale, teatro naturale stabile che ammette sfumature e variazioni infinitesime, è emblema che conserva la vivezza delle cose emblematizzate e anzi la fa palese, instancabilmente, implacabilmente, la riassume, la saggia, la rimette in gioco ogni volta entro un quadro e su uno sfondo costanti. Il tradizionale confronto tra Dante e Petrarca o meglio tra la *Commedia* e il *Canzoniere* non ha molto senso se viene attuato in rapporto a una scala di valori e con l'intento di stabilire un'astratta priorità; [...] Ne ha moltissimo se viene effettuato sul piano della lingua. Direi che in tal caso l'accertamento delle diversità serve a capire soprattutto Petrarca e a circoscrivere, a specificare il senso della sua arte. (pp. 142–3, italics in the original)

[15] Corti, ibid. 98; Sereni, ibid. 99.

[Think how the physicality of the sensory world comes alive in Dante, how his landscape lives and breathes, and the way, in Petrarch, it is fixed once and for all. In Dante it accompanies a specific event associated with this or that landscape [...] It is *that* place, *that* time, *that* particular circumstance, it flickers and radiates outwards in a discourse that leads elsewhere [...] Or else it supports a concept, fills out a simile, making it concrete and visible. [...] In Petrarch, it is an ideal place, an unchanging natural theatre that allows for infinitesimal shades of meaning and variations, it is the emblem that preserves the vividness of the things emblematized, makes that vividness visible, tirelessly, implacably, subsumes it within itself, tests it and puts it back into play each time within a constant frame and an unchanging backdrop. The traditional comparison between Dante and Petrarch or, better, between the *Commedia* and the *Canzoniere*, doesn't mean much if it is gauged in relation to a pre-established scale of values or with the aim of establishing an abstract notion of priority. [...] It means a great deal if undertaken at the level of language. I would say that in that case the acknowledgement of their differences aids an understanding above all of Petrarch and helps to circumscribe and specify the sense of his art.]

Dante's landscape lives and breathes, whereas Petrarch's possesses the kind of fixity of which Isella speaks—a form which, if it does not kill life (as Pirandello might have it), seriously prescribes the limits in which it comes to exist. This is both a strength and a limitation, as Sereni circumscribes Petrarch's art in terms of its synthetic power but also hints at the closure specified by that introversion. If, according to Sereni, landscape in Dante is predominantly mimetic while often being also supremely allegorical (in that it looks beyond itself to a higher purpose and is thus subordinate to the moral fabric of the poem), in Petrarch, it is intrinsic to how the poetry itself takes shape: landscape is forever changing and forever staying the same, rather in the same way that Petrarch's poetry looks forward by endlessly looking back. In both, landscape can be an expression of identity, but only in Petrarch does it become absolute. In turn, this absolute quality of Petrarch's verse is not so much an embodiment of the 'parola assoluta' [absolute word] favoured by the hermetics as of the properties of the lyric landscape in its inexorable, unfailing and unrelenting ubiquity as the 'luogo ideale' of the lyric subject itself.

As Contini notes in 'Preliminari sulla lingua di Petrarca' ['Preliminary Remarks on Petrarch's Language'], there is paradoxically nothing natural about Petrarch's landscape of nature: language and scenery are both constructed out of the antithetical structures of desire and the self which, thriving on lack, seek to embrace the phantasms of the Other (only mnemonically or imaginatively 'present') by relinquishing or eliding the 'true' perception of the effectively absent object. 'Il verso è dunque caratterizzato da una litote in senso vastissimo, in quanto non è soltanto negativo [...] ma è *negativo per immagini*, dunque conforme alla costante EVASIVITÀ di Petrarca (*sostanze, ma sostanze non attualizzate* [...]) [The line is thus characterized by a litotes in an extremely broad sense, insofar as it is not only negative [...] but negative in terms of images, and thus consistent with Petrarch's constant EVASIVENESS (substances, but substances that are not actualized).][16] 'Negativo per immagini', 'sostanze non attualizzate': these could also be the blueprint of Sereni's poetry in *SU* and *SV*, which similarly derives its identity from the figuration of the absence left by the departure of the desired object, which poetic language seeks to fill precisely by conjuring the phantasm of a fuller state, now lost (but increasingly, in Sereni, also forced to measure the shortfall between memory and desire, and so turned against the subject).

In both Petrarch and Sereni, the landscape is thus essentialized more than reduced, constructed upon the basis of a 'sguardo esclusivo' [exclusive gaze] intent upon transforming—in deictic fashion—'lontananza' [remoteness] (potentially all-consuming) into more manageable 'distanza' [distance] (which the 'I' can map, measure, and fix in relation to the self and thus somehow appropriate as its own): 'Per quanto stilizzato, il "terreno" ove si spazializza l'immagine e se ne celebra la sincronia è essenziale alla "fissazione" quanto quella' [However stylized, the 'terrain' where the image unfolds, and which celebrates its synchrony, is essential to the 'fixation' as such].[17] The difference between the two poets lies in the degree to which the 'I' can survive the vicissitudes of that desiring terrain—in other words, the extent to which it is in command of the idyll.

Idyllic memory, or the memory of the idyll

That idyll is properly the 'luogo ideale' that Petrarch seeks to create and sustain through the length of the *RVF*, but which he finds he can access only intermittently, and which must be renewed with each attempt to reclaim the originary vision (of Laura), or its memory. The sestina *RVF* XXX, which is the first of the anniversary poems and marks the time that has passed since Petrarch first saw his 'giovene donna sotto un verde lauro' [youthful lady under a green laurel], is a blueprint for this idyll, and its phantasmatic status. 'Idyll', from the Greek, is a diminutive of εἶδος, meaning 'form' or 'picture'. It is an apt word to use to describe the space of Petrarch's desire in this poem, since the scene that emerges betrays its

---

[16] Gianfranco Contini, 'Preliminari sulla lingua di Petrarca', in Petrarca, *Canzoniere*, pp. xxvii–lv (pp. lii–liii).
[17] Bertone, 'Gli occhi di Laura, i passi di Francesco', p. 115.

identity as a purely constructed landscape of the imagination, in which (memorial) phantasm and *locus amoenus* are completely fused:

> [...]
> e 'l suo parlare, e 'l bel viso, et le chiome,
> mi piacquen sí ch'i' l'ò *dinanzi agli occhi*,   5
> ed avrò sempre, *ov'*io sia, in poggio o 'n riva.
> [...]
> I' temo di cangiar pria volto et chiome   25
> che con vera pietà mi mostri gli occhi
> *l'idolo mio*, scolpito in vivo lauro:
> che s'al contar non erro, oggi à sett'anni
> che sospirando vo di riva in riva
> la notte e 'l giorno, al caldo ed a la neve.   30
>
> [...]
> [and her speech and her lovely face and her locks
> pleased me so that I have her *before my eyes*   5
> and shall always have *wherever* I am, on slope or shore.
> [...]
> I fear I shall change my face and locks   25
> before she with true pity will show me her eyes,
> *my idol* carved in living laurel;
> for, if I do not err, today it is seven years
> that I go sighing from shore to shore
> night and day, in heat and in snow.]   30

Since the subject always carries that image (idyll) with him, the implication in the first strophe is that he will never again be parted from it—note the miraculous deictic fusion of time, space, and subjectivity in the phrase, '*sempre, ov'io* sia' [*always, wherever I* am], of l. 6. However, by the fifth strophe the idyll, and the 'idolo' [idol] on which it depends, has revealed itself to be only a dead image carved into a living tree. More problematically, the phantasmatic traits of the lost object have been transferred to the 'I' itself ('viso' [face], l. 4 → 'volto' [face], l. 25; 'chiome' [locks], ll. 4, 24 → 'chiome', ll. 11, 15, 25, 32), which, now faced with the absence of his beloved, can recognize only his own reflection there, with the Narcissus-like discovery that 'the phantasm is me' ('iste ego sum').[18] The 'I' wastes away in contemplation of that image and the realization of the unequal and disproportionate response of the subject to (his) desire, and his ultimate loneliness. The 'occhi' [eyes] that shape the 'idolo' are finally the 'occhi' (l. 38) that will dissolve the 'I' completely, transforming

---

[18] Cf. Ovid, *Metamorphoses* III, 463. Available in English translation as *The Metamorphoses of Ovid*, trans. Allen Mandelbaum (San Diego, Calif.: Harvest, 1993).

the shore that is the privileged locus of the idyll into the shore of death, 'che menan gli anni sì tosto a riva' [that lead my years so quickly to shore] (l. 39).

As Sereni already recognizes in 'Petrarca, nella sua finzione', the phantasms of Petrarch's poetic universe thus incorporate not just the image of Laura but also the poet's image of himself: 'Al cospetto dello specchio che è Laura, Petrarca ha lavorato a formare la propria immagine. È a questa che parla nel parlare con Laura. Il punto in discussione è qui' [Before the mirror that is Laura, Petrarch worked on shaping his own image. It's to that image that he speaks when speaking to Laura. This is what is at issue] (p. 137). The object and the mirror fuse in the realm of the phantasm, which is also the space for interrogating the poet's subjective limits: the self's persona, its substance, or lack thereof. The phantasm arises, like a familiar yet unknown country, in the dialogue between author and text, or between life and work: a subtle dialectic that Sereni posits once again in a topographically liminal realm that shapes both memory and desire, time and space:

> Sempre meno l'esistenza promuove l'opera, è piuttosto l'opera a promuovere l'esistenza prolungandosi, insinuandosi in questa, come per una conversione d'energia. Tra il vivere e lo scrivere viene a formarsi come una fascia intermedia, una zona di riporto, *un paese immateriale abitato da alcuni fantasmi*. Laura, che è certamente esistita e che ha segnato alcuni momenti capitali nell'esistenza del poeta, è uno di questi fantasmi, certo il più importante; e in questo senso Petrarca ha avuto una doppia vita proiettata in una lunga ossessione. (p. 136)
>
> [It is less and less the case that existence fosters the work; rather, it is the work that fosters existence, prolonging itself, insinuating itself into it as though through a conversion of energies. Between living and writing a kind of intermediate zone comes to be formed, an in-between space, *an immaterial realm inhabited by phantasms*. Laura, who most certainly existed, and who marked some of the most important moments of the poet's existence, is one of these phantasms, undoubtedly the most important one; and in this sense, Petrarch lived a double life shaped by a lengthy obsession.]

Importantly, Sereni puts the emphasis not so much on the identity of Petrarch's original passion for Laura as on what that passion (desire) becomes in its transformation into text and poem. As the subject is drawn into the immaterial world peopled by phantasms, he finds his own subjectivity simultaneously created and dissolved. Since this passage is one which Sereni retains in every version of his article on Petrarch and is that on which the 'Amati Laura come io ti amo' ['Love Yourself, Laura, as I Love You'] version opens, we can surmise that Sereni finds the greatest consonance with Petrarch when he locates the essence of poetry in its doubling or schismatic effects upon the writing subject.

That latter dimension is in fact the one to which Sereni gives prominence in his own textual universe. Looking at the dialectic in evidence in *RVF* XXX, he plays most upon the negative dimension of Petrarch's vision and his experience of writing, emphasizing 'quella sorta di *sdoppiamento* che Petrarca ha operato rispetto al proprio mondo affettivo [...] quel proiettarsi di passioni in fantasmi, *non escluso il fantasma di un se stesso amante e poetante*' [that sort of *doubling* that Petrarch carried out with the world of his affections... the way passions are projected into phantasms, *not excluding the phantasm of a self loving and poetizing*].[19] For Sereni, this latter articulation in fact becomes the primary phantasm. It is none other than the essence of Petrarchan desire itself, 'una ossessione di prolungarsi oltre sé, una contraddizione assolutamente fertile in lui (dico sul piano espressivo) tra il dolce e l'amaro' [an obsession with going beyond himself, an absolutely fertile contradiction in him (on the expressive plane, I mean) between sweetness and bitterness]: the double helix of '*dolere*' and '*voluptas*' [pain and pleasure], 'trauma' and 'terapia' [trauma and therapy], between whose poles the poetic subject is suspended, most likely wilfully.[20]

Sereni's poem, 'Addio Lugano bella' [Beautiful Lugano Goodbye], in *SV*, revisits the landscape of *RVF* XXX in some significant ways. It is paradigmatic of the centrality of the memory-phantasm in Sereni's later poetry, and the way in which it is established by his reworking of an essentially Petrarchan scheme. However, where Petrarch fixes the image of Laura in the landscape, Sereni finds that it is rather he who is always already etched or posted there, and without the consistency or solidity enjoyed by Petrarch's image in its diamond-like steadfastness ('ch' Amor conduce a pie' del duro lauro | ch'à i rami di diamante et d'or le chiome' [that Love leads to the foot of the harsh laurel | that has branches of diamond and gold locks], *RVF* XXX, ll. 23–4). Instead, the Serenian 'I' finds that it is as uncertain and transitory as moving water, with no consistency of self:

---

[19] Sereni, 'Petrarca e i poeti d'oggi', pp. 94–5.
[20] The quotation comes from ibid. 95, 'da far congetturare che il trauma presupponga, nel momento stesso in cui si verifica, e preveda, l'intervento di una terapia' [leading us to conjecture that the trauma, at the very moment that it makes itself felt, presupposes and anticipates the intervention of a therapy]. For the dialectic between '*dolere*' and '*voluptas*', see Sereni, 'Petrarca, nella sua finzione', pp. 134–5.

[…]
incerte laghi transitori (*come me,*
ululante di estasi alle colline in fiore?
falso-fiorite, un'ora
di sole le sbrinerà).   25
[…]
Ne vanno alteri i gentiluomini nottambuli
Scesi con me per strada   30
              da un quadro
visto una volta, perso
di vista, rincorso tra altrui reminiscenze
o soltanto sognato.
         ('Addio Lugano bella', in *SV*, pp. 197–8)

      [uncertain
mountains, transitory lakes (*like me,*
howling ecstatically at hillsides in bloom?
false-flowering, an hour
of sun will defrost them),   25
[…]
Sleepwalking gentlemen go stately there
descending by road with me   30
              out of a picture
seen just once, lost
sight of, searched for amid others' memories
or dreamed only.]

    In Sereni's poem, the phantasm of the self barely takes shape before dissolving again. It almost completely fuses with the landscape to the point at which the two become indistinguishable, but is not permitted complete identification with it (note the question mark in line 23). The uncertainty that was the mark of the liminal or threshold subject, discussed in the previous chapter, again rears its head. In Petrarchan fashion, the self, howling with ecstasy at the flowering hills, constructs its voice in dialogue with the space of the idyll, but finds that voice, and its own appeal, misdirected, just as the poem has opened with the failed imploration to the Other to recognize the 'I''s place within that vision of desire:

        Dovrò cambiare geografie e topografie.
        Non vuole saperne,
        mi rinnega in effigie, rifiuta
        lo specchio di me (di noi) che le tendo.
        Ma io non so che farci *se la strada*   5
        mi si snoda di sotto
        come una donna (come lei?)
        con giusta impudicizia.

[I'll have to change landscapes and places.
She doesn't want to know,
denies me in effigy, refuses
the mirror of me (of us) I offer.
But I don't know what to do *if the road*   5
unwinds beneath me
like a woman (like her?)
with proper shamelessness.]

In Sereni's poem, the *congedo* in a sense comes too early, and already at the beginning it as though the 'I' ought to be leaving the space he is just about to enter. Instead, like the Petrarchan subject, he remains fixed at the point at which he becomes undone, unravelling along the road of desire that leads nowhere. By the end (ll. 29–33), the subject has described his departure from the picture (which is also the poem), out of which he walks, descending, but he has not relinquished the image (his 'idolo', if you like), which continues to plague him in his being unable to place it.

The experience might be only a dream, or something sought in the alienating place between ('*tra*') the memories of an Other/another's memories ('*altrui* reminiscenze', l. 32) which the 'I' cannot claim as its own. In Sereni's poem, like in Petrarch's, the identity of the phantasm extends to cover both subject *and* object of desire, but whereas Petrarch's subject effectively embraces the ambivalence of the idyll as the paradoxical path to recovering the phantasm of the lost object preserved deep inside the self, Sereni finds himself exiled from that space from the beginning, and facing a double loss (both of the previously desired object, now absent even as memory or image, and the present emptiness of the 'I' that is completely filled in the pursuit of its own image and thus leaves no space for anything else). In both poems, the subject is ultimately alone; only in Sereni's has it completely lost the other term against which to measure the self's solitude.

Thus, despite Sereni's assertion to the contrary in 'Petrarca, nella sua finzione', 'Chiedo scusa per avere divagato autobiograficamente, almeno in parte, sul paesaggio, sullo sfondo e il contorno' [I apologize for having strayed partially autobiographically onto the landscape, its background, and contours] (p. 129), it is precisely in his attraction to the topographical detail of Petrarch's *RVF* that his approach becomes autobiographical in essence. Landscape becomes charged with fetishistic value when, mixing memory and desire;[21] it becomes the symbolic substitute for the disguising of a loss that is real:

---

[21] From T. S. Eliot's *The Waste Land*, ll. 1–4, 'April is the cruellest month, breeding | Lilacs out of the dead land, mixing | Memory and desire, stirring | Dull roots with spring

Arrivavo a Luino per via stradale una certa volta dopo molti anni che mancavo. Adesso so bene a partire da che punto, non il presentimento, ma la presenza fisica di Luino comincia a rivelarsi nella sua identità concreta. Sempre da allora scocca immancabile a quel punto un verso del Petrarca, che non è il caso di citare qui. Ma il tuffo al cuore non si produce sempre allo stesso modo: a volte è rimprovero, a volte rassegnazione, altre volte impeto di irruzione in un paesaggio come se fosse nuovo. Fatti miei? eh sì, purtroppo, fatti miei; *idoli, che qualcuno potrà anche chiamare feticci.* Diciamo: *idoli della memoria*.[22]

[I reached Luino by road, one time, after an absence of many years. Now I know well at which point not the presentiment, but the physical presence of Luino, begins to make itself felt in its concrete identity. Always, from then on, at that point, a line from Petrarch—which it would be inappropriate to cite here—unfailingly comes to mind. But the sudden dive of the heart doesn't always occur in the same way: sometimes it comes as a reproach, sometimes as resignation, sometimes as the wish to burst onto the landscape as though it were new. Something particular to me? Yes, alas: *idols, which others might call fetishes.* Let's say: *idols of memory.*]

Sereni's 'idoli' bear the memory of Petrarch's own 'idolo' of *RVF* XXX, while baring at the same time their status as mere fetishes: a displaced and fragmentary seat of desire still purporting to be an end in itself. Luino is in a sense Sereni's Vaucluse; yet, as a path back towards the lost or absent object, this intensely personal version of landscape is unpredictable or somehow incomplete. The 'verso del Petrarca' which Sereni does not quote here is likely to be that which he does include in 'Petrarca, nella sua finzione' (p. 132) when talking about Petrarch's 'paesaggio amato e rivisitato irrevocabilmente illividire, incenerire, svuotarsi' [loved and revisited landscape irrevocably turning leaden, ashen, emptied], from *RVF* CCCXX (5–6, 14), 'Sento l'aura mia anticha' [I feel the old breeze], where the emphasis is on the interval between a fleeting vision of the fuller landscape of desire of the past ('i dolci colli | veggio apparire, *onde* 'l bel lume nacque [. . .]' [see appearing the sweet hills *where* the light was born [. . .]], (ll. 1–2) and the perception of its present emptiness, which is also the now empty experience of desire itself:

> O caduche speranze, o penser' folli!   5
> Vedove l'erbe e torbide son l'acque,

---

rain', in *Selected Poems* (London: Faber and Faber, 1975), pp. 49–74 (p. 51). Interestingly these entities again emerge from within landscape, just as Sereni's own version of that formula, 'Memoria che ancora hai desideri' [Memory you still have desires], is embedded within the context of a return to Bocca di Magra, first in 'Gli squali' ['The Sharks'] (p. 116), then reproduced as the incipit to Part III of *Un posto* (p. 227).

[22] Sereni, 'Negli anni di Luino' [In the Luino Years], in *ID2*, p. 135.

> [...]
> or vo piangendo il suo cenere sparso.   14

[Oh short-lived hopes, oh mad cares! The grass is bereaved and the waters troubled [...] now I go bewailing the scattering of its ashes].

As lines 7–8 of the sonnet clarify, the 'I' lies in the chamber ('nest'), where Laura once lay, and now lies dead, 'et vòto et freddo è 'l nido in ch'ella giacque | nel qual io vivo, et morto giacer volli'. The widowed landscape of the poem is not just the site of an absence, then, but of a *specific loss*, which instates a cycle of repeated mourning that however remains incomplete. As Robert Pogue Harrison states, Petrarch's poetry gains much of its force and identity from the 'perspective of the mourning voice', but only to the extent that it prolongs grieving, so that the memory of the lost object can be treasured and preserved, and the absence of its earthly referent lamented but not relinquished.[23] Mourning cedes to melancholia and to the 'retaining forever in phantasy what has long since been lost in reality'.[24] The gerund 'vo piangendo', together with the deictic 'now' of line 14 and the emphasis upon the 'scattered ashes' of the subject's passion, now spent, confirm the impossibility of rediscovering the totality or wholeness he seeks. But they also betray the fact that the poem is born from that desire *as lack* and cultivates it as its ambiguous but precious source of the images and memories it can still hold onto.

Sereni draws most upon the melancholy traits of the Petrarchan subject, and in *SU* he appropriates the last line of Petrarch's poem as a mark of the waning force of his poetic vision and the scattered ashes of a 'vainly' sown desire, viewed as beyond hope. This increased negativity is evident in 'Sopra un'immagine sepolcrale' ['On a Cemetery Photograph'], which concludes with the line, 'E quante lagrime e seme *vanamente sparso*' [And how much seed, what tears *vainly shed*] (p. 168), and in 'Le ceneri' ['The Ashes'], which presents a landscape that is like Petrarch's widowed, but without the compensatory store of (poetic) memory to preserve even a shadow of fullness:

> Che aspetto io qui girandomi per casa,
> che s'alzi un qualche vento
> di novità a muovermi la penna
> e m'apra a una speranza?

---

[23] Robert Pogue Harrison *The Body of Beatrice* (Baltimore, Md.: Johns Hopkins University Press, 1988), p. 101.
[24] See Esther Sánchez-Pardo's account of melancholia in her *Cultures of the Death Drive: Melanie Klein and Modernist Melancholia* (Durham, NC: Duke University Press, 2003), p. 53. The Serenian subject also increasingly moves toward melancholia, as discussed in the chapter that follows.

> Nasce invece una pena senza pianto 5
> né oggetto, che una luce
> per sé di verità da sé presume
> —e appena è un bianco giorno e mite di fine inverno.
> Che spero io più smarrito tra le cose:
> *Troppe ceneri sparge attorno a sé la noia,* 10
> la gioia quando c'è basta a sé sola.
>
> <div align="right">(In <i>SU</i>, p. 119)</div>
>
> [What am I waiting for turning round the house,
> for some breath of fresh air
> to lift then set my pen in motion
> and open me up to a hope?
>
> Instead a pain without lament 5
> or object's born, which a light
> of truth in itself from itself presumes
> —and it's barely a mild white day at winter's end.
>
> What do I hope for more lost among things.
> *Too much ash scatters boredom round itself,* 10
> joy when it's here in itself is enough.]

With no primordial vision left against which to measure its present loss or fall, even the status of the lost object is put in doubt, resulting in a 'pena senza pianto | né oggetto': the loss of a loss, or the loss of loss itself. That lack permeates the subject and his poem until he assumes the place of the object, 'io *più smarrito tra le cose*' (l. 9), and declares himself in a realm apart from joy or the hope of recovery. The ashes that 'noia' scatters around itself are the fragments of poetry expended in the endless search for a totality which always remains beyond them.

This brings us to the most suggestive of Sereni's definitions of what the memory of Petrarch represents in poetic terms. Concluding 'Petrarca, nella sua finzione', he states:

> Ancora oggi, se penso a un autore che più consenta di cogliere la poesia allo stato puro, di dare fugacemente un volto a quest'altro fantasma che è la poesia, penso per istinto al Petrarca. Ma anche questo istinto—lo riconosco—è viziato, tanto che un moto successivo porterebbe a sopprimere il discorso ora accennato. La poesia, voglio dire, non esiste, come non esiste il suo fantasma. Esiste questa o quella poesia, cioè esistono i suoi testi. (p. 145)

> [Still today, if I think of an author who most allows us to appreciate poetry in its pure state, to fleetingly give a face to this other phantasm that is poetry, I instinctively think of Petrarch. But this instinct too—I know—is vitiated to the extent that a later feeling would suppress the discourse to which I just alluded. Poetry, I mean to say, doesn't exist, nor does its phantasm exist. Only this or that poem exists, i.e. its texts exist.]

So the memory of Petrarch comes to reside in the space between the loss of, and nostalgia for, a myth of Poetry with a capital 'P'. In Sereni's own universe—in which that myth is problematically elusive—Petrarch's memory is merely disseminated from one text into another, without ever wholly claiming that territory as its own or being able to inhabit it completely. If Sereni's own versions of the phantasm can only be dismembered versions of the more compact and unified phantasms of the *RVF* played upon a single figure—Laura—then this is surely a sign also of a diminishing faith in the power of poetry itself to establish (an image of) wholeness. Locating the identity of poetry in the relationship between desire, word, and phantasm—which in the poetry of the Middle Ages constituted a powerful nexus that could incorporate the desired object (inevitably situated elsewhere) within its bounds[25]—but dissolving any unity between them, Sereni simultaneously affirms his distance from that concept of poetry as fulfilment or utopia.

The section of *SV* entitled *Traducevo Char* [*Translating Char*] is emblematic of this creative, intertextual tension, and of the fact that, by the time we reach the later phase of Sereni's production, there is no unmediated access to a mythicized (lyric) past. It shows how in Sereni's poetry of this period, his discourse has adapted to include a plurality of voices and a split subjectivity, which sit uneasily with the traditionally monologic lyric 'I' generally considered to derive from the Petrarchan heritage, still however conjured in the negative spaces left by its retreat from the poem. As the subject returns to the landscape of Vaucluse conjured through the Charian–Petrarchan dyad inherent in translating Char, he encounters again that original tension between desire for possession/belonging and the decantation (to recall Isella's term) of a firmly poetic reality.

Poems 'I' and 'IV' of the series are exemplary cases. Each bears the trace of the passage of the medieval author through Sereni's text, in poem 'I' via the designation of the 'falcate pulverolente | che una primavera dietro sé sollevano' [dust-covered strides | that raise a spring behind them], and in 'IV' with the final evocation of a landscape of desire which carries the (albeit distant) mark of Petrarch's 'disiata forma vera' [longed-for true form] of *RVF* XVI, 'È a un'ora di marcia | al sole dell'altra provincia | *la forma desiderata*' [It's an hour's march away | in the other province's sun | *the desiderated form*]. Moreover, in poem 'IV', the landscape actually

---

[25] See Giorgio Agamben, *Stanze: la parola e il fantasma nella cultura occidentale* (Turin: Einaudi, 1977), esp. Part III, Chapter VI, 'La "gioi che mai non fina"', pp. 146–55 (p. 152); in English as *Stanzas: Word and Phantasm in Western Culture*, trans. Ronald L. Martinez (Minneapolis: University of Minnesota Press, 1993), from which translations are taken.

speaks in a Petrarchan way of its haunted status, but with a voice that importantly also carries the memory of Leopardi and the *topoi* of the Romantic heritage, from which it cannot be extricated:

> [...]
> con *discorsi di siepi*
> *vaneggianti* tra setole e velluti
> scricchiolii di porte
> appena schiuse rimpalli
> d'echi gibigianne cucù.
> [...]
> ('Villaggio verticale' ['Vertical Village'], ll. 4–8, p. 242)[26]
>
> [with *the speech of hedges*
> *raving* among brambles and velvets,
> creaking of doors
> barely open, rebounding
> of *echoes, mirror gleams, cuckoos.*]

'Villaggio verticale'—a fourteen-line poem, divided into two strophes of eight and six, of which line 5 is one of only two hendecasyllables—thus conjures the ghost of Petrarch and Leopardi while simultaneously establishing itself as a kind of spectre of a sonnet, whose total form (whether desired or not) is therefore always elsewhere, and never wholly present in the text. Instead, Sereni's poem situates meaning in the gap between desire and fulfilment—or between memory and desire. The 'villaggio verticale' responds to the 'dubbio di un disguido' [fear of misunderstanding] (l. 2) with only a further dispersal or scattering of an elusive point of origin, which puts the locus of totality or wholeness only further out of reach and holds the dream of the poem in abeyance. The disproportion between what the subject seeks from the (poetic) landscape and what is given it in return leads me to make the assertion that in Sereni we are dealing with poetry as desire-space:

> On each occasion desire, announced at the outset as a term in search of a definition, is conscientiously removed from view during the defining process: it is not a state or a motion but a space, and not a unified space but a split and distorted one. Need and demand are its co-ordinates but they

---

[26] 'Vaneggiando' revisits Petrarch's own *vaneggiare* [raving] that the reader memorably encounters in *RVF* I, putting the entire collection under the sign of shame, 'et del mio vaneggiar vergogna è il frutto' [and of my raving, shame is the fruit] (l. 12). It recurs in *RVF* XXXII, LXII, CCXLIV, and CCLXX. The Leopardian intertexts refer predominantly to the *idillio minore* [minor idyll], 'L'infinito', Sereni's rewriting of which—'Non sovrumani spazi qui...' [No more-than-human spaces here...] (reproduced in full on pp. 800–1 of the critical appendix to Sereni's *Poesie*)—generated two other poems in *SV* besides this one: *Traducevo Char* 'I', and 'VIII'.

cannot be co-ordinated. It is a dimension in which the subject is always destined to travel too far or not far enough, in which any 'above' is always a new 'below', and in which each anticipated moment of plenitude brings with it a new vacancy. Desire-space is not just mobile and unmappable by the subject: it is a place of permanent catastrophe.[27]

The disorienting place of the phantasm

The quality of the phantasm as it emerges in the poems from Petrarch and Sereni just analysed bears a striking resemblance to Laplanche's and Pontalis's theoretical formulation of it in their study, *Fantasme originaire: Fantasmes des origines, origines du fantasme*, in which they declare that:

Le fantasme n'est pas l'objet du désir, il est scène. Dans le fantasme, en effet, le sujet ne vise pas l'objet ou son signe, *il figure lui-même pris dans la séquence d'images*. Il ne se représente pas l'objet désiré mais *il est représenté participant à la scène, sans que* [...] *une place puisse lui être assignée*.

Conséquence: tout en étant toujours présent dans le fantasme, le sujet peut y être sous une forme désubjectivée, c'est-à-dire dans la syntaxe même de la séquence en question.[28]

[Fantasy, however, is not the object of desire, but its setting. In fantasy the subject does not pursue the object or its sign: *he appears caught up himself in the sequence of images*. He forms no representation of the desired object, *but is himself represented as participating in the scene although* [...] *he cannot be assigned any fixed place in it* [...].

As a result, the subject, although always present in the fantasy, may be so in desubjectivized form, that is to say, in the very syntax of the sequence in question.]

As a result, the primary function of the phantasm is that of a *mise en scène* of desire (p. 74). Projected into the space of the phantasm (which Sereni designates in 'Petrarca, nella sua finzione' as the poetic locus of the 'paese *immateriale*' [*immaterial* realm]), the 'I' finds itself caught up in an alienating spectacle (reminiscent of Lacan's scopic drive) that would render it more divided than it already is and sets it only further apart from its desired object. Since the phantasm stands for the desiring self, as much as a true Other, the experience of desire that it foregrounds is one of

---

[27] Malcolm Bowie, *Lacan* (London: Fontana, 1991), pp. 137–8.
[28] Jean Laplanche and J. B. Pontalis, *Fantasme originaire: fantasmes des origines, origines du fantasme* (Paris: Hachette, 1985), p. 74. English translations are taken from Laplanche and Pontalis, 'Fantasy and the Origins of Sexuality', in *Formations of Fantasy*, ed. Victor Burgin, James Donald, and Cora Kaplan (London: Methuen, 1986), pp. 5–34. While 'fantasme' is translated here as 'fantasy', in French it does also carry the meaning of 'phantasm'.

a (radical) splitting of the subject, and its dissemination along a syntax of desire as expropriation. Where no position is assigned for it, it is inevitably misplaced: lacking or in excess of its proper place. As we saw in the discussion of the origins of the speaking subject in Chapter 1, the phenomenon of 'fading' through which it passes is intrinsically bound up with the birth of the phantasm: the 'splitting' [*Spaltung*] that constitutes the speaking subject in its subordination to the signifier.[29] Discussing the identity of the phantasm in these terms, Lacan writes:

> Disons, pour révéler la métaphore du Damourette et Pichon sur le moi grammatical en l'appliquant à un sujet auquel elle est mieux destinée, que le fantasme est proprement l'"étoffe' de ce Je qui se trouve primordialement refoulé de n'être indicable que dans le 'fading' de l'énonciation.[30]
>
> [Let us say, borrowing the metaphor used by Damourette and Pichon about the grammatical 'I' and applying it to a subject to which it is better suited, that the phantasy is really the 'stuff' of the 'I' that is originally repressed, because it can be indicated only in the 'fading' of the enunciation.]

The parallel between this designation, and Petrarch's consciousness of what in the *RVF* he terms his 'venir meno' is striking:

> Le treccie d'òr che devrien fare il sole
> d'invidia molta ir pieno,
> e 'l bel guardo sereno,
> ove i raggi d'Amor sí caldi sono
> *che mi fanno anzi tempo venir meno,*
> *et l'accorte parole,*
> rade nel mondo o sole,
> che mi fer già di sé cortese dono,
> *mi son tolte*;
>
> (*RVF* XXXVII, ll. 81–9)[31]
>
> [Those tresses of gold, which ought to make the sun go filled with envy, and that lovely clear gaze where the rays of love are so hot that *they kill me before my time*, and those *skilful words*, rare in the world, or unique, which gave themselves to me so courteously, *are taken from me*;]

This is the revelation of language (and desire) as difference, displacement, and splitting. In the passage from possession to dispossession, and from an emphasis on the Other to the obsession with the deprived self, lies the key

---

[29] Lacan, 'Subversion du sujet' ['The Subversion of the Subject'], in *Écrits* II (Paris: Éditions du Seuil, 1971), p. 296.
[30] Ibid. 297.
[31] See also *RVF* XXIII, XLVII, CVIII, CLXXXIV.

to fathoming Petrarch's concept of desire-space and Sereni's identification with it.

Citing Freud's arguments in 'Three Essays on the Theory of Sexuality', Lynn Enterline notes in her study of desire and mourning in early modern writing that, in relation to the phantasm, 'the "object" found for the subject is "never the same object" as the one that was lost. Between the losing and the "refinding" [...] the object becomes "something else".'[32] In this moment of 'slippage' (which is, in fact, the essential nature of desire), the phantasm assumes the place of the real object (of desire) and functions as a lure (image or screen), concealing the fact that the real object is not there in the first place. The subject gets tied up in knots pursuing the phantasm which never in fact leads him any closer to his real aim or target, but rather eternalizes the desire of which it is itself symptom and expression:

> L'"accesa voglia', il 'gran desio', il 'furor', di cui Petrarca attestava l'autenticità nella lettera al Colonna è dunque insieme *il movente* della parola, *l'oggetto* della parola, e *l'ostacolo* della parola: il 'dire', le 'rime' del *Canzoniere* saranno chiamate a colmare passo per passo, punto per punto, la mancanza che le sottende e le genera: la doppia mancanza dell'oggetto del desiderio (Laura, l'irraggiungibile, ma anche l'indicibile, nel sottrarsi della parola stessa che la dice) e del soggetto desiderante.[33]
>
> [The 'burning want', the 'great desire', the 'furore', to whose authenticity Petrarch attested in his letter to Colonna is thus simultaneously the *mover* of the word, *the object* of the word, and the *obstacle* to the word: step by step, stage by stage, the 'speech', the 'poems' of the *Canzoniere* are called upon to fill the absence that underscores and generates them—the double absence of the object of desire (Laura, the unreachable, but also the unsayable, in the subtraction of the word itself that speaks her) and the desiring subject.]

Returning to the memory of Petrarch's *RVF* XXX, we can appreciate the enclosure within the self of the image, which this implies, and the folding inwards of the subject's speech to the point at which inside and outside no longer figure, since the 'I' is only really addressing itself, 'L'idéal, si l'on peut dire, de l'auto-érotisme, ce sont "des lèvres qui se baisent elles-mêmes": *ici*, dans cette jouissance apparemment fermée sur soi, comme au plus profond du fantasme, *ce discours qui ne s'adresse plus à personne, tout répartition du sujet et objet est aboli*' [The ideal, one might

---

[32] Lynn Enterline, *The Tears of Narcissus: Melancholia and Masculinity in Early Modern Writing* (Stanford, Calif.: Stanford University Press, 1995), p. 30.
[33] Adelia Noferi, "Il *Canzoniere* del Petrarca: scrittura del desiderio e desiderio dellla scrittura', in *Il gioco delle tracce: studi su Dante, Petrarca, Bruno, il neo-classicismo, Leopardi, l'informale* (Florence: La Nuova Italia, 1979), pp. 43–67 (p. 52).

say, of auto-eroticism is 'lips that kiss themselves'. *Here*, in this apparently self-centred enjoyment, as in the deepest fantasy, in *this discourse no longer addressed to anyone, all distinction between subject and object has been lost*].[34]

In this space, which again dovetails with Sereni's conception of the 'paese' [realm] of the phantasm in Petrarch's *RVF*, subject and object completely fuse so as to become indistinguishable, as each dissolves into the phantasm of poetry. This is the ultimate, but also extreme (utmost) space of the lyric: what Sereni will refer to, in *SV*, as 'il belvedere di non ritorno' [belvedere of no return] ('Il poggio' ['The Knoll']):

> Quel che di qui si vede
> —mi sentite?—
> dal belvedere di non ritorno
> —ombre di campagne scale
> naturali e che rigoglio
> di acque che lampi che fiammate
> di colori che tavole imbandite—
> e quanto di voi di qui si vede
> e non sapete
> quanto più ci state.
>
> (p. 257)
>
> [What there is to see from here
> —you hear me?—from
> the belvedere of no return
> —shadows of countrysides
> natural stairs and what waters'
> bubbling, what flashes, what blazes,
> of colours, what tables well laid—
> is how much of you there's to see from here
> and none of you know
> how much longer you'll remain.]

One cannot help but hear an echo of Zanzotto's commentary of Petrarch's 'Che fai? Che pensi?' ['What are you doing? What are you thinking?'] (*RVF* CCLXXIII), in which he states that 'l'esperienza del *Canzoniere* si risolve in questi interrogativi che possono avere mille risposte ma sono destinate a rientrare in un'unica non risposta' [The experience of the *Canzoniere* resolves itself in these interrogatives that can receive a thousand responses but are destined to culminate in a single non-response].[35] In the failure of poetry to utter a response and the unanswered

---

[34] Laplanche and Pontalis, *Fantasme originaire*, pp. 72–3.
[35] Andrea Zanzotto, 'Petrarca fra il palazzo e la cameretta' (1976), in *Fantasie di avvicinamento* (Milan: Mondadori, 1991), pp. 261–71 (p. 264).

question that lingers over the whole of Sereni's poem, which contaminates the idyll and its memory, lie the spaces in the text where the spectre of Petrarch is both conjured and dissolved.

PLACES IN MEMORY: DEIXIS AT PHANTASMA AND THE QUESTION OF ENABLING ABSENCE

If landscape is the scene of the subject's creation myth and its fall, it is poetic language that allows us to map its trajectory in the poem. Having established the nature of Petrarch's legacy for Sereni in terms of the memory of the poetic place in which language, landscape, and phantasm meet, it is a question of determining how that realm comes to be established (or to interpose itself) in Sereni's own work. Again, deixis holds the key. As the figure opening up the possibility of establishing poetic presence as a (symbolic/poetic) surrogate of the lost object, while simultaneously foregrounding the fragility of the position of the speaking subject in relation to that object, deixis embodies the quintessential traits of the phantasm as a *mise en scène* of desire.

Making the absent memorable

As was explained in Chapter 2, Enrico Testa, in '*Sur la corde de la voix*', distinguishes between two distinct but complementary functions of deixis which he defines respectively as the 'funzione enunciativa' and the 'funzione astanziale'. Whereas the first category of deictic reference emphasizes its discursive context, and is used to foreground the speaking subject engaged in the present instance of discourse, the second category centres upon instances in which the discourse situation is merely imagined or remembered and in which the subject enjoys a unique ability to create presence from absence.[36]

The word 'astanziale', like the word 'fantasma' (from the Greek *phàntasma*), has its primary meaning in terms of a 'making present and visible' and putting the object 'within reach of' (literally 'next to' from 'ad' + 'stante') the subject. The function of this mode of deixis is thus to bring the absent object back within reach by situating it within a conceivable and perceptible location, so that, for example, it appears as 'là' [there], rather than 'al di là' [beyond/elsewhere] and tends always to be configured,

---

[36] See Enrico Testa, '*Sur la corde de la voix*: funzione della deissi nel testo poetico', in *Linguistica, pragmatica e testo letterario*, ed. Umberto Rapallo (Genova: Il Melangolo, 1996), pp. 113–46 (p. 129).

as deictics inevitably are, from the point of view of the subject at the centre of that universe.[37]

Karl Bühler draws these different strands together in a comprehensive study of what he calls deixis at phantasma ('at phantasma' also being translated as 'in the imagination'). He endeavours to explain why when we are called upon to orient ourselves, or another person or thing, within a purely imagined or fictional space, we still have recourse to deictic words normally reserved for standard situational deixis which always works on the basis of addresser and addressee having a shared context, especially a shared visual perspective:

> He who is led by phantasma cannot follow the arrow of the speaker's outstretched arm and pointed finger with his gaze to find the something out *there*; he cannot use the spatial origin quality of the voice's sound, to find the place of a speaker who says *here*; the voice character of an absent speaker saying *I* also does not belong to written language. And still, a rich variety of these and other deictic words are offered to one in vivid accounts of absent objects and by absent narrators.[38]

Looking at this category of deixis in more detail, it becomes clear why, as Bertone specifies (pp. 132–3), deictics are so prominent in Western literature and why they can be seen to be the measure of the desiring subject—a mark of how that subject is able to forge a relationship to the object of desire conceived of as absent or missing. When Bühler states that deixis at phantasma is reserved for the realms of the 'memorable absent' or 'constructive imagination' (p. 22), he is really talking about an absence that can be made memorable by its (poetic) treatment: guaranteed recuperation by the way in which the phantasm is processed.

This 'mimesis of the absent', as Bühler calls it (p. 23), depends upon being able to fix oneself and one's object at the privileged point in which memory, imagination, and desire intersect to ensure the endurance of the image (Petrarch's 'imagine') or phantasm (Sereni). As we have already seen, for both poets this auspicious site is almost always synonymous with a place, a locus to which they constantly, and often obsessively, return: where the subject literally fixes itself in the hope that the poetic miracle will take effect and the lost object will come back into view. Sharing several properties with the fetish in Freud's conception, these fetishized

---

[37] As Keith Green states, 'There is a centre of orientation in deixis that is inevitably egocentric', 'Deixis and the Poetic Persona', *Language and Literature* 1.1 (1992), pp. 121–34 (p. 122).

[38] 'The Deictic Field of Language and Deictic Words', in *Speech, Place and Action: Studies in Deixis and Related Topics*, ed. Robert J. Jarvella and Wolfgang Klein (Chichester: Wiley, 1982), pp. 13–30 (p. 23) (italics in the original).

places (or objects associated with them in symbolic fashion—Petrarch's 'aura' [breeze], 'colli' [hills], or 'erba' [grass] for example—are conjured precisely to maintain a connection with the object of desire that the subject is not yet ready to give up (mourn).[39] These places work fetishistically because they preserve the all-important relationship to the lost object intact whilst testifying to the fact that they are in themselves only part-objects (or in this case part-places), finally unable to restore that object fully to presence: 'A symbolic substitute—and symptom of a culturally demanded renunciation only nominally accepted—the fetish works by contradiction: it both affirms and denies the traumatic loss that it replaces (and preserves).'[40]

Moreover, this topographic or orientational approach, whereby the phantasm appears at a particular point within the imagined scene, brings it to life far more vividly than if it were to appear un-grounded, and lends it a naturalism that brings it closer to the 'real' object that it substitutes. As Bühler explains when discussing these situation phantasms, which often occupy a space of half-sleep or waking-dream so common to Sereni's *SU* and *SV*:

> What is being imagined, in particular if it is something movable like human beings, often comes to us, that is, into the indicated perceptual order-schema, and there, it may be, if not actually 'seen', then still localized. Results on eidetic imagery have taught us that there are multifarious nuances between the normal perception with the body's eye and the normal appearance of the object of imagination before the so-called mind's eye. But these nuances are programmatically less interesting than the simple fact that the imagined object appearing in the normal (non-eidetic) way before the mind's eye also may have a place before, beside, or behind me and directly among the objects in the room in which I find myself, the objects which I partly perceive, partly imagine.[41]

---

[39] See Freud's 'Three Essays on the Theory of Sexuality' (1905), in *SE* VII (1953), pp. 125–245, in which fetishism is discussed under the broader subject of 'Deviations in Respect of the Sexual Aim'. Particularly relevant passages for our discussion with respect to fetishized landscapes include the definition of the fetish as 'what is substituted for the sexual object is some part of the body (such as the foot or the hair) [...], *or some inanimate object which bears an assignable relation to the person whom it replaces* and preferably to that person's sexuality' (p. 153), and Freud's comment that 'in other cases *the replacement of the object by fetish is determined by a symbolic connection of thought*, of which the person concerned is usually not conscious' (p. 155).

[40] Lynn Enterline, 'Embodied Voices: Petrarch Reading (Himself Reading) Ovid', in *Desire in the Renaissance: Psychoanalysis and Literature*, ed. Valeria Finucci and Regina Schwartz (Princeton: Princeton University Press, 1994), pp. 120–45 (p. 129).

[41] 'The Deictic Field', p. 28.

Returning to the definition of the phantasm as the *mise en scène* of desire, it becomes clear the extent to which that *mise en scène* incorporates a linguistic mode that is deictic in essence. The purpose of deixis at phantasma is to allow the speaking 'I' to place itself and give its object a place in a scene that otherwise risks being a disconcerting proliferation of fleeting images. In several poems by Petrarch and Sereni, landscape appears to be born from the phantasm and not vice versa. However, deixis at phantasma would seek to create the illusion of the pre-existence of a place and a point of origin (of desire) to bolster the self's own substance.

As Harrison states in relation to the deictic force of the language of the *RVF*, 'Withdrawing from the realm of transcendent exteriority, Petrarch seeks to constitute lyric presence from within rather than without. [. . .] A lyric topology is founded upon an ideal present tense of vocalization' [i.e. the deictic present].[42] The phantasm foregrounds this miraculous force of the lyric, but also the fact that the presence is illusory and lasts only as long as the utterance can sustain itself in the here and now. Petrarch celebrates this poetic ambiguity and its extreme lyric potential, but also recognizes its perils. His emphasis upon finding the 'immagine vera' [*true* image] of Laura (*RVF* CXXVI, l. 60) is a sign of his awareness of the dangerously self-referential quality of the landscape and his desire to recover something of the Other that is true, which could appear to pre-exist the moment in which the (poetic) phantasm comes to be. As we have already seen, Sereni appears already to have relinquished that search, and his poetry articulates instead a state in which the very identity of the originally lost object is put in doubt, with emphasis falling more upon the subject that pursues its own phantasm of itself.

Petrarch and Sereni: a map of desire[43]

Taking this notion of landscape as a *mise en scène* of desire that implicates the subject as much as his object, Sereni is thus led to revisit the poetic heart of the Petrarchan idyll and to redefine it on his own terms. While in 'Petrarca, nella sua finzione', he gives priority to Petrarch's so-called *rime in morte* [poems written after the death of Laura], I believe that the greatest consonance between his poetry and the *RVF* actually resides in his memory of the 'luogo ideale' of the *rime in vita* [poems written during

---

[42] Harrison, *The Body of Beatrice*, pp. 96, 101.
[43] I borrow this notion of a map of desire from Elena Lombardi's analysis of the structures of desire underpinning Dante's *Commedia*, in *The Syntax of Desire: Language and Love in Augustine, the Modistae, Dante* (Toronto: University of Toronto Press, 2007), pp. 160–74.

the life of Laura] which finds its apex in two canzoni that take Vaucluse as their setting, 'Se 'l pensier che mi strugge' ['If the care that torments me'] (CXXV) and 'Chiare, fresche et dolci acque' ['Clear, fresh, sweet waters'] (CXXVI).[44] The attraction that they hold for him would appear to be both formal and thematic. As Barolini has stated, 'the canzone is the closest approximation to narrative in a lyric universe': for Sereni it potentially represents a more discursive and dialogic form than the sonnet; it covers greater ground in terms of experience and psychology, and includes a sometimes quite protracted self-questioning that mirrors his poetic attitude more closely.[45]

In addition, canzoni CXXV and CXXVI both embody the perennial tensions underlying Petrarch's particular conceptualization of desire and poetry, and form part of a series of canzoni which map, topographically, the effects upon the subject of a kind of spatialization of desire. Summarizing the effects of the sequence upon the writing subject, Barolini writes: 'the series takes the poet from the brink of escape in 125, to actual ec-stasis in 126, where momentarily the turning-back mechanism places him outside the temporal continuum, only to return him to the adamantine chains of time and narrative in 127, 128 and 129.'[46]

It is this spatialization, or what Bertone defines as '[l]'estetizzazione della soggetività' [the aestheticization of subjectivity] (p. 98), that I want to argue Sereni takes as the structural model for his own articulation of his landscape of desire. Reading Petrarch's canzoni CXXV and CXXVI against Sereni's 'Ancora sulla strada di Zenna' ['On the Zenna Road Again'] and 'Luino-Luvino', in which the relationship between landscape and phantasm reaches its height, allows us to measure the scope of that legacy and its impact upon the architecture of Sereni's lyric subject.

This desire-space comes to the fore in Sereni's dialogue with the Petrarchan subject who returns time and again to the locus of his 'original' encounter with Laura in Vaucluse.[47] Paradoxically for a poem constructed

---

[44] It should be noted that these titles for the two parts of the *RVF*, while in use since some time in the fifteenth century, do not exactly correspond to Petrarch's own division between poems I–CCLXIII and CCLXIV–CCCLXVI (in which Laura's death is only registered in *RVF* CCLXVII).

[45] Barolini, 'The Making of a Lyric Sequence: Time and Narrative in Petrarch's *Rerum vulgarium fragmenta*', *MLN* 104.1, Italian Issue (Jan. 1989), pp. 1–38 (p. 25).

[46] Ibid. As Barolini notes, ec-stasis means more than mere rapture: meaning as it does 'out of place' (histanai) and 'out of time' (stasis).

[47] In a letter (*Familiares* 2.9) to his friend Giacomo Colonna, defending Laura as a real woman against doubts that she was merely an allegory of the poetic laurel, Petrarch places the first sighting of her in the church of St Clare in Avignon. However, within the poetic universe of the *RVF*, Petrarch often transposes the vision to Vaucluse, which is privileged as the locus of the original encounter with the beloved. For further discussion of the elusive quality of the 'history' of Petrarch's love for Laura, see Peter Hainsworth, *Petrarch the Poet:*

on the basis of the memory of the *locus amoenus* as the site of a primary vision of Laura, canzone CXXV begins with what is effectively a negation of landscape. Either it is the empty space hollowed out by the speaking 'I''s 'pie' lassi' [weary feet] (l. 8) as he wanders 'per campagne et per colli' [through fields and across hills] (l. 9) in search of his beloved, or the privileged locus—still occupied by Love, 'ove si siede a l'ombra' [where he is sitting in the shade] (l. 22)—from which he is exiled. Whereas for the Middle Ages, as Paul Zumthor has stated, 'da nessuna parte c'è luogo senza presenza' [there can be no place without presence], for Petrarch almost the opposite is true: 'per lui il luogo può essere saturato da un'assenza o divenire astratto, farsi—dolorosamente, come in una nascita—spazio in rapporto a una spazialità generale, infinita e autonoma' [for him, places can be saturated by absence or become abstract, become— painfully, like at birth—spaces in relation to a broader spatiality, both infinite and autonomous].[48] Sereni is the heir to this legacy, recognizing Petrarch's modernity in conceiving of space in this way.

This potentially infinite but bewildering space/place as it emerges in *RVF* CXXV is that of the genesis of desire and language on the basis of an original act of loss/splitting. In fact the first four stanzas of the poem are all marked by an inherent negativity, with the speaking subject twice abandoned: by Laura, and by his own poetic voice. His only way out of the impasse is to entrust his voice to the landscape: the 'verde riva' [green shore] of the Sorgue, which, through one of Sereni's favourite tropes, prosopopoeia, is called upon to amplify his sighs, ensuring their afterlife. Combined with the adverb 'sempre' [always] (l. 51), Petrarch's linguistic gesture indicates the extension he seeks to give his voice in the landscape, and proves to be a highly effective, if somewhat ambiguous, path to harnessing the phantasmatic power of poetic discourse, which could stand in for the 'dolci rime leggiadre' the poet once possessed the power to create (in the first flushes of love), but has lost along the way and wants to rediscover:

> Dolci rime leggiadre
> che nel primiero assalto
> d'Amor usai, quand'io non ebbi altr'arme,
> chi verrà mai che squadre   30

An Introduction to the 'Rerum vulgarium fragmenta' (London: Routledge, 1988), pp. 108–18, and Robert M. Durling's introduction to *Petrarch's Lyric Poems* (Cambridge, Mass.: Harvard University Press, 1976), pp. 1–33 (pp. 4–7).

[48] See Bertone, 'Gli occhi di Laura, i passi di Francesco', p. 142, n. 22. The text he cites is Paul Zumthor, *La mesure du monde: représentation de l'espace au Moyen Âge* (Paris: Éditions du Seuil, 1993).

> questo mio cor di smalto
> ch'almen com'io solea possa sfogarme?
> [...]
> Come fanciul ch'a pena 40
> volge la lingua et snoda,
> che dir non sa, ma 'l più tacer gli è noia,
> cosí 'l desir mi mena
> a dire, et vo' che m'oda
> la dolce mia nemica anzi ch'io moia. 45
> Se forse ogni sua gioia
> nel suo bel viso è solo,
> et di tutt'altro è schiva,
> odil tu, verde riva,
> e presta a' miei sospiri sí largo volo, 50
> che sempre si ridica
> come tu m'eri amica.

[Sweet graceful rhymes that I used in the first assault of Love, when I had no other arms;

who will ever come who can shatter the stone about my heart, so that at least I can pour myself forth as I used to do? [...]

Like a child who can hardly move and untangle his tongue, who is not able to speak but hates to be silent any longer,

thus desire leads me to speak, and I wish my sweet enemy to hear me before I die.

If, perhaps, she takes joy only in her lovely face and flees everything else, do you, green shore, hear it and lend to my sighs so wide a flight that it be always remembered that you were kind to me.]

The restoration of voice that seems imminent at the end of stanza 4 thus turns out to be only the simulated dialogue staged with the 'verde riva' of the river Sorgue, which replaces rather than fulfils the truly desired contact with the beloved, but it is enough to placate the soul (ll. 64–5) and crucially to perform the poetic 'miracle' that takes place in stanza 6:

> *Ovunque* gli occhi volgo
> trovo un dolce sereno
> pensando: *Qui* percosse il vago lume.
> *Qualunque herba o fior colgo*
> credo che *nel terreno* 70
> *aggia radice*, ov'ella ebbe in costume
> gir fra le piagge e 'l fiume,
> et *talor* farsi un seggio
> fresco, fiorito et verde.
> Cosí nulla se 'n perde, 75
> et piú certezza averne fòra il peggio.
> Spirto beato, quale

se', quando altrui fai tale?
[...]

[*Wherever* I turn my eyes, I find a sweet brightness, thinking: '*Here* fell the bright light of her eyes.'
Whatever grass or flower I gather, I believe that it is *rooted in the ground* where she was wont
to walk through the meadows beside the river, and *sometimes* to make herself a seat, fresh, flowering, and green. Thus no part is omitted and to know more exactly would be a loss. Blessed spirit, what are you if you make another become such?]

The 'miracle' of the poem, when it happens, thus draws its force from the deictic strategy that can transform any number of spaces, grasses, or flowers, generic in themselves, into supreme *loci* for containing the memory of Laura. A desire that had risked being groundless can be rooted and any place at all ('ovunque'... 'qualunque') can be made to speak of the passage of the beloved through it so long as it is first appropriated imaginatively and subjectively as such by the 'I'/eye of the speaker. The poetic subject, initially exiled from the landscape, now inhabits it, though only to the extent that he divides it up as he gathers it, so betraying the paradox of his poetic project through the length of the *RVF*. The almost, but not quite, synthetic amalgam of deictic present and memorial/commemorative past historic in '*Qui percosse* il vago lume' (l.68) conserves the tension, as well as indicating the poetic power of a subject who, despite knowing that wholeness is a fantastic mirage born of fetishizing the image of the lost object, still embraces the part as an illusion of its presence.

It is therefore via phantasmatic recreation—the projection of a past history on a present space ('verde riva', the present interlocutor)—that in Leopardian fashion the imprecise and ill-defined provides the blank canvas or screen for the phantasmatic re-investment of a truly empty space, even the rediscovery of perhaps what was never there or never seen in the first place. But where 'nothing is omitted' (l. 65), there is also no space for the consciousness of a split subject and so the speaking 'I' is forced to deny himself as he affirms the Other. As we have seen, for Sereni this is the very essence of the Petrarchan idyll: the tension between fragmentation and unity—or the difference between the *rime sparse* and the *canzoniere*.

As several critics have noted, Petrarch's collection of lyric poems feeds precisely off this tension, and setting *RVF* CXXV alongside *RVF* CXXVI already hints at the extent to which Petrarch simultaneously evokes and diffuses a sense of narrative chronology or progression.[49] The scene with

---

[49] On this see at least Hainsworth, 'History', in *Petrarch the Poet*, pp. 108–18; Giuseppe Mazzotta, 'The *Canzoniere* and the Language of the Self'; and Barolini, 'The Making of a Lyric Sequence'.

which we are presented in 'Chiare, fresche et dolci acque' is essentially unaltered from 'Se 'l pensier' while being at the same time something different. This is already heralded at the start of the poem in the different configuration of the landscape, less on the basis of what is missing, which is rued as so, than on what is still memorially present, and celebrated as such, but which forces the poetic subject to lose himself in the process.

As Stefano Agosti emphasizes, the fetishized objects of Laura in *RVF* CXXVI lead the poet to Paradise, represented spatially in the transition from low to high. Yet, caught as he is in the double-bind which memory itself creates, the poet can only reaffirm that paradisiacal dimension via a return to those same fetishized objects (the trees, grass, and flowers) which are the symbolic ground in which to root the situation phantasms upon which his desire feeds. Since each object or part-object merely points to something which points back to it, the poet cannot reach a totality, even though his fixation to that favourable spot for the emergence of the phantasm—in this case '*questa* herba' [*this* grass]—is absolute:

> Da indi in qua mi piace
> *questa herba* sí, ch'altrove non ò pace.

[From then on *this grass* has pleased me so that elsewhere I have no peace.]

As Agosti notes:

> All'erba, *a questa erba*, indicizzata temporalmente e spazialmente dal mirabile deittico quasi pre-leopardiano, per di più sintomaticamente immune da elisione (*questa herba*), a questo postremo feticcio, metonimico della totalità del luogo ove si è verificato l'evento prodigioso, è affidato dunque proprio il compito opposto rispetto alla sua evidenziata contingenza: quello, ripetiamo, di farsi depositario dell'eternità del desiderio.[50]
>
> [To the grass, to *this grass* and last fetish—temporally and spatially indexed by the marvellous, almost pre-Leopardian deictic, symptomatically immune from elision (*questa herba*) and functioning as a metonymy for the totality of the place where the prodigious event occurred—is therefore entrusted precisely the opposite task to the one apparently in play: that, we repeat, of making itself a repository of the eternity of desire.]

'This grass' is a 'postremo feticcio' because it is the ultimate destination for an errant desire that, to quote Judith Butler on Lacan, 'constantly analogizes the lost object with the present object, and constructs false certainties on the basis of partial similarities', and from which there is no

---

[50] Stefano Agosti, *Gli occhi le chiome: per una lettura psicanalitica del 'Canzoniere' di Petrarca* (Milan: Feltrinelli, 1993), p. 44.

way back (in this poem, the poetic subject goes so far as to imagine himself dead).[51] The problem for the poet is that he has to face the 'altrove' [elsewhere] of desire, even if he would exclude it, since he exists far more in that dimension than the privileged one. He tries to bring the two poles closer together so that one is subsumed within the other (see l. 52, 'girando parea dir: *Qui* regna Amore' [turning about [it] seemed to say: '*Here* reigns Love'], referring to the vision), but there is always the risk that if he travels too far into memory it may become its own kind of 'oblio' [forgetfulness] and he will become consumed by it. There would no longer be differentiation between 'here' and 'elsewhere', and the tensions on which he thrives, the movement between the two domains in which he alone finds existence, would fall into monotony. Thus he has to rediscover the small or contingent object upon which he can rest or erect the self— literally, 'against *this* grass', where the deictic 'questa' is properly the measure of the desiring self in relation to its object at phantasma, posited there. As Harrison notes, this 'grassy (no) place', in which the linguistic act takes place, is the space of the anthology itself, and that unreal landscape the wondrous, but ultimately uncertain, domain of the speaking voice.[52]

The first stanza of Petrarch's poem already sets the parameters of the encounter with the phantasm. The grass and flowers are eroticized as fetishistic entities by the fact that Laura once draped herself over them. The relationship between the different elements is developed through the second, third, and fourth stanzas in which Petrarch emphasizes the memorial dimension as well as the ambiguity of Laura's appearance which is always half-concealed, first by the 'rain of flowers' and then by the cloud— love's cloud, possibly the threat of oblivion, or the cloud that consumes Eurydice in the myth of Orpheus' failed descent into the underworld to reclaim her:

> Da' be' rami scendea 40
> (dolce ne la memoria)
> una pioggia di fior' sovra 'l suo grembo;
> et ella si sedea
> humile in tanta gloria,
> coverta già de l'amoroso nembo. 45
> Qual fior cadea sul lembo,
> qual su le treccie bionde,
> ch'oro forbito et perle

---

[51] Judith P. Butler, 'Lacan: The Opacity of Desire', in *Subjects of Desire: Hegelian Reflections in Twentieth-Century France* (New York: Columbia University Press, 1987), pp. 186–204 (p. 193).
[52] Harrison, *The Body of Beatrice*, pp. 102–4 (p. 104).

> eran quel dí a vederle;
> qual si posava in terra, et qual su l'onde;   50
> qual con un vago errore
> girando parea dir: Qui regna Amore.

[From the lovely branches was descending (sweet in memory) a rain of flowers over her bosom,
 and she was sitting humble in such a glory, already covered with the loving cloud;
 this flower falling on her skirt, this one on her blond braids, which were burnished gold and pearls to see that day; this one was coming to rest on the ground, this one on the water, this one, with a lovely wandering, turning about seemed to say: 'Here reigns Love.']

Petrarch tries to give Laura an existence beyond his projection or imagination of her, but it is only ever hypothetical, and the projected future time of the third stanza, in which the poet flirts with the possibility that she might one day seek him (l. 33: 'cercandomi' [seeking me]), is here quickly displaced by the imperfect tense of memory (l. 40 onwards) and by the more passive articulation of her as a silent object for the poet to gaze upon, without that gaze being returned. The fact is that even when the vision reaches its height, it is the flowers that his eye follows which trace out the shape and form of his beloved, rather than her visible form, as though he might not be able to see her at all if it were not for the flowers leading the way. The importance of those fetishized objects of the landscape—the 'voi' [you] (l. 18)—cannot therefore be stressed enough, and only through a relationship with the ground, with limit, and with specificity can the poet hope to create a space and place from which the soul might soar upward.

The reconfiguration of the idyll

These tensions that frame Petrarch's idyll are also those which shape Sereni's successive returns to his own correlative of Vaucluse, Luino. While we do not find adjacent series of poems in *SU* and *SV* along the lines of the two Petrarchan canzoni just analysed, patterns of return to the same landscape still emerge which often bridge vast intervals of time and space. Sereni's 'Ancora sulla strada di Zenna' [On the Zenna Road Again], written in the early 1950s, is a case in point. While the literal context of the poem is provided by the poet's return to Zenna, the liminal pass connecting Varese (in Italy) with the Swiss province of Canton Ticino, as the title suggests—recalling Sereni's earlier poem, 'Strada di Zenna' [Zenna Road], in *Frontiera* (dating to 1938)—it is also a revisitation of his poetic past. This invites a Petrarchan dialogue between his later and his earlier work, as well as establishing an intertextual framework that extends from Petrarch to Leopardi, Montale, and Proust:[53]

'Ancora sulla strada di Zenna'

Perché quelle piante *turbate* m'inteneriscono?
Forse perché ridicono che il verde si rinnova
a ogni primavera, ma non rifiorisce la gioia?
Ma non è questa volta un mio lamento
e non è primavera, è un'estate,   5
l'estate dei miei anni.
Sotto i miei occhi portata dalla corsa
la costa va formandosi *immutata*
da sempre e *non la muta il mio rumore*
né, più fondo, quel repentino vento che la *turba*   10
e alla prossima svolta, forse, finirà.
E io potrò per *ciò che muta* disperarmi
portare attorno il capo bruciante di dolore...
ma l'opaca trafila delle cose
che là dietro indovino: la carrucola nel pozzo,   15
la spola della teleferica nei boschi,
i minimi atti, i poveri
strumenti umani avvinti alla catena
della necessità, la lenza
buttata a vuoto nei secoli,   20
le scarse vite che all'occhio di chi torna
e trova che nulla nulla è veramente *mutato*
si ripetono identiche,
quelle agitate braccia che presto ricadranno,
quelle inutilmente fresche mani   25
che si tendono a me e il privilegio
del moto mi rinfacciano...
Dunque pietà per le *turbate* piante
evocate per poco nella spirale del vento
che presto da me arretreranno via via   30
salutando salutando.
Ed ecco *già mutato il mio rumore*
s'impunta un attimo e poi si sfrena

---

[53] 'Strada di Zenna', whose first 'stesura' [version] dates to 1938, was originally entitled 'Zenna', and published as such in *Frontiera* (1941) and *Poesie* (1942). It received its definitive title in Sereni's reworking of *Frontiera* for the 1966 reprint, reinforcing the dialogue the poet wanted to establish with its successor, 'Ancora sulla strada di Zenna' (published in *SU*, 1965). On the genesis of the two poems, see Silvio Ramat, 'Un poeta sulla Strada di Zenna: due liriche di Vittorio Sereni', *Italica* 62.3 (Autumn 1985), pp. 246–63 (p. 247).

fuori da sonni enormi
e un altro paesaggio gira e passa.   35
              (In *SU*, pp. 113–14)

['On the Zenna Road Again'

Why do these *troubled* branches touch me?
Maybe because *they repeat* the green renews
each spring, but joy doesn't flourish afresh?
But this time it's not my lament
and it's not spring, it's summer,   5
the summer of my years.
Under my eyes, the coastline brought on
by the road is forming itself
always *unchanged* and *not changed by my motor*
nor, lower, that sudden wind which *troubles* it   10
and at the next bend will, perhaps, die down.
And I'll be able to despair *for what changes*,
carry round a burning head of sorrow...
but the obscure threading of things
I suppose back there, the pulley in the well,   15
the wheels of cable ways through woods,
the least acts, the poor
human implements bound to the chain
of necessity, the fishing line
cast for nothing through centuries,   20
the meagre lives that for the eye of one returning
who finds nothing, not a thing has really *altered*
repeat themselves identically,
those flurrying arms that will soon fall back,
those hands pointlessly fresh   25
stretching towards me and the privilege
of motion they reproach me...
So pity them for the *troubled* branches
called forth a moment in the spiral of wind
that will soon drop away from me   30
waving goodbye goodbye.
And now *already changed the motor*
checks an instant and then is released
from immense sleep
and another landscape turns and goes by.]   30

What has been lost in the transition from 'Strada' to 'Ancora' is the ability to map desire, or the landscape, on a scale that the 'I' can comprehend; in other words, the 'I' has lost the power to place itself at the *origo* of the scene. In 'Strada', the emphasis had been on measure, 'Questa misura ha il silenzio' [The silence has this cadence] (l. 13), but now all measure is gone. Where earlier the 'I', taking shelter in the 'noi' [we], found meaning in being placed at the heart of a scene still to some extent projected towards a future, and in a process of becoming, by 'Ancora', he has moved to occupy—alone—the marginal space around it, left behind—'l'*esteso* strazio [...] *per chi resta* nei sogni | di pallidi volti feroci' [the *extended* torment [...] *for whoever remains* in dreams | of pallid faces] ('Strada', ll. 22–3). Whereas in 'Strada', the voices of the dead were a constant accompaniment to the journey of life, 'forse è vostro | il gemito che va tra le foglie' [it may be the wail | going through the leaves is yours] (ll. 32–3), by the time we reach 'Ancora', the landscape is silent, there is no interlocutor beyond the self (cf. *RVF* CXXV), and the wind is only a mechanical force driven by the car. The earlier myth, of the 'strade che rasentano l'Eliso' [streets that border Elysium] ('Strada', l. 7), is dismantled. The 'reality' that stands in its place offers none of the support or direction the 'I' seeks.

The idyll is marred not so much because the subject's perception of it has changed ('Ma non è questa volta un mio lamento', l. 4) but because what had earlier presented itself as a place of joy and rebirth (even through or beyond death, as 'Strada' intimated) is revealed to have been one only of sterility and stasis, which is far more damning than the shadow of death itself. The landscape has not died—it has not even aged—and that is where its menace lies, in forcing the subject to accept its impenetrability and otherness from himself (he can pass through it, but not enter), and the foreclosure of the journey that had already been threatened at the earlier landing, and now seems definitive, at least for the 'I'', 'Ma torneremo taciti a ogni approdo. | Non saremo che un suono | di volubili ore noi due | o forse brevi tonfi di remi | di malinconiche barche' [But we'll return silent at each approach to shore, | be no more than a sound, | you and I, of voluble hours | or perhaps short thuds of oars | from disconsolate boats] ('Strada', ll. 26–30).

To this extent even the landscape is revealed to be a phantasm—especially the poetic landscape of the earlier collection which has now dissolved, leaving only its negative counterpart, which is somehow felt to have been implicit in it all along but only able to be retrospectively recuperated as a pre-existing or foundational loss: 'la lenza | buttato *a vuoto* nei secoli, | le *scarse* vite che all'occhio di chi torna | e trova che nulla nulla è veramente mutato | si ripetono identiche...' ('Ancora', ll. 19–23) The landscape is paradoxically something other than it appeared, while being more than ever what it was before. Forced to acknowledge the power the landscape has over him, at the same time as recognizing his dependency upon it, the 'I' finds itself, in Petrarchan fashion, bound to a place whose animation is tied to his own but in which there is no clear division between what comes before and what comes after.

In this way, the relationship between 'Ancora' and its counterpart in *Frontiera* can be considered Petrarchan in essence, to an extent mirroring that between the second and the first parts of the *RVF*. In Peter Hainsworth's words:

> The dominant note of Part 2 is regressive or recursive, not progressive. Petrarch does not surrender old pleasures lightly. Whether he looks backward or forward, or to the equally uncertain present, it is Laura as she was, or as he thought she was, who occupies him. [...] Knowing that the tracing of old ground is not a restoration, does not prevent the action of the imagination or of the desire that guides it from continuing to repeat itself. [...] There is so little reorientation that Part 2 seems overall a more concentrated, darker rewriting of Part 1, its transposition into a minor key.[54]

While the reorientation taking place from *Frontiera* to *SU* is more pronounced than Petrarch's, and the textual landscape more radically altered from one phase of Sereni's poetry to the next (arguably shifting *to* a major *from* a minor key), at the same time his underlying preoccupation is still with fathoming the identity of the present from the perspective of its previous topographic incarnation in the past. The Laura figure, never present to begin with, not even in 'Strada', is more than ever remote, yet the posthumous quality of the landscape of Sereni's later poem with respect to the first works to create what Silvio Ramat has termed 'un [...] romanticismo postremo ovvero sfigurato in chiave "decadentistica"' [a romanticism *in extremis* or, better, one twisted in a decadent key], in which the objects of desire (Sereni's 'piante'), now disfigured in the present, are coloured blacker still by the memory of how they had appeared before.[55]

If, as Ramat suggests, 'la leggerezza di ["Strada di] Z[enna"] era garantita [...] da *un'assenza di memoria* (il che vale pressappoco per l'intero libro d'esordio) [the lightness of ["Strada di] Z[enna"] was guaranteed [...] by *an absence of memory* (something which holds for pretty much the whole of the first book)]', the counterweight of 'Ancora' is precisely the presence of memory—both personal and poetic—from which the subject cannot extricate himself.[56] To this extent, one structural and phantasmatic model of 'Ancora' is sonnet CCIX of the *RVF*, whose 'sweet hills', where the 'I' left himself, are always in front yet always behind him, partly

---

[54] *Petrarch the Poet*, pp. 162–3.
[55] 'Zenna', pp. 254–5.
[56] Ibid. 259–60.

perceived or imagined, and partly remembered, both inside and outside the self:

> I dolci colli ov'io lasciai me stesso,
> partendo onde partir già mai non posso,
> mi vanno innanzi, et èmmi ognor adosso
> quel caro peso ch'Amor m'à commesso.   4
> Meco di me mi meraviglio spesso,
> ch'i' pur vo sempre, et non son anchor mosso
> dal bel giogo piú volte indarno scosso,
> ma com' piú me n'allungo e piú m'appresso.   8
> [...]
> di duol mi struggo, et di fuggir mi stanco.   14

[The sweet hills where I left myself, when I departed from the place I can never depart from, are before me as I go, and still behind me is that sweet burden Love has entrusted to me.

Within myself I am often amazed at myself, for I still go and yet have not moved from the sweet yoke that I have shaken off in vain many times, but the farther I go from it the closer I come.

[...]

[I] am tormented by sorrow and weary myself with fleeing.]

Although Sereni keeps almost nothing of Petrarch's lexicon in 'Ancora', he arguably intensifies the situation of the Petrarchan subject, who is depicted as turning in circles about a fixed point. Remaining and leaving are equally fraught and equally illusory alternatives, and the only thing the 'I' can really know is that the further he travels, the more he re-enters himself. At first glance, Sereni's poem seems less introspective, or more capable of resisting the egocentric pull of desire, but finally it too acknowledges a fixation with the self that subtends every attempt to liberate oneself from it. The fact that the memory of the idyll is always projected in front, while being located behind the subject, confirms its identity as a desire-space in the Lacanian sense—a perspective also written into Sereni's poem in that while in the first part of the poem the subject moves to embrace the landscape, it ultimately retreats and withdraws from him.

Thus, whilst in 'Ancora' it seems that what has brought the landscape to 'life' has only been the wind generated by the passing car, in turn that intimation of movement, initially aligned with the 'I', is later absorbed by his surroundings, to the point at which he too is caught up in the phantasmatic realm ('fuori da sonni enormi', l. 34). The 'I' breaks loose by the end but he is also forced to leave everything behind him, losing more than he gains from his passage through the scene. The landscape, in retreat from him, withdraws into its own exteriority and otherness, in the characteristically Petrarchan pose of *congedo*, 'che presto *da me* arretreranno via via | salutando salutando' ('Ancora', ll. 30–1). As the poetic voice declares, his 'rumore' (passage) was unable to change the landscape, but he has nonetheless been imperceptibly altered (*già mutato*) by its refusal to open itself up to him, and in the process of writing the poem.

The dialogue that Sereni's text simultaneously establishes with Proust reinforces this fugitive quality of the landscape, as well as the subject's attachment to it as a site for the 'remembrance of things past'. Sereni's lakeside wind conjures the memory of the 'soft marine breeze' which in Proust's *Sodome et Gomorrhe* II mediates contact between the protagonist Marcel and his beloved Albertine, in her absence from him:

> Même à une assez grande distance d'Albertine j'avais la joie de penser que si mes regards ne pouvaient pas aller jusqu'à elle, pourtant plus loin qu'eux cette puissante et douce brise marine qui passait a côté de moi devait dévaler, sans être arrêtée par rien jusqu'à Quetteholme, venir agiter les branches des arbres qui ensevelissent Saint-Jean-de-la-Haise sous leur feuillage, en caressant la figure de mon amie, et jeter ainsi un double lien d'elle à moi dans cette retraite indéfiniment agrandie, mais sans risques, comme dans ces jeux où deux enfants se trouvent par moments hors de la portée de la voix et de la vue l'un de l'autre, et où tout en étant éloignés ils restent réunis. [...] De fantômes poursuivis, oubliés, recherchés à nouveau, quelquefois pour une seule entrevue et afin de toucher à une vie irréelle laquelle aussitôt s'enfuyait, ces chemins de Balbec en était pleins.[57]

> [Even at a considerable distance from Albertine I had the joy of thinking that, even if my eyes could not reach her, the powerful, soft sea breeze that was following past me, carrying further than they, must sweep down, with nothing to arrest it, as far as Quetteholme, until it stirred the branches of the trees that bury Sant-Jean-de-la-Haise in their foliage, caressing my beloved's face, and thus create a double link between us in this retreat indefinitely enlarged but free of dangers, as in those games in which two children find themselves momentarily out of sight and earshot of one another, and yet while far apart remain together. [...] Of phantoms pursued, forgotten, sought anew, sometimes for a single meeting, in order to establish contact with an unreal life which at once faded away, these Balbec roads were full.]

The connection between Proust and Sereni is unlikely to be coincidental, not least because the passage in question precedes by just a few lines the section Sereni quotes from *À la recherche* in a letter to Attilio Bertolucci (20 October 1941) in which he pronounces, 'Proust è ormai il mio autore' [Proust is by now my author]. Identifying with the artistic dilemma facing the French writer, whose 'sort était de ne poursuivre que des fantômes'

---

[57] Proust, *Sodome et Gomorrhe II: Chapitre III*, in *À la recherche*, pp. 1516–17.

[fate was to chase only phantasms],[58] Sereni acknowledges the power of Proust's soft sea breeze to open up the path to the object of desire, outstripping and out-travelling the gaze and instigating the boundaries of that fetishized space which fuses the landscape of the natural world with the phantasm. In turn, the tree branches are transformed into a double of the self, as they fuse with the writer's arms to caress the beloved's face. As in *RVF* CCIX, the distance the 'I' has moved becomes immaterial. Since the loss of the Other is never accepted—or, more properly, mourned—as irrevocable, the subject's hold over it is kept intact, however 'indefinitely enlarged' the intervening space becomes. The deprived self basks in the light of a fullness that can only be imagined, and a glimpse ('entrevue') of the phantasm ('fantôme') is enough to renew the search each time the original object is lost from view.

This is in direct contrast to the tone of resignation that characterizes Sereni's poem. More negatively than Petrarch or Proust, Sereni's entry into the field of desire is marked from the outset by a feeling of anxiety (note the emphasis upon 'turbate'), as though memory itself has become a hostile place, where for the earlier author it could potentially be the haven from the traumatic effects of the present. Like Petrarch, Sereni is intent on measuring the time that has passed, but as Ramat notes:

> Oltre che di ripetizione e di conflitti fra i due modi-tempi di uno stare in luogo, o meglio del toccare un luogo (dotato d'un suo proprio nome ricco di potere evocativo) di sfuggita, in Sereni hanno rilevanza massima le corrispondenze, come a suggerire una continuità *sui generis* tra passato e presente anche là ove il riscontro del divario tra quello e questo paia provocare la persona a disperati bilanci esistenziali, nell'orbita scontatissima del compianto dell'età perduta.[59]
>
> [In addition to the repetition and clashes between the two moods and tenses associated with staying in one place or, better, momentarily touching a place blessed with a name rich in evocative power, correspondences in Sereni have a crucial importance, as though to imply a continuity *sui generis* between past and present even where the acknowledgement of the gap dividing one time from the other seems to provoke the 'I' to desperate existential balances, in the entirely predictable sphere of regret for a lost age.]

The metaphorical fall (out of Eden) on which the poem opens is repeated as the second fall of the arms/branches of the trees, which simultaneously reproach the poetic subject for his 'privilegio | del moto' (ll. 26–7), which turns out not to be an advantage at all. The phantasm is

---

[58] See *Attilio Bertolucci–Vittorio Sereni: una lunga amicizia, Lettere 1938–82*, ed. Gabriella Palli Baroni (Milan: Garzanti, 1994), p. 38 and note on p. 39.
[59] 'Zenna', p. 247

not a woman, or even an Other, but landscape itself—the poetic phantasm or *mise en scène* of desire conjured by the intimately Leopardian 'piante' who invite the opening question/reflection on the self. However, the repetition of the deictic 'quelle' to designate these (vegetal) phantasms, which emerge from the current of wind and carry the poetic memory of Leopardi's 'L'infinito' ['The Infinite'], sets the subject's encounter with them at some distance, and reinforces the useless quality of their seeming vitality, or his own, which stops short of being properly generative since it is always already fixed or past.

While lines 28–9 of Sereni's poem, 'Dunque pietà per le turbate *piante* | evocate *per poco* nella spirale del *vento*', echo the central passage of Leopardi's 'L'infinito', 'sedendo e mirando interminati | spazi di là da quella, e sovrumani | silenzi, e profondissima quiete, | io nel pensier mi fingo, ove *per poco* | il cor non si spaura. E come il *vento* | odo stormir tra queste *piante*' [sitting here and gazing, I find that endless | Spaces beyond that hedge and more-than-human | Silences, and the deepest peace and quiet | Are fashioned in my thought; so much that *almost* | my heart fills up with fear. And as I hear the *wind* rustle among the *leaves*], his version lacks the subjective agency of the Leopardian one. His plants seem to be evoked by the wind more than the 'I', destined to be short lived ('evocate *per poco*') but having a very disconcerting effect on the subject's consciousness of itself nonetheless. In turn, the miraculous experience of the Leopardian 'naufragar' [sinking] is recast as a kind of controlled hallucination whose gaze into the beyond 'che *là dietro* indovino' (l. 15) is not an escape, but only another dead end: the revelation of a Montalian 'male di vivere' [pain of living][60] reduced to a series of objects of memory largely drawn from *Ossi* and *Le occasioni*, here hypostatized in a single pose.

Characteristic of a journey of desire which, in Petrarchan fashion, now consists in denying any journey at all, this is the ultimate declaration of the immobility of the 'I' and its tenacity to the scene of its fall. As Laplanche and Pontalis describe, there is no way for the subject to locate himself in relation to that phantasmatic scene; instead we find a subject who can only 'figure lui-même *pris* dans la séquences d'images' [appear *caught up* himself in the sequence of images]. He also perceives himself as somehow unbalanced, disproportionate to the space afforded him in the landscape, and merely a witness to the game of desire played ad infinitum which, in Petrarchan fashion, would appear to continue beyond the poem even though it seems to exhaust itself there.

---

[60] Cf. Montale's 'Spesso il male di vivere ho incontrato...' [Often I have met what's wrong in life...'], in *Ossi*, p. 33.

Consequently, this poem presents a spatialization of desire very close to the one we encounter in the *RVF*, with the pose of the subject also revisiting the characteristic Petrarchan state of a repeated and prolonged mourning for something felt to be problematically elsewhere but unable to be relinquished or moved on from. For Dal Bianco, 'Ancora' is in fact the prime example of Sereni's Petrarchan tendency toward *variatio*, which he argues is a synonym for a kind of fetishism of return, or even a masochism, in Sereni's response to Petrarch and the version of the lyric he would represent:

> In realtà, Sereni è un grande poeta della variazione; se indulge in procedimenti iterativi [...] non è soltanto per una sorta di scommessa sulla capacità del discorso poetico di accogliere 'l'orrore del vuoto nella ripetizione', è anche *per farsi del male*, per una sorta di *masochismo etico-stilistico, per castigare in sé il petrarchista.*[61]
>
> [In reality, Sereni is a great poet of variation; if he indulges in repetitive procedures... it is not only because of a kind of wager as to the capacity of poetic discourse to grasp 'the horror of the void in repetition' but also *to do harm to himself*, through a kind of *ethical-stylistic masochism, to castigate the Petrarchist inside him.*]

According to Dal Bianco, it is this attitude which shapes the 'forma interna' [internal form] of Sereni's poetry in the terms in which Mengaldo describes it, as a mode of syntactic traction or torsion mirroring the patterning of a twisted psyche, the distorted relationship between the poetic subject and language, always threatened by aphasia, and the resistance of Sereni's poetry to linearity.[62] In this reading, the introversion posed (threatened) by the Petrarchan lyric 'I'—a topographic folding of the subject and its scenery upon themselves—are resisted precisely because they are on some level inevitable. The net in which the Serenian subject is caught incorporates Petrarch to the extent to which their experiences of desire as negativity meet in the realm of memory and the phantasm:

> Ridotta, per via di contenuti o d'astrazione, alle sue componenti, rivela in sè anche la traccia di quella che sarà in altri la sua ripetitività, la musica facile; e per altro verso *la piega mentale derivante dal ricorrente assetto psicologico tra luce e ombra*, lo sviluppo e la chiusa d'obbligo sulla scatto d'un 'ma' espresso o taciuto, *un vizio dello spirito, una distorsione stabilizzata*; in una parola: la maniera.[63]

---

[61] 'Vittorio Sereni', p. 191.
[62] See Pier Vincenzo Mengaldo, 'Sereni traduttore di poesia', introduction to Sereni, *Il musicante di Saint-Merry*, pp. v–xxvii (esp. pp. xvi–xvii).
[63] Sereni, 'Petrarca, nella sua finzione, p. 133.

[Reduced to its component parts by means of contents or abstraction, it also reveals within itself the trace of what in other poets becomes repetitiveness, facile music; and elsewhere *a mental attitude that derives from the recurring psychological stand-off between light and shade*, the opening and obligatory closure at the click of a 'but' expressed or held back in silence, *a vice of the spirit, a distortion that becomes stable*, in a word: mannerism.]

Sereni's 'Ancora' is structured on this play of *variatio*, which embodies the struggle to find an adequate language to articulate the emptiness of desire as lack and non-fulfilment. This 'syntax of desire', to borrow Lombardi's phrase, extends from the kaleidoscopic repetition of words centred on the dyad 'mutabile'/ 'immutabile', in which both the 'I' and its landscape are implicated, to the triad of 'turbate... turba... turbate', and finally the phrasal repetition of 'il mio rumore', which importantly confirms the motion of desire to be passive and not active.

In 'Ancora', Sereni's castigation of the Petrarchan element of himself, if we can call it that, thus takes place in the reconfiguration of the textual landscape, and particularly in the negative reappropriation (expropriation) of the earlier landscape of desire from 'Strada'. It is also apparent in his mediation of Petrarch through the other authors (phantasms) that simultaneously speak through the landscape, from Leopardi to Montale and Proust. The latter, whose presence carries the memory of a narrative discourse of desire which tempers the lyrical one, seems closest to Sereni's own articulation of it, but in fact no single figure dominates: all are threaded together in an intertextual web that draws its particular qualities from the undecidability, or hybridity, of those discourses.

That undecidability also underscores the similarly Petrarchan/anti-Petrarchan matrix of Sereni's 'Luino-Luvino', which stages a dialogue with the landscape that incorporates a markedly self-reflexive dimension between the 'I' and the language of poetry:

'Luino-Luvino'

Alla svolta del vento
per valli soleggiate o profonde
stavo giusto chiedendomi se fosse
argento di nuvole o innevata sierra
cose di cui tuttora sfolgora l'inverno   5
quand'ecco
la frangia su quella faccia spiovere
restituirla a un suo passato d'ombra
di epoche lupesche
e ancora un attimo gli occhi trapelarono   10
da quella chioma spessa
lampeggiarono i denti

per rinselvarsi poi nella muta
assiepantesi attorno
dei luoghi folti dei nomi rupestri   15
di suono a volte dolce
di radice aspra
Valtravaglia Runo Dumenza Agra.
            (In *SV*, p. 264)

[At the wind's turning
through the deep or sun-filled valleys
I was just asking myself if it were
silver of clouds or snowy sierra
things which still set the winter ablaze   5
when look
the fringe falling over that face
restored her shadowy past
of lupine epochs
and still a moment her eyes leaked   10
out through the those thick locks
the teeth flashed
only to draw back into the woods
into the pack hedged round
with places thick with rocky names   15
with sweet sounds sometimes
from bitter roots
Valtravaglia Runo Dumenza Agra.]

    An example of Sereni's attention to the texture of poetic language, 'Luino-Luvino' confirms that place-names hold a certain fascination for him as sites of personal and/or cultural memory. Their particular appeal for him seems to reside as much in their sound quality or image-bank (tied to their etymology) as in their landscape proper, which is a Petrarchan attitude to language in essence. Sereni's topography includes, once again, layered echoes of similar desire-spaces in Leopardi ('assiepantesi attorno', l. 14, being most likely a reference, once again, to 'L'infinito') and Montale ('la frangia' recalling his sonnet beginning 'La frangia dei capelli che ti vela...' ['The fringe that hides...'], in *La bufera*, p. 195; and the 'nomi rupestri' the terrestrial place-name Valmorbia in *Ossi*, p. 41), as well as the familiar Petrarchan elements of the 'occhi' (l. 10) and 'chioma' (l. 11), and the juxtaposition of 'dolce' with 'di radice aspra' (ll. 16–17). In turn the 'chioma' seems to contain something also of Baudelaire's 'La chevelure' ['Hair'], a poem similarly centred upon memory, whose 'souvenirs dormant dans cette chevelure' [memories sleeping in these tresses] are 'awakened' by Sereni at the turn in line 6 ('quand'ecco'), which is also the moment at which the 'I' registers the return of the resurrected image of the desired object from the past, into which it falls again almost immediately.[64]

To this extent, 'Luino-Luvino' is a prime example of how Sereni uses deixis at phantasma to encode psychological as well as spatial proximity and distance. Typically, the boundaries between perception and memory are blurred, and the phantasm (once again a female figure enjoying a marked connection to place, as well as being herself a place-name) possesses the familiar quality of presence within absence which the unique qualities of deictic reference foreground: 'Il deittico non afferra e non si lascia afferrare: con esso si aderisce al vuoto e dal vuoto ci si accomiata' [The deictic grasps nothing and cannot itself be grasped: with it one clings to nothingness and from nothingness one returns].[65]

What the poet sees in the present is what is simultaneously being given back to the past. The deictic phrase 'quand'ecco' (l. 6) does signal the making visible of the fringe, which restores the face to view, but only by reconfining it to the shadows of the past. The poet recovers the female figure but his (poetic) action re-covers her, putting in place another veil, and she can only ever be present as the projection of what is essentially a shadow, a no-thing. To this extent the fringe is also a kind of horizon which is reaffirmed twice in the poem: firstly, as the 'chioma spessa' from which the eyes literally tumble out in an action which mirrors the first, and secondly in the Leopardian 'assiepantesi attorno' which reaffirms the 'siepe', the barrier to the beyond, as well as reiterating the action of opening and closing over again.

It is interesting that lines 10–11 recall the moment we have just looked at in Petrarch's canzone CXXVI, lines 40–52, but here the female figure is yet further 'morcelée' [fragmented] (to use the Lacanian term) and not quite equal to the sum of her parts since her true form remains always in shadow.[66] Just like the 'bionda e luttuosa passeggera' [the blonde and mournful passerby] of 'L'equivoco', she is the Petrarchan flower ('fior') become wilted ('de-flowered' in the sense of 'corrupted'):

---

[64] From *Spleen et idéal*, in Charles Baudelaire, *Les fleurs du mal*, ed. Graham Chesters (London: Bristol Classical Press, 1995), p. 23.
[65] Testa, '*Sur la corde de la voix*', p. 138.
[66] See Lacan, 'Le stade du miroir', p. 96, in which the *imago* or ego of the subject is haunted by 'Ce corps morcelé' [This fragmented body], which 'se montre régulièrement dans les rêves, quand la motion de l'analyse touche à un certain niveau de désintégration agressive de l'individu [usually manifests itself in dreams when the movement of the analysis encounters a certain level of aggressive disintegration in the individual].

> [...]
> Fu il lento barlume che a volte
> vedemmo lambire il confine dei visi
> e, nato appena, in povertà sfiorire.
> (ll. 11–13, p. 112)
>
> [It was the gradual glimmer we sometimes saw
> lap the faces' margin
> and, barely kindled, in weakness shrink away.]

As Sereni himself commented in a letter to Fortini dated 7 May 1958, the last line of this poem epitomizes 'la vendetta proustiana dell'amore che fatalmente si riconosce valido solo per quanto il soggetto ha sofferto, gioito, mentre l'oggetto si spoglia, si intristisce, perde consistenza. Al solito [...] vuol dire che i mezzi, le parole, non furono adeguati [the Proustian vendetta of love which fatally recognizes itself as a thing of value only insofar as the subject has suffered and exalted, while the object despoils itself, languishes, loses density. Usually [...] it denotes that the means, the words, were not up to the task].[67]

The loss the poem registers is also linguistic. Sereni emphasizes the failure of language to recuperate its object and the ensuing damage to the Other (poetic phantasm) that results. While, in similar fashion to Petrarch, the exterior landscape in 'Luino-Luvino' is transformed into its symbolic counterpart, there is not the same degree of fetishistic investment or talismanic import, and the fusion between the two dimensions Petrarch managed to achieve by creating the natural and essential link between where the flowers fall and where Laura resides is not present in Sereni. He maintains a certain sense of fluidity and progression from one element to the next, but it is ambiguous: 'spiovere' and 'trapelare' both suggest a flowing down, but also out, emphasizing that something is potentially lost in the process of re-emerging. Notwithstanding the cluster of words relating to parts of the body (especially the head) and the relatively consistent intercession of words relating to time—the deictics 'quand'ecco' (l. 6), 'ancora' (l. 10), 'poi' (l. 13), and deictic verbs '*re*stituire' (l. 8) and '*ri*nselvarsi' (l. 13) that have an implicit temporal encoding—the succession of elements seems to be a property of their own half-enclosed, half-disclosed nature rather than some superior order sought out to justify their very existence. This is set in opposition to Petrarch's 'flower-logic' as justification for Laura's appearance in that place under the trees, and in the space of the poem, in *RVF* CXXVI.

---

[67] As noted earlier, Sereni's correspondence with Fortini is preserved in the Archive in Luino, APS VII 24 (L 1246).

Moreover, if Sereni is playing in a Petrarchan way with the etymology of words—the fact that Luino has its roots in Luvino, the 'wolf place'—we have to consider that his approach is much less systematic than Petrarch's. Sereni does return to the notion of place-names as inherently poetic or phantasmatic—for example in 'Nell'estate padana' ['Summer in the Po Valley'][68] and Poem VIII of the *Traducevo Char* section of *SV*, which ends with a colon followed by the quintessentially Charian (but also Petrarchan) Vaucluse, as though that single place-name, in its unfathomable mystery, might be able to subsume the nine lines of verse preceding it. However, like these other appearances of place-names, it seems both absolute and incomplete, not so much a symbolism as a personal homage to Sereni's intensely topographic, psychological and emotional map:

VIII

Bastava un niente
e scavalcava un anno
una costa splendente
una vallata ariosa
viene a cadere qui
e s'impiglia tra i passi
negli indugi della mente
la foglia che più resiste—
voglia intermittente: Vaucluse.

(In *SV*, p. 246)[69]

[A nothing sufficed
and leaped over a year
a resplendent coast
an airy valley
come to fall here
and be ensnared amid steps
in the mind's delays
is the most stubborn leaf—
intermittent desire: Vaucluse.]

Ultimately, this poem measures the disproportion that is the mark of all of Sereni's landscapes of desire. Between nothingness and the steadfastness of a name, which can leap coasts and valleys but still falls into the trap of

---

[68] See ll. 1–2 and 9: 'Campitello Eremo Sustinente | luoghi di fascini discreti [...] oggi nomi di spettri della calura' [Campitello Eremo Sustinente | places of discrete charms [...] today naming specters of the heat] (p. 258).

[69] As discussed earlier, this is one of the poems generated from Sereni's 'rewriting' of Leopardi's 'L'infinito'.

an intermittent desire, the subject acknowledges his being caught in a Petrarchan labyrinth. Inherently double, the leaf (both thing of nature and phantasm of poetry) resists—resists time and resists capture. The fact that desire is intermittent is what makes arriving at a totality impossible: what cannot be wholly grasped also cannot be transcended and does not allow the speaking subject either to fully embrace or to relinquish the desired object. Unable to be got beyond, the place—Vaucluse—into which the poem leads reveals itself to be just another figuration of liminality or limbo. The loss of desiring force combined with a tenacity to the place of hesitation or delay ('indugi') leads the subject nowhere except back inside. Vaucluse—Petrarchan, Charian space of memory—is properly the absent centre of the poem, symbolically pushed to the outside: 'un centro come non-luogo, non-centro, anch'esso ubiquitario e disperso' [a centre as a non-place, a non-centre, it too omnipresent and scattered].[70] Nowhere is Sereni's debt to Petrarch's memory clearer than in this figuration of desire-space.

Desire without end?

Consequently, like Petrarch, Sereni often finds himself posited at the edge of an abyss, with an experience of desire that borders on self-annihilation. However, his experience of liminality has few of the compensatory pleasures that Petrarch still finds in the material of poetry as a space for the celebration of desire and the beloved, however transitory or flawed the experience may be. Instead he aligns himself with those moments in Petrarch when the desiring journey seems to have reached a point of no return, which the poet is not sure how he entered and from which he cannot see an escape. Reading the *congedo* of *RVF* CXXVI alongside that of Sereni's 'La malattia dell'olmo' ['The Disease of the Elm'] (in *SV*) helps to identify the point at which the poets' paths converge and diverge again:

> Quante volte diss'io
> allor pien di spavento:
> Costei per fermo nacque in paradiso.   55
> Cosí *carco d'oblio*
> il divin portamento
> e 'l volto e le parole e 'l dolce riso
> m'aveano, et *sí diviso*
> *da l'imagine vera*,   60
> *ch'i' dicea sospirando*:

---

[70] Noferi, 'Il *Canzoniere* del Petrarca', in *Il gioco delle tracce*, p. 53.

> Qui come venn'io, o quando?;
> credendo esser in ciel, non là dov'era.
> Da indi in qua mi piace
> questa herba sí, ch'altrove non ò pace. 65
> Se tu avessi ornamenti quant'ài voglia,
> *poresti* arditamente
> *uscir del boscho*, et gir in fra la gente.

[How many times did I say to myself then, full of awe: 'She was surely born in Paradise!'
Her divine bearing and her face and her words and her sweet smile had so *laden me with forgetfulness and so divided me from the true image, that I was sighing*: 'How did I come here and when?' thinking I was in Heaven, not there where I was. From then on this grass has pleased me so that elsewhere I have no peace.

If you had as many beauties as you have desire, *you could* boldly *leave this wood* and go among people.]

Like his poem, Petrarch is ultimately unwilling or unable to leave the wood of memory once he has entered it and, as Nancy Vickers argues, what we are presented with is 'a painfully ambiguous expression of the dangers of delectation in the memory of that image' (the image of Laura, but also I would argue the poet's own self-image as he stages the scene of recollection).[71] Desire and its poetic expression are responsible for dividing the poet from himself, suspended as he is between the lure of the phantasm and its defeat, pursuing memory to such excess that it leads to total forgetfulness of his reality (ll. 56–60). As Mazzotta has argued, this fact underlines the negativity of a poem which on the surface appears positive but in reality can no more redeem the subject that he can his own verse:

> The *envoi* places the poem in a landscape of nature, which is neither the landscape of vision nor that of memory: it acknowledges the failure of the lyric to live up to the poet's ideas, but it also seals the poem's unavoidable loneliness. From this point of view song 126, which begins by being antithetical to its sister song, ends in the same recognition of a voice that can never coincide with a vision, or, to put it differently, of an understanding that can never be at one with its lyrical origin.[72]

Sereni takes this identity of poetry as the locus of 'an understanding that can never be at one with its lyrical origin' and radicalizes it yet further. The

---

[71] Nancy Vickers, 'Re-membering Dante: Petrarch's "Chiare, fresche et dolci acque"', *MLN* 96.1, Italian Issue (Jan. 1981), pp. 1–11 (p. 10).
[72] Mazzotta, 'Petrarch's Song 126', Appendix I to *The Worlds of Petrarch*, pp. 167–80 (p. 179).

slide towards unreality makes itself felt in his poetry too, in a poem which similarly deals with the dangers of a memory and a phantasm which become engrossing to the point of expiration. Returning the subject to the landscape of Bocca di Magra, where it has been consumed before, the *congedo* of 'La malattia' stages the final descent on a journey of desire which, like Petrarch's, can never truly forget its past history:

> Vienmi vicino, parlami, tenerezza,
> —dico voltandomi a una 20
> vita fino a ieri a me prossima
> oggi così lontana—scaccia
> da me questo spino molesto,
> la memoria:
> non si sfama mai. 25
> È fatto—mormora in risposta
> nell'*ultimo chiaro*
> quell'ombra—adesso dormi, riposa.
>   Mi hai
> tolto l'aculeo, non
> il suo fuoco—*sospiro abbandonandomi a lei* 30
> *in sogno con lei precipitando già.*
>   ('La malattia dell'olmo', in *SV*, pp. 254–5)
>
> [Come near to me, speak to me, tenderness,
> —I say turning back towards
> a life until yesterday close to me
> today so remote —drive out
> from me the insistent thorn,
> the memory:
> it is never satisfied. 25
> It's finished—that shadow
> murmurs a reply
> in *the last light*—sleep now, rest.
>   You've
> removed the thorn, but not
> its burning—*I sigh as I give myself up to her* 30
> *in dreams with her already falling.*]

Topographically speaking, Petrarch's wood is stripped bare; night falls and the poet is cast out. The overwhelming nature of the experience in Sereni's case does nothing to reconfigure or transform his own condition; there is no meeting of heaven and earth and no possibility of transcendence. Where Petrarch courts 'oblio' [forgetfulness] in *RVF* CXXVI and tastes eternity in that dimension, however fallacious it may be, the turning back of memory in Sereni's case merely precipitates time (note the deictic 'già' with which the poem ends) and death—his own death, and the death of the poem.

That Sereni's voice in this poem is also a 'sigh' (l. 30 recalls Petrarch's, 'ch'i' dicea sospirando', l. 61) seals his fate as a desiring subject whose pursuit of the phantasm ultimately leads him into a dimension of dream which, like Petrarch's 'dreams' of the dead Laura, becomes all-consuming. From this space there is no exit, merely a fall projected beyond the last word of the poem, which, as we have already seen, makes Sereni's version of desire-space ever more synonymous with poetry itself, the ultimate phantasm which no amount of speaking can temper and no silence deny.

The poetic space that is conjured as phantasm is the only space capable of placating desire, but lasts only as long as the conceit. Reminiscent once more of Laplanche's and Pontalis's definition of the phantasm as a disconcerting *mise en scène* of desire rather than a proper (or dependable) surrogate for the lost object, this phantasm, for the Serenian and Petrarchan subject, is not the space of wish fulfilment but rather a perpetual struggle to come to terms with the emptiness of desire itself. The birth of desire and the birth of the phantasm are one and the same, and the 'I' falls at the genesis of them both.[73] Every *locus amoenus* is simultaneously a *locus horridus* and each penetrates the poetic idyll as a landscape of desire.

BEYOND PETRARCH

The last four lines of 'La malattia dell'olmo' just quoted could also be a metaphor for Sereni's relationship to Petrarch's *RVF*. Even when the memory of that 'first prick of the thorn' should be fading, somehow its effects are felt far into the future and are proof of the fact that poetic memory itself is tenacious, perhaps dangerously so. In Sereni's later work, in which the Petrarchan landscape seems distant from the poet's present concerns, there is still a resistance to giving it up as well as a commitment to charting new territories which might counter its dominance.

While it is typical for elements of the Petrarchan text to be disseminated over a wide radius in *SU* and *SV*, somehow, because of the nature of Sereni's own relationship to space and language, they become

---

[73] Cf. Laplanche and Pontalis, *Fantasme originaire*, p. 69: 'entre les deux temps de l'expérience réelle et de sa reviviscence hallucinatoire, entre l'objet qui comble le signe qui inscrit à la fois l'objet dans son absence: moment mythique du dédoublement de la faim et de la sexualité en un point d'origine' [between the two stages represented by real experience and its hallucinatory revival, between the object that satisfies and the sign which describes both the object and its absence: a mythical moment at which hunger and sexuality meet in a common origin].

concentrated at certain points to become almost a constant: a point of attraction or fixation which Sereni as a lyric poet in essence cannot fully renounce, even when other forces are in play to lead him in different directions. Whilst retaining relatively little of Petrarch's lexicon, echoes of the *RVF* do still live on as fragments of a much wider poetic mosaic, often mediated through Sereni's experience of the work of other poets and authors which gives his particular brand of 'Petrarchism' a depth and complexity, but also an ambiguity, that is unique.

In focusing on Sereni's topography, it is evident the extent to which his recourse to deictic strategies in the dialogue with the Other is reminiscent of the coordination of memory and desire-spaces in Petrarch's topography, particularly where Laura herself becomes synonymous with some aspect of place, or cannot be distinguished from the setting in which her phantasm appears. In rooting his own phantasms in landscape, Sereni is able to preserve the Petrarchan attitude to topography whilst leaving himself room to graft something entirely personal upon it. In this way, he evokes and diffuses the memory of the ideal space of the lyric, which leads him back to Vaucluse as a poetic precursor of his own privileged loci of Luino and Bocca di Magra, while simultaneously foregrounding its remoteness or otherness from his own topography of desire.

In revisiting Petrarch's deixes, Sereni encourages us to read them as important constants not only for the development of his own poetry but also for the development of lyric poetry more generally, particularly with regard to the dialogue with absence and the representation of the lost or absent object. As Peter Hainsworth states, 'the landscape [of the *RVF*] resembles Laura in taking many forms whilst remaining the same. It also merges with her: it evokes her, substitutes for her, marks her absence, sometimes [...] performing all three functions in barely separable succession'.[74] It is the inseparability of poetry, landscape, and phantasm, together with the realization that none can stand alone, which constitutes the poetic force of the *RVF* but also its greatest bind. Sereni remains a 'Petrarchist' to the extent that he recognizes the irreducibility of that triad, the always mediated access to the desired object, and the revelation of desire as the lack of a totality that can be imagined as absent but never wholly grasped as present. Paradoxically, he will become a 'Dantist' for the same reasons, 'trattando l'ombre come cosa salda' [treat[ing] [...] shades as bodied things] (*Purg.* XXI, 138). Like the two faces of Lacan's Moebius strip, which ultimately become one, Sereni's dialogue with Dante begins where the one with Petrarch ends, and vice versa.

---

[74] *Petrarch the Poet*, p. 134.

5

'Memorie triste', 'passi perduti'

The Melancholy Journey and the Return to Dante[1]

> We are born with the dead:
> See, they return, and bring us with them.
> (T. S. Eliot, 'Little Gidding')

If Sereni's memory of Petrarch, communicated through a return to the hypostatized landscape of the *RVF*, ultimately becomes synonymous with stasis or regression, his memory of Dante is employed to further mark the distance that divides the subject from his desired goal. As Sereni's experience of desire turns from fulfilment to frustration, and from the promise of progression to the absence of transcendence, another ghost rears its head to evoke the knowledge of what could have been but is no longer. That ghost is Dante, but a Dante mediated through a shadow of melancholia that eclipses every attempt to embrace the lost object or to recuperate the distant territory of an ideal poetic past.

This chapter explores how, in choosing to configure his desiring quest as a journey, Sereni is both engaging with the dimension of the *Commedia* that deals with desire as spiritual motion and redefining it in the context of his own experience 'così l'animo preso entra in disire, | ch'è moto spiritale, e mai non posa | fin che la cosa amata il fa gioire' [just so the mind, just seized, achieves desire, | a movement of the spirit never resting | as long as

---

[1] These tropes, best translated here as 'memories of sin/sorrow' and 'lost steps', come respectively from: Dante Alighieri, *Purg.* XXXI, ll. 10–12, 'Poco sofferse; poi disse: "Che pense? | Rispondi a me; ché *le memorie triste* | in te non sono ancor da l'acqua offense"' [For a moment she held back, then asked: | 'What are you thinking? Speak, for your memories | of sin have not been washed away by water yet']; Sereni, 'Italiano in Grecia' ['Italian in Greece'], ll. 11–17, in *DA* (p. 63), 'sono un tuo figlio in fuga che non sa | nemico se non la propria tristezza | o qualche rediviva tenerezza | di laghi di fronde *dietro i passi* | *perduti*, | sono vestito di polvere e sole, | vado a dannarmi a insabbiarmi per anni' [I'm one of your sons in flight who knows | no enemy if not his own sorrow | or some reawakened tenderness | of lakes, of fronds *behind the steps* | *that are lost*, | I'm clothed in sun and dust, go to damn and bury myself in sand for years].

it enjoys the thing it loves] (*Purg.* XVIII, 31–3). From his growing fixation with loss, to his subject's repeated inability or refusal to redirect an errant or regressive desire, to the frustrated search for a pre-lapsarian state of linguistic fullness, Sereni's dialogue with Dante can be mapped in his reworking of an essential purgatorial paradigm, one which finds its ideal culmination in the Garden of Eden. Where, in that supreme landscape of desire, Dante stages the reunion with his beloved Beatrice and indicates that, beyond the pull of the 'memorie triste' [memories of sin/sorrow] (*Purg.* XXXI, 11) associated with the melancholy experience of her death, a full redemption of the past is possible, Sereni will find in his own 'memorie triste' only the confirmation of the irredeemable qualities of the self and the dangers of a second fall.

DA, which first registers Sereni's journey of desire as a perverse purgatory, in which the subject can only travel backwards not forwards, and inaugurates the experience of desire as lack and not fulfilment (*gioire*), receives particular consideration in what follows. Marking a more determinate return to Dante after the largely Petrarchan experimentation of *Frontiera*, in desiring terms it also instigates a hiatus between a 'before' and 'after', the memory of which haunts the subject right into *SU* and *SV*. Recreating that spiral of desire[2] that rests at the heart of Dante's *Commedia*, it holds the key to understanding why Sereni's purgatorial journey fails where Dante's succeeds, and why Sereni's melancholy strategy for repossession of the lost object of desire necessarily condemns him to return to the 'selva oscura', to make his Eden more of a road that leads back to Hell than a gateway that leads on to Paradise.

SERENI AND DANTE: AN OVERVIEW

While Sereni's evolving relationship to Dante in the course of his career has not been viewed precisely in these terms, it has been discussed with respect both to Dante's anti- or counter-Petrarchan credentials and to the attraction of the second canticle of the *Commedia* for a poet who, particularly in his later poetry, almost comes to inhabit the purgatorial state of the in between.

Studies often begin by emphasizing Dante's value as a model of *plurilinguismo* [plurilingualism] and historical objectivity, an alternative to the selective language and high lyricism of the Petrarchan poetic

---

[2] The notion of a spiral of desire is one I take from Teodolinda Barolini, 'Purgatory as Paradigm: Traveling the New and Never-Before-Traveled Path of This Life/Poem', in *The Undivine 'Comedy': Detheologizing Dante* (Princeton, NJ: Princeton University Press, 1992), pp. 99–121 (p. 101).

universe which, as we have seen, can continue to find a place in Sereni's poetry only as part of a world of phantasms.[3] Dantean elements do also penetrate the phantasmatic plane, but there is a greater commitment where Dante is concerned to integrating the poetic and existential dimensions of subjectivity. The opening up of Sereni's poetry towards a more dialogic mode and towards history, especially from *SU* onwards, is generally seen in light of his greater proximity to Dante at that stage in his career. However, as with the evolving nature of his 'Petrarchism', Sereni's *dantismo* should not be considered as an event confined to a single time period but rather as a kind of poetic disposition activated more or less depending on his specific artistic choices.

As Luigi Scorrano has shown, Dante is effectively present in Sereni's poetry from the beginning, even if the transparency of the *Commedia* as a source text only really comes to the fore in the mature phase of Sereni's production.[4] Paradoxically, the more rich and forceful Dante's presence in Sereni becomes, and the more widespread, the fewer the number of direct references and the higher the incidence of textual echoes (what Scorrano calls 'stampi' (p. 44), 'suggestioni' and 'richiami' [danteschi] [[Dantesque] marks, suggestions, and allusions] (p. 59)), employed with increasing naturalness and maturity:

> La 'trasversalità' del dantismo sereniano [...] costituisce in sé 'una critica attiva'; questa recupera brani di memoria dantesca e li restituisce, là dove più ragionatamente essi vengono utilizzati, soprattutto nelle modalità consentite a un discorso che registra più domande che risposte e, dunque, non appoggia su basi di certezza ma sul dubbio costitutivo della coscienza novecentesca.
>
> [The 'transversality' of Sereni's Dantism, as it emerges from this study, constitutes in itself an 'active critique'; it recuperates passages of Dantesque memory and reinstates them, where they most logically come to be used, above all in the modalities permitted by a discourse that registers more questions than answers and consequently does not rest on secure foundations but instead on the doubt that constitutes twentieth-century consciousness (p. 75).]

It is this reflective, self-questioning, quality of Sereni's *dantismo*, combined with its obliqueness (p. 57), that constitutes its transversality according to Scorrano: its ability to cut across the material out of which it is formed and in so doing to undertake an active critique of its own memorial

---

[3] See e.g. Paolo Baldan, 'Tra storia e memoria: *Diario d'Algeria* di Vittorio Sereni', *La rassegna della letteratura italiana* 77 (1973), pp. 599–618, and Pierluigi Pellini, 'Brevi note su Dante nella poesia del Novecento italiano: con una lettura sereniana', in *Le toppe della poesia: saggi su Montale, Sereni, Fortini, Orelli* (Rome: Vecchiarelli, 2004), pp. 171–99.

[4] Luigi Scorrano, 'Dantismo "trasversale" di Vittorio Sereni', *Alighieri: Rassegna Bibliografica Dantesca*, n.s. 40.14 (July–Dec. 1999), pp. 41–76.

operation. It is a dynamic form of intertextuality in which Sereni engages analytically with those aspects of Dante's text with which he feels a particular consonance (which in a sense transcend the particular historical and cultural conditions in which Dante was writing), while acknowledging the distance that separates the modern from the medieval mind:

> Oggi, leggendo Dante, possiamo essere culturalmente interessati dal fatto che la sua posizione politica era quel che era in quel determinato momento, però non c'è dubbio che di fronte alla costruzione terrena e metafisica della *Divina Commedia* noi ci fermiamo su determinati punti, dove sentiamo che è la poesia che trionfa su tutto il resto. Ora dire che differenza c'è tra noi e Dante è un discorso inutile, perché noi facciamo una lettura particolare di Dante, di Petrarca, che li rende attuali; per cui sentiamo che certi aspetti della nostra sensibilità ed esperienza si rispecchiano perfettamente in loro. Quindi non c'è una poesia del passato e una poesia del presente, c'è una evoluzione. Di diverso tra noi e i poeti del passato c'è il nostro lavoro in formazione, che noi compiamo in quanto siamo soggetti diversi da quelli che c'erano prima.[5]

> [Today, reading Dante, we can be interested culturally in the fact that his political position was what it was in that particular moment, but there is no doubt that when faced with the earthly and metaphysical structure of the *Divina Commedia* we focus our attention on specific points, in which we feel that it is the poetry that triumphs over everything else. Today, saying what difference there is between us and Dante is a senseless discourse since we undertake a particular reading of Dante and Petrarch which makes them contemporary, to the extent that we feel that certain aspects of our sensibility and experience are perfectly reflected in theirs. Consequently, there is not a poetry of the past and a poetry of the present but an evolution. What differs between us and the poets of the past is our project in the making, which we undertake insofar as we are different subjects from those who came before us.]

Sereni's intertextual dialogue with Dante thus pivots upon moments of experience, both autobiographical and poetic, that are consistent and yet evolving from one dimension into the other. Critics who have underlined the 'purgatorialità' [purgatoriality] of Sereni's poetry post-*DA* recognize that at least part of the attraction of Dante's second canticle resides in its resemblance to the particular temporal and spatial conditions that he inhabited as a prisoner of war in Algeria. The effects of Sereni having himself lived through a form of Purgatory cast their shadow beyond the immediate period of imprisonment, and his poetic subject is slow to shake off the stigma of his 'dannazione' [damnation]:[6]

---

[5] Sereni, *Sulla poesia: conversazione nelle scuole*, ed. Giuliana Massani and Bruno Rivalta (Parma: Pratiche, 1981), pp. 41–62 (pp. 43–4).
[6] 'Vado a dannarmi a insabbiarmi per anni' [I go to damn and bury myself in sand for years], Sereni, 'Italiano in grecia' ['Italian in Greece'] (l. 17), in *DA*, p. 63.

E ancora in sogno d'una tenda s'agita
il lembo. Campo d'un anno fa
cui ritorno tentoni
ma qui nessuno più
a ginocchi soffre
solo la terra soffre
che nessuno più
soffra d'essere qui
e tutto è pronto per l'eternità
il breve lago diventato palude
la mala erba cresciuta alle soglie
né fisarmonica geme
di perdute domeniche
tra cortesi comitive
di disperati meno disperati
più disperati. Io dico:
—Dov'è il lume
che il giovane Walter vigilava
fiammante nell'ora tarda
all'insonne compagnia...—.
Sidi-Chiami, ottobre 1944
(In *DA*, p. 80)

[And again in a dream the tent's edge
is flapping.
Camp of a year ago
I drag myself back to
but no one any longer
suffers here on their knees
only earth suffers
that people no longer
suffer being here
and all's made ready for eternity
the brief lake become marshes
evil weeds grown to the thresholds
nor does accordion groan
of lost Sundays
amongst fond gatherings
of the desperate less desperate
more desperate. I say:
—Where is the lamp
young Walter watched over
to the wakeful company...—.
Sidi-Chiami, October 1944]

According to Ramat, Sereni's 'purgatorialità' is most evident in the dimension of 'visione' [vision] that underpins much of his poetic experience in *SU* and elsewhere (note the opening of this poem, 'E ancora in sogno...'). It is consolidated through the failure of the poet to find, even in memory, a 'segno-guida' [guiding-sign] who could lend him ratification from the outside and lead him beyond the more limited frame of his own hallucinatory reality. Ramat's comparative reading of Sereni's 'La spiaggia' ['The Beach'] and Mario Luzi's 'La notte lava la mente' ['Night Washes the Mind'] demonstrates how the visibly suspended quality of Sereni's form of Purgatory vis-à-vis its Luzian counterpart derives above all from the uncertainty of there being anything more, even when the signs in the landscape seem to suggest that an alternative space is opening up.[7] Luzi, on the other hand, as a clearer heir of the *stilnovisti*, preserves the sacredness of the *tu* [you] figure intact, which signals the possibility of an epiphanic or utopian moment largely negated in Sereni's universe. As was the case with Petrarch, so in the dialogue with Dante, the greatest hole in Sereni's poetry is in effect left by the absence of a female figure capable of offering salvation, and Sereni's desiring journey always in a sense begins from a minus point, trying to get back to zero.

Sereni's numerous Dantesque encounters with the dead, in a penumbral zone of half-sleep or waking-dream reminiscent of the *Commedia*'s opening, are generally a symptom of this lack underlying his desiring quest, a substitute for the absent dialogue with a true Other we still find in, for example, Montale. Much has been written about the ambiguous nature of Sereni's poetic encounters with his 'ombre' [shades]: their often arbitrary, intermittent, or occasional quality in a Montalian sense, and their tendency to bring the subject up short or to reproach him for something in his past, drawing him into an uncertain space where the realm of the living infiltrates that of the dead, and vice versa.[8] Often, these shades are no more than phantasms—incarnations or projections of the subject's desire—that rarely take on a more substantial quality. As Mazzoni notes:

> Anche quando l'apparizione ha la struttura del dialogo col proprio doppio—
> e dunque presuppone, nella realtà, non un'intuizione istantanea, ma un
> pensiero che si è protratto per molto tempo—, nel testo l'incontro dell'io

---

[7] Silvio Ramat, 'Purgatorio e inesistenza in due testi poetici medionovecenteschi (M. Luzi, *La notte lava la mente*; V. Sereni, *La spiaggia*)', *Paradigma* 3 (1980), pp. 383–403.

[8] See at least Giorgio Bàrberi Squarotti, 'Gli incontri con le ombre', in *La poesia di Vittorio Sereni: atti del convegno*, ed. Stefano Agosti et al. (Milan: Librex, 1985), pp. 68–90; Pier Vincenzo Mengaldo, 'Il solido nulla', in *La tradizione del Novecento: nuova serie* (Florence: Valecchi, 1987), pp. 377–86.

con la voce che gli si oppone viene sempre rappresentato come se fosse improvviso. L'io rievoca mentalmente, in forma mimetica o allegorica, una verità, un'immagine, un ricordo che, in modo traumatico e istantaneo, riemergono e si rivelano.[9]

[Even when the apparition has the structure of a dialogue with the double of the 'I'—and so, in effect, presupposes not a sudden intuition, but a thought process that has evolved over time—, in the text the 'I''s encounter with the voice that opposes it is always represented as though it were sudden. The 'I' mentally re-evokes, in either a mimetic or allegorical form, a truth, an image, or a memory, which, in traumatic and instantaneous fashion, re-emerge and disclose themselves to view.]

In Sereni's words, that memorial dimension 'è *morto tempo* da spalare al più presto' [is *dead time* to shovel away with all haste] ('Il tempo provvisorio' ['The Provisional Time'], *SU*, p. 105): his journey is inevitably one that leads him back to sites of trauma, or rather that reiterates an itinerary which has failed in the past but whose destination he hopes, by revisiting, he may be able to rewrite. In the most literal of ways, he thus again courts a purgatorial topography but one whose efficacy is yet to be confirmed, and all the dialogues he undertakes with shades whose origin and destination is unknown serve to reinforce the sense that the meaning of his otherworld journey is yet to be determined.

In 'Tempo e memoria in Sereni' ['Time and Memory in Sereni'], Pier Vincenzo Mengaldo reiterates this view when he writes that what is at play in Sereni is a 'memoria che può protendersi verso il non vissuto come nostalgia' [a memory that can project itself toward the non-yet-lived like nostalgia],[10] a view echoed by Sereni in an interview of 1982 in which he defines the unique powers of memory in constructing an identity for the subject. Here, Sereni clarifies the presence of that parabola in his poetry that essentially turns time and space inside out, uniting time present and time past and reviving apparently dead or aborted moments of experience so that they can be relived in the present. Memory here functions as an intensely imaginative experience as well as being, more negatively, a path to unreality. By turning nostalgically towards what has never been, it can recuperate fragments of an as yet unlived reality as recollections, to create a phantasm of something that could not exist otherwise:

---

[9] Guido Mazzoni, 'Verifica dei valori: saggio su *Gli strumenti umani*', *Allegoria*, n.s. 6.18 (1994), pp. 45–81 (p. 70).
[10] In *La tradizione del Novecento: quarta serie* (Turin: Bollati Boringhieri, 2000), pp. 220–38 (p. 227).

D. La memoria dei trapassati è memoria anticipata di se stesso; la morte anzi è già qui, nel presagio di certezza. E sa di sopravvivenza.
R. Effettivamente tendo a vivere certi momenti del presente col senso che siano già passati. Paradossalmente sono i più intensi. Una poesia significativa in questo senso è 'Autostrada della Cisa', inserita nell'ultimo libro.[11]
[Q. Memory of the dead is the advance memory of oneself; in fact death is already here, in the certainty of a presentiment. And it is like living on.
A. I admit I tend to live certain moments in the present with the sense that they are already past. Paradoxically they are the most intense. A significant poem from this point of view is 'Autostrada della Cisa', included in the last book.]

If, as Barolini states, the quintessence of Dante's purgatorial experience lies in 'the journey back through time to the place of beginnings [...] a journey whose goal is the undoing of time through time', Sereni's quest is always already intimately purgatorial while being at the same time invertedly so, always preoccupied more with the inevitability of loss than with the potential for restoration.[12] Overall, his preoccupation with death must be understood in the context of his 'culto della memoria' [cult of memory] and 'patologia della ripetizione' [pathology of repetition][13] that are symptomatic of a melancholy condition which prevents the poetic subject from changing or moving forward, 'da me passato come storia passato | come memoria' [from me gone past like history gone past | like remembrance] ('L'alibi e il beneficio' ['The Alibi and the Benefit'], *SU*, p. 152). In more general terms, that fixation cements Sereni's purgatorial condition as one indebted not only to Dante but also to a range of other twentieth-century authors 'da Eliot a Pound a Mann a Kafka con i loro ambienti carcerarii, sanatoriali, ospedalieri' [from Eliot to Pound, Mann, and Kafka with their prison, sanatoria, and hospital settings], so that in this area especially his *dantismo* is almost certainly one mediated through the modernist tradition.[14]

---

[11] Interview with Paola Lucarini, 'Intervista a Vittorio Sereni', *Firme nostre*, Sept. 1982, p. 3.
[12] Teodolinda Barolini, *Dante's Poets: Textuality and Truth in the 'Comedy'* (Princeton, NJ: Princeton University Press, 1984), p. 47.
[13] Mengaldo, 'Tempo e memoria in Sereni', p. 226.
[14] Laura Barile, 'Amore e memoria: il rammemorare e il mare di Sereni', *Autografo* 13 (1988), pp. 33–60 (p. 57, n. 12). Barile is summarizing Paolo Baldan's arguments on the subject, in 'Gozzano petit maître di Sereni: Lo "scalpore" di una tesi', in *Guido Gozzano: i giorni, le opere: atti del convegno nazionale di studi, Turin, 26–28 October 1983* (Florence: Olschki, 1985), pp. 43–60.

A modernist Dante? Sereni, Montale, and T. S. Eliot

Just as Leopardi and Char were key textual mediators in Sereni's revision of Petrarch, so Montale and Eliot come to have a central role in the filtering of Dante's text into the space of Sereni's poetry. Most critics who have written about Dante's reception in the twentieth century have emphasized the importance of T. S. Eliot for Dante's reintroduction into the field of lyric poetry, both in Italy and elsewhere, and it seems that Sereni too comes to Dante via Eliot—or, at the very least, that his interest in the two poets develops side by side.

In 'Dante e i poeti del Novecento' ['Dante and the Poets of the Twentieth Century'], Anna Dolfi contends that if we continue to think of the *Commedia* as a 'colossale esperienza conoscitiva e fideistica' [a colossal cognitive and fideistic experience], 'l'allegoria dantesca sarà sempre inconciliabile con la moderna analogia; Dante e il Novecento saranno insomma, come talvolta avviene in geometria, grandezze incommensurabili' [Dantean allegory will always be irreconcilable with modern analogy; in short, Dante and the twentieth century will remain, as happens sometimes in geometry, incommensurable magnitudes].[15] If, on the other hand, we allow for a more dialectical approach to intertextuality, then we can more readily understand how Dante comes to be reintroduced into the *Novecento*, reinterpreted in the context of contemporary culture. For Dolfi, the key exponents of this kind of active intertextuality with Dante are Montale and Eliot, especially in their debates about the possibility of achieving a measure of objectivity in lyric verse, which hinged upon their reading of the *Commedia*. She also underlines the centrality of Montale's 'lettura eliotiana di Dante' [Eliotian reading of Dante] for understanding how his own *dantismo* takes shape, and she notes how the three authors function organically as a triangle 'come se insomma il difficile rapporto tra i due poeti moderni [...] dovesse necessariamente passare, schermarsi, coinvolgere il nome di Dante' [in short, as though the difficult relationship between the two modern poets [...] necessarily had to pass through, conceal, or involve Dante's name].[16]

Silvio Ramat too, even though he does not believe that any dramatic turn away from Petrarch towards Dante occurred in the twentieth century, still admits in his 1970 article 'Il Novecento e una traccia dantesca' ['The Twentieth Century and a Dantean Trace'] that:

---

[15] Anna Dolfi, 'Dante e i poeti del Novecento', *Studi danteschi* 58 (1986), pp. 307–42 (p. 319).
[16] Ibid. 325.

Qualcosa negli ultimi decennî si è mosso in una direzione insolita e che il Dante europeo individuato da T. S. Eliot nel 1929 suggeriva contemporaneamente a Montale un'impostazione del proprio lavoro che per qualche segno pareva dantesca o almeno gli consentiva di proporre alcune varianti alla tradizione aperta dal Petrarca e poi così capillare, persuasiva, necessaria nella linea della nostra cultura poetica.[17]

[Something in the last few decades has moved in an unusual direction and that the European Dante singled out by T. S. Eliot in 1929 simultaneously afforded Montale a framework for his own work which to some degree appeared Dantesque or at least allowed him to propose some variation with respect to the tradition inaugurated by Petrarch that had subsequently become so widespread, persuasive, and fundamental to the evolution of Italian poetic culture.]

Reading Zygmunt G. Barański's article 'The Power of Influence: Aspects of Dante's Presence in Twentieth-Century Italian Culture', we can surmise that the cross-fertilization that occurred between Dante, Montale, and Eliot prefigured a similarly enriching poetic dialogue between Contini, Montale, and Dante in the late 1930s to early 1940s. Effectively presenting Dante as a model of how twentieth-century literature could reconnect with contemporary realities, Contini indicated the path towards future renewal that lay in an 'emphasis on objectivity rather than subjectivity, the sense of community rather than individuality, and the belief that art is more than just an aesthetic pursuit but that it has responsibilities towards the world'.[18]

These are all aspects of the Dantean text which are likely to have attracted Sereni and which would have been confirmed by his readings of Montale and Eliot in the 1940s, the same period in which Dante's presence in Sereni's poetry becomes more pronounced, and his poetry begins to adapt—in *DA*—to accommodate a less compact, more disjointed or dislocated lyric subject forced to confront its own disunity and alienation. Both Montale and Eliot provide Sereni with a model for how Dante can be reshaped to fit with contemporary poetic practice, whilst recognizing the extent to which their appropriation of the *Commedia* depends upon their ability to look beyond the traditional limits of interpretation and to transcend conventional categories of literary and historical analysis:

---

[17] Silvio Ramat, 'Il Novecento e una traccia dantesca', *Forum italicum* 4.3 (1970), pp. 311–30 (p. 311).

[18] Zygmunt G. Barański, 'The Power of Influence: Aspects of Dante's Presence in Twentieth-Century Italian Culture', *Strumenti Critici*, n.s. 1.3 (1986), pp. 343–76 (p. 360).

Il culto della poesia di Dante, sonnecchiante allo stato di vasto sottinteso negli interessi odierni, non manca da qualche tempo in qua di dare vigorosi indizi di risveglio. Lo studio dell'opera poetica e critica di T. S. Eliot, l'attenzione suscitata dalla sua teoria del 'correlativo oggettivo', esemplata appunto su Dante in forme non propriamente ortodosse rispetto alla tradizione critica, la sua rivalutazione di aspetti e di strumenti, quali l'uso dell'allegoria, solitamente confinati tra gli elementi 'caduchi' del poema, hanno irrobustito l'opinione che fa della *Commedia*—della sua struttura, della sua finalità, delle sue allusioni—un blocco compatto profondamente radicato in un'epoca, in una situazione storica.[19]

[The cult of Dante's poetry, lying dormant as a pervasive and allusive presence in today's affairs, has recently begun to show vigorous signs of a reawakening. The study of T. S. Eliot's poetry and criticism, the interest generated by his theory of the 'objective correlative', specifically modelled on Dante in less than orthodox ways with respect to the critical tradition, his revaluation of elements and tools, such as the use of allegory, normally relegated to 'frail' elements of the poem, have strengthened the view of the *Commedia*—its structure, its aims, and its allusions—as a compact unit, deeply rooted in a specific era and a particular historical situation.]

As was the case in his relationship with Petrarch and *petrarchismo*, Sereni is attracted to more hybrid forms of *dantismo* which are in a sense enriched by this process of cross-fertilization that he seeks to cultivate in his own poetry. It is characteristic of *SU* and *SV* in particular that Dantean echoes should appear alongside those of other poets and authors including Eliot, Montale, and Proust, all of which are at one time or another called upon to reaffirm, refute, or redefine the Dantean context.

The mediation of Dante through Eliot is a case in point. In addition to the example given above from Sereni's essay on Dante, 'Si può leggere Dante come un poeta "puro"?' ['Can Dante be Read as a "Pure" Poet?'], in which Eliot and Dante appear in close proximity to one another, there are other instances too in which Eliot occupies a prominent space in Sereni's critical writings. For example, in his review of Montale's *Quaderno di traduzioni* [*Notebook of Translations*], the one poem Sereni chooses to quote in Montale's translation is Eliot's 'Song of Simeon' ('Il canto di Simeone').[20] Further evidence of Sereni's familiarity with Eliot's work in Montale's translation is provided, as we shall see, by *Un posto*, in which the poetic figure of the 'animula' is one which appears to derive from the

---

[19] Sereni, 'Si può leggere Dante come un poeta "puro"?' ['Can Dante be Read as a "Pure" Poet?'], first publ. in *Milano Sera*, 23–4 Oct. 1950, p. 3, now in *SG*, pp. 28–33 (p. 28).

[20] Sereni's '*Quaderno di traduzioni* di Eugenio Montale'—an article on the first *Meridiano* edition of Montale's collected works in translation, *Quaderno di traduzioni* (Milan: Mondadori, 1948) —is preserved amongst Sereni's 'prose' in APS IV 190 (F 425).

eponymous poem by Eliot.[21] Eliot's 'animula' is itself a reworking of Emperor Hadrian's original use of the term, and if we consider the following translation of Eliot's poem by Montale, we see that the network of intertextual references extends also to Dante since Montale translates Eliot's 'simple soul' as the 'semplice anima' of Dantean derivation:[22]

> [...]
> The pain of living and the drug of dreams
> Curl up *the small soul* in the window seat
> Behind the *Encyclopaedia Britannica*.
> Issues from the hand of time *the simple soul*
> Irresolute and selfish, misshapen, lame,
> Unable to fare forward or retreat,
> Fearing the warm reality, the offered good,
> Denying the importunity of the blood,
> Shadow of its own shadow, spectre in its own gloom,
> Leaving disordered papers in a dusty room;
> Living first in the silence after the viaticum.
> [...][23]

> [...]
> Pena di vita e narcotico di sogni torcono *l'anima piccoletta* che accanto alla finestra
> siede al riparo dell'*Enciclopedia Britannica*.
> Lascia la mano del tempo *la semplice anima*, incerta
> ed egoista, storta e zoppicante,
> incapace di starsi avanti o indietro,
> teme la realtà calda, l'offerto bene,
> rifiuta il sangue come un importuno,
> ombra delle sue ombre e spettro del suo buio,
> disperde le sue carte tra buio e polvere
> e comincia la vita nel silenzio che segue il viatico.
> [...][24]

---

[21] 'la | farfugliante animula', *Un posto* IV, 13–14 (pp. 228–9). I will return to this moment of intertextuality between Sereni, Montale, and Eliot in the final section of this chapter.

[22] The Emperor Hadrian is meant to have uttered on his deathbed, 'Animula, vagula, blandula, | hospes comesque corporis, | quae nunc abibis in loca, | pallidula, rigida nudula | Nec, ut soles, dabis iocos...' ['Little soul, gentle and drifting, guest and companion of my body, now you will dwell below in pallid places, stark and bare; there you will abandon your play of yore']. See Marguerite Yourcenar, *Memoirs of Hadrian*, trans. Grace Frick (London: Readers' Union, 1955), pp. 6 (passage in Latin verse), and 303 (prose translation).

[23] T. S. Eliot, 'Animula', ll. 21–31, in *Ariel poems*, in *Selected Poems* (London: Faber and Faber, 1975), pp. 101–2.

[24] Eugenio Montale, 'Animula', *Quaderno di traduzioni 1896–1981*, 2nd edn (Milan: Mondadori, 1982), pp. 118–21 (pp. 119–21). 'La semplice anima' (l. 24) recalls both

From other statements that Sereni makes about Eliot, we can gather that he had also read both 'The Love Song of J. Alfred Prufrock' and the *Four Quartets*, and that the formative period with respect to Eliot was the early 1940s.[25] A copy of the 1941 Fenice edition of Eliot's poems in translation, entitled *Poesie*, survives as part of Sereni's personal library in the Archive in Luino and Sereni's correspondence with Alessandro Parronchi in 1946 confirms that Eliot had left a profound mark on him when he had read him several years earlier:

> Rispondo alla tua domanda su Eliot. Non sbagli. Anzi, hai tanta ragione che non posso non confessarti che i primi due versi (che non sono poi, io credo, i migliori) sono nati dalla suggestione del primo verso di *East-Coker*:
>
> **In my beginning is my end.**
>
> È un riferimento del tutto esteriore, ma ha avuto un senso l'averne la musica nell'orecchio. Strana poesia, non so come venutami tutta insieme nel dormiveglia di una delle più grigie e oppresse domeniche della mia vita. [...] Oggi come oggi è probabile che io vada verso Eliot. Chissà.[26]
>
> [In answer to your question about Eliot, you're not mistaken. Actually, you're so right that I should confess that the first two lines (not, in my opinion, the best) were inspired by the first line of *East Coker*:
>
> **In my beginning is my end.**
>
> It's a reference that is utterly external, but it was useful having the music of it in my ears. A strange poem, I don't know how it came to me from beginning to end somewhere between waking and sleep one of the greyest and most oppressive Sundays of my life. [...] Right now, I think I'm moving towards Eliot. Who knows.]

Sereni's description of the circumstances of this moment of intertextuality with Eliot suggests that he regarded the integration of apparently distant or disparate intertexual elements as capable of opening up areas of debate in his own poetry which—to return to Scorrano's definition of intertextuality as a form of active critique—we can see as evidence of a dialogue with the past that is both active and ongoing. Similarly, Sereni's

---

Dante's 'anima semplicetta' [simple infant soul] (*Purg*. XVI, 88), and the 'anima piccoletta' of the previous lines.

[25] 'The Love Song of J. Alfred Prufrock' is discussed by Sereni alongside other authors in the context of the theme of 'solitudine' which was the introduction to a disc on the topic commissioned by *La Cetra* (see n. 27 below). Sereni quotes from the second of Eliot's *Four Quartets* in the letter to Parronchi (1946) cited next, in which he admits that inspiration for the opening of 'Via Scarlatti' (originally entitled 'Il colloquio') came from 'East Coker'.

[26] From Letter 27 (1946) sent by Sereni to Parronchi, in *Un tacito mistero: il carteggio Vittorio Sereni–Alessandro Parronchi*, ed. Barbara Colli and Giulia Raboni (Milan: Feltrinelli, 1994), pp. 73–4. The influence discussed is on the first two lines of 'Via Scarlatti', 'Con non altro che te | è il colloquio' [With none other than you | is the word].

comments about Eliot's 'The Love Song of J. Alfred Prufrock' (1911), in his presentation from the 1950s on the theme of 'Solitudine' [Solitude], reveal as much about his own poetry, and his relationship to the other authors under discussion, as to Eliot himself—an indicator of Eliot's central importance for our understanding of Sereni's relationship to the poetic tradition more generally:

> *Il canto d'amore di J. Alfred Prufrock* di T. S. Eliot e i versi *Alla luna* di Leopardi stanno forse ai termini opposti della situazione di solitudine: in questi vive ancora, sotto forma di caro inganno, l'illusione che in quello verrà poi a degradarsi nello squallore dell'uomo moderno, tanto più solo quanto più materialmente gremito è il mondo che gli si stipa attorno, e delle sue frequentazioni.[27]
>
> ['The Love Song of J. Alfred Prufrock' by T. S. Eliot and Leopardi's 'To the Moon' perhaps stand at opposite ends of the state of solitude: in Leopardi, illusion lives on in the form of a cherished deception but in Eliot this illusion is degraded in the squalor of modern man—all the more alone the more materially chock-a-block is the world that teems around him—and the people and places he frequents.]

What is at stake in this changed landscape of the lyric is also a degradation of the myth of poetry itself. Eliot's subject is all the lonelier for being surrounded by the chaos and oppressive materiality of the world, whose perceived finitude, like the self's, leads to the foreclosure of experience and a premature end to its dreams of desire, 'I have heard the mermaids singing, each to each. || I do not think that they will sing to me. [. . .] We have lingered in the chambers of the sea | By sea-girls wreathed with seaweed red and brown | Till human voices wake us, and we drown' ('The Love Song', ll. 124–5, 129–31).[28] Where in Leopardi's 'Alla luna', language holds 'la ricordanza' [the remembrance] of the joyous era of youth, 'quando ancor lungo | la speme e breve ha la memoria il corso' [when hope's course is still long to run and memory's short] (ll. 13–14), albeit lost and dependent now on painful recollection of lost time, the speaking

---

[27] 'Solitudine' was a presentation Sereni wrote for a disc recording by the same name for *La Cetra*, 'collana letteraria "documento"', directed by Nanni de Stefani. The poems which Sereni discusses were chosen by him as representative of the theme, and were recorded by G. Albertazzi (Rome: 1957). They are: Leopardi's 'Alla luna' ['To the Moon'], Apollinaire's 'Le Pont Mirabeau' ['Mirabeau Bridge'], Cardarelli's 'I ricordi' ['Memories'], Saba's 'Quest'anno' ['This Year'], Pavese's 'Lavorare stanca' ['Work's Tiring'], Salinas's 'No te veo' ['I don't see you'], Auden's *The Rise of F6* and Eliot's 'The Love Song of J. Alfred Prufrock'. The full version of Sereni's text is preserved in the archive materials of his prose writings, APS IV 9.2 (F 158) and can also be read in abridged form in 'da Apollinaire', in *ID2*, pp. 59–60, as post-face to Sereni's translation of 'Le pont Mirabeau'.

[28] T. S. Eliot, 'The Love Song of J. Alfred Prufrock', in *Selected Poems*, pp. 11–16 (p. 16).

subject of Eliot's poem registers only what it is not and cannot express, prefiguring his poetic stance in 'Burnt Norton' (1935), in which 'Words strain, | Crack and sometimes break, under the burden, | Under the tension, slip, slide, perish, | Decay with imprecision, will not stay in place, | Will not stay still. Shrieking voices | Scolding, mocking, or merely chattering, | Always assail them' (V, 13–19).[29]

In aligning himself with this dimension of Eliot's text in counterpoint to the more intact and monologic universe of the Leopardian lyric, Sereni confirms his descent into the realms of a more infernal, confused, or frustrated speech, 'Neither plenitude nor vacancy. Only a flicker | Over the strained time-ridden faces [...] The loud lament of the disconsolate chimera' ('Burnt Norton' III, 10–11; V, 22). This phantasm of poetry, near relation to the tormented souls of Dante's *Inferno* as well as to the poetic subject of Petrarch's *RVF*, shapes Sereni's dialogue with his 'ombre', particularly where his preoccupation with the weight yet insubstantiality of shadows mirrors his reflections on the subject's relationship to the universe of his own discourse.

Part V of Sereni's *Un posto*, in which the poetic 'I' encounters the shade of Elio Vittorini, is perhaps one of the clearest examples we have of how a hybrid intertextuality with Eliot and Dante functions dialectically to evoke and distort the memory of Dante's *sacrato poema* [sacred poem] (*Par.* XXIII, 62):

[...]
Viene uno, con modo e accenti di truppa da sbarco
mi si fa davanti avvolto nell'improbabile di chi,
stato a lungo in un luogo in un diverso tempo
e ripudiatolo, si riaffaccia per caso, per un'ora:
'Che ci fai ancora qui in questa bagnarola?'.   30
'Elio!' riavvampo 'Elio. Ma l'hai amato
anche tu questo posto se dicevi: una grande cucina,
o una grande sartoria bruegheliana...' Ci pensa
                              [un poco su
'Una cucina, ho detto?'. 'Una cucina.'
'Con cuochi e fantesche? bruegheliana?'
                              ['Bruegheliana'   35
'Ah,' dice 'e anche sartoria? con gente che taglia
                              [e cuce?'
'Con gente che taglia e cuce' 'Ma' dice 'dove ce le
                              [vedi adesso?'

---

[29] Leopardi, 'Alla luna', in *Canti*, p. 115; my translation. T. S. Eliot, 'Burnt Norton', no. 1 of *Four Quartets* (London: Faber and Faber, 1959), pp. 13–20 (p. 19).

'Eh,' dico eludendo 'anche oggi pescano, al
                                                [rezzaglio'.
'Ma tu' insiste 'tu che ci fai in questa bagnarola?'
'Ho un lungo conto aperto' gli rispondo.   40
'Un conto aperto? di parole?' 'Spero non di sole
                                                [parole.'
Oracolare ironico gentile sento che sta per sparire.
Salta fossi fora siepi scavalca muri
e dai belvederi ventosi
non mi risparmia, già lontano, l'irrisione   45
di paesi gridati come in sonno irraggiungibili.
Ne echeggia in profondo, nel grigiore,
l'ora del tempo la non più dolce stagione.
            (*Un posto* V, 26–48, pp. 230–1)[30]

[Up comes on with troop landing manners and
                                                [tones
standing before me, wrapped in the unlikelihood
of somebody who, after years at one time in a place
and disowning it, for an hour by chance reappears:
'What are you doing here still in this old tub?'   30
'Elio,' I burst out again, 'Elio. But even you
loved this place if you said: a big kitchen
a big tailor's as in Breughel...' He thinks on that a
                                                [while:
'Did I say kitchen?' 'A kitchen.'
'With cooks and maidservants? As in Breughel?'
                                                ['In Breughel.'   35
'Ah,' he says, 'and tailors too? With those who cut
                                                [and sew?'
'Who cut and sew.' 'But', he says, 'where'd you
                                                [see them now?'
'Eh,' I say, eluding him, 'they fish *al rezzaglio*
                                                [even today.'
'But you,' he insists, 'what are you doing in this old
                                                [tub?'
'I've a long account open,' I reply.   40
'An open account? of words?' 'Not just words I
                                                [hope.'
Oracular, ironic, kindly, he's about to disappear I
                                                [sense.
He leaps ditches, pierces hedges, scales walls
and from blustery belvederes

---

[30] 'Avvolto' and 'riavvampo' are both potentially of Dantean derivation. See e.g. for 'avvolto': *Inf.* VII, 14 and *Inf.* XX, 44; for 'riavvampo': *Purg.* V, 84 and *Par.* XXV, 82.

doesn't spare me, already distant, the derision 45
of places cried out as in sleep, unattainable.
It echoes in the depths, in the greyness
the weather now, the no longer tender season.]

[...]
I met one walking, loitering and hurried
As if blown towards me like the metal leaves
Before the urban dawn wind unresisting.
And as I fixed upon the downturned face
That pointed scrutiny with which we challenge 90
The first-met stranger in the waning dusk
I caught the sudden look of some dead master
Whom I had known, forgotten, half recalled
Both one and many; in the brown baked features
The eyes of a familiar compound ghost 95
Both intimate and unidentifiable.
So I assumed a double part, and cried
And heard another's voice cry: 'What! Are *you*
 [here?'
Although we were not. I was still the same,
Knowing myself yet being someone other— 100
And he a face still forming; yet the words
 [sufficed
To compel the recognition they preceded.
And so, compliant to the common wind,
Too strange to each other for misunderstanding,
In concord at this intersection time 105
Of meeting nowhere, no before and after,
We trod the pavement in a dead patrol.
[...]
But, as the passage now presents no hindrance 120
To the spirit unappeased and peregrine
Between two worlds become much like each other,
So I find words I never thought to speak
In streets I never thought I should revisit
When I left my body on a distant shore. 125
[...]
The day was breaking, in the disfigured street
He left me, with a kind of valediction,
And faded on the blowing of the horn.
 ('Little Gidding' II, 86–107, 120–5, 147–9)[31]

---

[31] T. S. Eliot, No. 4 of *Four Quartets*, pp. 41–8 (pp. 43–4) (italics in the original).

Even before discussing Dante's and Eliot's presence, it should be noted that the primary intertextual model in play here is in fact Vittorini's own *Conversazione in Sicilia* [*Conversation in Sicily*]. As Giovanna Cordibella argues, by mimicking the distinctive traits of Vittorini's narrative style—especially his penchant for repetition and dialogue—Sereni displays a 'mimetic intent' that connects him to the novelist, while enabling him to splice his lyric universe with more narrative, dialogic, and prosaic structures. Since the results are ultimately parodic, the conversation has a double significance: on the one hand, it functions like the repeated refrain of *Un posto* ('non scriverò questa storia' [I'll not write this story]) to simultaneously stimulate and dispel the impetus to write; on the other, it ends any aspiration toward poetic unity and highlights the impossibility of ever wholly incorporating another model—here, Vittorini's 'eteredosso bildungsroman' [heterodox *bildungsroman*]—into the ever-evolving (fragmenting, dissolving) fabric of the lyric, perhaps because it is not even desired (Cordibella notes that the veiled critique of Vittorini is in line with Sereni's view of him as too ideologically entrenched in predetermined ideas).[32]

This intertextual self-staging is rendered even more dramatic when we consider that the dialogic nature of the confrontation is undoubtedly also indebted to the *Commedia*, particularly Dante-pilgrim's encounters with the souls of the dead in *Inferno* and *Purgatorio*. These had also provided Vittorini with a model for his protagonist's own Dantesque descent into an underworld of memories and places in *Conversazione in Sicilia*,[33] and so come to be doubly present in the scene, both in Sereni's literal memory of Vittorini and in the more figurative one associated with Eliot.

It is not by chance that the point of interchange develops out of the identity of the phantasm: the 'familiar compound ghost' drawn from 'Little Gidding', which at the same time evokes the spectre of Brunetto Latini (*Inf.* XV), now reincarnated in the figure of Vittorini, who, if he can be mistaken for a 'cosa salda' [solid thing] by the poet at the beginning, is all too ready to dissipate at the end. 'Hying to his confine'—in imitation of the 'erring spirit' of Shakespeare's *Hamlet*, which Piero Boitani also recalls in describing the nature of Virgil's disappearance in *Purgatorio* XXX—we are left with the

---

[32] Giovanna Cordibella, *Di fronte al romanzo: contaminazioni nella poesia di Sereni* (Bologna: Pendragon, 2004), pp. 97, 101.
[33] For this, and a summary of other key thematic and stylistic traits of Vittorini's novel, see Ann Hallamore Caesar and Michael Caesar, *Modern Italian Literature* (London: Polity Press, 2007), pp. 177–8.

sense that the more meaningful return belongs to the dead figure rather than the living, although of course they are inextricably linked.[34]

Linguistically and syntactically, Sereni and Vittorini's discourses almost mirror each other to the letter, adding weight to the hypothesis that the latter is merely a projection of the former, a phantasm constructed in the poet's mind from memory to try to resolve the 'conto aperto' which the subject experiences as incomplete. Yet, ironically, the tautologous nature of the exchange and the endless, potentially hollow and circling repetition of words and phrases mean that all that the subject may have is the 'sole parole' (l. 41) he endeavours to counter, and the unfinished quality of the experience for both parties contaminates the language of the encounter so that it too 'goes nowhere'. Combined with the way in which the Serenian subject is abandoned by his interlocutor at the end, recalling the doubly bereft subject of 'Little Gidding; ('When I *left* my body [...] he *left* me'), and is left staring, paralysed and alone, into the greyness of the negated landscape, these associations already indicate the extent to which Sereni's journey diverges from (or reverses) the more productive Dantean model, or rather turns back to it only at the point at which all hope is lost.

The effect is heightened by the fact that the passage cited from *Un posto* contains one of only two instances (the other being in 'Intervista a un suicida' ['Interview with a Suicide'])[35] of Sereni directly reappropriating a full line from Dante, in this case with a minimal but nonetheless important distortion in his negativization of the line with the addition of a 'non più' (l. 48):

> Temp' era dal principio del mattino,
> e 'l sol montava 'n sù con quelle stelle
> ch'eran con lui quando l'amor divino
> mosse di prima quelle cose belle;
> sì ch'a bene sperar m'era cagione
> di quella fiera a la gaetta pelle
> *l'ora del tempo e la dolce stagione*;
> (*Inf.* I, 37–43)
>
> [It was the hour of morning,
> when the sun mounts with those stars

---

[34] 'At the "trumpet to the morn" sounded by Beatrice's dawn epiphany, Virgil silently "hies to his confine", and Dante inconsolably weeps. [...] Shades have indeed become solid things... and irremediably returned to their "emptiness"': Piero Boitani, *The Tragic and the Sublime in Medieval Literature* (Cambridge: Cambridge University Press, 1989), pp. 166–7.

[35] 'Mia donna venne a me di val di Pado' [My wife came from the valley of the Po] (*Par.* XV, 137) reproduced—in quotation marks—as line 31 of 'Intervista a un suicida', in *SU*, p. 164.

> that shone with it when God's own love
> first set in motion those fair things,
> so that, despite that beast with gaudy fur,
> I still could hope for good, encouraged
> *by the hour of the day and the sweet season,*]

Sereni's introduction of an additional syllable produces an *endecasillabo straniato* and *ipermetro* [distorted and hypermetric hendecasyllable] which also mirrors the distance (fall) from the ideal landscape of Dante's text, which is rooted in a divine act of creation and sustained by the 'sustanza di cose sperate' [substance of things hoped for] (*Par.* XXIV, 64) that underpin Dante's faith (and the pilgrim's) in the hope of better things. Sereni's poem revisits the spiritual comfort Dante-pilgrim gains from the 'hour of the morning and the sweet season' only as an impossibility, and leaves his subject in little doubt, instead, as to the loss of his friend and his failure to find recompense for it in the surrounding landscape.

Dantean lexicon therefore leaves its mark on this episode, interspersed with recollections of Vittorini's *Conversazione in Sicilia* and Eliot's 'Little Gidding', seamlessly threaded together in Sereni's construction of a dialogue that is intrinsically also his own, a highly personal re-enactment of an affectionate friendship that spanned many years and will survive many more years in the poem. Sereni's commitment to moving towards a more narrative, anti-lyric form of poetry, capable of housing a number of voices simultaneously, is reproduced in miniature here, reinforced through the greater space given to dialogic elements, whose roots are to be found in the *Commedia* and other models of *plurilinguismo* like Eliot himself. In turn, the hybridity of that discourse prevents the poem from settling into any single mode completely, whether in its desire for a totality of form or in the dream of a whole subjectivity.

While the first intimation of this evolution can be detected in some of the poetry of *DA*—which Sereni would have been working on in the 1940s—it seems most likely that his redefinition of the lyric form began in earnest in the 1950s and 1960s. These were key decades not only for the genesis and development of *Un posto*, but also for the reworking of parts of *DA* itself, a revised edition of which was published at the same time as *SU* in 1965. Taking all of this into account, we must acknowledge that Sereni's return to Dante is unlikely to have occurred in any absolute or definitive way. Rather, it is likely to have been the result of a process of gradual filtration of the *Commedia* into Sereni's creative consciousness, which began early on in his career but gained more prominence as his own poetry adapted to reflect his changing ideas about the lyric form, and whose plurivocality looked back to Dante whilst at the same time looking forward to the new path which opened up for the redefined lyric subject of *SU* and *SV*.

The meeting of poetry and history: Sereni's reading of Dante

Sereni's own essay on Dante, 'Si può leggere Dante come un poeta "puro"' (1950), gravitates around the notion of identity in the *Commedia* and sets it in the context of the poetic versus the historical value of Dante's text. In one respect, Sereni's essay re-engages with the debates that had stemmed in large part from Croce's scholarship on Dante, and specifically the distinction Croce had drawn between 'poesia' [poetry] and 'non poesia' [non-poetry] in the *Commedia*.[36] In other respects, it moves beyond more binary approaches such as these, with Sereni seeking to demonstrate how one ought to have a dialectical view of history and poetry in the way in which these two fields interact in the space of Dante's poem.

In order to clarify what is at stake in this dimension, Sereni focuses on Dante's representation, in the *Commedia*, of the figure of Pope Boniface VIII and on Giuseppe Petronio's essay *Bonifacio VIII*, importantly subtitled 'un episodio della vita e dell'arte di Dante' [an episode of the life and art of Dante].[37] He agrees with Petronio's attempt to elucidate 'l'operazione che permette di cogliere il passaggio, o i successivi passaggi, dal fantasma di vita all'immagine poetica e definitiva che gli corrisponde' [the operation that allows us to grasp the shift, or successive shifts, from the living phantasm to the definitive poetic image that corresponds to it] (p. 31), but is critical of his tendency still to work with a too black and white view of the relationship that poetry can entertain with history and reality:

---

[36] Benedetto Croce, *La poesia di Dante* (Bari: Laterza, 1921). See e.g. Croce's assessment of the role and function of allegory in Dante's poem, which begins: 'Nella poesia, l'allegoria non ha mai luogo [...] L'altro caso è che non lasci sussistere la poesia o non la lasci nascere, e al suo posto ponga un complesso d'immagini discordanti, poeticamente frigide e mute, e che perciò non sono vere immagini ma semplici segni; e in questo caso, non essendoci poesia, non c'è neppure oggetto alcuno di storia della poesia, ma solo l'avvertenza del limite di questa, del poeticamente fallito e nullo, del brutto' [In poetry, allegory never occurs [...] The other case is when allegory does not allow the poetry to exist, or stops it from being born, and in its place puts a group of discordant images, poetically silent and cold, which consequently are not true images but simple signs; and in this case, since there is no poetry, there is not even an object of the history of poetry, but only the awareness of its limits, of the poetically flawed and nullified, and of ugliness], pp. 21–2.

[37] Giuseppe Petronio, *Bonifacio VIII: un episodio della vita e dell'arte di Dante* (Lucca: Lucentia, 1950).

D'accordo che Dante non può essere letto 'come un qualsiasi poeta puro' e 'fermandosi solo all'abilità dell'artista', o in omaggio al 'culto dannunziano della parola'. Ma ecco: qui mi pare che il Petronio abbia proceduto a una eccessiva semplificazione polemica, tanto da ricostruire, nella sua forma più grezza, il vecchio dualismo tra 'contenuto' e 'forma'. (p. 32)

[Granted, Dante cannot be read 'as just any pure poet', nor by 'limiting oneself to the abilities of the artist', nor in homage to 'a Dannunzian cult of the word'. Yet, it seems to me that here Petronio has arrived at a polemical over-simplification, reconstructing, in its crudest form, the old dualism between 'content' and 'form'.]

Instead, Sereni advocates a more nuanced approach to the interaction between the poetic and the real or historical, whether the former be the product of the latter or something from which the latter can be reconstructed:

Si tratta insomma di vibrare all'unisono col poeta, identificando per quanto possibile la nostra coscienza del tempo, non trascurando, in quanto inutili sovrastrutture, quelli che erano i motivi estremamente seri dei conflitti e della vita ideale e pratica dell'epoca. Solo così, dal Bonifacio che vive allo stato di fantasma—un fantasma terribilmente concreto—nello spirito di Dante, si può passare all'immagine del Bonifacio sinistramente presente, si può dire, in tutta quanta la *Commedia*: dall'originaria *magnanimità*, nel senso di imponenza e di forza—di cui successivamente si colora la sperimentata nefandezza del personaggio, in modo da farlo apparire, *comunque*, grande—al suo farsi simbolo dell'errore e della corruzione universale, caricandosi di significati sempre più vasti e annullandosi dunque in essi nel senso cui il Petronio accenna. (pp. 30–1; italics in the original)

[In short, it is a question of vibrating in unison with the poet, identifying where possible our consciousness of time, without dismissing as useless superstructures the extremely serious reasons behind the conflicts and the ideal and practical life of the age. Only in this way, moving from the Boniface that exists as a ghost—a terribly real ghost—in Dante's mind, is the image of a sinisterly present Boniface revealed, it can be said, in the *Commedia* as a whole: from his original *magnanimity*, in the sense of grandeur and strength—which subsequently colours the proven wickedness of his character, in a way that gives him, *nevertheless*, the appearance of greatness—to his becoming a symbol of sin and universal corruption, taking upon himself broader and broader meanings and nullifying himself as a consequence within them, in the sense suggested by Petronio.]

In advocating an integral approach to reading Dante that considers the interplay of the personal and the universal, Sereni comes close to mirroring Contini's view of him, which likewise emphasized the existence of a 'doppio piano' [double level] in Dante's text centred on the way in which 'nell' "io" di Dante convergono l'uomo in generale, soggetto del vivere e dell'agire, e l'individuo storico, titolare di un'esperienza determinata *hic et nunc*, [...] Io trascendentale (con la maiuscola) [...] e "io" (con la minuscola) esistenziale' [Dante's 'I' incorporates both man in general (the living and acting subject) and the historical individual (someone participating in an experience in the here and now) [...]: both the transcendental 'I' (with a capital letter) and the existential, lower-case 'I'].[38] While Sereni's choice of the terms 'fantasma' and 'immagine' to correspond to the historical and poetic-allegorical dimensions, respectively, perhaps reveal a shift away from the more concrete eschatological framework of the *Commedia* towards something more intangibile, his consciousness of the dialogue between the two levels is paramount. In returning us once again to a consideration of memory and phantasm ('un fantasma terribilmente concreto—nello spirito di Dante') and their interactions with history, including the history of the writing subject, Sereni indicates the point at which he himself can re-enter the realms of this tantalizing poetic equation.

Again it is Montale who appears to facilitate the transition for Sereni between one mode of writing and the other. It becomes clear, for example, from what Sereni writes of history in relation to Montale's poetry, that the Dantean dimension to which he is drawn in the Ligurian poet has much less to do with Montale's reincarnation of Beatrice in the figure of Clizia—a modern reworking of the *stilnovist* figure of the 'donna angelicata' [angelicized lady]—than with the situation of his poetic subject whose identity comes to be shaped, like Dante's own, through a particular interaction of history with personal, cultural, and poetic memory. Sereni writes of Montale's 'Il ritorno' ['The Return']:

> La voce che esce dal fonografo (dal *cofano*) appartiene a una presenza (il *tu* ben noto, imprecisato ma polivalente) che s'inserisce nello spazio storico—storico nel senso che è ricordato.[39]

> [The voice coming from the phonograph (from the *chest*) belongs to a presence (the well-known *you*, undefined but polyvalent) which occupies the historical space—historical in the sense that it is remembered.]

Sereni is far from adhering to an objective view of history, then, and any history made in the light of memory will necessarily be subject to partiality and distortion even as it is engaged in the process of reconstructing a truth.

---

[38] Gianfranco Contini, 'Dante come personaggio-poeta della *Commedia*', in *Un'idea di Dante: saggi danteschi* (Turin: Einaudi, 1976), pp. 33–62 (pp. 34–5). As Contini acknowledges, the original distinction is inspired by Charles Singleton's work on the subject.
[39] Sereni, 'Il ritorno', p. 152.

As the dimension of epiphany promised by Sereni's encounters is increasingly relegated to a past time and space, which the subject must revisit in order for the true meaning of his experience in the present to be fathomed, so the vicissitudes of desire and memory come to dovetail with the uncertain identity of the recollected Other.

All this implies not only that Dante's influence on Sereni penetrates to the very heart of his poetry but also that it is made manifest on a variety of levels, ranging from the topographical and personal to the poetic and historical. A first look at how Dante is absorbed into the 'rete intertestuale' [intertextual web][40] of Sereni's poetry in fact suggests that he fits the twentieth-century model of *dantismo* put forward by Zygmunt Barański in 'Powers of Influence' insofar as there is a rich and multilayered play of associations that are likely to range between a more conscious *dantismo* and one that may be unconscious or somehow inevitable. In either case, *Un posto* testifies to Dante's presence in Sereni's poetry being assured by the early 1970s (we remember that *Un posto* was published in definitive form in 1973)—a view confirmed by Sereni's words to Attilio Bertolucci in a letter of 20 December 1970, which reveal how intrinsic a part Dante has become to his creative consciousness. Articulating his troubled state of mind and his propensity towards self-doubt and poetic impasse, Sereni literally speaks with a Dantean voice, reappropriating a line from *Inferno* VIII, 63 that embodies his innermost thoughts and anxieties: 'Io sono in questi giorni, ma non solo, una specie di cane rabbioso—e *in me medesmo mi volgo coi denti*, anche perché ce l'ho parecchio con me stesso [These days, but not only, I'm a kind of rabid dog—and *gnaw at myself with my own teeth*, because, among other things, I really am mad with myself].[41]

The episode Sereni recalls here is Dante's meeting with the Florentine Filippo Argenti. It develops through a particularly bitter exchange in which the pilgrim, like Argenti, suffers from a form of anger and desire for revenge that ultimately lead the damned soul to turn upon, and devour, himself. The scene seems to have been one that marked Sereni's imagination in a profound way, and we find echoes of it in several of his

---

[40] Cesare Segre, *Avviamento all'analisi del testo letterario* (Turin: Einaudi, 1985), p. 89. Segre uses this term to refer to the 'rete intertestuale ben fitta' [dense intertextual web] that characterizes the opening of Ariosto's *Orlando Furioso*, but it applies equally well to Sereni, especially in *Un posto*.

[41] *Attilio Bertolucci–Vittorio Sereni: una lunga amicizia. Lettere 1938–1982*, ed. Gabriella Palli Baroni (Milan: Garzanti, 1994), p. 225. The other possible point of intertextual reference, besides *Inf.* VIII, 61–3, is *Par.* XXX, 25–7, in which there is evidence of a similar grammatical construction, 'ché, come sole in viso che più trema, | così lo rimembrar del dolce riso | *la mente mia da me medesmo scema*' [for, like sunlight striking on the weakest eyes, | the memory of the sweetness of that smile | *deprives my mind of my mental powers*], a different incarnation of the mind reflecting on itself, and this time Dante's own.

poems: from the 'occhio intento' [intent eye] of *Un posto*, which marks an unusual conjunction of foresight and hindsight, prolepsis and analepsis—characteristics of the space of the melancholy subject, as I will show[42]—to the even more fundamental preoccupation Sereni shares with Dante at this point regarding the dangers of memory, or rather a particular kind of memory that is turned upon itself in destructive fashion:

> Quei fu al mondo persona orgogliosa;
> bontà non è che sua memoria fregi:
> *così s'è l'ombra sua qui furïosa.*
> Quanti si tengon or là su gran regi
> che qui staranno come porci in brago,
> di sé lasciando orribili dispregi!'.
> [...]
> Tutti gridavano: 'A Filippo Argenti!';
> e 'l fiorentino spirito bizzarro
> *in sé medesmo si volvea co' denti.*
> (*Inf.* VIII, 46–51, 61–3)

> ['In the world this man was full of arrogance.
> Not one good deed adorns his memory.
> *That is why his shade is so enraged.*
> 'How many now above who think themselves
> great kings will lie here in the mud, like swine,
> leaving behind nothing but ill repute!'
> [...]
> All cried: 'Get Filippo Argenti!'
> And that spiteful Florentine spirit
> *gnawed at himself with his own teeth.*]

This cannibalistic—and, as I will go on to define it, melancholy—form of memory that leads the tortured soul to ravage itself is one to which Sereni seems to be drawn, particularly in his later poetry. The shift of his desire away from the pursuit of a true object to a form of narcissistic regression in which desire has no real object, but rather endlessly generates its own destructive phantasm which leaves the self sinking ever deeper into its own mire, suggests that Sereni's *dantismo* is increasingly concentrated around key points in the *Commedia* which haunt him as correlatives of his own, at times, infernal situation.

---

[42] Cf. *Un posto* VI, 14–21 and *Inf.* VIII, 64–6, 'Quivi il lasciammo, che più non ne narro; | ma ne l'orecchie mi percosse un duolo, | per ch'io avante *l'occhio intento* sbarro' [Of him I say no more. Then we moved on, | when such a sound of mourning struck my ears | *I opened my eyes wide* to look ahead].

REWRITING THE MELANCHOLY JOURNEY

The melancholy dimension of the *Commedia* that Sereni draws upon and intensifies, in the articulation of his own desiring *quête*, is one I believe to be focused around the first two *cantiche* of Dante's poem. It comes to a head in the Earthly Paradise cantos of *Purgatorio* (especially XXX and XXXI), which in a sense review all of the melancholy experiences Dante has so far encountered (both in the *Commedia* and outside of it—most importantly, in the *Vita nova*) and reworks them in light of the path now opening up for the pilgrim (and the poet) as he prepares to enter Paradise. Whether we are dealing with the melancholia that has become the permanent condition of the damned in Hell, or with the shadow of melancholia that still makes its presence felt in the subject (if only momentarily) at the summit of Mount Purgatory, the source of anxiety undoubtedly lies in memory and in a complex autobiographical and salvific equation rooted in desire that Sereni cannot help but re-evoke in his own aspirations towards transcendence.

The model journey: remembering Dante

As Lino Pertile argues in his study of desire in the *Commedia*, there are several articulations of desire that coexist within Dante's text and the metaphor of the journey is the privileged vehicle for their manifestation since all imply the subject beginning from a point of exile and seeking a destination, more or less happy or more or less available to him, depending upon the route through life he chooses to take:

> Col termine *desiderio* si designa in generale un impulso psicologico verso una soddisfazione che può essere sia fisica sia spirituale. L'impulso è neutro in se stesso, ma acquista significato morale diverso a seconda dell'oggetto verso il quale si orienta. Secondo Sant'Agostino, gli uomini sono viaggiatori in cerca di una felicità che esiste soltanto nella loro vera patria. In questo senso desiderio ed esilio coincidono.[43]

> [The term *desire* generally designates a psychological impulse towards an experience of satisfaction that can be either physical or spiritual. The impulse is neutral in itself but acquires a particular moral significance according to the object towards which it is directed. According to St Augustine, men are

---

[43] Lino Pertile, *La punta del disio: semantica del desiderio nella 'Commedia'* (Fiesole: Cadmo, 2005), p. 26.

travellers in search of a happiness that exists only in reaching the true homeland. In this sense, desire and exile coincide.]

The pilgrim's journey similarly begins from a point of exile and evolves to incorporate the full gamut of possible endings for desire, both negative and positive. Desire also underpins the project of the poet and infuses the very language of his poem, which is constantly negotiating the space between (diminishing) lack and (increasing) fulfilment, and—particularly in the *Purgatorio* and *Paradiso*—mirrors the upward trajectory of the pilgrim's desire as it journeys to return to its Maker. The overcoming of physical and psychological obstacles, the renunciation of the 'via smarrita' [lost way] for the 'via diritta' [straight way], the increase in understanding that permits progress in intellectual terms too—all these transitional moments form part of Dante's desiring journey and all are orchestrated by the author for the benefit of his character and for his reader.[44] Importantly for our discussion in relation to the Serenian journey, they also imply a duality, a pair of forces or situations that the pilgrim must choose between and which only properly gain meaning from what they are not, what they prevent, or, in the case of *Purgatorio*, what they undo and in undoing redeem. For Dante-poet the journey is consequently neither so direct nor so clear-cut, and the residue of past experiences (past falls, the memory of past transgressions) is constantly being evoked and diffused in light of the present demands of the poem.

As Teodolinda Barolini has argued in *The Undivine 'Comedy': Detheologizing Dante*, the relationship between memory, temporality, and subjectivity is most pronounced in Dante's second canticle, which can be termed an 'Augustinian realm' insofar as the penitent soul undertakes a pilgrimage of desire in which he must learn to turn his desire from mortal objects to immortal ones, 'objects of "brief use"' to objects the soul can enjoy indefinitely'.[45] Earthly objects, even those that in Augustine's words can be 'perfectly legitimate in themselves', must be relinquished since, in their 'vanità' or mortality, they will ultimately fail to placate desire (p. 102).[46] However, this cannot be carried out without regret, and episodes like the

---

[44] Cf. *Inf.* I, 1–3, 'Nel mezzo del cammin di nostra vita | mi ritrovai per una selva oscura, | ché la diritta via era smarrita' [Midway in the journey of our life | I came to myself in a dark wood, | for the straight way was lost].

[45] *The Undivine 'Comedy'*, p. 103.

[46] The passage from the *Enchiridion* is cited by Jacques Le Goff, *The Birth of Purgatory*, trans. Arthur Goldhammer (Chicago: University of Chicago Press, 1981), p. 71. As Barolini shows, *vanità* is a highly charged word in Dante's poetics, bridging the identity of something insubstantial or not enduring (and ultimately fallacious) with the lure of the *donna gentile* and the 'altra novità' (mis-directions in desire) that led Dante astray following Beatrice's death.

meeting with Dante's friend Casella in *Purg.* II testify to the nostalgia that persists beyond the end of the soul's earthly life.[47]

This dialectic constitutes what Barolini terms a 'spiral of conversion that moves away from the noble temporal goods for which the soul feels a backward-turning love in the direction of their eternal counterparts [...] paradigmatically rendered in the concluding verses of *Purgatorio* XXVIII, where the pilgrim "lapses" towards his classical poets and "converts" to Beatrice' (p. 102).[48] Memory, as the nostalgic locus of this lapse, mediates between previously errant and newly redeemed desire, helping to create the 'bittersweet elegiac poetry of *Purgatorio*' (p. 102) and the tension that sustains the entirety of the second realm. In a process that ultimately involves 'mastering the lesson of death', the relationship (tension) between memory and desire is paramount (p. 107).[49]

I believe that it is this dimension of Dante's journey to which Sereni is drawn each time his own subject confronts the problematic nature of its relationship to its object(s) of desire (destined to fail him), and its struggle to master or relinquish the loss of them. However, Sereni appropriates the parabolic relationship between memory—located backwards and behind the subject—and the destination of the desiring journey—located through and beyond it—,which constitutes the spiral of desire in Dante's *Purgatorio*, as a more negative process of involution by which desire turns back upon itself and becomes stuck in an earlier state. Caught in a melancholy cycle of regression and incorporation that endlessly defers the moment at which the past might be relinquished, his subject becomes trapped inside a form of memory that ends all hope of redemption, either personally or poetically.

'Male del reticolato': privileging the backwards gaze[50]

In order to understand how this more negative spiral of desire comes to take hold in Sereni's poetry, it is necessary to go back to the beginning—to the first articulations of the desiring journey in *Frontiera*, and to the poet's

---

[47] On the significance of Dante-pilgrim's meeting with Casella, see Barolini, '"Amor che ne la mente mi ragiona"', in *Dante's Poets*, pp. 31–40.

[48] See *Purg.* XXVIII, 145–8, 'Io mi rivolsi 'n dietro allora tutto | a' miei poeti, e vidi che con riso | uditi avëan l'ultimo costrutto; | poi a la bella donna torna' il viso' [*I turned around then to my poets | and saw that they had listened | to her final utterance with a smile. | Then I turned back to the fair lady*]. The lady is in fact Matelda, but the implication holds.

[49] Cf. Barolini, *The Undivine 'Comedy'*, pp. 107–8, on Beatrice's rebuke to Dante in *Purg.* XXX–XXXI.

[50] As alluded to earlier, 'Male del reticolato' ['Barbed-Wire Fever'] is the title of a prose piece that Sereni wrote in 1945 about his experiences as a prisoner of war in Algeria, now in *ID2*, pp. 16–20.

first encounters with the past and the world of the dead. From here we can trace the evolution in Sereni's journey through *DA* and on to *SU* and *SV*, which are characterized by the even greater prominence given to memory, and its contamination by a series of phantasms called upon to mediate the desiring quest, that leave the subject open to the pull of a more regressive desire. The backwards gaze, so integral to the subject's survival during his period of incarceration in the war camps of Algeria, becomes pathological on his return, merely substituting one self-imposed form of imprisonment for another, real kind, to create a 'psychic tomb' of the kind Kristeva talks about in *Soleil noir*:[51]

> Mai eravamo stati prigionieri come in quel momento, a dispetto di ogni indizio ormai lampante di prossimo rilascio. Mai ci eravamo tanto infognati nella nostra condizione di vinti come ora che stavamo per uscirne. Andava maturando un assurdo amore per le abitudini, i luoghi della segregazione, un regredire (raccolto? meditativo? accorato? lirico? rabbioso?) dentro una disposizione d'animo solitario, in un prolungato amplesso portato sulle cose e sulle voci di lì, dall'angolo più remoto del campo la vista di quella nave che navigava a perdita d'occhio dentro l'Atlantico all'ora del tramonto, i brusii della notte africana oltre la soglia della baracca inondata dal plenilunio.[52]

> [Never had we been such prisoners as at that moment, in spite of what by now were clear signs of our imminent release. Never had we considered ourselves with the slime of defeat so much as now when we were about to emerge from it. An absurd love of habits, the places of our segregation, was developing, withdrawal (spiritual? meditative? aggrieved? lyrical? enraged?) into a solitary spiritual disposition, a prolonged ecstasy bringing on the swell of things and voices from beyond, from the remotest corner of the camp to the sight of a vessel toiling its way out of sight in the Atlantic at sunset, the faint whir of the African night beyond the threshold of the hut bathed in the full moon's light.]

In *Frontiera*, a regressive desire of this kind was at times identifiable in the way in which Sereni processed memories, but it was differently configured, directed less towards solitary activity and much more towards securing the potentially restorative force of another (a *tu* [you] figure) who inhabits the past but can perhaps be brought back into the present.[53] In

---

[51] 'La représentation incertaine que j'en garde et que j'orchestre dans la chambre noire de ce qui devient en conséquence *mon tombeau psychique, situé d'emblée mon malaise dans l'imaginaire*' [the blurred representation that I keep and put together in the darkroom of what thus becomes *my psychic tomb, this at once locates my ill-being in the imagination*] Julia Kristeva, Soleil noir: dépression et mélancolie (Paris: Gallimard, 1987), p. 72. This is a notion from Kristeva to which I will return. The traits of melancholia she describes in the section of *Soleil noir*, entitled 'Un passé qui ne passe pas' ['A Past That Does Not Pass By'] (pp. 70–2), find very strong resonance in Sereni's poetry.
[52] Sereni, 'L'anno quarantacinque' ['The Year '45'], p. 100; trans. Robinson–Perryman.
[53] 'Ritorno' ['Return'] (p. 19), 'Temporale a Salsomaggiore' ['Storm at Salsomaggiore'] (p. 20), and 'Diana' (p. 23) are good examples of this.

Frontiera, the retrospective perspective that will later predominate as a sign of the poet's melancholia is only at a nascent stage, and it competes for space with the more positive impetus towards the discovery of the unknown, and the charting of still unexplored territories. Thus while in *Frontiera* Sereni does at times display an obsession with death, and especially with the image or memory of the dead, this still forms part of a poetics of revelation in which what the poet seeks from the past is often returned to him unexpectedly, or is something to which he can gain access with a minimum of anxiety and displacement. The need for the penitential journey is not yet fully established and if a Dantean dimension does exist, it is perhaps Virgilian more than Comedic proper, part of an 'otherworld' journey in more general terms—a certain affinity with the world of the dead, or an opening up of space in their direction:

> II
> Questo trepido vivere nei morti.
> Ma dove ci conduce questo cielo
> che azzurro sempre più azzurro si spalanca
> ove, a guardarli, ai lontani
> paesi decade ogni colore.
> Tu sai che la strada se discende
> ci protende altri prati, altri paesi,
> altre vele sui laghi:
> > il vento ancora
> turba i golfi, li oscura.
> Si rientra d'un passo nell'inverno.
> E nei tetri abituri si rientra,
> a un convito d'ospiti leggiadri
> si riattizzano i fuochi moribondi.
> [...]

('Strada di Creva', II.15–27, *Frontiera*, pp. 40–41)

> [This timorous living among the dead.
> But where this bluer, always bluer,
> sky opens wide and leads us
> to the distant villages,
> gazing, every colour decays.
> You know that if the road descends
> to us it extends other fields, other villages,
> other sails on the lakes:
> > again the wind
> disturbs the bay, obscures them.
> We go back a step into winter.

> And to the gloomy dwellings we go back,
> at a banquet of enchanting guests,
> dying fires are rekindled.]

Like the descent into darkness figured in Sereni's classically-inspired *Versi a Proserpina* [*Poems to Proserpine*] (also in *Frontiera*), the underworld that beckons here is perhaps closer to Hades than Hell, and consequently able to house a topography that spreads ('si spalanca') from the Avernus-like Lake Maggiore to something like Elysium (cf. 'le strade che rasentano l'Eliso' [streets that border Elysium], in 'Strada di Zenna', l. 7). Although—as the title of the collection suggests, and as the previous study of deixis in *Frontiera* has shown—movement is generally configured in relation to a boundary that sets a limit on experience, a certain amount of movement and possession of space is still afforded the subject in the space between one border and the other. While there is at times the potential for the subject to veer off course, or to succumb to the pull of a death-oriented desire that may lead him in the wrong direction, he generally knows which way he ought to be travelling to rediscover what he has lost. Overall, he strives to reach a beyond that is still, at this point in his poetics, understood to be located in a space forwards and in front of him, even if there are hints that it will not stay there indefinitely.

This is in sharp contrast to the situation that develops in subsequent collections, beginning from *DA*, in which progressive motion comes up against, and largely unravels beneath, a regressive pull in desire, centred on memory. Although Sereni is increasingly drawn to Dante's Edenic topography and particularly to the tension implicit in it that sets the recollection of the Fall against the promise of salvation, his own journey back to the origins of desire and the self leads him to getting stuck at the level of his 'memorie triste' (*Purg.* XXXI, 11). Unable to make a passage beyond them to something else, he becomes caught in a downward spiral that ends the journey at the point when it ought to be beginning.

'Riaffiorata febbre': remembering Algeria[54]

Looking at *DA*, it becomes clear that this spiral of desire takes hold in the subject during his experiences as a prisoner of war in Africa, when he too is forced to live through his own kind of Purgatory:

---

[54] From 'Algeria', ll. 5–7, in *DA*, 'Come mi frughi *riaffiorata febbre* | che mi mancavi e nel perenne specchio | ora di me baleni' [How you rifle through me *reawakened fever* | that I lacked and in the perennial mirror | of me now flashes] (p. 85).

'Memorie triste', 'passi perduti'

> In piena coscienza bisogna dire che nessuno stato di detenzione è stato più blando del nostro, di noi caduti in mano americana. I vari drammi individuali maturati in rapporto a quella situazione sono un altro discorso. Ma il nostro vero guaio era lì, in quella blanda, torpida, semidillica prigionia.[55] [In all conscience, it must be said that—us having fallen into American hands—no state of detention could have been blander. The various individual dramas that developed in relation to that state are another matter. But our real hardship consisted precisely in that bland, torpid, semi-idyllic imprisonment.]

As Sereni tells us elsewhere, 'un'alta collina boscosa di forma troncoconica, da montagna del Purgatorio' [a high wooded hill in the shape of a truncated cone, like the Purgatorial Mountain][56] towered over one of the camps in which he was stationed, and he even goes so far as to label the prisoner of war camps 'veri e propri paradisi terrestri' [consummate earthly paradises] whose remote location leads to a severing of all contact with the outside world.[57] As 'un campo di meditabondi, in pratica un campo-deposito, una riserva limbale o purgatoriale [a camp of brooders, virtually a camp-repository, a limbo or purgatorial reservation], Sereni's prison environment fast becomes a chamber for the listless subject of melancholy whose time, in the absence of action, is spent contemplating a by now irretrievable past, an irrecuperable loss:[58]

> Quest'uomo doveva essere tormentato dai ricordi, aveva la mania delle date e dei nomi di luoghi in calce alle singole liriche. Volti, figure, paesaggi del passato... pietà di sé e del proprio passato, delle ore e degli incontri che vogliono in qualche modo durare.
> Sì, ma questi ricordi non sono poeticamente felici: non hanno spicco, non sono evidenti, non hanno forza di comunicazione. E c'è di peggio: un sovrabbondare di tenerezza, un pericoloso abbandono a una poeticità diffusa, affidata al soggetto patetico, al tema suggestivo... [59]
> [This man must have been tormented by memories, he had the habit of always putting the date and place name at the foot of every single lyric. Faces, people, bygone landscapes... self-pity and pity for his past, for the hours and the meetings that somehow want to survive.
> Yes, but these memories are not poetically felicitous: they do not stand out, do not reveal themselves, have no communicative force. And worse:

---

[55] Sereni, 'L'anno quarantacinque', p. 95, trans. Robinson–Perryman.
[56] 'Algeria '44', first publ. in *ID1*, pp. 26–9, now in *ID2*, pp. 13–16 (p. 14).
[57] 'Le sabbie dell'Algeria' ['Algerian Sands'], first publ. in *Storia illustrata* 16.178 (Sept. 1972), pp. 102–7, now in *TDP*, pp. 249–57 (p. 251).
[58] Ibid. 254.
[59] 'Male del reticolato', p. 18, trans. Robinson–Perry man.

there is an excess of sentimentality, a dangerous abdication to a vulgar poeticality, to the pathetic fallacy, to the emotive theme...]

The 'orizzontalità' [horizontality][60] which characterizes the subject of Sereni's second collection, his evident fixation on memories that all too often take the form of hallucinatory presences that rise mirage-like from the desert, reveal how his 'mal d'Africa' [African sickness] is precisely that—both a psychological sickness (a Montalian 'male di vivere' [pain of living]) that takes hold of him as a result of his confinement to this 'angolo morto della storia' [dead corner of history] and the recurring nostalgia for Africa that persists long after his return to Italy at the end of the war.[61]

The poem 'Il male d'Africa' ['The African Sickness'], in *DA* (pp. 92–5) maps this process very visibly, and suggests that Sereni is both establishing the purgatorial journey as paradigm and reworking its final destination. Revisiting the central dynamic of Dante's *Purgatorio*, it charts the subject's attempts to atone for an experience by working through his most painful memories of it. The expiation is a failed one, however, whose incompleteness prevents the subject being able to move beyond memory once he has engaged in it. Since the poet's own journey back to Italy at the end of the war is simultaneously grafted upon the parallel journey undertaken in reverse by his friend Giansiro Ferrata (over twelve years later), there can also be no complete possession of the past or the present, only the shadowy double play of desire and memory that complicates the Dantean scheme even as it recalls it.[62]

The dedication carried by the poem, '*A Giansiro che va in Algeria (1958)*' [*For Giansiro going to Algeria (1958)*], also gives us a clue as to its unique status within *DA* as a whole, since it was written well after the end of the war and was originally intended to be included in *SU* (which retains a fragment of it, p. 151). In typical Serenian fashion it is thus also a chance for the poet to revisit an earlier phase in his poetics so that the time that he feels he is missing—his haunting by all those 'passi perduti' [lost steps] that he has failed to take—also implicates a poetic road and a poetic

---

[60] 'Ci si domandava, noi rimasti nel campo-deposito, se non fosse andata meglio a quelli che la sorte aveva assegnato al movimento dei reparti di lavoro che non a noi *confinati nella posizione orizzontale*' [Those of us who were left behind in the camp-repository wondered whether those whom fate had assigned to the to-ing and fro-ing of working parties didn't actually have it better than us, *confined as we were to the horizontal position*], 'Le sabbie dell'Algeria', p. 257.

[61] Sereni, 'L'anno quarantacinque', p. 99, trans. Robinson–Perryman.

[62] Giansiro Ferrata was a critic and writer whose friendship with Sereni spanned several decades. The Archive in Luino houses a number of letters and postcards sent by Ferrata to Sereni in the period from the early 1940s to the late 1970s: APS VI 182 (F 414).

journey that have been distorted in a similar fashion to memory and desire.

The obstacles written into the poem suggesting a resistance or delay to forward movement (beginning with the intimately purgatorial figure of the 'anima attardata' [soul delayed], l. 4), or an inability to reconnect with a home that ought to be 'familiare' [his family's] but in which the poet finds himself a stranger, are therefore emblematic less of a physical restraint than a psychological one, centred upon 'qualche groppo | convulso di ricordo' [some convulsive | chokings of memory] (ll. 68–9) and 'questo groppo da sciogliere' [this tangle to unravel] (l. 100), which he cannot get beyond. The repeated 'eco' that rebounds from the past back to the present, from Algeria to Milan and back again, shows the extent to which all paths lead back to Africa and the 'male' of the title is thus an intimately personal kind of illness—a melancholia precisely—that is the result of a too-strong attachment to memory, and worst of all to a memory that is itself deficient, that leaves Sereni as he himself tells us 'incompleto per sempre' [forever incomplete].[63]

That sense of lack, combined with an unhealthy fixation upon the site of loss, leads to the genesis of a backward-looking desire, whose point of origin (Algeria) is synonymous with its final destination, in a finite and closed circle that actually puts the unsurpassable memory of Casablanca in place of the Logos:

> Pensa—dicevo—la guerra è sul finire   15
> e ponente ponente mezzogiorno
> *guarda che giro per rimandarci a casa.*
> [...]
>   *Rimbombava*
> la eco tra viadotti e ponti lungo
> un febbraio di fiori intempestivi

---

[63] 'Cominciavi a renderti conto in concreto di tante cose—le donne, i viaggi, i libri, la città, la poesia; cominciavi a vivere con pienezza, uscito una buona volta dallo sbalordimento giovanile. Venne la guerra e rovinò ogni cosa. Ti pareva di spiegare così la crisi che colse te e alcuni tuoi coetanei dopo il '45, di ritorno dalla guerra e dalla segregazione (e dell'esserti sentito escluso dalla Liberazione, privato della sua lotta *come di un'esperienza che ti è mancata lasciandoti incompleto per sempre*)' [You began to take stock, concretely, of many things—the women, the journeys, the books, the city, poetry; you began living fully, once definitively beyond the bewilderment of youth. Came the war, and everything was ruined. That's how you thought to explain the crisis that overcame you and some others of your age after '45, back from the war and imprisonment (and feeling yourself excluded from the Liberation, deprived of its struggle as *of an experience you've missed, leaving you forever incomplete*], Vittorio Sereni, 'Cominciavi' ['You Began'] (1960), first publ. in *ID1*, pp. 98–9, now in *ID2*, pp. 64–5 (p. 64); trans. Robinson–Perryman.

'Memorie triste', 'passi perduti' 219

> *ritornava* a un sussulto di marmitte
> che al sole fumavano allegre 25
> *e a quel febbrile poi sempre più fioco*
> ritmo di ramadàn
> che giorni e giorni ci durò negli orecchi
> ci fermammo e fu,
> *calcinata nel verbo* 30
> *sperare nel verbo desiderare,*
> *Casablanca.*
>   ('Il male', pp. 92–3)
> To think—I said—the war's ending 15
> and west-southwest,
> *what a roundabout way to send us home.*
> [...]
>   [...] Between viaducts
> and bridges the echo *rebounded*
> through a February of untimely flowers,
> *returned* to spitting stewpots
> steaming gaily in the sun 25
> *and to that feverish, then ever fainter*
> rhythm of Ramadan
> persisting day after day in our ears,
> we halted there,
> *chalked within the verb* 30
> *to hope, the verb to desire,*
> *was Casablanca.*]

The last lines echo the beginning of the Gospel of St John, 'In principio era il Verbo, e il Verbo era presso Dio e il Verbo era Dio' [In the beginning was the Word and the Word was with God, and the Word was God] (John 1: 1). However that 'place' is not the site of an original act of creation but of a repeated loss and fall only intensified by the distance the subject moves away, which puts him equidistant from the self he has left behind and the one he is still to reunite with, from which he is also estranged:

> e quando più non si aspettava quasi 40
> fummo sul flutto sonoro
> diretti a una vacanza
> di volti di là dal mare, da una
> *nereggiante distanza,* in famiglia
> coi gabbiani che fidenti 45
> *si abbandonavano* all'onda.
> Ma caduta ogni brezza, navigando
> oltre Marocco all'isola dei Sardi
> una febbre fu in me:
> *non più* quel folle 50

ritmo di ramadàn
                              ma un'ansia
una fretta d'arrivare
quanto più nella sera
d'acque stagnanti e basse
l'onda s'ottenebrava   55
rotta da luci fiacche—e
              Gibilterra! un latrato,
il muso erto d'Europa, della cagna
che accucciata lì sta sulle zampa davanti:
Tardi troppo tardi alla festa
—scherniva la turpe gola—   60
troppo tardi! e altro di più confuso
sul male appreso verbo
della bianca Casablanca.
                  (pp. 93–4)

[and when we'd stopped expecting it almost   40
we were on resounding swell,
heading for a holiday
of faces over there beyond the sea,
from *a blackish distance*, in the family
with seagulls that trustful   45
gave themselves up to the wave.
But every breeze dropped, past
Morocco sailing for the isle of Sards
a fever grew in me:
no longer that maddening   50
rhythm of Ramadan
                  but an eagerness,
a fretting to arrive
the more so on evenings
of stagnant low water
when the wave darkened,   55
broken by feeble glimmers—and
              Gibraltar! a howl,
the raised snout of Europe,
from the bitch crouched there on front paws:
Late, too late for the feast
—the foul throat taunted —
too late! and another thing more confused
about *the ill-comprehended*
verb of white Casablanca.]

Thus what has the potential to be a cathartic, penitential, and ultimately redemptive process, more in keeping with the purgatorial slant of the poem suggested by the early appearance of the 'anima attardata', ends up becoming something more negative or infernal in quality. The lexicon that Sereni reappropriates from Dante's *Commedia* is evidence of this, since the word 'groppo', which appears twice in Sereni's poem, is one that Dante uses above all to reinforce the stasis and immobility that characterizes those in Hell. It indicates a misdirection in desire: a turning inwards, or folding back over oneself—similar to that already identified in the Argenti episode—which marks a kind of implosion, an endless circling of self-destruction.

This 'groppo' in Sereni's poem recalls the knot that characterizes the twisted trunks of the imprisoned souls in the suicide wood of *Inferno* XIII, the clump one of the spendthrifts ('sproloqui') reduces himself to, echoing the pose of the suicides who have literally been joined to their bushes, 'E poi che forse li fallia la lena, | di sé e d'un cespuglio fece un groppo' [Then, almost out of breath, he pressed himself | into a single tangle with a bush] (*Inf.* XIII, 122–3), and perhaps more significantly still, the knot of frozen tears which characterizes the impossible weeping of the souls in Cocytus that ends weeping altogether:

> *Lo pianto stesso lì pianger non lascia,*
> e 'l duol che truova in su li occhi rintoppo,
> *si volge in entro* a far crescer l'ambascia;
> *ché le lagrime prime fanno groppo,*
> e, sì come visiere di cristallo,
> rïempion sotto 'l ciglio tutto il coppo.
> (*Inf.* XXXIII, 94–9)

> [*The very weeping there prevents their weeping,*
> for the grief that meets a barrier at the eyelids
> *turns inward* to augment their anguish,
> *since their first tears become a crust*
> that like a crystal visor fills
> the cups beneath the eyebrows.]

Finally, it revisits the 'groppo' which the pilgrim experiences in *Inf.* XI when he meets an obstacle to his understanding which crucially coincides with a physical delay to his and Virgil's progress through Hell, a literal blocking of the way whose knot must be dissolved before further progress can be made:

> '*Lo nostro scender conviene esser tardo,*
> sì che s'ausi un poco in prima il senso
> al tristo fiato; e poi no i fia riguardo'.
> [...]
> *Ancora in dietro un poco ti rivolvi'*,
> diss' io, 'là dove di' ch'usura offende
> la divina bontade, *e 'l groppo solvi'*.
> (*Inf.* XI, 10–12, 94–6)

['*We must delay descending* so our sense,
inured to that vile stench,
no longer heeds it.'
[...]
'*But go back a little way,*' I said,
'to where you told me usury offends
God's goodness, and *untie that knot for me*.]

Recovering old ground, returning to an earlier point that demands clarification, can thus be positive for Dante, negative for Sereni. Like the frozen tears of Cocytus, memory in Sereni's poem leads only to the negation of memory, or rather the inability to form memories in such a way that they can be positive. This experience is made more traumatic still by the feeling the subject has that his true self may reside back there, still imprisoned in that 'reticolato' [barbed wire] he may never properly have left and which he cannot see beyond. By the end of 'Il male d'Africa', Sereni has to accept that the real phantasm may not be his memory at all but his present self, which he does not recognize himself in and which is missing ten years that cannot be repaid. He regresses to a point in the past where he hopes he might reconnect with a path that could lead him to a future, beyond the Hell he inhabits; instead he finds himself attached only to what he has forgotten or cannot bring to light, 'Questa ciarla non so se di rincorsa o fuga | vecchia di dieci o più anni | di un viaggio tra tanti.. . —s'inquietano i tuoi occhi— | e nessuna notizia d'Algeria. | No, nessuna—rispondo' [This chit-chat catch-up or flight I don't know, | now ten or more years old | about one journey among many... —your eyes grow troubled— | and no news of Algeria. | No, none—I reply] (l. 64–8).

Sereni's journey is no longer unique as it was in *Frontiera*, and his failure to find a 'viaggio' to call his own leads him to renouncing the journey altogether, wishing it on his interlocutor (no doubt, Ferrata himself):

Portami tu notizie d'Algeria—
quasi grido a mia volta—di quanto
passò di noi fuori dal reticolato,   90
dimmi che non furono soltanto
fantasmi espressi dall'afa,
di noi sempre in ritardo sulla guerra
ma sempre nei dintorni
di una vera nostra guerra... se quanto   95
proliferò la nostra febbre d'allora
è solo eccidio tortura reclusione
o popolo che santamente uccide.
[...]

'Memorie triste', 'passi perduti'

<blockquote>

ma *a te* fortuna e buon viaggio
borbotta borbotta la pentola familiare.   104
(pp. 94–5)

[Bring me news of Algeria
—*I almost shout in return*—about
what of us passed beyond the barbed wire,   90
tell me they weren't only
ghosts pressed from the heat haze,
of us always late for the war
but always on the outskirts
of a real war of our own... if what   95
our fever of that time was spreading
is only slaughter, torture, isolation,
or a people that religiously kill.
[...]
but to you good luck and *bon voyage*,
the family pot's bubbling, bubbling.]   104

</blockquote>

Significantly, this final desire on the part of the subject to comprehend what part of him, if any, has managed to liberate itself and return from the camp, and what remains caught in the wire, is left unvoiced. What is called forth are only the disturbing visions or *phantasmata* that designate the uncertain, liminal presence of a posthumous self for whom there can be no homecoming, either in space or time, only the Montalian awareness of an unchangeable landscape which registers the unyielding force of memory:

<blockquote>

È scritta là. Il sempreverde
alloro per la cucina
resiste, la voce non muta,
Ravenna è lontana, distilla
veleno una fede feroce.
Che vuole da te? Non ti cede
voce, leggenda o destino...
Ma è tardi, sempre più tardi.
('Dora Markus', II.26–33, *Le occasioni*, pp. 126–7)

[It's written there. The evergreen
laurel for the kitchen lasts,
the voice won't change. Ravenna's far,
a savage faith distils its venom.
What does it want from you?
Voice, legend, destiny—
nothing's surrendered...
But it's late, always later.]

</blockquote>

Looking at another of Montale's poems, 'Voce giunta con le folaghe' ['Voice That Came with the Coots'] (from *La bufera*), we can understand to what extent the success or failure of Sereni's journey actually comes down to the choice between two kinds of memory. In Montale's poem, an infernal memory, characterized by a desire that is excessive or incomplete (and thus mis-directed or deficient in some way), is set against another, purgatorial, one. This latter form of memory, unlike the first, can be useful because it leads to self-knowledge and frees the subject from those sins, insufficiencies, or transgressions which it also forces him to revisit, allowing him to jump clean over them, rejoining his path further up:

> [...] *Memoria*
> non è peccato fin che giova. Dopo
> è letargo di talpe, abiezione
> *che funghisce su sé...* —
>   Il vento del giorno   45
> confonde l'ombra viva e l'altra ancora
> riluttante in un mezzo che respinge
> le mie mani, e il respiro mi si rompe
> nel punto dilatato, nella fossa
> che circonda lo scatto del ricordo.   50
> Così si svela prima di legarsi
> a immagini, a parole, *oscuro senso
> reminiscente, il vuoto inabitato*
> che occupammo e che attende fin ch'è tempo
> *di colmarsi di noi, di ritrovarci*...   55
>   ('Voce giunta con le folaghe', ll. 42–55,
>   in *La bufera*, p. 250)

[*Memory is no sin while it avails.
After it's molelike torpor, misery
That mushrooms on itself...*'   45
        The wind of day
melds the living shadow
and the other, still reluctant one
in an amalgam that repels my hands,
and the breath breaks out of me at the swelling point,
and in the moat that surrounds the release of memory.   50
So it reveals itself before attaching
to images, or words, *dark reminiscent
sense, the unlived-in void* we occupied
that waits for us until the time has come
to fill itself with us, to find us again...]   55

Whilst Sereni too aims for a 'memoria [...] che giova', he is increasingly drawn back to a form of more abject memory that is the result, precisely, of his commitment to a melancholy strategy for repossession of the lost object of desire—that 'oscuro senso | reminiscente' outlined above by Montale (ll. 52–3). Fashioned by an errant desire, it tends towards an overvaluation of the past, tying the 'I' to an image that may have little to do with the recollection of an actual experience and much more to do with an imaginary return to a place that has perhaps never existed before but which the subject still seeks as the (pre-existing) origin of his desire, 'il vuoto inabitato [...] che attende fin ch'è tempo | di colmarsi di noi, di ritrovarci' (ll. 53–5).

By configuring as a return what cannot be one, the poet establishes the paradigm of his desiring journey as one directed backwards, towards a mythical version of the past (and an unreal possession) sought out as restitution for an absence or loss felt in the present. However, as inherently phantasmatic in character, memory of this kind is potentially dangerous, as it contaminates perception and leads to a disorientation that comes both from its proximity to death and from its resemblance to dream. It is the same memory, in fact, that Dante is called upon to revisit in the final cantos of *Purgatorio*, on the other side of which lies the gate to Paradise and the true Beatrice but which on its near side also recalls in the process the dangers of Hell and the trials of Purgatory only just now left behind.

The symptoms of regression: defining melancholia

In order to clarify why this shift towards a more negative and regressive form of desire occurs in Sereni, and how it is related (whether negatively or positively) to the model of the desiring journey put forward in the *Commedia*, it is important to establish the coordinates of a melancholy desire that can explain the phenomena so far discussed. The starting point for my theoretical discussion in this part of the chapter is Freud's 1917 essay 'Mourning and Melancholia', but I also refer to two other works on melancholia which present us with a practical application of Freud's theories to the study of literature—Kristeva's *Soleil noir* and Agamben's *Stanze: la parola e il fantasma nella cultura occidentale* [*Stanzas: Word and Phantasm in Western Culture*]—which both provide an insight into melancholy as a decidedly poetic response to dealing with loss, or figuring it in language.

Already in 'Il male d'Africa' we have seen evidence of a regressive tendency in Sereni's poetry that results from a particular relationship between desire and memory. For him, poetic memory is always a double construct incorporating a desire for return within the premonition of a future loss:

D. Che cosa è la memoria per il poeta?

R. Per quanto mi riguarda, direi che è in stretta connessione col desiderio e, per altro verso, con *una particolare forma di presagio istantaneo che di un fatto vissuto fa, appunto, oggetto di memoria.*[64]

[Q. What is memory for a poet?

A. As far as I'm concerned, it is strictly related to desire and, in another way, with a *particular form of sudden premonition which makes of a lived event an object of memory.*]

The fact that Sereni already knows that he will be going back turns the trajectory of desire from prospective yearning to pre-emptive nostalgia. In poetic terms, it also divides the subject between competing temporalities and locates his desire in a misperception of what has existed or already ceased to exist. This is a mechanism of which we find echoes in Montale's poem 'La casa dei doganieri' ['The House of the Customs Men'] in *Le occasioni*, and it is helpful to consider the resonance which this poem has for an understanding of Sereni's attitude to memory, and the nature of his growing melancholy experience:

> *Tu non ricordi* la casa dei doganieri
> sul rialzo a strapiombo sulla scogliera:
> *desolata t'attende dalla sera*
> *in cui* v'entrò lo sciame dei tuoi pensieri
> e vi sostò irrequieto.   5
> Libeccio sferza da anni le vecchie mura
> e il suono del tuo riso non è più lieto:
> la bussola va impazzita all'avventura
> e il calcolo dei dadi più non torna.
> *Tu non ricordi; altro tempo frastorna*   10
> *la tua memoria*; un filo s'addipana.
>
> Ne tengo ancora un capo; ma s'allontana
> la casa e in cima al tetto la banderuola
> affumicata gira senza pietà.
> Ne tengo un capo; ma tu resti sola   15
> né qui respiri nell'oscurità.
>
> *Oh l'orizzonte in fuga*, dove s'accende
> rara la luce della petroliera!
> Il varco è qui? (Ripullula il frangente
> ancora sulla balza che scoscende...).   20
> *Tu non ricordi la casa di questa*

---

[64] Interview with Domenico Porzio, 'In viaggio verso me', *Panorama*, 22 Mar. 1982, pp. 117–21 (p. 121).

mia sera. Ed io non so chi va e chi resta.
                                    (p. 161)

[*You don't recall* the house of the customs men
high on the bluff that drops sheer to the reef:
it's been waiting, *deserted, since the evening
your thoughts swarmed in*
and hovered, nervously.

Sou'westers have lashed the old walls for years
and your laugh's not carefree any more:
the compass needle staggers crazily
and the dice no longer tell the score.
*You don't remember: other times
assail your memory*; a thread gets wound.

I hold one end still; but the house recedes
and the smoke-stained weathervane
spins pitiless up on the roof.
I have one end; but you're alone,
not here, not breathing in the dark.

Oh the vanishing horizon line,
where the tanker's light shines faint!
Is the channel here? (The breakers
still seethe against the cliff that drops away...)
You don't recall the house of this, my evening,
And I don't know who's going or who'll stay.]

The point about this poem is that Montale chooses to configure as a memory what cannot be one, or rather that can only be a part-memory from which the portion that he really seeks—the part that belongs to the *tu* figure—is missing or elsewhere, '*altro tempo* frastorna | la tua memoria' (ll. 10–11). As Montale admitted in a letter to Alfonso Leone dated 19 June 1971:

La casa dei doganieri fu distrutta quando avevo sei anni. La fanciulla in questione non poté mai vederla; andò ... verso la morte, ma io lo seppi molti anni dopo. Io restai e resto ancora. Non si sa chi abbia fatto scelta migliore. Ma verosimilmente non vi fu scelta.[65]

[The custom men's house was destroyed when I was six years old. The girl in question could never have seen it: she ... was heading towards death, but I learned of it many years later. I remain and remain still. I don't know who made the better choice. But most likely there was no choice.]

---

[65] In *Lingua nostra*, 38.3–4 (Sept.–Dec. 1977), p. 118, cited in the appendix to *L'opera in versi*, p. 917.

Thus with the funereal strategy that carries the *tu* figure off towards death, the poet serves only to reinforce rather than to counter the sense that she (the unnamed Arletta) belongs to another world from the start, and that his own determination to remain attached to this place, devoid of her from the beginning, means that he will always be looking for her in the wrong place.[66] Reading Giorgio Agamben's definition of melancholia in *Stanze*, we can begin to understand how this kind of misdirection of desire—the hankering after the phantasm of an object which, being lost forever, takes on the properties of a supreme Other overvalued in and of itself—functions at the basis of the melancholy disposition into which the bereft subject willingly leads itself:

> E come il recesso dell'accidioso non nasce da un difetto, ma da una concitata esacerbazione del desiderio, che si rende inaccessibile il proprio oggetto nel disperato tentativo di garantirsi così dalla sua perdita e di aderire ad esso almeno nella sua assenza, così si direbbe che il ritrarsi della libido malinconica non abbia altro scopo che quello di rendere possibile un'appropriazione in una situazione in cui nessun possesso è, in realtà, possibile. [...] Ricoprendo il suo oggetto coi funebri addobbi del lutto, la malinconia gli conferisce la fantasmagorica realtà del perduto; ma in quanto essa è il lutto per un oggetto inappropriabile, la sua strategia apre uno spazio all'esistenza dell'irreale e delimita una scena in cui l'io può entrare in rapporto con esso e tentare un'appropriazione che nessun possesso potrebbe pareggiare e nessuna perdita insidiare.[67]
>
> [As, in the case of *acedia*, the withdrawal not from a defect, but from a frantic exacerbation of desire that renders its object inaccessible to itself in the desperate attempt to protect itself from the loss of that object and to adhere to it at least in its absence, so it might be said that the withdrawal of melancholic libido has no other purpose than to make viable an appropriation in a situation in which none is really possible. [...] Covering its object with the funereal trappings of mourning, melancholy confers upon it the phantasmagorical reality of what is lost; but insofar as such mourning is for an unobtainable object, the strategy of melancholy opens a space for the existence of the unreal and marks out a scene in which the ego may enter into relation with it and attempt an appropriation such as no other possession could rival and no loss possibly threaten.]

Montale's choice of the adjective 'desolata' for his 'casa' is emblematic of this melancholy strategy, since it implies that the house is not just

---

[66] On the significance of 'La casa dei doganieri' as an Arletta poem, see Jonathan Galassi, in *Eugenio Montale: Collected Poems 1920–1954* (New York: Farrar, Straus, and Giroux, 2000), pp. 511–12.

[67] Giorgio Agamben, *Stanze: la parola e il fantasma nella cultura occidentale* (Turin: Einaudi, 1977), pp. 25–6.

empty but specifically devoid of the Arletta figure and thus in expectation of her return ('desolata *t'attende* dalla sera | in cui v'entrò lo sciame dei tuoi pensieri', ll. 3–4), though, as we know from Montale's comments, she has never been there in the first place. Once again it is deictic reference that betrays the strong element of self-delusion: what she fails to remember, because she cannot possibly remember it, is 'la casa di *questa | mia serà*' (ll. 21–2), the poet's own chamber that is also the space of his poem, what he lovingly prepares for her in order that she might one day fill it and come back to him.

Yet all that he is left with is his own tormented circling about an absence that the Dantesque action of the 'libeccio' that 'sferza da anni le vecchie mura' (l. 6) brings home to him, wearing away at the impossible memory of her 'no longer happy laugh' and leaving him unable to determine the direction his desiring journey should take.[68] The point of escape (the 'varco') is no longer certain, and since she will not come or, as he sees it, will not come back, he is left stranded with his own thoughts. His torment is thus double: he cannot bear to stay here, in this 'casa', if she is not with him, but he can also never leave until she returns, a clear manifestation of the stasis (*acedia*) that strikes down the melancholic in his haunting by a perennially lost object, wholly inaccessible but never relinquished as such, which turns mourning into something pathological and obsessive.

In 'Mourning and Melancholia', Freud began his discussion from just this point, observing that in order to explain the traits of melancholia— which point to a loss in regard to the ego more than to an object— something must have shifted in the melancholic to transform standard mourning (the reaction to the real loss of a loved object) into a pathological form of mourning (a response to the feared and constantly reinstated loss 'of a more ideal kind').[69] As Freud goes on to emphasize, this leads to the melancholic making a dangerous '*identification* of the ego with the abandoned object' and causes him to succumb to a form of narcissistic regression that paradoxically stems from the failure of the subject to properly mourn the passing of one object of his desire, so that the drives are turned inwards, preserving a form of the object intact in its fusion with

---

[68] Cf. *Inf.* XVIII, 73–5, 'Quando noi fummo là dov' el vaneggia | di sotto per dar passo a li *sferzati*, | lo duca disse: "Attienti, e fa che feggia"' [When we came to the point above the hollow | that makes a passage for *the scourged*, | my leader said: 'Stop, let them look at you']; *Purg.* XIII, 37–9, 'E 'l buon maestro: "Questo cinghio *sferza* | la colpa de la invidia, e però sono | tratte d'amor le corde de la ferza' [And the good master said: 'This circle | *scourges* the sin of envy, and thus | the cords of the scourge are drawn from love'].

[69] Sigmund Freud, 'Mourning and Melancholia' (1917), in *SE* XIV (1957), pp. 243–58 (p. 245).

the ego (p. 249, italics in the original). It is this which becomes the melancholy object that obsesses the depressed subject and instigates a constant and prolonged cycle of mourning for this more phantasmatic loss, designed to prevent any real loss from occurring again:

> There is no difficulty in reconstructing this process. An object-choice, an attachment of the libido to a particular person, had at one time existed; then, owing to a real slight or disappointment coming from this loved person, the object-relationship was shattered. The result was not the normal one of a withdrawal of the libido from this object and a displacement of it to a new one, but something different, for whose coming-about various conditions seem to be necessary. The object-cathexis proved to have little power of resistance and was brought to an end. But the free libido was not displaced on to another object; it was withdrawn into the ego. [...] Thus the shadow of the object fell upon the ego, and the latter could henceforth be judged by a special agency, as though it were an object, the forsaken object. (pp. 248–9)

The opposition to abandoning a prior libidinal position, even when the subject knows the object to be dead, can be so intense that 'a turning away from reality takes place and a clinging to the object through the medium of an hallucinatory willful psychosis' leads to the existence of the lost object being 'psychically prolonged' beyond where it should have been relinquished (p. 244). According to Freud, it is an 'unknown loss' (p. 245), not necessarily historically identifiable, that obsesses the melancholic, not wholly confronted nor understood, never properly accepted, and so never mourned.

In this way, the ego comes to be 'overwhelmed by the object' which, by introjecting it, the melancholic would both wish to preserve and at times has fantasies of destroying—a nod to the original tension implicit in narcissistic identification in which, inevitably according to Freud, 'hate comes into operation on the substitutive object, abusing it, debasing it, making it suffer and deriving sadistic satisfaction from its suffering' (p. 251). The self-reproaches that make themselves manifest as symptoms of melancholy desire undoubtedly stem from this process, as does the space that melancholy opens up in the subject for the promotion of the death-drive (which Freud terms *Thanatos*) over the life instinct (*Eros*), or rather the endless sliding of the latter towards the former which is implied by the desire to return to an anterior state.

Sereni's familiarity with the topography of death's space in poems such as 'Le sei del mattino' ['Six in the Morning'] (*SU*, p. 120) and 'Autostrada della Cisa' (*SV*, pp. 261–2) testifies to a death-oriented desire of this kind, and with returns to places and landscapes where he has been before, he succeeds only in swapping one form of absence for another. The 'luogo incerto' [indefinite place] that his melancholy subject inhabits is precisely the space Freud and Kristeva talk about in which the subject seeks both to affirm and to deny the loss of an object that he would both seek to preserve and destroy:

> Spesso per viottoli tortuosi
> *quelque part en Algérie*
> del luogo incerto
> che il vento morde,
> la tua pioggia il tuo sole 5
> tutti in un punto
> tra sterpi amari del più amaro filo
> di ferro, spina senza rosa...
> ma già un anno è passato,
> è appena un sogno: 10
> siamo tutti sommessi a ricordarlo.
>
> Ride una larva chiara
> dov'era la sentinella
> e la collina
> dei nostri spiriti assenti 15
> deserta e immemorabile si vela.
>   *Sidi-Chiami, novembre 1944*
>   (In *DA*, p. 81; italics in the original)

[Often through tortuous alleys
quelque part en Algérie
of the indefinite place
that the wind gusts bite,
your rainfall your sunlight 5
all at one point
amongst bitter briars of the more
bitter iron wire, thorn with no rose...
but already a year's gone by,
it is barely a dream: 10
we're all subdued to remember.

A clear phantom laughs
where the sentry was
and the hillside
of our absent spirits 15
deserted and beyond recall veils over.
            Sidi-Chiami, November 1944]

This poem in *DA* recreates the play of substitution at the basis of the melancholy disposition—substituting the 'larva' for something that really existed, transporting the 'I' endlessly back to a point that also may not have existed in the first place but which becomes the chamber for an absent self he is trying to rediscover that slips further from view the closer he comes to reaching it. What the subject is forced to remember is a haunting absence that ends up covering everything else, so that he is fixated on an ellipsis—an empty space—where he looks for himself but where he cannot be. Mengaldo notes in this regard:

> È trascorso un anno da altre località e circostanze e tutti sono lì 'sommessi a ricordarlo' ma il ricordo si annichila in quanto tale perché ciò che essi possono ricordare non è che un fantasma, un vuoto, e il luogo, la collina, fatta deserta di loro che sono assenti e vi vivono ormai solo come 'spiriti', non è veramente ricordabile, non è quello che era, è un segno meno.[70]
>
> [A year has passed since they left that place and that situation, and everyone is there 'subdued to remember [it]'. But any real memory is destroyed as such because what they can remember is only a phantasm, a void, and the place, the hill, emptied of them who are absent and live there now only as 'spirits', cannot really be remembered, it is not what it was: it is a minus sign.]

The 'luogo incerto' thus figures the poet's exile from the 'luogo ideale' of the lyric in decidedly linguistic-topographic terms. Memory is not the mythicized space it once was (for example, in *Frontiera*), but a minus sign, hinting at the failure to find meaning in a place still sought out as the locus of signification. What follows is the introjection-incorporation of the external landscape as a repository of lost time, but without the hope of working through that loss to something else. Sereni's 'punto', a Dantean syntagm which recurs in *Un posto di vacanza*, is here already a negative articulation of the God-point of *Par.* XVII, 16–18:

> così vedi le cose contingenti
> anzi che sieno in sé, mirando *il punto*
> in cui tutti li tempi sono presenti.
>
> ['so you, gazing on *the point* that holds all time,
> are able to discern contingencies
> before they are apparent in themselves.]

Sereni's 'point' elides time only to the extent that it draws the subject progressively further back until he reaches, together with his ghostly companions, a place immemorial, beyond memory or knowledge, which now mists over: 'e la collina | dei nostri spiriti assenti | deserta e immemorabile si vela' (ll. 14–16). As a correlative of the melancholy object of desire, this hill is cast as a prehistoric yet unforgettable lost Other, which, however, cannot be refound as it once was. The larva or shadow which laughs in the disturbing scene marks the spot that is 'empty' yet 'full' of

---

[70] 'Tempo e memoria', p. 232.

the spirits of those who have moved on without moving anywhere at all. And so Sereni returns to Petrarch's 'dolci colli ov'io lasciai me stesso' ['sweet hills where I left myself'] (*RVF* CCIX), recast as the nightmarish vision of the loss of/to the self. If Montale's 'La casa dei doganieri' is a tabernacle of melancholy time ('t'attende *dalla sera in cui*...'), Sereni's poem instead cultivates the enclosure of melancholy space and the *venir meno*, or fading, of the subject in the face of that (self-)dispossession.

What dominates in 'Spesso per viottoli tortuosi' is an infernal register that extends from the verb *mordere*, which recalls the melancholy self-destruction of the damned,[71] to the 'sterpi amari' of the suicide wood in *Inf.* XIII.[72] Like the souls trapped in the *poena damni* or pain of loss which constitutes their eternal separation from God and the self's ultimate deprivation, the poetic subject of Sereni's poem is forced to remember that which torments him most now that it is irrecoverable. To this extent, Algeria assumes the role of something like the 'verdi colli' [green hills] instrumental in Maestro Adamo's punishment in *Inferno* XXX, where the landscape itself causes the suffering sinner's sighs to come faster, and turns memory into an instrument of God's justice and divine punishment, to fittingly make the self the source of its own damnation as it had been in life:

> Li ruscelletti che d'i verdi colli
> del Casentin discendon giuso in Arno,
> faccendo i lor canali freddi e molli,
>   sempre mi stanno innanzi, e non indarno,
> ché l'imagine lor vie più m'asciuga
> che 'l male ond' io nel volto mi discarno.
> La rigida giustizia che mi fruga
> tragge cagion del loco ov' io peccai
> a metter più li miei sospiri in fuga.
>   (*Inf.* XXX, 64–72)

> [The streams that, in the Casentino,
> run down along green hillsides to the Arno,
> keeping their channels cool and moist,
>   flow before my eyes forever, and not in vain,
> because their image makes me thirst still more
> than does the malady that wastes my features.
>   The rigid justice that torments me
> employs the landscape where I sinned
> to make my sighs come faster.]

---

[71] See e.g. *Inf.* VI, 28–30; IX, 100–2; XIX, 118–20; XXX, 25–7; XXXIV, 58–60.
[72] e.g. *Inf.* XIII, 7–9, 'Non han sì aspri sterpi né sì folti | quelle fiere selvagge che 'n odio hanno | tra Cecina e Corneto i luoghi cólti' [No rougher, denser thickets make a refuge | for the wild beasts that hate tilled lands | between the Cècina and Corneto].

Landscape becomes a permanent site of trauma, an open wound. The unquenchable thirst of *l'idropico* [the dropsy sufferer] is renewed through the image, always in his mind's eye, of the water of the 'ruscelletti':

> L'immagine incisa nella carne, dalla carne si proietta davanti al soggetto che parla in un fotogramma fisso per l'eternità, che è la figura sinestetica di una fissazione psicologica e morale. In quel corpo dilatato il paesaggio nasce cinesteticamente da una dolorosa assenza non colmabile e si fissa al volto. [...] Il paesaggio reale (non l'idillio, non il giardino: i luoghi reali della Toscana) nasce come inferno del corpo devastato.[73]
>
> [The image carved into the flesh, by the flesh, is projected in front of the subject who speaks in a photogram fixed for all eternity, which becomes the synaesthesic symbol of a psychological and moral fixation. In that distended body, the landscape is born kinaesthetically from a painful absence that cannot be filled and fixes itself on the face. [...] The real landscape—not the idyll, not the garden, but the real places in Tuscany—is born hell-like in the ravaged body.]

Infernal memory of this kind is so negative because it offers no hope of change or renewal. The backwards gaze is once again turned in on itself, with desire vainly pursuing the memory of something which is now but a mirage, a fast-disappearing shimmer on the surface of a dream. Sereni can perhaps appropriate as his own Montale's conclusion in 'Stanze':

> [...] La dannazione
> è forse questa vaneggiante amara
> oscurità che scende su chi resta.
> (ll. 38–40, in *Le occasioni*, p. 164)
> [It may be damnation is the bitter
> raving darkness that descends
> on those who remain.]

Unable to recover the origins of his beloved, or to follow her on her journey of transcendence, the Montalian 'I' ultimately aligns itself with those left behind, who remain in darkness. For Sereni too, desire and damnation dovetail where the subject falls victim to a *vaneggiare* which confuses the phantasmatic with the real and elides the memory of the lost object with the dream of the ultimate, utopic, and indefinitely remote object of melancholy desire known as *La Chose*. From this object all paths of desire stem and to it they all return in an endless, hollow circling that pushes the true destination of desire only further out of reach:

---

[73] Giorgio Bertone, *Lo sguardo escluso: l'idea del paesaggio nella letteratura occidentale* (Novara: Interlinea, 2000), p. 92.

Depuis cet attachement archaïque, le dépressif a l'impression d'être déshérité d'un suprême bien innommable, de quelque chose d'irreprésentable, que seule peut-être une dévoration pourrait figurer, une *invocation* pourrait indiquer, mais qu'aucun mot ne saurait signifier. Aussi, aucun objet érotique ne saura-t-il remplacer pour lui l'irremplaçable aperception d'un lieu ou d'un pré-objet emprisonnant la libido et coupant les liens du désir. (*Soleil noir*, p. 23; italics in the original)

[Ever since that archaic attachment the depressed person has the impression of having been deprived of an unnameable, supreme good, of something unrepresentable, that perhaps only devouring might represent, or an *invocation* might point out, but no word could signify. Consequently, for such a person, no erotic object could replace the irreplaceable perception of a place or a preobject confining the libido or severing the bonds of desire.]

Like *das Ding* (*the Thing*) of Freudian theory, *La Chose* is 'un oggetto oltre gli oggetti [. . .] "un reale ribelle alla significazione"' [an object beyond all objects [. . .] 'the real that rebels against signification']:[74] something that will remain even when every other condition of desire is fulfilled and so consolidates the reality of desire as lack. In other words, not an imaginary object but, in Lacanian terms, part of the register of the Real which can only exist *before* or *elsewhere than* the ostensible locus of the (speaking) subject in the Symbolic order and is thus irreducible to language.[75] Kristeva here labels it, in topographic fashion, as 'un lieu ou un pré-objet': a non-object (or not-yet-object) inhabiting a (no-)place, confined to a time before the subject existed discretely from the (m)Other, and so outside the sign system. Once the subject has 'seen' that place it can look at nothing else, but can also never find the words (because they do not exist) to bring it into the realm of the Symbolic.

It is this resistance to symbolization/signification that constitutes the unsurpassable nature of the loss in melancholia, as opposed to that in mourning; where no articulate desire exists, no meaning can either. The play of substitution on which language and desire depend is immobilized and the attachment to *La Chose* is not reduced but intensified. This constitutes the gravitational pull of the melancholic towards regression: the pre-linguistic space of silent 'thing-ness' which exists before the birth of the sign, 'qui vu à rebour par le sujet déjà constitué, apparaît comme l'indéterminé, l'inséparé, l'insaisissable' [that, seen by the already constituted subject looking back, appears as the unspecified, unseparated, the

---

[74] Elio Gioanola, *Leopardi: La malinconia* (Milan: Jaca Books, 1995), p. 260. The part in quotation marks corresponds to where Gioanola quotes from Kristeva's *Soleil noir*.
[75] On Lacan's notion of the Real, see Malcolm Bowie, *Lacan* (London: Fontana, 1991), pp. 94–5.

elusive].[76] Returning to Sereni's 'Spesso per viottoli tortuosi', this is the point at which memory fails because the subject is passing beyond memory to something else that only looks like it: the phantasmatic chamber of desire into which the 'I' falls every time it seeks to refind an object which cannot, in fact, be found.

Paradise regained: desire and memory in Dante's Eden

The distance between this model of desire and the one that triumphs in Dante's *Commedia* is immediately recognizable, but that is not to say that melancholy desire is absent from Dante's poem, only that it is present to be overcome, as Hell must be transcended to reach Purgatory, and Purgatory, Paradise. There is one episode in Dante's *Commedia* in particular—Dante's reunion with Beatrice in the Earthly Paradise—which I believe embodies the tension between memory and desire to which Sereni is drawn each time his subject is forced to confront the potentially overwhelming nature of loss, and the possibility of language (specifically poetic language) redeeming that loss in the present. The dream of Eden, which has been shown to be progressively negated within the boundaries of Sereni's universe, nevertheless incorporates the enormity of the task which poetry is set, particularly in the wake of Dante, and Sereni's own failure to transcend persistently evokes as its anti-type the miraculous scene of redemption of subjectivity and language in Dante's Earthly Paradise.

The scene is all the more miraculous when we consider how far, and in what ways, the pilgrim-Dante had apparently fallen when he lost his way in the dark wood and Beatrice, moved by Heaven, intervened for his salvation, such that there was no way to save him 'fuor che mostrarli le perdute genti' [except to make him see souls in perdition] (*Purg.* XXX, 138) and his way to Paradise would remain barred 'se Letè si passasse [...] sanza alcuno scotto | di pentimento che lagrime spanda' [should Lethe be crossed [...] without payment of some fee: | his penance that shows itself in tears] (*Purg.* XXX, 143–5). Yet despite all the signs to the contrary earlier in the *Commedia*, the reunion with Beatrice, anticipated since the earliest cantos of *Inferno*, and prefigured by Virgil's repeated invocations of the beloved at key points of transition for the pilgrim, is not the harmonious meeting we expect, or that the pilgrim desires.[77] Foreshadowing

---

[76] Julia Kristeva, *Soleil noir*, p. 22, n. 10.
[77] See e.g. Virgil's words in Purg. VI, 46–8, and especially Purg. XXVII, 34–42, in which the name of the beloved is able to transform the pilgrim's fear into desire, 'Quando mi vide

Sereni's own Dantesque encounters with the past, the event of Beatrice's return is in fact a highly fraught drama of selfhood for a 'borderline' subject caught between memory and desire, and between the painful recollection of past transgressions and the journey toward self-knowledge, still incomplete and needing to be driven forward:[78] 'Guardaci ben! Ben son, ben son Beatrice. | Come degnasti d'accedere al monte? | non sapei tu che qui è l'uom felice?' ['Look over here! I am, I truly am Beatrice. | How did you dare approach the mountain? | Do you not know that here man lives in joy?'] (*Purg.* XXX, 73–5).

Several critics have commented upon the profoundly retrospective slant to the encounter with Beatrice, and the effect which this has on the moment of rebirth of the new Christian subject at the summit of Mount Purgatory, which can only take place beyond memory (specifically, the memory of Beatrice's death)—a dimension of Dante's poem to which I feel Sereni would have felt an affinity in his own desire (obsession) to liberate himself from the excessive attachment to the past which is at the root of his subject's melancholia.[79] In Dante's case, the problematic loci of grief and loss needing to be worked through are poignantly thrown into relief with Virgil's disappearance in *Purg.* XXX, at the very moment at which the force of Dante's 'ancient love' for Beatrice transports the subject back to his first encounter with her and to the earliest pages of his 'libro de la memoria', *Vita nova*:

> Tosto che ne la vista mi percosse
> l'alta virtù che già m'avea trafitto
> prima ch'io fuor di püerizia fosse,   42
> volsimi a la sinistra col respitto
> col quale il fantolin corre alla mamma
> quando ha paura o quando elli è afflitto,   45
> per dicere a Virgilio: 'Men che dramma
> di sangue m'è rimaso che non tremi:
> conosco i segni de l'antica fiamma.'   48

star pur fermo e duro, | turbato un poco disse: "Or vedi, figlio: | tra Bëatrice e te è questo muro". [. . .] così, la mia durrezza fatta solla, | mi volsi al savio duca, udendo il nome | che ne la mente sempre mi rampolla' [When he saw me stay, unmoved and obstinate, | he said, somewhat disturbed: 'Now look, my son | this wall stands between Beatrice and you' | [. . .] just so, my stubbornness made pliant, I turned | to my wise leader when I heard the name | that ever blossoms in my mind].

[78] On the notion of Dante-pilgrim's 'borderline' or 'threshold' subjectivity in the Earthly Paradise, see Gary Cestaro, *Dante and the Grammar of the Nursing Body* (Notre Dame, Ind.: University of Notre Dame Press, 2003), p. 69.

[79] See Cestaro, *Dante and the Grammar of the Nursing Body*, p. 144; and Lino Pertile, 'La ferita d'amore', in his *La puttana e il gigante: dal Cantico dei Cantici al Paradiso terrestre di Dante* (Ravenna: Longo, 1998), pp. 87–133.

> Ma Virgilio n'avea lasciati scemi
> di sé, Virgilio dolcissimo patre,
> Virgilio a cui per mia salute die'mi;　　　　　　51
> né quantunque perdeo l'antica matre,
> valse a le guance nette di rugiada
> che, lagrimando, non tornasser atre.　　　　　　54
> 'Dante, perché Virgilio se ne vada
> non pianger anco, non piangere ancora,
> ché pianger ti conven per altra spada'.　　　　　57
> Quasi ammiraglio che in poppa e in prora
> viene a veder la gente che ministra
> per li altri legni, e a ben far l'incora;　　　　　60
> in su la sponda del carro sinistra,
> quando mi volsi al suon del nome mio,
> che di necessità qui si registra,　　　　　　　　63
> vidi la donna che pria m'appario
> velata sotto l'angelica festa,
> drizzar li occhi ver' me di qua dal rio.　　　　66
> (*Purg.* XXX, 40–66)

> [As soon as that majestic force,
> which had already pierced me once
> before I had outgrown my childhood, struck my eyes,　42
> I turned to my left with the confidence
> a child has running to his *mamma*
> when he is afraid or in distress　　　　　　　　45
> to say to Virgil: 'Not a single drop of blood
> remains in me that does not tremble—
> I know the signs of the ancient flame.'　　　　48
> But Virgil had departed, leaving us bereft:
> Virgil, sweetest of fathers,
> Virgil, to whom I gave myself for my salvation.　51
> And not all our ancient mother lost
> could save my cheeks, washed in the dew,
> from being stained again with tears.　　　　　54
> 'Dante, because Virgil has departed,
> do not weep, do not weep yet—
> there is another sword to make you weep.'　　57
> Just like an admiral who moves from stern to prow
> to see the men that serve the other ships
> and urge them on to better work,　　　　　　　60
> so on the left side of the chariot—
> as I turned when I heard her call my name,
> which of necessity is here recorded—　　　　　63
> I saw the lady, who had just appeared
> veiled beneath the angels' celebration,
> fix her eyes on me from across the stream.]　66

Feeling the force of the ancient flame, and the terrifying weight of desire and memory, Dante-pilgrim turns back to Virgil but finds that Virgil is not there. The thrice repeated name of Dante's *maestro*, which echoes the loss of Eurydice in the Orphic myth, embodies what Lombardi terms terms desire as *de sideribus*, whose primary meaning in Latin antiquity was 'pain and regret for something or somebody that no longer exists and is forever lost'.[80] Perceiving Virgil's disappearance as an irreplaceable loss of this kind, the pilgrim's face turns dark again with tears and he lapses towards a more 'sinister retrospection',[81] reversed only by the counter-pull in desire exerted by Beatrice's calling of his name (62–6) and her reminder that weeping in Eden should not be for the loss of Virgil but, at the very least, for all that humanity lost at the Fall (here overshadowed by the weight of personal grief, ll. 52–4), and above all for the shame and the knowledge of one's own sins. As Piero Boitani states, 'The "theophany" with which the scene opened becomes "recherche du temps perdu" and at the same time anagnorisis.'[82] At this pivotal moment in the text, the key to Dante's salvation lies in his being able to substitute one kind of weeping or 'tristezza' for the other: he must learn to transcend the classical response to loss, embodied in the figure of Virgil, to embrace instead the redeeming Christian desire embodied by Beatrice, newly returned from the dead.

Almost all of the Dantean intertexts that we can identify in Sereni's poetry ultimately treat this kind of recollection of loss ('temps perdu') without, however, being able to recreate the transcendent framework that guarantees the reconciliation of the subject to his past (including his poetic past), or the recovery of the lost object. To this extent, Sereni holds most tenaciously to Dante's 'memorie triste', evoked in the passage from Fall to salvation and in the liminal space between 'empty' and 'full' speech that precedes the pilgrim's final confession and absolution:

> Poco sofferse; poi disse: 'Che pense?
> Rispondi a me; ché *le memorie triste*
> in te non sono ancor da l'acqua offense.'   12
> Confusione e paura insieme miste
> mi pinsero un tal 'sì' fuor de la bocca
> al quale intender fuor mestier le viste.   15

---

[80] Elena Lombardi, *The Syntax of Desire: Language and Love in Augustine, the Modistae, Dante* (Toronto: University of Toronto Press, 2007), p. 11 (italics in the original). The most haunting expression of this kind of desire as loss is the motif of the failed embrace we find in Virgil, so poignantly reworked by Dante in the *Purgatorio*, later resurfacing in Sereni's own 'Autostrada della Cisa' indebted to both classical and medieval models.
[81] Cestaro, *Dante and the Grammar of the Nursing Body*, p. 145.
[82] *The Tragic and the Sublime in Medieval Literature*, p. 164.

> Come balestro frange, quando scocca
> da troppo tesa, la sua corda e l'arco,
> e con men foga l'asta il segno tocca, 18
> sì scoppia' io sottesso grave carco,
> fuori sgorgando lagrime e sospiri,
> e la voce allentò per lo suo varco. 21
> (*Purg.* XXXI, 10–21)
>
> [For a moment she held back, then asked:
> 'What are you thinking? Speak, for your *memories*
> *of sin* have not been washed away by water yet.' 12
> Confusion and fear, mixed together,
> drove from my mouth a *yes*—
> but one had need of eyes to hear it. 15
> As a crossbow breaks with too much tension
> from the pulling taut of cord and bow
> so that the arrow strikes the target with less force, 18
> thus I collapsed beneath that heavy load
> and, with a flood of tears and sighs,
> my voice came strangled from my throat.] 21

Those memories of sin/sorrow are an almost overwhelming force, which simultaneously reenact the fallen history of the subject's desire. As Dante-pilgrim suddenly finds himself bewildered and unable to speak, the voice momentarily held inside recalls the 'grande reticenza' [great reticence] and 'preterizione' [paralepsis] that characterized the grieving subject of the *VN* who, in the aftermath of Beatrice's death, fell into the negativity of desire and, at least for a while, found compensation for her loss in the wrong direction.[83] In thrall to that loss and the lure of the new, Dante did not immediately follow Beatrice to her new place in Heaven but, with his 'penne in giuso' [wings turned downward], found himself trapped in the mortal coil of the 'cose fallaci' [deceitful things], a locus of sin now laid bare, like the 'femmina balba' [stammering woman] of *Purg.* XIX, as something purely chimeric:

> pon giù il seme del piangere e ascolta:
> sì udirai come in contraria parte
> mover dovieti mia carne sepolta. 48
> Mai non t'appresentò natura o arte
> piacer, quanto le belle membra in ch'io

---

[83] See Domenico De Robertis' notes to ch. XXVIII of Dante's *Vita nuova*, in which he points out: 'Tutti i capitoli XXVIII–XXX sono una grande "reticenza" o preterizione' [All the chapters from XXVIII-XXX constitute a great 'reticence' or paralepsis], in Dante Alighieri, *Vita nuova*, ed. Domenico De Robertis, *Opere minori*, 2 vols (Milan: Ricciardi, 1979–88), I.1 (1984), pp. 3–247 (p. 191).

rinchiusa fui, e che so' 'n terra sparte; 51
e se 'l sommo piacer sì ti fallio
per la mia morte, qual cosa mortale
dovea poi trarre te nel suo disio? 54
Ben ti dovevi, per lo primo strale
de le *cose fallaci*, levar suso
di retro a me *che non era più tale*. 57
Non ti dovea gravar le penne in giuso,
ad aspettar più colpo, o pargoletta
o altra novità con sì breve uso. 60
(*Purg.* XXXI, 46–60)

[stop sowing tears and listen.
Then you shall hear just how my buried flesh
should have directed you to quite a different place. 48
Never did art or nature set before you beauty
as great as in the lovely members that enclosed me,
now scattered and reduced to dust. 51
And if the highest beauty failed you
in my death, what mortal thing
should then have drawn you to desire it? 54
Indeed, at the very first arrow
of *deceitful things*, you should have risen up
and followed me who *was no longer of them*. 57
You should not have allowed your wings to droop,
leaving you to other darts from some young girl
or other novelty of such brief use.] 60

The experience was melancholic to the extent that there was some fundamental misrecognition on Dante's part of what Beatrice had represented *in death*. Her loss threatened to engulf the ego in its dangerous identification with those phantasmata that had sought to replace her in her absence.[84] However, in opposition to the Freudian model, the libido— rather than being immobilized through loss—was all too easily displaced onto other objects, which led the subject only further away from the true locus of desire as fulfilment, 'di là dal quale non è a che s'aspiri' [beyond which there is nothing left to long for] (*Purg.* XXXI, 24). This left the self deprived not only of Beatrice but also of any hope of reparation or recovery until she intervened to rescue him (as recounted in *Inf.* II). That deprivation, melancholically self-inflicted, had to be paid for by

[84] These included not only the *donna gentile* (as recounted in *Vita nova*), but also potentially the experience of the *rime*, especially the *petrose* [stony rhymes]. For a fuller discussion of this, see my 'Lost for Words: Recuperating Melancholy Subjectivity in Dante's Eden', in *Dante's Plurilingualism: Authority, Knowledge, Subjectivity*, ed. Sara Fortuna, Manuele Gragnolati, and Jürgen Trabant (Oxford: Legenda, 2010), pp. 193–210.

the journey to the very bottom of Hell and up Purgatory, progressively undoing the separation from God and from Beatrice. Now in Eden, and in the full presence of his beloved, the gate to Paradise is once more open. Dispelling the phantasmata of the past shrouded in the shadow of death, the subject's desire and his language can finally embrace the 'new life' of the resurrected object, transforming (earthly) lack into (heavenly) ubiquity in a true moment of conversion:

> Di pentèr sì mi punse ivi l'ortica
> che di tutte altre cose qual mi torse
> più nel suo amor, più mi si fe' nemica.   87
>   Tanta riconoscenza il cor mi morse,
> ch'io caddi vinto; e quale allora femmi,
> salsi colei che la cagion mi porse.   90
>   Poi, quando il cor virtù di fuor rendemmi,
> la donna ch'io avea trovata sola
> sopra me vidi, e dicea: 'Tiemmi, tiemmi!'.   93
> [...]
>   La bella donna ne le braccia aprissi;
> abbracciommi la testa e mi sommerse
> ove convenne ch'io l'acqua inghiottissi.   102
>   Indi mi tolse, e bagnato m'offerse
> dentro a la danza de le quattro belle;
> e ciascuna del braccio mi coperse.   105
>   (*Purg.* XXXI, 85–93, 100–105)

> [*The nettle of remorse so stung me then*
> that whatever else had lured me most to loving
> had now become for me most hateful.   87
>   *Such knowledge of my fault was gnawing at my heart*
> *that I was overcome*, and what I then became
> she knows who was the reason for my state.   90
>   then, when my heart restored my vital signs,
> I saw the lady I first found alone above me,
> saying: 'Hold on to me and hold me fast!'   93
> [...]
>   The lovely lady spread her arms,
> then clasped my head, and plunged me under,
> where I was forced to swallow water.   102
>   then she drew me out and led me, bathed,
> into the dance of the four lovely ladies
> as each one raised an arm above my head.]   105

As Kristeva states in *Soleil noir*, 'La capacité imaginaire de l'homme occidental qui s'accomplit avec le christianisme est la capacité de transférer du sens *au lieu même où il s'est perdu dans la mort et/ou dans le non-sens*'

[The imaginative capability of Western man, which is fulfilled within Christianity, is the ability to transfer meaning to *the very place where it was lost in death and/or non-meaning*] (p. 115). In distinction to the Lacanian model of desire as perennial lack and displacement from one emptiness to another, through which the Serenian subject takes shape, Dante presents a model of subjectivity and desire newly restored to fullness and the possibility of eternal transcendence. As the imminent experience of the *Paradiso* will confirm, heavenly beatitude is not the end of desire but the end of desire as lack—the transition to a desire actualized and fulfilled for all eternity. In Lombardi's words:

> In the economy of salvation the notion of desire-as-lack that pervades human time and history can be turned into a loss (by sin and the subsequent damnation) or into *fulfilment*. This notion of fulfilment is very easy to explain and very difficult to grasp: it is an 'actualized' version of desire rather than the cessation and absence of it. Fulfilment at once contains both desire and its satisfaction. Desire as fulfilment is not pacified, but rather stimulated and satisfied at the same time. The medieval notion of fulfilment is best described by the mystical experience on earth, and by the blessedness of heaven: in fulfilment desire is 'now'.[85]

Refusing Lethe: melancholy regression and the end of Eden

In Sereni's case perhaps, that last axiom could be rephrased as 'in desire, fulfilment was "then"', or even, 'outside of fulfilment, desire is always'. In the absence of a salvific Other, the Serenian subject withdraws in Cavalcantian fashion into the 'haunted interiority of the solitary psyche' and the memory of Dante's drama of desire is (re)cast as the frustrated search for an originary locus of joy and fulfilment, only figurable as lost, from which the desiring subject has been (definitively) exiled.[86] This exile without hope of return, nevertheless fixated upon the memory of a prior moment of plenitude potentially only imagined, is what shapes the landscapes of desire of Sereni's later poetry. The disproportion between memory and desire which is the impetus for poetry at the same time makes of the poem a place of lack and not fulfilment, and of the impossible redemption of a

---

[85] Lombardi, *The Syntax of Desire*, p. 12 (italics in the original).
[86] On Cavalcanti's 'radical phantasmology of the self', see Robert Pogue Harrison, *The Body of Beatrice* (Baltimore, Md.: Johns Hopkins University Press, 1988), pp. 69–90 (p. 74).

past which, unlike Dante's (but like Petrarch's), remains in part submerged, resists symbolization or being brought into language, anchored to an unknown loss which, since it cannot be properly remembered, can also not be properly mourned, forgotten, or got beyond.

It is that unknown loss, or mirage of *La Chose*, that increasingly haunts the Serenian subject. Some hint of it is present in almost all of Sereni's later work, but it is most vividly mapped in the postwar landscapes of Bocca di Magra and in a series of poems set in that posthumous realm, which includes 'Gli squali' ['The Sharks'], *Un posto*, and 'La malattia dell'olmo' ['The Disease of the Elm']. All three poems invoke or address memory; in each, the subject seeks out a poetic presence to counter an underlying absence and loss, associated Dantesquely with some past transgression needing to be atoned for; all situate the desiring subject at a point *in extremis* in the poetic landscape. The recurring dictum, 'memoria che ancora hai desideri' [memory you still have desires], which is carried from 'Gli squali' into *Un posto*, and is rephrased in 'La malattia' as 'la memoria: | non si sfama mai' [the memory: | it is never satisfied], presents the faultline of Sereni's poetics—melancholia as the insatiable remembrance of, and desire for, a perennially lost object and the constantly renewed fantasy of its recovery; or, in other words, the enduring quality of his 'memorie triste' in distinction to their Dantean counterparts.

In 'La malattia dell'olmo' [The Disease of the Elm], Sereni directly engages with the episode just analysed from Dante's Earthly Paradise, revisiting the Edenic topography of Dante's poem and reshaping it on his own terms. However, all that he seems to achieve is a renewal and intensification of his 'memorie triste', rather than their purging, being forced to succumb to a personal and poetic fall for a second time:

> Se ti importa che ancora sia estate
> eccoti in riva al fiume l'albero squamarsi
> delle foglie più deboli: roseogialli
> petali di fiori sconosciuti
> —e a futura memoria i sempreverdi   5
> immobili.
>
> Ma più importa che la gente cammini in allegria
> che corra al fiume la città e un gabbiano
> avventuratosi sin qua si sfogli
> in un lampo di candore.   10
>
> Guidami tu, stella variabile, fin che puoi...
>
> —e il giorno fonde le rive in miele e oro
> le rifonde in un buio oleoso
> fino al pullulare delle luci.
>   Scocca

'Memorie triste', 'passi perduti'

da quel formicolio
un atomo ronzante, a colpo
sicuro mi centra
dove più punge e brucia.

Vienmi vicino, parlami, tenerezza,
—dico voltandomi a una
vita fino a ieri a me prossima
oggi così lontana —scaccia
da me questo spino molesto,
la memoria:
non si sfama mai.

È fatto—mormora in risposta
nell'ultimo chiaro
quell'ombra—adesso dormi, riposa.
                  Mi hai
tolto l'aculeo, non
il suo fuoco—sospiro abbandonandomi a lei
in sogno con lei precipitando già.
            (pp. 254–5)

If it matters to you it's still summer
look here how on the river bank the tree
flakes its more tenuous leaves:
rosy-yellow petals of unknown flowers
—and to future memory the evergreens
motionless.

But it matters more the people step gaily,
the city rush to the river and a seagull,
ventured as far as here, be unleafed
in a flare of brilliant white.

Lead me, variable star, as long as you're able...
—and the day casts the banks in honey and gold
and recasts them in an oily dark
until the teeming of the lights.
                  It darts
out from that swarm,
the humming atom, hits me
with unswerving aim
where it most stings and burns.

Come near to me, speak to me, tenderness,
—I say turning back towards
a life until yesterday close to me

>   today so remote – drive out
>   from me the insistent thorn,
>   the memory:
>   it is never satisfied.   25
>   It's finished—that shadow
>   murmurs a reply
>   in the last light—sleep now, rest.
>   You've
>   removed the thorn, but not
>   its burning—I sigh as I give myself up to her   30
>   in dreams with her already falling.]

Like the decaying elm tree at its heart, Sereni's Eden, in distinction to Dante's, is revealed to be a purely terrestrial space that has mortal (l'albero *squamarsi* | delle foglie più deboli', ll. 2–3) as well as immortal extensions ('i sempreverdi | immobili', ll. 5–6). Subject to the passing of the seasons, what is viewed as enduring is only that which will be able to cheat time and death, the phrase 'a futura memoria' indicating the vestiges of a loss that will be carried by the memory of the landscape once the speaking voice—fused with the dying tree in a way that recalls the hybrid speech of the imprisoned souls of the suicide wood in *Inf.* XIII—is no more.[87]

Hybridity as a lack of differentiation between subject and object is also the condition that spells out the impossible reconciliation of the subject to itself, since the shade ('ombra') of the poet's past life, whilst initially viewed as the source of a possible salvation, reveals itself to be only the 'other' of the memory the subject seeks to purge, which perpetuates rather than eradicates the degenerate arc of desire. In distinction to Dante's, Sereni's 'Edenic' language is thus further contaminated by memory, rather than purified of it, making it impossible for the subject to redeem himself or his poem. More problematically, the composite nature of speech, here combined with the intimately melancholy activities of turning back ('dico *voltandomi*', l. 20) and sighing ('sospiro *abbandonandomi*', l. 30), which deictically encode a backward look into language, actually forces the subject to regress. Whereas in *Purg.* XXXI, 31, Dante-pilgrim's 'sospiro amaro' [bitter sigh] signals the liberation from sin, and the breakthrough from aphasic silence to fully voiced confession, Sereni's 'sigh' figures instead the retreat or defeat of discourse which finally gives up the

---

[87] Cf. *Inf.* XIII, 43–5, 'sì de la scheggia rotta usciva insieme | parole e sangue; ond' io lasciai la cima | cadere, e stetti come l'uom che teme' [so from the broken splinter oozed | blood and words together, and I let drop | that twig and stood like one afraid], and the article by Leo Spitzer, 'Speech and Language in *Inferno* XIII', *Italica* 19.3 (Sept. 1942), pp. 81–104.

ghost, unable to assuage the subject's desire or put out the fire of memory. Sereni's poem consequently ends with a masochistic gesture reminiscent of the cannibalistic dream of the melancholic described by Kristeva:

> La cannibalisme mélancolique, qui a été souligné par Freud et Abraham et qui apparaît dans nombre de rêves et fantasmes de déprimés, traduit cette passion de tenir au-dedans de la bouche [...] l'autre intolérable que j'ai envie de détruire pour mieux le posséder vivant. [...] Il manifeste l'angoisse de perdre l'autre en faisant survivre le moi, certes abandonné, mais non séparé de ce qui le nourrit encore et toujours et se métamorphose en lui—qui ressuscite aussi—par cette dévoration. (*Soleil noir*, p. 21)
>
> [Melancholy cannibalism, which was emphasized by Freud and Abraham and appears in many dreams and fantasies of depressed persons, accounts for this passion for holding within the mouth [...] the intolerable other that I crave to destroy so as to better possess it alive. [...] It manifests the anguish of losing the other through the survival of self, surely a deserted self but not separated from what still and ever nourishes it and becomes transformed into the self—which also resuscitates—through such devouring.]

With respect to the Dantean model, degeneration and fall thus occur in Sereni's poem in language as much as in desire.[88] The lost other is incorporated into the self, where it is alternately resuscitated and consumed, but never fully relinquished nor possessed. What is lost in the passage from the medieval to the modern author is the belief in the power of the poetic word to transform absence into presence, or to overcome language's inherent negativity. In more ways than one, Sereni's poem ends up being the space of a failed conversion, bringing us back to Petrarch and to the memory of *RVF* CXXVI, discussed in the previous chapter also in relation to 'La malattia'. Sereni's river (Lethe), beyond which the end of memory can be imagined but never reached, similarly remains uncrossed. More negatively than Petrarch, however, Sereni's affirmation of the eternal but annihilating force of memory culminates with a fall into time and death, but out of the garden (Eden) whose promise of redress is not borne out. The phantasms of Petrarch and Dante, which are both in the final moment left behind, each contribute in their different ways to Sereni's staging of a modern, 'deracinated subjectivity', whose dreams of metaphysical and poetic integration are well and truly shattered.[89]

---

[88] On this point, see also my 'Performative Desires: Sereni's Re-staging of Dante and Petrarch', in *Aspects of the Performative in Medieval Culture*, ed. Manuele Gragnolati and Almut Suerbaum (Berlin: de Gruyter, 2010), pp. 165–96.

[89] See Theodore J. Cachey Jr., 'Between Petrarch and Dante: Prolegomenon to a Critical Discourse', in *Petrarch and Dante: Anti-Dantism, Metaphysics, Tradition*, ed. Zygmunt

SUSPENDING THE POETICS OF TRANSITION: THE DISCOURSE OF THE MELANCHOLIC

To put things another way, the deviating journey of desire is at one with the errancy of discourse. Melancholia is a failed narrative of frustrated speech: a 'discours vide' [empty speech], 'langue étrangère' [foreign language] or 'lettre morte' [dead letter] which leads nowhere.[90] As Sereni writes in conclusion to his short story, *Ventisei* [*Twenty-Six*] (1970), in which he has sought to trace out the elusive phantasm of creative discourse:

> Una cosa sola è chiara: sono fermo al limite a cui mi sono sempre fermato ogni volta che ho messo righe sulla carta. Nel punto dove la vera avventura, l'impresa vera incomincia. [...] Mi sta contro una selva, le parole, da attraversare seguendo un tracciato che si forma via via si cammina, in avanti (o a ritroso) verso la trasparenza, se è questa la parola giusta del futuro.[91]
>
> [One thing only is clear: I am standing at the limit where I've always stopped myself whenever I put pen to paper. The point at which the true adventure, the true undertaking begins. [...] There stands before me a wood, the words, to travel through following a line that gradually forms as you walk, forwards (or back) towards the transparency, if that is the right word for the future.]

This passage consolidates our sense of the author being stuck in what is effectively a 'textual selva oscura' or 'poetic wandering'.[92] The end may be just another beginning, but the beginning is also the end, as past and future time collapse into one another and the writing subject, finding himself confronted each time with a dark wood of words, can find a way through only along the still-forming path he will himself create. However, perceiving that meaning may be behind rather than in front of him, this is also the place where he gets stuck, or chooses to remain.

For Sereni, 'poetry is not [...] the language of desire. It is, as Dante saw it, the desire of language.'[93] However, since Sereni's poetic journey receives no sanction or assistance from the outside, and is not supported by any higher teleology, his struggles with self-expression do not find resolution in the same way in which they do in Dante. Rather, they merely

---

G. Barański, and Theodore J. Cachey Jr. (Notre Dame, Ind.: University of Notre Dame Press, 2009), pp. 3–49 (p. 13).

[90] See Kristeva, *Soleil noir*, pp. 75, 66, and 73 respectively.
[91] Sereni, 'Ventisei', p. 202; trans. Robinson–Perryman.
[92] I borrow both these notions from Barolini, *Dante's Poets*, p. 29.
[93] Lombardi, *The Syntax of Desire*, p. 176.

lead to the intensification of a crisis that is as much poetic as it is existential, and in which the failure to complete the poetic journey satisfactorily is just another symptom of the melancholy disease that contaminates that dimension of the subject's existence too. In Kristeva's words:

L'être parlant [...] exige à sa base une rupture, un abandon, un malaise. La dénégation de cette perte fondamentale nous ouvre le pays des signes, mais le deuil est souvent inachevé. Il bouscule la dénégation et se rappelle à la mémoire des signes en les sortant de leur neutralité signifiante. [...] Jusqu'à ce que le poids de la Chose originaire l'emporte, et que toute traductibilité devienne impossible. La mélancolie s'achève alors dans l'asymbolie, la perte de sens: si je ne suis plus capable de traduire ou de métaphoriser, je me tais et je meurs. (*Soleil noir*, p. 54)

[Speaking beings [...] demand a break, a renunciation, an unease in their foundations.

The negation of that fundamental loss opens up the realm of signs for us, but the mourning is often incomplete. It drives out negation and revives the memory of signs by drawing them out of their signifying neutrality. [...] Until the weight of the primal Thing prevails, and all translatability becomes impossible. Melancholia then ends up in asymbolia, in loss of meaning: if I am no longer capable of translating or metaphorizing, I become silent and I die.]

If successful speech resides in the subject being able to concatenate—in his submission to the metonymic chain of desire that drives him forward towards a possession that is, if not inevitable, then at least construed as possible—the melancholic's speech functions in the opposite direction. Directing the desiring gaze and the metonymic chain backwards, it pulls the subject towards a form of undifferentiated silence akin to the prelinguistic space of primary narcissism, through which the subject withdraws from the demands of the Symbolic order and suspends the signifying chain.

Since *La Chose* can never be brought into language, desire and language are severed in the search for an impossible possession that always lies beyond them. This is figured in Sereni's *Un posto* in the successive but failed attempts by the poetic subject to bridge the abyss between words and things, desire and its object, by which Sereni transmutes the journey of desire into one of language and poetry:

IV
Mai così—si disse rintanandosi
tra le ripe lo scriba—mai stato
così tautologico il lavoro, ma neppure mai
ostico tanto *tra* tante meraviglie.
Guardò lo scafo allontanarsi *tra* due ali di fresco,   5
sfucinare nell'alto – e *già* era fuori di vista, nel turchino,

rapsodico dattilico fantastic<u>ante</u>
perpetuandosi nell'indistinto di altre estati.
Amò, semmai servissero al disegno,
quei transit<u>anti</u> un attimo come persone vive 10
e int<u>anto</u>
sull'omissione il mancamento il vuoto che si pose
tra i dileguati e la sogguard<u>ante</u> la
farfugli<u>ante</u> animula *lì*
crebbe il mare, si smerigliò il cristallo 15
di poco prima, si frantumò
e un vetro in corsa *di là dalla* deriva
raggiò sopravento l'ultimo enigma estivo.
Passano—tornava a dirsi—tutti assieme gli anni
e *in un punto s'incendiano*, che sono io 20
custode non di anni ma di attimi
—e più nessuno che giungere doveva e era atteso
più nessuno verrà sulle acque spopolate.
[...]
Di fatto si stremava su un colore 30
o piuttosto sul nome del colore da distendere
sull'omissione, il
mancamento, il vuoto:
        l'amar<u>anto</u>
luce di stelle spente che nel raggiungerci ci infuoca
o quale si riverbera frangendosi su un viso 35
infine ravvisato, mentre la barca vira...).
Tutto salpava, tutto
metteva vela sotto lo sguardo vetrino
tutto diceva addio sull'onda del venti di agosto.
Restava, colto a volo, quel colore 40
tirrenico, quel nome di radice amara,
la grama preda dello scriba
still<u>ante</u> altra insonnia dai mille soli
d'insonnia luccic<u>ante</u>
dei marosi. 45
    (*Un posto* IV, 1–23, 30–45, pp. 228-9)

[Never quite so—the scribe taking shelter
between the banks told himself—never been
quite so tautological, the work, never so
troublesome among so many splendors.
Between two wings of freshness he watched the launch diminish, 5
forging off into high seas—and *already* out of sight in the turquoise,
rhapsodic dactylic daydreaming
prolonging itself in the haze of other summers.

> He loved them, should they ever suit his design,
> those in transit a moment like persons living 10
> and meanwhile
> over the absent the missing the nothingness that settled
> *between* the disappeared and the peering
> the stuttering animula there
> sea swelled, the crystal of just before 15
> turned emerald, shattered
> and a windshield advancing on the far side of the drift
> radiated upwind summer's last enigma.
> The years—he was telling himself once more—pass as one
> *and burst into flame at a point*, which is me 20
> custodian not of years but moments
> —and nobody else who, expected, should have come,
> no one else will come upon abandoned waters.
> [...]
> He wore himself out on a color in fact 30
> or better on the name of a color to extend
> over the absent
> the missing, nothingness: the amaranth
> light of dead stars that in reaching us inflame us
> or such as reverberate breaking on a face 35
> recognized at last, just as the boat veers...).
>
> Everyone up-anchored, everyone
> under the glazed look hoisted sail,
> all said farewell on the wave of August twentieth.
> Caught in flight, that Tyrrhenian 40
> colour staged, the name with bitter root,
> the scribe's paltry prey dripping
> other insomnia from the thousand suns
> of glittering insomnia
> in the tidal waves.] 45

This brings Sereni into dialogue with Dante as the poet not only of *Inferno* and *Purgatorio* but also of *Paradiso*. While there is not space here to fully treat the depth and complexity of the intertextual relationship with Dante's third canticle, it is important to recognize the extent to which, topographically and linguistically speaking, Sereni's *Un posto*—in figuring the journey of poetry itself—also absorbs the memory of Dante's writing of the *Paradiso*.[94]

---

[94] For a fuller exploration of this topic, see my '*"Per-tras-versioni" dantesche*: Post-Paradisiacal Constellations in the Poetry of Vittorio Sereni and Andrea Zanzotto', in

As we have already seen in the way that Sereni configures his intertextual dialogue with Montale, *Un posto* is a poem that, like the *Paradiso*, speaks of its own fraught genesis. It is also a sustained exploration of the possibilities and limits of poetic language, and deals in a different way with the threatening collapse of meaning and language into silence, which is the particular ground of the *Paradiso*. In many respects, it retropes Dante's experience of 'oltraggio', turned by Sereni from a condition of linguistic-memorial ec-stasis, in the face of the uncontainable abundance of God, to that of a linguistic-memorial paralysis in the face of an all-consuming space of absence and lack—'posto di *vacanza*' [where *vacanza* means vacancy as well as holiday]:

> Da quinci innanzi il mio veder fu maggio
> che 'l parlar mostra, ch'a tal vista cede,
> e cede la memoria a tanto *oltraggio*'
> (*Par.* XXXIII, 55–7)
>
> [From that time on my power of sight exceeded
> that of speech, which fails at such a vision,
> as memory fails at such *abundance*.]

In the passage from Part IV of *Un posto*, the Serenian subject, immobilized by his overwhelming perception of 'l'omissione il mancamento il vuoto' (ll. 12, 26–7), renounces all hope of speaking of other things and withdraws further into the self. In the space of just a few lines, this turns the subject from the Dantesque figure of 'lo scriba' (*Par.* X, 27), who fully embraces the challenge of writing God's universe,[95] into 'la sogguardante la | farfugliante animula' (ll. 13–14), which, in recalling Eliot's poem and Montale's translation of it, embodies instead the stuttering, simple soul, in retreat from both language and the world. Frozen in a single gesture of seeing (literally peering) and speaking, but never wholly articulating, a loss that has always already occurred ('il vuoto che si pose | tra i dileguati e la sogguardante . . . '), the subject becomes trapped in the melancholy state of frustration and immobility in which desire becomes blocked.

Sereni's main grammatical innovation in *Un posto* is his wide use of present participles and infinitives in a mode of syntactic suspension, which indicates a resistance to transposition in a linguistic sense, a failure to

---

Metamorphosing Dante: Appropriations, Manipulations and Rewritings in the Twentieth and Twenty-First Centuries, ed. Manuele Gragnolati, Fabio Camilletti, and Fabian Lampart (Vienna: Turia + Kant, 2011), pp. 153–74.

[95] 'Messo t'ho innanzi; omai per te ti ciba; | ché a sé torce tutta la mia cura | quella materia ond'io son fatto scriba' [I have set your table. From here on feed yourself, | for my attention now resides | in that matter of which I have become the scribe] (*Par.* X, 25–7).

concatenate. Part IV is emblematic in this respect, with its high incidence of present participles in an adjectival role, whose repeated endings in 'ante' (as underlined above) convey invariability and stasis. In their combined effects, these syntactic and phonologic aspects embody the frozen gestures of the subject and the hypostatized motions of objects, always begun but never ended. They suspend the signifying chain, pulling the subject simultaneously in a backwards as well as a forwards direction, towards an unresolved moment of the past or a future state that remains incomplete, turning the poetic subject into the 'mémoire étrange' [strange memory] of which Kristeva speaks in *Soleil noir* who is 'cloué' [nailed down] to 'une expérience indépassable' [an unsurpassable experience] that skews both time and space.[96]

'*Quei* transitanti' (*Un posto* IV, 10)—the momentary phantasms conjured by desire ('Amò...')—are already passing into memory, coloured by it, and moving out of reach, as the landscape of the poem is turned from the transcendent to the in-between, with the repetition of 'tra' and the continual receding of what lies beyond it. This effectively recasts the transitional poetics of the *Commedia*, especially the *Paradiso*, as one of liminality or limbo. Whereas 'tra-' is a prefix Dante uses to emphasize transgression in the positive sense of moving beyond the self and nearing eternity (e.g. *tra*sumanar [to go beyond the human], *tra*smodar [to transcend], *tra*svolare [to soar beyond]),[97] in Sereni's poem it figures instead the unbridgeable distance dividing the subject from his goal and the consequent state of being suspended between two incomplete dimensions of experience:

> Chissà che *di lì traguardando* non si allacci nome a cosa
> ... (la poesia sul posto di vacanza).
> Invece torna a tentarmi in tanti anni quella voce
> (era un disco) *di là, dall'altra riva*. Nelle sere di polvere e sete
> quasi la si toccava, gola offerta alla ferita d'amore
> sulle acque. *Non scriverò questa storia*.
>
> (*Un posto* I, 22–7, p. 224)

---

[96] See Kristeva, *Soleil noir*, p. 71, 'Une temporalité décentrée [...] *un moment* bouche l'horizon de la temporalité dépressive, ou plutôt lui enlève tout horizon, toute perspective. Fixé au passé, régressant au paradis ou à l'enfer d'une expérience indépassable, le mélancolique est une mémoire étrange: tout est révolu, semble-t-il dire, mais je suis fidèle à ce révolu, j'y suis cloué, il n'y a pas de révolution possible, pas d'avenir' [A skewed time sense [...] a *moment* blocks the horizon of depressive temporality or rather removes any horizon, any perspective. Riveted to the past, regressing to the paradise or inferno of an unsurpassable experience, melancholy persons manifest a strange memory: everything has gone by, they seem to say, but I am faithful to those bygone days, I am nailed down to them, no revolution is possible, there is no future] (italics in the original).

[97] See e.g. *Par.* I, 70; XXX, 19; and XXXII, 90.

[Who knows *if on arrival over* there name's not conjoined to thing
... (the poem on the holiday place).
Instead that voice returns to tempt me many years
(a record, it was) *from over there, the far shore.* Dusty, thirsty evenings
you almost touched it, throat offered to the wound of love
upon the waters. *I'll not write this story.*]

Despite what he might hope, the poet cannot in fact see beyond at all, and all that is returned to him is his lack of foresight, his inability to make the two sides join up. The deictic 'lì' [there] towards which the subject projects himself, and from which he can only imagine looking back to where he is now, is of course the 'altra riva' he cannot reach, and so the higher perspective aligned with that point is not one to which he can have access. Instead, a voice returns to haunt him, dangling itself tantalizingly within reach but receding just enough into the past ('Nelle sere') to delay its capture indefinitely. Already at the point of failing, another journey is cut short: 'Non scriverò questa storia' (l. 27). A path opens momentarily to close over again.

As the passage from Part IV confirms, 'Lo scriba' has nothing to write, or writes nothing, revisiting the 'sentenza' [sayings] of the Sibyl in Sereni's similarly Dantesque poem, 'Autostrada della Cisa', 'non lo sospetti ancora | che di tutti i colori il più forte | il più indelebile | è il colore del vuoto?' [do you not still suspect | that of all the colours the strongest | the most fast | is the colour of nothingness?] (*SV*, p. 263), a message which, if it is not lost as it is in *Paradiso* XXXIII, still figures a lack and one which does not presume a prior state of meaning or fullness.[98] The word 'amaranto' [amaranth], to which Sereni's desiring pursuit is directed, embodies that ghost of a revealed emptiness. It turns out to be a hall of mirrors, an impossible web of desire in which the subject is caught.

As Giovanna Gronda notes in her study of *Un posto*, 'amaranto', besides being part of a complex system of words in the poem that includes 'amore' [love], 'amare' [to love], 'amaro' [bitter], 'marea' [tide], 'intento' [intent], 'intanto' [meanwhile], also creates a bridge with a network of verbal forms ending in '-ante', '-ente', '-anti', and '-enti'.[99] In pursuit of the mirage of the whole from all of these parts, the subject wears himself out ('*si stremava su un colore*', IV, 24). Finally, in its complete elsewhereness, or nonexistence,

---

[98] Cf. *Par.* XXXIII, 64–6, 'Così la neve al sol si disigilla; | così al vento ne le foglie levi | *si perdea* la sentenza di Sibilla' [Thus the sun unseals an imprint in the snow. | Thus the Sibyl's oracles, on weightless leaves, | lifted by the wind, *were swept away*].

[99] Giovanna Gronda, '"Un posto di vacanza" iuxta propria principia', in *Tradizione traduzione società: saggio per Franco Fortini*, ed. Romano Luperini (Rome: Edizioni Riuniti, 1989), pp. 177–203 (p. 183, n. 16).

'amaranto'—more phantasm than object proper—comes to represent the utopia of Sereni's poetic universe. Coinciding with the 'punto' of Dantean derivation (*Un posto* IV, 20), which bridges the full gamut of desire, from that punished in the second circle of Hell to that celebrated in the furthest reaches of the Empyrean, Sereni's 'point' carries the same doubleness and ambiguity as Dante's (see also *Un posto* I, 11; II, 3; V, 7; VII, 18).[100] As Christian Moevs argues with respect to the *Commedia*:

> The *punto* for Dante [...] becomes the moment of conversion, the dimensionless now in which the soul either awakens to its ground or falls under the hypnosis of the senses and mortal desire. Indeed, in [...] *Paradiso* 33, Dante sets up the timeless instant of transcendent understanding, the *lumen gloriae*, against the entire history of human desire and exploration in time ('Un punto solo m'è maggior letargo | che venticinque secoli a la 'mpresa | che fé Nettuno ammirar l'ombra d'Argo').[101]

Whatever Sereni's 'punto' represents (and in the passage from *Un posto* IV it could even represent the subject), its being a point of consummation of time ('gli anni [...] *s'incendiano*') but not memory (which endures) means that it is intrinsically bound up with a melancholy obsession with loss, the perception of fragmentation, and the fall into discontinuity and difference, 'che sono io | custode non di anni ma di attimi | e più nessuno che giungere doveva e era atteso | più nessuno verrà sulle acque spopolate' (IV, 20–3). Whereas at the summit of *Purgatorio*, Dante's passage through Lethe leaves him free of sin and ready to ascend to the stars, Sereni's refusal of Lethe—his inability to conceive of an end to memory—keeps those stars forever at a distance. Unable to ascend to the heavens, he tries to bring the heavens down to him, but the light of dead stars can inflame or torment, but not placate desire, and he ends up haunted not only by the echoes of his failed voyage but also by the fragments of a failed poetry.

---

[100] 'Nel punto, per l'esattezza, dove un fiume entra nel mare' [At the point, to be precise, where a river flows into the sea]; 'si restringe su un minimo | punto di luce dove due s'imbucano spariscono nel sempreverde' [is reduced to a minimal | point of light where two take cover, disappear in evergreens]; 'Esplode in più punti e dilaga la sparatoria dei clic-clac' [It explodes here and there and spreads, the click-clack's gunfire]; 'il disegno profondo | nel punto dove si fa più palese' [At the point | where it became most clear | the deep design was grasped].

[101] Christian Moevs, 'Subjectivity and Conversion in Dante and Petrarch', in *Petrarch and Dante: Anti-Dantism, Metaphysics, Tradition*, ed. Zygmunt G. Barański, and Theodore J. Cachey Jr. (Notre Dame, Ind.: University of Notre Dame Press, 2009), pp. 226–59 (p. 235). Moevs expressly compares the 'punto' of *Inf.* V with the 'punto' of the *Paradiso*, noting: 'Dante symmetrically and ironically contrasts this *punto* of Christic revelation, which conquers him in *Paradiso* 28 [...] to the *punto* of text and time that conquered Francesca and Paolo in *Inferno* 5 [...] ensnaring them in lust and the lure of mortal beauty.'

Having earlier renounced his own history, then the history of another, in the final stages of his journey Sereni abdicates the search for the poetic word, and finally desire itself. Addressing his poem in its impassive, unyielding totality, which in its readiness to move on fails to reflect his static and dissolutional poetics, the writing 'I' beseeches it to leave him behind:

> Ma tu specchio ora uniforme e immemore
> pronto per nuovi fumi
> di sterpaglia nei campi per nuove luci
> di notte dalla piana per gente
> che sgorghi nuova da Carrara o da Luni
>
> tu davvero dimenticami, non lusingarmi più.
> (*Un posto* VII, 28–33, p. 233)
>
> [But you, mirror, uniform now without memory
> ready for new smoke plumes
> from stubble in fields for new lights
> at night from the plain for people
> who anew you disgorge from Luni or Carrara
>
> truly disremember me, flatter me no more.]

For Sereni, the end of desire is conceivable only in the absence of memory or the total annihilation of the self, whereas for Dante, in the closing lines of the *Paradiso*, it is synonymous with the ecstatic union of a perfected self with God, which dissolves language and memory but leaves some essential part of the 'I' intact:

> A l'alta fantasia qui mancò possa;
> ma già volgeva il mio disio e 'l *velle*
> sì come rota ch'igualmente è mossa
> l'amor che move 'l sole e l'altre stelle.
> (*Par.* XXXIII, 142–45; italics in the original)
>
> [Here my exalted vision lost its power.
> But now my will and my desire, like wheels revolving
> with an even motion, were turning with
> the Love that moves the sun and all the other stars.]

If, as Barolini states, 'it is [...] possible to experience the end of this [Dante's] poem as a being stranded in an eternal present, on a very high peak that was attained by dint of following behind the voice, the all-making voice, that suddenly is no more', by contrast, the poetic voice in Sereni's poem, no longer wanting to be inveigled, absents itself.[102] His

---

[102] Barolini, *The Undivine 'Comedy'*, p. 256.

poem must carry on its journey alone; the speaking subject desires only to be forgotten.

BEYOND DANTE

Staring into the mirror of poetry, Sereni thus finds not only a dissociated image of himself but also the revelation of the exiled poetic voice that only asserts itself through negation, particularly of any hope of reaching the ideal Dantean space ('luogo ideale') implicit in a return to the beginning.

Reflecting this double process of restoration and nullification of an ideal poetic past, Sereni's recourse to Dantean lexicon and Dantean tropes, because of the way in which they are almost seamlessly inserted into the fabric of the text, creates a poetic world that is inclusive of a Dantean dimension without being reducible to it. His (poetic and desiring) journey is in many senses one modelled on Dante, and yet at the same time continually departs from that model, refuses to come to completion, and even at times resists starting out. In this way, the dialogue with Dante is concentrated around key points in Sereni's poetry which can be read as emblematic of the presence of a melancholy subject, symbolically situated on the banks of Lethe that are also those of the Acheron, at the point at which the light of Paradise fades and the black chamber of Hell opens up to receive him.

Sereni's reappropriation of Dantean motifs, and their simultaneous disavowal, mirrors a tension in his own relationship to memory and poetry, which divides him between a mythicized past, to which he endeavours to return, and a bitter awareness of the doomed nature of that pursuit. More than this, however, his approach serves to redefine those pathways of desire that, in a secular world and in the absence of God, find themselves redirected to new ends and ideally to new beginnings. And yet, as we have seen, the spiral of desire into which Sereni's subject falls increasingly merely equates one with the other, so that ending both, he may perhaps reappropriate Eliot's conclusion: 'I can only say, *there* we have been: but I cannot say where.'[103]

---

[103] *Burnt Norton*, p. 15 (italics in the original).

Conclusion

'Sei più in là'

The Destination of Poetry, the Limits of Identity[1]

> Smettila di corteggiarmi—disse al viaggiatore il paesaggio innevato
> su tutta la sua estensione—smettila di starmi attorno con parole.[2]
> (Vittorio Sereni, 'Dovuto a Montale')

By focusing upon Sereni's redefinition of the lyric 'I', and his establishment of new and highly original modes for its construction in poetic space, this study has sought to reinterpret his contribution to the Italian lyric tradition. While Sereni cannot be considered an experimental poet in the sense of some of his contemporaries, he does exercise a unique form of radicalism in the way in which he shapes aspects of the tradition as facets of a self which, like its Petrarchan counterpart, 'finds poetic identity in all the forms it takes, however uncertain it may be about their meaning and status'.[3] In turn, this dialectical way of writing—in which the poet looks backwards as much as forwards—emerges as the necessary creative condition for an author unsure of what path remains open to him to navigate in the future.

As a sustained exploration of how Sereni constructs his subject on the basis of an evolving poetic topography—which incorporates an important and systematic intertextual dimension—the study challenges the view that his poetry is one anchored purely or mainly in the author's (attempts to define his) empirical identity, and shifts the focus more towards an understanding of the evolution of his subjectivity in language. By rereading Sereni's work in light of the presence of a desiring subject, whose

---

[1] 'Sei più in là | ti vedo nel fondo della mia serachiusascura | ti identifico tra i non i sic i sigh | ti disidentifico' [You're further over there | I see you at the bottom of my closed dark evening | I identify you among the nos the sics the sighs | I disidentify you], Andrea Zanzotto, 'Oltranza oltraggio' ['Excess Outrage'], ll. 7–10, in *La beltà, Le poesie e prose scelte*, ed. Stefano Dal Bianco and Gian Mario Villalta (Milan: Mondadori, 1999), p. 267.

[2] [Stop courting me—said the landscape, covered in snow as far as the eye could see, to the traveller—stop hounding me with words.]

[3] Peter Hainsworth, *Petrarch the Poet: An Introduction to the 'Rerum vulgarium fragmenta'* (London: Routledge, 1988), p. 19.

existence impacts in definitive fashion upon his poetic form and whose quest is linguistic as much as experiential, it becomes possible to explain both his decision to establish a textual landscape through a set of recurring grammatical features—deictics—and how these are related to his assumption of a poetic identity, which becomes more fragmentary and phantasmatic in character as his poetry develops.

Deictics embody the discourse of displaced desire that never allows the word to coincide with its object or, better, only represents the object by dint of its absence and final illocality within the signifying field. Liminality, as an experience, is the unsettling realization of this fact and, as a recurring trope of Sereni's poetry (and Montale's before him), attests to the diminishing hold of the poetic 'I' over its landscape (of desire). The dominant presence of deictics in Sereni's universe, and the fact that they survive (albeit altered) into the changed landscape of his postwar poetry, suggests that his concern with finding a space to inhabit, a 'luogo ideale' [ideal place], remains intact even when that 'luogo' is understood as endlessly deferred and disseminated through successive and incomplete figurations, none by itself capable of restoring the 'I' or its lost object fully to presence. Deictics mediate in the space between possession and dispossession: even as they carry the memory of a lyric power that could establish poetic presence as a symbolic substitute for the lost object, they foreground the transient quality of the speaking subject that is sustained only as long as the utterance.

Whereas, in *Frontiera*, deictics are a response to the more unsettling parts of liminality, they soon become contaminated by it so that they too contribute in their increasing unreality to the liminal predicament of the subject, becoming the textual equivalent of limbo or Purgatory. Establishing a place for oneself in the world and discovering one's poetic voice go hand in hand, and the poet's most desired object might just be the complete poem or the total identity that elude him:

Altri di noi non c'è qui che lo specimen
anzi l'imago perpetuantesi
a vuoto—
    ('Altro posto di lavoro' ['Other Place of Work'], ll. 4–6, in *SV*, p. 253)

[Here there is nothing of us but the specimen
or rather the imago of self-perpetuating
for nothing—]

The definition of deictics as the empty signs of language is also one that, poetically speaking, betrays their foundations in nothingness and something as insubstantial and transitory as the voice. As an analysis of Sereni's poetry reveals, deictics actually allow us to glimpse the identity of language as negativity as well as the potential miracle of a poetic language that could counter that negativity, substituting presence for absence and offering some (albeit imaginary or illusory) compensation for an original lack. It is this double quality of deixis, and the ambivalent nature of its power rooted in the phantasm, that Sereni draws upon most in the reconfiguration of his own textual and desiring landscape.

Faced with the disintegration of the poetic idyll that was once sustained by a more generative poetics, his subject falls out of an imagined plenitude into a perceived state of deprivation. Unable to stake its ground topographically or poetically speaking, it finds itself denied or even actively expelled by the created universe: 'Non ti vuole ti espatria | si libera di te | rifiuto dei rifiuti | la maestà della notte' [It doesn't want you expatriates you | frees itself of you | refusal of refusals | the majesty of night] ('Notturno' ['Nocturne'], ll. 5–8, in *SV*, p. 224). Exile in fact becomes the permanent condition of writing, only exacerbated in Sereni's case by the feeling that he has also been cast out from the poetic circle which once celebrated 'l'unione senza fine del desiderio e del suo oggetto' [the endless union of desire and its object], and he stands at the extreme end of a line of poets for whom desire is the foundation of poetry, and its fulfilment the increasingly elusive goal:

> Nel corso di un processo storico che ha in Petrarca e in Mallarmé le sue tappe emblematiche, questa essenziale tensione testuale della poesia romanza sposterà il suo centro dal desiderio al lutto e Eros cederà a Thanatos il suo impossibile oggetto d'amore per recuperarlo, attraverso una funebre e sottile strategia, come oggetto perduto, mentre il poema diventa il luogo di un'assenza che trae però da quest'assenza la sua specifica autorità.[4]
>
> [Over the course of a poetic process whose emblematic temporal extremes are Petrarch and Mallarmé, this essential textual tension of Romance poetry will displace its centre from desire to mourning: Eros will yield to Thanatos its impossible love object so as to recover it, through a subtle and funereal strategy, as lost object, and the poem will become the site of an absence yet nonetheless draws from this absence its specific authority.]

Earlier models of desire in the work of poets such as Dante, Petrarch, and Montale are rescued and ennobled in order for Sereni to be able to communicate his remoteness from these, and the bathetic nature of his own desiring quest is measured against the shadow of a series of poetic phantasms whose total form eludes the poet as much as the poetic identity he seeks to rebuild from among their vestiges. They provide ratification to

---

[4] Giorgio Agamben, *Stanze: la parola e il fantasma nella cultura occidentale* (Turin: Einaudi, 1977), p. 154.

a degree, but also the unsettling discovery of the inability to rediscover the same conditions for their appropriation that existed for the earlier author. Sereni's identity takes shape from amongst these 'ragged remainders' and 'evanescent margins' of a poetic world he would desire to recreate but which eludes his grasp, and the different 'selves' the poet encounters in his work are all versions of the same predicament, all shreds of a poetic selfhood that refuses to come to completion.[5]

The melancholy subject who comes to inhabit that textual Purgatory is a direct progeny of a poetic space that is made up of 'contiguità laceranti e alternative compresenti: cioè un destino tutto terrestre' [lacerating contiguities and co-present alternatives: that is, an entirely terrestrial destiny].[6] Like the Montalian subject of the *Ossi*, he is one of the 'razza | di chi rimane a terra' [race | who are earthbound] ('Falsetto', p. 13), forced to watch from a distance as his horizon slips further from view. Sereni is denied both Dante's right of ascension to the paradisiacal dimension that lies beyond and Petrarch's ability to transform hollow spaces into an enchanted wood of memory (as in *RVF* CXXVI). While the visionary dimension in the strictest sense becomes more important as Sereni's poetry develops (in which phantasmatic objects increasingly coexist or fuse with their real counterparts and the poet is at pains to distinguish between them), it also becomes more ambivalent in its effects and less capable of transfiguring reality or the self beyond the more limited frame of hallucination.

In looking to the Montalian universe, Sereni aligns himself most with elements that deal with the failure to totalize or to transcend, and he distances himself from the epiphanic dimension of Clizia and her correlatives who rarely find a place in his poetic universe, from which the constant dialogue with a female Other is also notably absent. Emphasis shifts upon a loss which cannot be recuperated (not even within the bounds of poetry), and Sereni moves closer to Zanzotto, whose own configuration of a beyond similarly expresses itself in the tension towards an object which recedes indefinitely from his grasp, more intangible than ever:

---

[5] 'With the ragged remainders and evanescent margins of a world desired by the subject the subject himself is fashioned and upholstered', Malcolm Bowie, *Lacan* (London: Fontana, 1991), p. 168. These are both features that Bowie attributes to desire-space, which, as I argue in Ch. 4, are at the basis of Sereni's desiring landscape too.

[6] Vittorio Sereni, 'Giorgio Seferis' (1971), first publ. as the preface to Giorgio Seferis, *Le opere: poesia, prosa*, trans. Filippo Maria Pontani (Milan: Club degli Editori, 1971), pp. ix–xxx, now in *Letture preliminari*, pp. 115–35 (pp. 127–8).

> [...]
> ti fai più in là
> intangibile—tutto sommato—
> tutto sommato   5
> tutto
> sei più in là
> [...]⁷
>
> [You move further over there
> intangible—all in all
> all in all   5
> all
> you're further over there]

That *tu* is language, or the part that evades expression, or the poem itself in its 'oltranza' [excess/going beyond]—something which enacts a fall for the subject more than a path to salvation. The deictic 'là', like Sereni's own, is used less to describe a landscape than to create one, and every locus is the scene of a battle, between the self and the Other, and between the poet and his 'materia' [material].

This suggests not only that the deictic phenomena so far discussed can shed light upon the projects of more poets than just Sereni, but also that the liminal predicament of a subject exiled by language may be the founding condition of Italian poetry of the second half of the twentieth century. Perhaps poetry of this period is defined by space more than time (if time is the privileged store of narrative) or at any rate communicates the expatriation of the lyric subject in topographic fashion, as a result of finding oneself stranded in a textual landscape which seems remote or unfamiliar.

That said, Sereni also has a deep concern with temporality, and in making liminality a condition of memory he succeeds in moulding deixis to that dimension too. Textually speaking, the melancholy self is just another manifestation of a subject *in limine* whose reiterative qualities reaffirm the sense that no single moment is sufficient to rewrite the whole of history or the sum total of an identity. Deictics in this case foreground the bathos of the poetic moment, or the eternal return to the point of loss, which the poet paradoxically covets in refusing to accept and move on. The multitude of voices that intercede to mediate his poetic quest merely exacerbate the moment of dispossession, and divide him between an irrecoverable past and the equally elusive phantasms which inhabit the present.

---

[7] Zanzotto, 'Oltranza oltraggio', ll. 3–7, p. 267.

Textual anaphora is the main vehicle for this splitting or dissemination of identity, and it helps to reconfigure the traditional parameters of the lyric text to incorporate a more heterogeneous conception of the writing process and the subject engaged in it. By allowing Dante, Petrarch, and Montale to coexist in a poetically composite space, Sereni foregrounds the similarities as well as the differences between them, and where their voices intersect we often find examples of what, following Barolini's study of textuality in the *Commedia*, can be termed moments of 'textual stress', where Sereni must choose which poetic path to follow and often vacillates between them.[8] His attraction to the epic qualities of Dante's text, which he finds himself unable to recreate, feeds into the lyric fragmentation originating on the Petrarchan plane, and his poetic phantasms are inevitably degraded versions of what has come before. Montale and Leopardi mediate between the two, at one moment restoring perspective to a subject in decline within his own textual universe, at another exacerbating further his sense of distance from a concept of poetry as fulfilment or utopia. Where poetry was once the site where the fracture between desire and its unattainable object could be healed, it is now synonymous with the fracture itself.[9]

Each poetic fissure which intertextuality brings to light, in the gap that opens up between Sereni and the earlier author, reiterates his position at the limits of expression and the necessity of rediscovering the meaning of poetry as desire or chasm. Liminality is also a feature of this textual uncertainty and of Sereni's propensity to measure his own poetry against what has come before. His anxiety extends also to his awareness of writing poetry 'nei perigliosi paraggi della prosa' [in the perilous environs of prose],[10] which brings him into close contact with Umberto Saba and a range of other authors who had similar formal concerns, from Proust and

---

[8] Teodolinda Barolini, *Dante's Poets: Textuality and Truth in the 'Comedy'* (Princeton, NJ: Princeton University Press, 1984), p. 30.

[9] I am once again drawing upon Agamben's theory of the relationship between desire, word and phantasm in *Stanze*, pp. 146–55.

[10] 'Difficile, forse il più difficile "esercizio di lettura", quello che si può fare su Saba. Accertata la nascita della sua poesia *nei perigliosi paraggi della prosa*, resta poi affidata senz'altri appigli alla pura sensibilità del lettore l'individuazione dei luoghi in cui la voce s'abbandona al gorgo del canto: punti delicati sempre in un poeta che professa il suo amore per le "trite parole" che nessuno osa' [Hard, perhaps the hardest 'exercise in reading', is the one that can be attempted for Saba. Acknowledging that his poetry is born *in the perilous environs of prose*, it is then left to the sole sensibility of the reader, unaided, to pinpoint the place in which the voice abandons itself to the whirl of song: always delicate points in the work of a poet who professes his love for the 'trite words' no one dares use]. Vittorio Sereni 'Gli uccelli sono un miracolo' ['Birds Are a Miracle'], first publ. in *La scuola*, 47.8 (Aug. 1951), pp. 151–2, now in *SG*, pp. 43–7 (pp. 46–7).

Fortini to poets Sereni translated such as René Char, Ezra Pound, and William Carlos Williams:

> Si convive per anni con sensazioni, impressioni, sentimenti, intuizioni, ricordi. Il senso di rarità o eccezionalità che a ragione e a torto si attribuisce ad essi, forse in relazione con l'intensità con cui l'esistenza li impose, è la prima fonte di insoddisfazione creativa, anzi di riluttanza di fronte alla messa in opera, che si traduce (peggio per chi non la prova) in nausea metrica, in disgusto di ogni modulo precedentemente sperimentato... Si convive con le proprie intenzioni, con spettri di poesie non scritte... Un poeta invidierà sempre a un narratore, sia questi o no di stampo tradizionale, quella specie di sortilegio evocativo con cui l'altro dà corpo, illusorio fin che si vuole, a figure, situazioni, vicende, ben oltre la voce, l'accento, la formulazione lirica immediata.[11]
>
> [You live for many years with sensations, impressions, feelings, intuitions, memories. The sense of rare or exceptional character, which rightly or wrongly you attribute to them, is due perhaps to the intensity with which life had impressed them upon you. This is the first source of creative dissatisfaction, of reluctance even before the work at hand, which is translated (worse for those who don't feel it) into metrical nausea, into disgust with every form previously tried. You live with your intentions, with ghosts of unwritten poems... A poet will always envy a novelist—whether of the conventional type or not—for that kind of sorcery by which he conjures up characters, events, situations that have nothing to do with voice, accent, or immediate lyric formulation.]

If Sereni views prose as more enduring, if less intense or effulgent, than lyricism, it is revealing that the most prominent of the narrative voices we have discovered is Proust's, which also operates in a 'zona limitrofa' [border zone] between the two.[12] The contiguity of narrative and lyric elements in Sereni's work is another kind of liminal predicament, and one which no doubt feeds into the other aspects of desire-space already discussed.

Sereni's poetry is consequently an intertext in the most literal of senses: a cross-hatch of other voices and discourses drawn from his rich poetic heritage; the arena in which, in the absence of a true interlocutor, he is free to dialogue with himself; and the transitory space for the housing of a subject that has its home in the interstices between words or in the shifting realm of deictic reference, in which 'gli *shifters*, nel momento in cui

---

[11] Sereni, 'Il silenzio creativo' ['Creative Silence'], p. 76; trans. Robinson–Perryman.
[12] Laura Barile, 'Gli alberi e la metamorfosi nella poesia di Vittorio Sereni', first publ. in *Lettere italiane* 45.3 (July–Sept. 1993), pp. 376–97, now in *La poesia di Vittorio Sereni: se ne scrivono ancora*, ed. Alfredo Luzi et al. (Grottammare: Stamperia dell'Arancio, 1997), pp. 89–108 (p. 91).

alludono ad una possibilità d'enunciazione, misurano gli intervalli tra l'intenzionalità dei segni e il loro senso, pausano gli indugi di un dire "impreciso", ne indicano il margine' [the *shifters*, in the moment in which they allude to the possibility of enunciation, measure the interval between the intentionality of the signs and their meaning, pause the delays inherent in an 'imprecise' way of speaking, indicate its margins].[13] All the authors who act as intermediaries in Sereni's poetic quest contribute to this complex and dynamic *mise-en-scène* of a subject caught in the textual labyrinth, dark wood, or waste land of his own desire, and many reiterate the experience of writing as one of displacement or disorientation, of fragmentation more than synthesis.

This leads Sereni to explore regions of poetry that are in one sense the epitome of the modern complexes of exclusion and separation, and in another emerge as the paths which lead back to the foundational experience of literature and the common concern with a loss which perhaps only poetry can recuperate or embody. Distances which open up in his poetry between the desiring subject and the desired object testify to this dilemma, as well as to the ability of poetry to negotiate territories traditionally reserved for philosophy or other abstract principles.

Those distances are also metaphysical, and deixis is the linguistic tool which Sereni uses (like Dante, Petrarch, Leopardi, and Montale before him) to incorporate epistemological concerns into poetry. It is perhaps unsurprising in this respect to find that deixis has also been the focus of philosophical study, notably by Heidegger, who in *Poetry, Language, Thought* deals with its value as that which 'gathers being' to itself, reiterating its importance as a marker of individual experience and identity:

> Even when mortals turn 'inward', taking stock of themselves, they do not leave behind their belonging to the fourfold. When, as we say, we come to our senses and reflect on ourselves, we come back to ourselves from things *without ever abandoning* our stay among things. Indeed, the loss of rapport with things that occurs in states of depression would be wholly impossible if even such a state were not still what it is as a human state: that is, a staying *with* things. Only if this stay already characterizes human being [*sic*] can the things among which we are also *fail* to speak to us, *fail* to concern us any longer.[14]

These are all features of Sereni's conception of poetry as desire-space, and it would be interesting to extend linguistic and psychoanalytic

---

[13] Enrico Testa, '*Sur la corde de la voix* : funzione della deissi nel testo poetico', in *Linguistica, pragmatica e testo letterario*, ed. Umberto Rapallo (Genova: Il Melangolo, 1996), pp. 113–46 (p. 125; italics in the original).

[14] Martin Heidegger, *Poetry, Language, Thought*, trans. Albert Hofstadter (New York: Perennial Classics, 2001), p. 155 (italics in the original).

discourses treated here to questions of ontology and the notion of 'dwelling poetically'.[15] In exploiting the boundary-making properties of language and poetic form, the poet 'makes space' for a version of the self which does not find expression elsewhere, highlighting its dependency upon the external world for its existence, and the being-affirming properties of the in-between. In this conception, the more ambiguous traits of liminality in Sereni's work could be redeemed as facets of a much wider concern with the terrestrial origins of the self, its tendency to measure itself 'against the heavenly', and the identity that results that is specifically human: 'This measure taking has its own *metron*, and thus its own metric.'[16]

In privileging a textual universe and a poetic identity over their experiential counterparts, Sereni re-evaluates where the true meaning of his identity lies, as well as that of a whole range of poets whose work is reassessed in line with his own. Whether his gaze is directed backwards to a more complete time and place accessible now only intermittently, or upwards to a heavenly or utopian dimension he cannot access, which only becomes more remote, desire resides always in the potential for movement or its frustration, and in the constant renewal of a journey which may already be complete when the poet starts out but in which he continues to put all future store of his own happiness:

> Non resta più molto da dire
> e sempre lo stesso paesaggio si ripete.
> Non rimane che aggirarlo [...]
> ('A un compagno d'infanzia' I, ll. 1–3, in *SU*, p. 170)
>
> [Not much remains to be said
> and the same landscape's always repeated.
> Nothing's left but to move around it]

In one way Sereni can never go back, in another that is all he does, in the same way that landscape is paradoxically the locus for an identity that never succeeds in finding a stable resting place. Everything has been said or nothing has been, but the world remains as it always was: the space in which the poet's identity finds its limits—where his voice is extinguished, his poetic vista cut short—and the scene of its accession, where the poet leaves one world behind to embrace the next. He is at one with the landscape; he is at odds with it. But it is all he knows.

---

[15] '"Poetically, man dwells..." Poetry builds up the very nature of dwelling. Poetry and dwelling not only do not exclude each other; on the contrary, poetry and dwelling belong together, each calling for the other', ibid. 225.
[16] Ibid. 218, 219.

APPENDIX:

Guide to Index of Archive Catalogue, Archivio Vittorio Sereni, Luino (Varese)

References made to archive documents correspond to those used in the Archive's catalogue. This catalogue retains the mode of classification used when the archive was still housed in Sereni's private abode [Archivio Privato della famiglia Sereni] in via P.A. Paravia 37, Milan, later transferred to Villa Hüssy, Pizza Risorgimento 2, Luino (VA), when it was acquired by the Comune di Luino on 10 December 1998:

APS I   notebooks and folders with manuscript texts in verse, prose, and translation
APS II   loose sheets and files of manuscript and typescript texts in verse
APS III   editorial proofs of works by Sereni (many annotated by the author)
APS IV   loose sheets and files of manuscript and typescript texts in prose
APS V   notebooks, loose sheets, and files of manuscript and typescript texts in translation
APS VI   letters written to Sereni from various correspondents
APS VII   letters written by Sereni to various correspondents

In addition, during the process of digitalization of these documents into a central database, each file was also given a letter and a numeral in order to identify it by type and number.
Each letter corresponds to the typology of the document:

Type of document	Corresponding letter
Notebook/diary	Q
Letter	L
File of loose papers	F

Each number identifies a document uniquely amongst all similar documents. e.g. APS VII 24 (L 1246) = Letter 1246 written by Sereni (to Fortini).

Bibliography

WORKS BY VITTORIO SERENI

Poetry
Frontiera (Milan: Corrente, 1941);
2nd rev. edn, *Poesie* (Florence: Vallecchi, 1942);
3rd rev. edn, *Frontiera* (Milan: All'Insegna del Pesce d'Oro, 1966).
Diario d'Algeria (Florence: Vallecchi, 1947);
2nd rev. edn, *Diario d'Algeria* (Milan: Mondadori, Collezione 'Lo Specchio', 1965; 1979).
Gli strumenti umani (Turin: Einaudi, 1965).
Stella variabile (Milan: Garzanti, 1981). A 'pre-edition' (Verona: Cento Amici del Libro, 1979) was printed in 130 copies, accompanied by lithograph prints by Ruggero Savinio.
Un posto di vacanza (Milan: All'Insegna del Pesce D'Oro, 1973), first publ. in *L'Almanacco dello specchio* 1 (1971).

All in:
Poesie, ed. Dante Isella, 4th edn (Milan: Mondadori, 2000).
Translations of a selection of Sereni's poetry and prose are available in English as: *The Selected Poetry and Prose of Vittorio Sereni: A Bilingual Edition*, ed. and trans. Peter Robinson and Marcus Perryman (Chicago: University of Chicago Press, 2006).

Anthologies
Il grande amico: poesie 1935–1981, ed. Gilberto Lonardi and Luca Lenzini (Milan: Rizzoli, 1990) = *GA*.
Un posto di vacanza e altre poesie, ed. Zeno Birolli (Milan: All'Insegna del Pesce d'Oro, 1994) = *Un posto*.

Prose works
Collected works
Gli immediati dintorni (Milan: Il Saggiatore, 1962) = *ID1*.
Letture preliminari, ed. Pier Vincenzo Mengaldo et al. (Padua: Liviana, 1973).
Il sabato tedesco (Milan: Il Saggiatore, 1980). Now in *La tentazione della prosa*, ed. Giulia Raboni (Milan: Mondadori, 1998), pp. 203–24.
Graziano: collezione della Galleria d'arte Il Catalogo (Salerno: Il Catalogo, 1982).
Gli immediati dintorni: primi e secondi, ed. Maria Teresa Sereni (Milan: Il Saggiatore, 1983) = *ID2*.
Senza l'onore delle armi (Milan: All'Insegna del Pesce d'Oro, 1986) = *SOA*.

Sentieri di gloria: note e ragionamenti sulla letteratura, ed. Giuseppe Strazzeri (Milan: Mondadori, 1996) = *SG*.

La tentazione della prosa, ed. Giulia Raboni (Milan: Mondadori, 1998) = *TDP*. This incorporates the whole of *ID2* and the posthumous prose work, *La traversata di Milano*, which Sereni was working on when he died.

Autobiographical writings
'Algeria '44' (1944), first publ. in *ID1*, pp. 26–9, now in *ID2*, pp. 13–16.
'Male del reticolato' (1945), first publ. in *La Rassegna d'Italia* 1.5 (May 1946), pp. 56–9, now in *ID2*, pp. 16–20.
'Esperienza della poesia' (1947), first publ. in *ID1*, pp. 41–6, now in *ID2*, pp. 25–8.
'Saba e l'ispirazione', first publ. as Appendix to R. Martinoni, 'Bricciche svizzero-italiane per Vittorio Sereni: Piero Bianconi, il Premio "Libera Stampa" e una collaborazione radiofonica (1947)', *Versants* 16 (1989), 64–6, now in *SG*, pp. 154–8.
'Un omaggio a Rimbaud' (1954), first publ. in abridged form as 'Sans ombre qu'on est soi-même', in *Omaggio a Rimbaud, di poeti italiani viventi*, ed. V. Scheiwiller (Milan: All'Insegna del Pesce d'Oro, 1954), pp. 31–2, now in *ID2*, pp. 46–50.
'Da Apollinaire' (1957), in *ID2*, pp. 59–60.
'Cominciavi' (1960), first publ. in *ID1*, pp. 98–9, now in *ID2*, pp. 64–5.
'Il silenzio creativo' (1962), first publ. in *ID1*, pp. 112–16, now in *ID2*, pp. 74–8.
'Senza vantaggio?', *Questo e altro* 3 (1962), 25–8.
'La cattura', first publ. in *Pirelli: rivista d'informazione e di tecnica* 16.1 (Feb. 1963), section entitled *Italia 1943*, 6, now in *TDP*, pp. 153–60. Also in *SOA*, pp. 9–20.
'L'anno quarantatre' (1963), in *ID2*, pp. 80–8, later repr. in *SOA*, pp. 21–32.
'L'opzione', first publ. in *Queste e altro* 8 (1964), pp. 33–45, repr. in *L'opzione e allegati* (Milan: All'Insegna del Pesce d'Oro, 1964) and in *Il sabato tedesco*, pp. 17–55, now in *TDP*, pp. 161–89.
'L'anno quarantacinque' (1965), in *ID2*, pp. 93–101. Also in *SOA*, pp. 33–44.
'Ventisei', first publ. in *Forum italicum* 4.4 (December 1970), pp. 576–89. Also in *SOA*, pp. 45–63, now in *TDP*, pp. 190–202.
'Le sabbie dell'Algeria', first publ. in *Storia illustrata* 16.178 (Sept. 1972), pp. 102–7, now in *TDP*, pp. 249–57.
'Poesia: per chi?', *Rinascita* 32.37 (19 Sept. 1975), pp. 21–2.
'Il mio lavoro su Char', in *Premio Città di Monselice per una traduzione letteraria*, ed. l'Amministrazione Comunale (Monselice, 1977), pp. xxv–xxviii.
'Autoritratto' (1978), first publ. in *La Rassegna della letteratura italiana* 85, ser. 7.3 (Sept.–Dec. 1981), pp. 427–9, now in *ID2*, pp. 127–32.
'Negli anni di Luino' (1979–81), first publ. in instalments in *La Rotonda, Almanacco Luinese 1979*, 1 (Luino: Nastro, 1978), pp. 31–9; *La Rotonda, Almanacco Luinese 1981*, 3 (Luino: Nastro, 1980), pp. 33–8, with the title

'Materie prime'; and *La Rotonda, Almanacco Luinese 1982*, 4 (Luino: Nastro, 1981), pp. 89–90, now in *ID2*, pp. 133–8.
'Infatuazioni' (1982), first publ. in *Sul porto* (Cesenatico), numero unico (1983), p. 32. Also in *Un posto*, pp. 72–3, now in *ID2*, p. 147.

Writings on literature and other authors
'In margine alle *Occasioni*' [on Montale], first publ. in *Tempo* 4.62 (1 Aug. 1940), 45, now in *SG*, pp. 56–60.
'Si può leggere Dante come un poeta "puro"?', first publ. in *Milano Sera*, 23–4 Oct. 1950, p. 3, now in *SG*, pp. 28–33.
'Gli uccelli sono un miracolo' [on Saba], first publ. in *La scuola* 47.8 (Aug. 1951), pp. 151–2, now in *SG*, pp. 43–7.
'Ognuno riconosce i suoi' [on Montale], *Letteratura* 30.79–81, n.s. 13 (Jan.–June 1966), pp. 305–10.
'"Satura" di Eugenio Montale', *L'Approdo letterario* 17.53 (1971), pp. 107–16.
'Giorgio Seferis', first publ. as 'Preface' to G. Seferis, *Le opere: poesia, prosa*, trans. Filippo Maria Pontani (Milan: Club degli Editori, 1971), pp. ix–xxx, now in *Letture preliminari*, pp. 115–35. Also in *Il verri* 38 (Feb. 1972), pp. 6–21.
'Petrarca, nella sua finzione la sua verità', in *SG*, pp. 127–46.
Other complete versions of the text are available as 'Petrarca: nella sua finzione la sua verità', in *AA.VV. Francesco Petrarca nel VI centenario della morte* (Bologna: Boni, 1976), pp. 69–78, and in Vittorio Sereni, *Petrarca, nella sua finzione la sua verità* (Vicenza: Neri Pozza, 1983), pp. 9–27.
Earlier versions of the essay (in abridged form) were published as 'Sì dolce è del mio amaro la radice', *Corriere del Ticino*, 22 June 1974, pp. 36–7, and as 'Amati Laura come io ti amo', *Il Giorno*, 14 July 1974, pp. 11–12.
'Petrarca e i poeti d'oggi: problemi e illuminazioni', *L'Approdo letterario* 20.66 (1974), pp. 93–100.
'Ci appassionò alla vita' [on Montale], first publ. in *Epoca* 26.1309 (8 Nov. 1975), pp. 35–8, now in *SG*, pp. 86–9.
'Intervento', in *Incontro con Eugenio Montale* on the occasion of Montale's award of the Nobel Prize, ed. Servizio Stampa and the Public Relations Office of Radio Televisione della Svizzera Italiana (Bellinzona: Istituto grafico Casagrande, 1976), pp. 29–32, under the title 'Sereni'.
'Il ritorno' [on Montale], first publ. in *Letture montaliane*, ed. Comune di Genova (Genova: Bozzi, 1977), now in *SG*, pp. 147–53.
'Il nostro debito verso Montale', in *La poesia di Eugenio Montale: Atti del Convegno Internazionale (Milano 12/13/14 settembre, Genova 15 settembre 1982)* (Milan: Librex, 1983), pp. 37–9.
'Dovuto a Montale' (1983), first publ. in *La Rotonda*, 6 (Almanacco Luinese per il 1984, Luino: Nastro, 1983), pp. 6–12, now included as Appendix to *ID2*, pp. 159–66.

INTERVIEWS WITH SERENI

Interview with Ferdinando Camon, in Ferdinando Camon, *Il mestiere di poeta* (Milan: Lerici, 1965), pp. 121–8.
Interview with Franco Brioschi, *Fogli di letteratura* 4 (1967), pp. 1–3.
Interview with Massimo Grillandi, in Massimo Grillandi, *Sereni* (Florence: La Nuova Italia, 1972), pp. 1–6.
Interview with Alessandro Fo, 'Un'intervista a V.S.', ed. Alessandro Fo, in *Studi per Riccardo Ribuoli* (Rome: Edizioni di storia e letteratura, 1986), pp. 55–75.
Sulla poesia: conversazione nelle scuole, ed. Giuliana Massani and Bruno Rivalta (Parma: Pratiche, 1981), pp. 41–62.
Interview with Domenico Porzio, 'In viaggio verso me', *Panorama*, 22 Mar. 1982, pp. 117–21.
Interview with Paola Lucarini, 'Intervista a Vittorio Sereni', *Firme nostre*, Sept. 1982, p. 3.
Interview with Ottavio Rossani, 'È vero, io rido poco ma so cos'è la gioia', *Il Giornale della Lombardia*, Feb. 1982, pp. 22–3.
Interview with Anna del Bo Boffino, 'Il terzo occhio del poeta: Vittorio Sereni l'erede di Montale', *Amica*, 28 Sept. 1982, p. 156.

PUBLISHED CORRESPONDENCE

Attilio Bertolucci–Vittorio Sereni: una lunga amicizia. Lettere 1938–1982, ed. Gabriella Palli Baroni (Milan: Garzanti, 1994).
Un tacito mistero: il carteggio Vittorio Sereni–Alessandro Parronchi, 1941–1982, ed. Barbara Colli and Giulia Raboni (Milan: Feltrinelli, 2004).

TRANSLATIONS

Collected translations
Il musicante di Saint-Merry e altri versi tradotti (Turin: Einaudi, 2001).

Single-author works
Char, René, *Ritorno sopramonte e altre poesie* (Milan: Mondadori, 1974).
——*Due rive ci vogliono: quarantasette traduzioni inedite*, ed. Elisa Donzelli (Rome: Donzelli, 2010).
Williams, William Carlos, *Poesie*, ed. Cristina Campo and Vittorio Sereni (Turin: Einaudi, 1961).

MANUSCRIPT AND ARCHIVE DOCUMENTS

During my visit to the Archivio Vittorio Sereni in Luino, I consulted many documents that it would be impossible to list here in their entirety. Instead, I include only those to which I make specific reference. For a guide to the indexing system of the catalogue, please see the Appendix.

'Un lungo sonno', APS I 21 (F 21).
'Solitudine', APS IV 9.2 (F 158).
'*Quaderno di traduzioni* di Eugenio Montale', APS IV 190 (F 425).
Correspondence with Giansiro Ferrata, APS VI 182 (F 414).
Correspondence with Franco Fortini, APS VI 198 (L 803); APS VII 24 (L 1246).

OTHER WORKS

Agamben, Giorgio, *Stanze: la parola e il fantasma nella cultura occidentale* (Turin: Einaudi, 1977); in English as *Stanzas: Word And Phantasm In Western Culture*, trans. Ronald L. Martinez (Minneapolis: University of Minnesota Press, 1993).

——*Language and Death: The Place of Negativity*, trans. Karen E. Pinkus and Michael Hardt (Minneapolis: University of Minnesota Press, 1991).

Agosti, Stefano, *Cinque analisi: il testo della poesia* (Milan: Feltrinelli, 1982).

——'Interpretazione della poesia di Sereni', in *La poesia di Vittorio Sereni: atti del convegno*, ed. Stefano Agosti et al. (Milan: Librex, 1985), pp. 33–46.

——*Gli occhi le chiome: per una lettura psicanalitica del 'Canzoniere' di Petrarca* (Milan: Feltrinelli, 1993).

Alighieri, Dante, *Vita nuova*, ed. Domenico De Robertis, *Opere minori*, 2 vols (Milan and Naples: Ricciardi, 1979–88), I.1 (1984), pp. 3–247.

——'*La Commedia*' secondo l'antica vulgata, ed. Giorgio Petrocchi, Società Dantesca Italiana, Edizione Nazionale, 2nd rev. edn, 4 vols (Florence: Le Lettere, 1994).

——*De vulgari eloquentia*, ed. and trans. Steven Botterill (Cambridge: Cambridge University Press, 1996).

——*Comedy*, trans. Robert Hollander and Jean Hollander, 3 vols (New York: Doubleday, 2000–2007).

Anceschi, Luciano, *Linea lombarda* (Varese: Magenta, 1952).

Augustine, Saint, *Confessions*, trans. Henry Chadwick (Oxford: Oxford University Press, 1992).

Baffoni Licata, Maria Laura, *La poesia di Vittorio Sereni: alienazione e impegno* (Ravenna: Longo, 1986).

Baldan, Paolo, 'Tra storia e memoria: *Diario d'Algeria* di Vittorio Sereni', *La rassegna della letteratura italiana* 77 (1973), pp. 599–618.

——'Gozzano petit maître di Sereni: Lo "scalpore" di una tesi', in *Guido Gozzano: i giorni, le opere. Atti del convegno nazionale di studi, Turin, 26–28 October 1983* (Florence: Olschki, 1985), pp. 43–60.

Barański, Zygmunt G., 'The Power of Influence: Aspects of Dante's Presence in Twentieth-Century Italian Culture', *Strumenti Critici*, n.s., 1.3 (1986), pp. 343–76.

——and Theodore J. Cachey Jr., eds, *Petrarch and Dante: Anti-Dantism, Metaphysics, Tradition* (Notre Dame, Ind.: University of Notre Dame Press, 2009).

Bàrberi Squarotti, Giorgio, 'Gli incontri con le ombre' in *La poesia di Vittorio Sereni: atti del convegno*, ed. Stefano Agosti et al. (Milan: Librex, 1985), pp. 68–90.

Barile, Laura, 'Amore e memoria: il rammemorare e il mare di Sereni', *Autografo* 13 (1988), pp. 33–60.

——'Gli alberi e la metamorfosi nella poesia di Vittorio Sereni', first publ. in *Lettere italiane* 45.3 (July–Sept. 1993), pp. 376–97, now in *La poesia di Vittorio Sereni: se ne scrivono ancora*, ed. Alfredo Luzi et al. (Grottammare: Stamperia dell'Arancio, 1997), pp. 89–108.

——*Sereni* (Palermo: Palumbo, 1994).

——'Alcuni materiali per "Un posto di vacanza"', in *Un posto di vacanza e altre poesie*, ed. Zeno Birolli (Milan: All'Insegna del Pesce d'Oro, 1994), pp. 95–109.

——'Una luce mai vista: Bocca di Magra e *Un posto di vacanza* di Vittorio Sereni', *Lettere italiane* 51.3 (July–Sept. 1999), pp. 384–404.

Barolini, Teodolinda, *Dante's Poets: Textuality and Truth in the 'Comedy'* (Princeton, NJ: Princeton University Press, 1984).

——'The Making of a Lyric Sequence: Time and Narrative in Petrarch's *Rerum vulgarium fragmenta*', *MLN* 104.1, Italian Issue (Jan. 1989), pp. 1–38.

——*The Undivine 'Comedy': Detheologizing Dante* (Princeton, NJ: Princeton University Press, 1992).

Baudelaire, Charles, *Les fleurs du mal*, ed. Graham Chesters (London: Bristol Classical Press, 1995).

Bazzocchi, Marco A., ed., *Autobiografie in versi: sei poeti allo specchio* (Bologna: Pendragon, 2002).

——ed., *La poesia del Novecento: modi e tecniche* (Bologna: Pendragon, 2003).

Benveniste, Émile, *Problèmes de linguistique générale* (Paris: Gallimard, 1966); in English as *Problems in General Linguistics*, trans. Mary Elizabeth Meek (Coral Gables, Fla.: University of Miami Press, 1971).

Bertone, Giorgio, *Lo sguardo escluso: l'idea del paesaggio nella letteratura occidentale* (Novara: Interlinea, 2000).

Blanchot, Maurice, *L'espace littéraire* (Paris: Gallimard, 1955); in English as *The Space of Literature*, trans. Ann Smock (Lincoln: University of Nebraska Press, 1982).

Boero, Matteo, 'La grana della voce: ritmo e intonazione negli *Strumenti umani*', *Stilistica e metrica italiana* 6 (2006), pp. 177–98.

Boitani, Piero, *The Tragic and the Sublime in Medieval Literature* (Cambridge: Cambridge University Press, 1989).

Bowie, Malcolm, *Lacan* (London: Fontana, 1991).

Boyde, Patrick, '"Ecfrasi ed ecceità" in Leopardi's *Canti*', *Italian Studies* 43 (1988), pp. 2–20.

Brose, Margaret, 'Leopardi's "L'infinito" and the Language of the Romantic Sublime', *Poetics Today* 4.1 (1983), pp. 47–71.

——'The Spirit of the Sign: Oppositional Structures in Montale's *Ossi di seppia*', *Stanford Italian Review* 4 (1984), pp. 147–75.

Bühler, Karl, *Sprachtheorie: die Darstellungsfunktion der Sprache* (Jena: Fischer, 1934); in English as *Theory of Language: The Representational Function of Language*, trans. Donald Fraser Goodwin (Amsterdam: Benjamins, 1990).

——'The Deictic Field of Language and Deictic Words', in *Speech, Place and Action: Studies in Deixis and Related Topics*, ed. Robert J. Jarvella and Wolfgang Klein (Chichester: Wiley, 1982), pp. 13–30.

Burgin, Victor, James Donald, and Cora Kaplan, eds, *Formations of Fantasy* (London: Methuen, 1986).

Butler, Judith P., *Subjects of Desire: Hegelian Reflections in Twentieth-Century France* (New York: Columbia University Press, 1987).

Cachey, Jr., Theodore J., 'Between Petrarch and Dante: Prolegomenon to a Critical Discourse', in *Petrarch and Dante: Anti-Dantism, Metaphysics, Tradition*, ed. Zygmunt G. Barański and Theodore J. Cachey Jr. (Notre Dame, Ind.: University of Notre Dame Press, 2009), pp. 3–49.

Caesar, Ann Hallamore, and Michael Caesar, *Modern Italian Literature* (London: Polity Press, 2007).

Cestaro, Gary, *Dante and the Grammar of the Nursing Body* (Notre Dame: University of Notre Dame Press, 2003).

Collot, Michel, *La poésie moderne et la structure d'horizon* (Paris: Presses Universitaires de France, 1989).

Contini, Gianfranco, *Un'idea di Dante: saggi danteschi* (Turin: Einaudi, 1976).

——'Preliminari sulla lingua di Petrarca', in Francesco Petrarca, *Canzoniere* (Turin: Einaudi, 1992), pp. xxvii–lv.

Cordibella, Giovanna, 'La tensione autobiografica nella poesia di Vittorio Sereni: il caso di *Un posto di vacanza*', in *Autobiografie in versi: sei poeti allo specchio*, ed. Marco A. Bazzocchi (Bologna: Pendragon, 2002), pp. 67–85.

——*Di fronte al romanzo: contaminazioni nella poesia di Sereni* (Bologna: Pendragon, 2004).

Cortellessa, Andrea, ed., *Un'altra storia: Petrarca nel Novecento italiano. Atti del Convegno di Roma, 4–6 ottobre 2001* (Rome: Bulzoni, 2004).

Croce, Benedetto, *La poesia di Dante* (Bari: Laterza, 1921).

Dal Bianco, Stefano, 'Vittorio Sereni: Petrarca come forma interna', in *Un'altra storia: Petrarca nel Novecento italiano. Atti del Convegno di Roma, 4–6 ottobre 2001*, ed. Andrea Cortellessa (Rome: Bulzoni, 2004), pp. 185–99.

D'alessandro, Francesca, *L'opera poetica di Vittorio Sereni* (Milan: Vita e Pensiero, 2001).

De Man, Paul, 'Autobiography as De-Facement', *MLN* 94.5, Comparative Literature (Dec. 1979), 919–30.

Di Bernardi, Alessandro, *Gli specchi multipli di Vittorio Sereni: 'Un posto di vacanza' e la crisi italiana degli anni Sessanta* (Palermo: S. F. Flaccovio, 1978).

Dolfi, Anna, 'Dante e i poeti del Novecento', *Studi danteschi* 58 (1986), pp. 307–42.

——*Terza generazione: ermetismo e oltre* (Rome: Bulzoni, 1997).

Donzelli, Elisa, *Come lenta cometa: traduzione e amicizia poetica nel carteggio tra Sereni e Char* (Turin: Aragno, 2009).

Eliot, Thomas Stearns, *Four Quartets* (London: Faber and Faber, 1959).
—— *Selected Poems* (London: Faber and Faber, 1975).
Enterline, Lynn, 'Embodied Voices: Petrarch Reading (Himself Reading) Ovid', in *Desire in the Renaissance: Psychoanalysis and Literature*, ed. Valeria Finucci and Regina Schwartz (Princeton, NJ: Princeton University Press, 1994), pp. 120–45.
—— *The Tears of Narcissus: Melancholia and Masculinity in Early Modern Writing* (Stanford, Calif.: Stanford University Press, 1995).
Ferretti, Giancarlo, 'L'ultima spiaggia di Sereni', in *La letteratura del rifiuto* (Milan: Mursia, 1968), pp. 179–93.
Flora, Francesco, *La poesia ermetica* (Bari: Laterza, 1936).
Fortini, Franco, *L'ospite ingrato* (Bari: De Donati, 1966).
—— *Saggi italiani* (Milan: Garzanti, 1987).
—— *Nuovi saggi italiani* (Milan: Garzanti, 1987).
Fortuna, Sara, Manuele Gragnolati, and Jürgen Trabant, eds, *Dante's Plurilingualism: Authority, Knowledge, Subjectivity* (Oxford: Legenda, 2010).
Freud, Sigmund, 'Three Essays on the Theory of Sexuality' (1905), in *The Standard Edition of the Complete Psychological Works of Sigmund Freud* [= *SE*], ed. James Strachey, 24 vols (London: Hogarth Press, 1953–74), VII (1953), pp. 125–245.
—— 'The Unconscious' (1915), in *SE* XIV (1957), pp. 161–215.
—— 'Mourning and Melancholia' (1917), in *SE* XIV (1957), pp. 243–58.
—— 'The Uncanny' (1919), in *SE* XIV (1957), pp. 219–56.
—— 'Beyond the Pleasure Principle' (1920), in *SE* XVIII (1955), pp. 7–64.
—— 'The Ego and the Id' (1923), in *SE* XIX (1961), pp. 3–66.
Frye, Northop, 'Approaching the Lyric', in *Lyric Poetry: Beyond New Criticism*, ed. Chaviva Hošek and Patricia Parker (Ithaca, NY: Cornell University Press, 1985), pp. 31–7.
Gioanola, Elio, *Leopardi: la malinconia* (Milan: Jaca, 1995).
Gragnolati, Manuele, Fabio Camilletti, and Fabian Lampart, eds, *Metamorphosing Dante: Appropriations, Manipulations and Rewritings in the Twentieth and Twenty-First Centuries* (Vienna: Turia + Kant, 2011).
—— and Almut Suerbaum, eds, *Aspects of the Performative in Medieval Culture* (Berlin: de Gruyter, 2010).
Green, Keith, 'Deixis and the Poetic Persona', *Language and Literature* 1.1 (1992), pp. 121–34.
Grignani, Maria Antonietta, '"Lavori in corso": addetti e dintorni', in *La poesia di Vittorio Sereni: atti del convegno*, ed. Stefano Agosti et al. (Milan: Librex, 1985), pp. 119–34.
—— *Prologhi ed epiloghi: sulla poesia di Eugenio Montale; con una prosa inedita* (Ravenna: Longo, 1987).
—— *La costanza della ragione: soggetto, oggetto e testualità nella poesia del Novecento* (Novara: Interlinea, 2002).
Grillandi, Massimo, *Vittorio Sereni* (Florence: La Nuova Italia, 1972).

Gronda, Giovanna, '"Un posto di vacanza" iuxta propria principia', in *Tradizione traduzione società: saggio per Franco Fortini*, ed. Romano Luperini (Rome: Edizioni Riuniti, 1989), pp. 177–203.

Hainsworth, Peter, *Petrarch the Poet: An Introduction to the 'Rerum vulgarium fragmenta'* (London: Routledge, 1988).

Harrison, Robert Pogue, *The Body of Beatrice* (Baltimore, Md.: Johns Hopkins University Press, 1988).

Heidegger, Martin, *Poetry, Language, Thought*, trans. Albert Hofstadter (New York: Perennial Classics, 2001).

Hošek, Chaviva, and Patricia Parker, eds, *Lyric Poetry: Beyond New Criticism* (Ithaca, NY: Cornell University Press, 1985).

Isella, Dante, 'La lingua poetica di Sereni', in *La poesia di Vittorio Sereni: atti del convegno*, ed. Stefano Agosti et al. (Milan: Librex, 1985), pp. 21–32.

——*Giornale di 'Frontiera'* (Milan: Archinto, 1991).

Jakobson, Roman, 'Les embrayeurs, les catégories verbales et le verbe russe', in *Essais de linguistique générale* (Paris: Minuit, 1963), pp. 176–96; in English as 'Shifters and Verbal Categories', in Roman Jakobson, *On Language*, ed. Linda R. Waugh, and Monique Monville Burston (Cambridge, Mass.: Harvard University Press, 1990), pp. 386–92.

Jarvella, Robert J., and Wolfgang Klein, eds, *Speech, Place and Action: Studies in Deixis and Related Topics* (Chichester: Wiley, 1982).

Jay, Paul, *Being in the Text: Self-Representation from Wordsworth to Roland Barthes* (Ithaca, NY: Cornell University Press, 1984).

Kristeva, Julia, *La révolution du langage poétique. L'avant-garde à la fin du xixe siècle: Lautréamont et Mallarmé* (Paris: Éditions du Seuil, 1974); in English as *Revolution in Poetic Language*, trans. Margaret Waller (New York: Columbia University Press, 1984).

——*Polylogue* (Paris: Éditions du Seuil, 1977).

——*Soleil noir: dépression et mélancolie* (Paris: Gallimard, 1987); in English as *Black Sun: Depression and Melancholia*, trans. Leon S. Roudiez (New York: Columbia University Press, 1989).

Lacan, Jacques, 'Le stade du miroir comme formateur de la fonction du Je telle qu'elle nous est révélée dans l'expérience psychanalytique', in *Écrits I (Nouvelle édition, texte intégral)* (Paris: Éditions du Seuil, 1999 [1966]), pp. 92–9.

——'L'instance de la lettre dans l'inconscient ou la raison depuis Freud', in *Écrits I*, pp. 490–526.

——'La direction de la cure et les principes de son pouvoir', in *Écrits II (Nouvelle édition, texte intégral)* (Paris: Éditions du Seuil, 1999 [1966]), pp. 62–123.

——'Remarque sur le rapport de Daniel Lagache: "Psychanalyse et structure de la personnalité"', in *Écrits II*, pp. 124–62.

——'Subversion du sujet et dialectique du désir dans l'inconscient freudien', in *Écrits II*, pp. 273–308. Selections of Lacan's *Écrits* are available in English in *Écrits: A Selection*, trans. Alan Sheridan (London: Routledge, 1977).

——*Séminaire XI: les quatre concepts de la psychanalyse*, text established by Jacques-Alain Miller (Paris: Éditions du Seuil, 1973); in English as *The Four*

Fundamental Concepts of Psychoanalysis, ed. Jacques-alain Miller, trans. Alan Sheridan (Harmondsworth: Penguin, 1979).

——'Das Ding (II)', in *Le séminaire de Jacques Lacan. Livre VII: L'éthique de la psychanalyse, 1959–1960*, text established by Jacques-Alain Miller (Paris: Éditions du Seuil, 1986), pp. 71–86; available in English in *The Ethics of Psychoanalysis, 1959–1960: The Seminar of Jacques Lacan, Book VII*, ed. Jacques-alain Miller, trans. Dennis Porter (London: Routledge, 2008).

Laplanche, Jean, and J. B. Pontalis, *Fantasme originaire: fantasmes des origines, origines du fantasme* (Paris: Hachette, 1985); in English as: 'Fantasy and the Origins of Sexuality', in *Formations of Fantasy*, ed. Victor Burgin, James Donald, and Cora Kaplan (London: Methuen, 1986), pp. 5–34.

Le Goff, Jacques, *The Birth of Purgatory*, trans. Arthur Goldhammer (Chicago: University of Chicago Press, 1981).

Leopardi, Giacomo, *Canti*, ed. Niccolò Gallo, and Cesare Garboli (Turin: Einaudi, 1993).

——*The Canti: with a Selection of His Prose*, trans. J. G. Nichols (Manchester: Carcanet, 1994).

——*Zibaldone*, edizione integrale diretta da Lucio Felici; premessa di Emanuele Trevi; indici filologici di Marco Dondero; indice tematico e analitico di Marco Dondero, Wanda Marra (Rome: Grandi Tascabili Economici Newton, 1997).

Lombardi, Elena, *The Syntax of Desire: Language and Love in Augustine, the Modistae, Dante* (Toronto: University of Toronto Press, 2007).

Lorenzini, Niva, 'Nuove configurazioni del paesaggio testuale', in *La poesia italiana del Novecento: modi e tecniche*, ed. Marco A. Bazzocchi (Bologna: Pendragon, 2003), pp. 213–29.

Luperini, Romano, ed., *Tradizione traduzione società: saggio per Franco Fortini* (Rome: Edizioni Riuniti, 1989).

Lyons, John, *Semantics*, 2 vols (Cambridge: Cambridge University Press, 1977).

Lyotard, Jean François, *Discours, Figure* (Paris: Klincksieck, 1971).

Mazzoni, Guido, 'Verifica dei valori: saggio su *Gli strumenti umani*', *Allegoria*, n.s. 6.18 (1994), pp. 45–81.

Mazzotta, Giuseppe, *The Worlds of Petrarch* (Durham, NC: Duke University Press, 1993).

Mclaughlin, Martin, and Letizia Panizza, with Peter Hainsworth, eds, *Petrarch in Britain: Interpreters, Imitators and Translators over 700 years* (Oxford: Oxford University Press for the British Academy, 2007).

Memmo, Francesco Paolo, *Vittorio Sereni* (Milan: Mursia, 1973).

Mengaldo, Pier Vincenzo, *La tradizione del Novecento: nuova serie* (Florence: Valecchi, 1987).

——*La tradizione del Novecento: quarta serie* (Turin: Bollati Boringhieri, 2000).

——'Sereni traduttore di poesia', introduction to Vittorio Sereni, *Il musicante di Saint-Merry* (Turin: Einaudi, 2001), pp. v–xxvii.

Moevs, Christian, 'Subjectivity and Conversion in Dante and Petrarch', in *Petrarch and Dante: Anti-Dantism, Metaphysics, Tradition*, ed. Zygmunt

G. Barański, and Theodore J. Cachey Jr. (Notre Dame, Ind.: University of Notre Dame Press, 2009), pp. 226–59.
Montale, Eugenio, 'Strumenti umani', first publ. in *Corriere della sera*, 24 October 1965, now in *Sulla poesia*, ed. Giorgio Zampa (Milan: Mondadori, 1976), pp. 328–33.
——*L'opera in versi*, ed. Rosanna Bettarini, and Gianfranco Contini (Turin: Einaudi, 1980).
——*Quaderno di traduzioni 1896-1981*, 2nd edn (Milan: Mondadori, 1982).
——*Eugenio Montale: Collected Poems 1920–1954*, rev. bilingual edn, trans. and annotated by Jonathan Galassi (New York: Farrar, Straus, and Giroux, 2000).
Neri, Laura, *Vittorio Sereni, Andrea Zanzotto, Giovanni Giudici: un'indagine retorica* (Bergamo: Bergamo University Press, 2001).
Noferi, Adelia, *Il gioco delle tracce: studi su Dante, Petrarca, Bruno, il neoclassicismo, Leopardi, l'informale* (Florence: La Nuova Italia, 1979).
Ó Ceallacháin, Éanna, *Eugenio Montale: The Poetry of the Later Years* (Oxford: Legenda, 2001).
Ovid, *The Metamorphoses of Ovid*, trans. Allen Mandelbaum (San Diego, Calif.: Harvest, 1993).
Pagnanelli, Remo, *La ripetizione dell'esistere: lettura dell'opera poetica di Vittorio Sereni* (Milan: All'Insegna del Pesce D'Oro, 1980).
——*Studi critici: poesia e poeti italiani del secondo Novecento*, ed. Daniela Marcheschi (Milan: Mursia, 1991).
Papi, Fulvio, *La parola incantata e altri saggi di filosofia dell'arte* (Milan: Guerini, 1992).
Pellini, Pierluigi, *Le toppe della poesia: saggi su Montale, Sereni, Fortini, Orelli* (Rome: Vecchiarelli, 2004).
Pertile, Lino, *La puttana e il gigante: dal Cantico dei Cantici al Paradiso terrestre di Dante* (Ravenna: Longo, 1998).
——*La punta del disio*: semantica del desiderio nella 'Commedia' (Fiesole: Cadmo, 2005).
Petrarca, Francesco, *Petrarch's Lyric Poems: the 'Rime sparse' and Other Lyrics*, ed. and trans. Robert M. Durling (Cambridge, Mass.: Harvard University Press, 1976).
——*Canzoniere*, ed. Gianfranco Contini (Turin: Einaudi, 1992).
Petronio, Giuseppe, *Bonifacio VIII: un episodio della vita e dell'arte di Dante* (Lucca: Lucentia, 1950).
Petrucciani, Mario, *La poetica dell'ermetismo italiano* (Turin: Loescher, 1955).
Prete, Antonio, *Il pensiero poetante: saggio su Leopardi* (Milan: Feltrinelli, 1980).
Proust, Marcel, *À la recherche du temps perdu*, ed. Jean-Yves Tavié (Paris: Gallimard, 1999); in English as *In Search of Lost Time*, trans. C. K. Scott Moncrieff and Terence Kilmartin, revised by D. J. Enright, 6 vols (London: Chatto & Windus, 1992).
Ramat, Silvio, *L'ermetismo* (Florence: La Nuova Italia, 1969).
——'Il Novecento e una traccia dantesca', *Forum italicum* 4.3 (1970), pp. 311–30.

——'Purgatorio e inesistenza in due testi poetici medionovecenteschi (M. Luzi, *La notte lava la mente*; V. Sereni, *La spiaggia*)', *Paradigma* 3 (1980), pp. 383–403.

——'Un poeta sulla Strada di Zenna: due liriche di Vittorio Sereni', *Italica* 62.3 (Autumn 1985), pp. 246–63.

Renzi, Lorenzo, et al., eds, *Grande grammatica italiana della consultazione*, 3 vols (Bologna: Il Mulino, 1995).

Riccobono, Rossella, 'The Question of Liminality and the Dissolution of Spatiotemporal Dimensions in Montale's Poetry: "Sul limite", "Vasca" and "Carnevale di Gerti"', *The Italianist* 17 (1997), pp. 74–98.

Ricoeur, Paul, *Soi-même comme un autre* (Paris: Éditions du Seuil, 1990); in English as *Oneself as Another*, trans. Kathleen Blamey (Chicago: University of Chicago Press, 1992).

Rimbaud, Arthur, *Lettres du Voyant*, ed. Gérald Schaeffer (Geneva: Minard, 1975).

Robinson, Peter, and Marcus Perryman, eds. and trans., *The Selected Poetry and Prose of Vittorio Sereni: A Bilingual Edition* (Chicago: University of Chicago Press, 2006).

Sánchez-pardo, Esther, *Cultures of the Death Drive: Melanie Klein and Modernist Melancholia* (Durham, NC: Duke University Press, 2003).

Saussure, Ferdinand De, *Cours de linguistique générale*, publíe par Charles Bally et Albert Sechehaye, avec la collaboration de Albert Riedlinger (Paris: Payot, 1972).

Scorrano, Luigi, 'Dantismo "trasversale" di Vittorio Sereni', *Alighieri: rassegna bibliografica dantesca*, n.s. 40.14 (July–Dec. 1999), pp. 41–76.

Segre, Cesare, *Avviamento all'analisi del testo letterario* (Turin: Einaudi, 1985).

Solmi, Sergio, 'Volontà classica del Novecento' (1946), in *La letteratura italiana contemporanea*, ed. Giovanni Pacchiano, 2 vols (Milan: Adelphi, 1992–8), II (= *Opere di Sergio Solmi*, III), pp. 511–19.

Southerden, Francesca, 'Performative Desires: Sereni's Re-staging of Dante and Petrarch', in *Aspects of the Performative in Medieval Culture*, ed. Manuele Gragnolati, and Almut Suerbaum (Berlin: de Gruyter, 2010), pp. 165–96.

——'Lost for Words: Recuperating Melancholy Subjectivity in Dante's Eden', in *Dante's Plurilingualism: Authority, Knowledge, Subjectivity*, ed. Sara Fortuna, Manuele Gragnolati, and Jürgen Trabant (Oxford: Legenda, 2010), pp. 193–210.

——'"Per-tras-versioni" dantesche: Post-Paradisiacal Constellations in the Poetry of Vittorio Sereni and Andrea Zanzotto', in *Metamorphosing Dante: Appropriations, Manipulations and Rewritings in the Twentieth and Twenty-First Centuries*, ed. Manuele Gragnolati, Fabio Camilletti, and Fabian Lampart (Vienna: Turia + Kant, 2011), pp. 153–74.

Spitzer, Leo, 'Speech and Language in *Inferno* XIII', *Italica* 19.3 (Sept. 1942), pp. 81–104.

Tandello, Emmanuela, 'Between Tradition and Transgression: Amelia Rosselli's Petrarch', in *Petrarch in Britain: Interpreters, Imitators and Translators over 700 years*, ed. Martin Mclaughlin and Letizia Panizza with Peter Hainsworth (Oxford: Oxford University Press for the British Academy, 2007), pp. 301–17.

——*Amelia Rosselli: la fanciulla e l'infinito* (Rome: Donzelli, 2007).

Testa, Enrico, 'Sur la corde de la voix: funzione della deissi nel testo poetico', in *Linguistica, pragmatica e testo letterario*, ed. Umberto Rapallo (Genova: Il Melangolo, 1996), pp. 113–46.

——*Dopo la lirica: poeti italiani 1960–2000* (Turin: Einaudi, 2005).

Ungaretti, Giuseppe, *Vita d'un uomo: tutte le poesie*, ed. Leone Piccioni (Milan: Mondadori, 1970).

Valentini, Alvaro, *Leopardi: l'io poetante* (Rome: Bulzoni, 1983).

Vattimo, Gianni, and Pier Aldo Rovatti, eds, *Il pensiero debole* (Milan: Feltrinelli, 1983).

Vickers, Nancy, 'Re-membering Dante: Petrarch's "Chiare, fresche et dolci acque"', *MLN* 96.1, Italian Issue (January 1981), pp. 1–11.

Vigorelli, Giancarlo, *Carte d'identità: il Novecento letterario in 21 ritratti indiscreti* (Milan: Camunia, 1989).

Virgil, *Eclogues, Georgics, Aeneid I–VI*, trans. H. Rushton Fairclough (Cambridge, Mass.: Harvard University Press, 1974).

West, Rebecca, *Eugenio Montale: Poet on the Edge* (Cambridge, Mass.: Harvard University Press, 1981).

Wright, Elizabeth, *Speaking Desires Can be Dangerous: The Poetics of the Unconscious* (Cambridge: Polity Press, 1999).

Yourcenar, Marguerite, *Memoirs of Hadrian*, trans. Grace Frick (London: Readers' Union, 1955).

Zanzotto, Andrea, *Fantasie di avvicinamento* (Milan: Mondadori, 1991).

——*Aure e disincanti nel Novecento letterario* (Milan: Mondadori, 1994).

——*Le poesie e prose scelte*, ed. Stefano Dal Bianco, and Gian Mario Villalta (Milan: Mondadori, 1999).

Zumthor, Paul, *La mesure du monde: représentation de l'espace au Moyen Âge* (Paris: Éditions du Seuil, 1993).

Index

absence 74, 77, 97, 116, 118, 225, 229–32
　of desired object 69, 89, 121, 140–1, 171, 183 n., 241, 259
　function in deixis 27–9, 57–9, 73, 98–9, 155–6, 160, 177, 184
　gaze as an index of 111, 122–4
　poetic 5, 26, 147, 153, 169, 190, 243–4, 247, 252, 260
　see also lack, loss
acedia 228–9
　see also melancholia
Acheron 124–5, 257
Agamben, Giorgio 75, 149 n., 225, 228, 260 n., 263 n. 9
Agosti, Stefano 39, 48, 137 n. 13, 163
Albertazzi, Giorgio 198 n. 27
Algeria 15, 188
　Oran 13
　in Sereni's writings 213, 215–20, 222–3, 231–3
anamorphosis 107 n., 118
　see also gaze
Anceschi, Luciano 9
aphasia 122–5, 174, 246–53
Apollinaire, Guillaume 1 n. 2, 3, 9, 17, 23, 198 n. 27
Augustine, Saint 42, 210–11
autobiography 4, 32, 34–5, 145, 188, 210

Baffoni Licata, Maria Luisa 18 n. 42, 32 n.
Baldan, Paolo 187 n. 3, 192 n. 14
Banfi, Antonio 8
Barański, Zygmunt G. 194, 208
Bàrberi Squarotti, Giorgio 190 n. 8
Barile, Laura 9, 11 n. 22, 14, 21 n. 51, 49–50, 100 n. 16, 119, 192 n. 14, 264 n. 12
Barolini, Teodolinda 27 n. 159, 162 n., 186 n., 192, 211–12, 248 n. 92, 256, 263
Baudelaire, Charles 176
Benveniste, Émile 43, 52, 53 nn. 5–6, 58 n. 18, 87
Bertolucci, Attilio 7 n., 171, 172 n. 58, 208
Bertone, Giorgio 64 n. 28, 130 n. 5, 140 n. 17, 156, 159–60, 234 n.
Bigongiari, Piero 9
Blanchot, Maurice 45

Bocca di Magra, *see* Liguria
Boero, Matteo 55 n. 11
Boitani, Piero 202, 203 n. 34, 239
Bonfanti, Maria Luisa 13
border spaces:
　geographic 7, 99
　poetic 48–9, 59–60, 70, 84, 92, 104, 215, 264
　psychological 39
　'sentimento di frontiera' [feeling of being on the border] 12
　see also liminality
Bowie, Malcolm 43 n. 32, 111, 127 nn., 151 n. 27, 235 n. 75, 261 n. 5
Boyde, Patrick 84 n.
Brose, Margaret 58, 59 n. 19, 94
Bühler, Karl 52, 55 n. 12, 156–7
Butler, Judith P. 163, 164 n. 51

Caesar, Ann Hallamore 202 n. 33
Caesar, Michael 202 n. 33
Cachey, Jr., Theodore J 30 n. 66, 247 n. 89
Cantoni, Remo 8
Caproni, Giorgio 37, 49
Carducci, Giosuè 9
Carta, Giuliano 8
Cestaro, Gary 237 n. 78, 239 n. 81
Cézanne, Paul 5
Char, René 22–3, 193, 264
　Sereni's intertextual dialogue with 5 n. 17, 129–32, 149, 150 n., 179–80
Charon 93 n. 9
La Chose/Das Ding, *see* psychoanalysis
Collot, Michel 70 n.
commitment [*impegno*] 18–19, 21 n. 49
Contini, Gianfranco 138–40, 194, 206, 207 n. 38
Cordibella, Giovanna 32 n., 202
Corneille, Pierre 23
Croce, Benedetto 205

Dal Bianco, Stefano 135, 174
damnation 184 n., 188, 208, 210, 233–4, 243
D'Annunzio, Gabriele 9
Dante Alighieri 133
　desire in 158 n. 43, 210–12
　melancholia in 225, 236–41

Dante Alighieri (*cont.*)
  place in lyric tradition 1, 25–6, 135–9, 193–7, 229
  Sereni's intertextual dialogue with 15, 29–30, 93, 184–8, 190, 192, 199, 207–10, 243–4
    in *Diario d'Algeria* 217, 221–2
    in *Frontiera* 214–15
    in *Stella variabile* 125 n., 200 n., 202–05, 232, 246–8, 251–7, 260–1, 263, 265
    in *Gli strumenti umani* 133–4
  Sereni's writings on 205–07
death 6, 15, 97, 100, 141–2, 186
  dialogue with the dead 28, 96
    in Dante 134, 190
    in Sereni 56–7, 86–8, 112–16, 168, 202–03
  drive, *see* psychoanalysis
  landscape and 131–2, 168
  language and 75 n. 36, 147, 158, 183, 242–3, 248
  and memory 225, 227–8, 246–7
  -oriented desire 164, 230, 237–41
  Sereni's preoccupation with 192, 212–15
  see also elegy
de Carlo, Giancarlo 21
deixis:
  and desire 89, 124–5, 155, 259
  and the exile of the poetic subject 29
  in Leopardi 57–9
  and liminality 90–1, 98–100, 262
  and the lyric voice 34, 51, 54–5, 89, 137, 158, 184, 259–60
  in Montale 93–4, 229
  Orphic power of 28
  in Petrarch 138, 140–1, 147, 162–4
  at phantasma 156–8
  in Sereni:
    Frontiera 56–7, 60–2, 65–74, 215
    Stella variabile 116–17, 177–8, 182, 246, 254
    Gli strumenti umani 74–89, 173
  theory of (linguistic) 52–3
  and the thetic 62–4
de Man, Paul 34
desire:
  as fulfilment 242–3
  and the gaze 103–05, 107–11, 121–5
  journey of 6, 182, 185–6, 210–15, 257
  and language 33, 38, 40–3, 47, 156, 249–57, 259
  and liminality 28, 75, 89–91, 94, 97–9, 102, 115, 126–7

  as loss/lack 28–30, 139–41, 144–7, 263–6
  melancholy 215–27, 231–4, 240–1, 243–9
  theory of 228–30, 235–6
  and memory 236–40
  object of 50–1
  and phantasm 128, 143, 149–58, 190–1, 209
  and poetry 4, 73–4, 142, 182, 260–1
  -space 150–1, 159–60, 162–5, 167–84, 264
  subject of 48, 62–4, 156, 183
  for transcendence 26, 210
Di Bernardi, Alessandro 39
discourse:
  anaphoric, in Sereni 77
  of desire 25, 30, 40, 91, 175, 259
  as distinguishing feature of Sereni's *Gli strumenti umani* 77, 80, 133–4
  failure of 246, 248–9
  and identity 35, 38, 48
  intersubjective 47, 74
  lyric 2, 52, 149
  negative foundations of 75
  poetic 21, 75, 89, 138, 160, 174, 187, 264
  subject of 26–7, 32, 41–2, 46, 62–4, 199
  universe of, in deixis 53–4, 58, 69, 155
  see also language, speech, voice
displacement:
  desire as 33, 146, 230, 243, 259
  geographical 13, 15, 218
  linguistic 28, 48, 77, 152
  in perception 121
  poetic 34, 69, 265
  see also exile
Dolfi, Anna 37 n. 19, 193
doubleness:
  of the 'I' as an instance of discourse 43 n. 33
  perceptual 53, 91, 101–03, 108, 111, 117
  of poetic memory 225, 257
  of poetic space 67, 114–15, 118–26, 255
  of the poetic subject 38, 68, 80–1, 131, 143, 172, 191, 207
  temporal 87, 96, 180
dreams 31–2, 39, 83, 157, 168, 177 n. 66, 189–90, 198, 236
  and phantasms 182–3, 225, 234–5, 246–7
  space of 74–5, 77, 85–7, 118, 144–5

Index

Earthly paradise 29, 210, 216, 236–44
  see also Eden
Eden:
  fall out of 172, 247
  Garden of 30, 186, 215, 237–43
  language of 246
  memory of 59, 116, 236
  -ic unity 40
  see also Earthly paradise
ego, *see* psychoanalysis
elegy 20, 57, 83–4, 116, 212
Eliot, Thomas Stearns 9, 37 n. 18, 145 n., 185, 257
  Sereni's intertextual dialogue with 15, 192–202, 204, 252
Elysium 60, 168, 215
Enterline, Lynn 153, 157 n. 40
epistemology 33, 265
Erba, Luciano 9 n. 17
ermetismo, *see* hermeticism
eros, *see* psychoanalysis
ethics 18, 20, 74, 139, 174, 210, 234
Eurydice 68, 164, 239
exile 13, 26, 160–2
  from fulfilment 30, 145, 243
  linguistic 28, 42, 48, 77, 262
  as origins of the desiring journey 210–11
  poetic 15, 27, 35, 64, 127, 232, 257, 260
existentialism (movement) 19
  existential anxiety 88 n., 137, 172, 249
  existential concerns in poetry 32, 40, 53, 62, 64 n. 27, 135, 187, 207

fall/Fall:
  Edenic 172–3, 183, 186, 204, 215, 239–40, 244–7
  of the subject 6, 30, 91, 155, 211, 236, 255
    linguistic 219
    perceptual 28, 91, 111
    poetic 40, 102, 148, 260, 262
fantasy 33, 151, 154, 244
Ferrata, Giansiro 91 n., 217, 222
Fortini, Franco 5 n., 11 n. 21, 18–19, 20 nn. 46–7, 21, 178, 264, 267
Freud, Sigmund:
  Das Ding in 30 n. 65, 235
  on desire 33 n. 4, 63, 153, 241
  discovery of the unconscious 41
  on dreams 39
  on drives 35, 47 n. 41, 107
  on the fetish 156–7
  on melancholia 225, 229–31, 247
  on narcissism 40
  the uncanny in 86
Frye, Northop 34 n. 7

Galassi, Jonathan 6 n. 8, 90 n. 1, 96, 115 n. 38, 228 n. 66
Gallo, Niccolò 18, 112
García Lorca, Federico 9
Gatto, Alfonso 9
gaze:
  backwards, in melancholia 213, 234, 249, 266
  double, in poetry 102
  elusive fabric of the 28
  as an index of desire 91, 97–8, 103–05, 116, 121, 165
  as interacting with the voice in deixis 54, 89, 122, 140, 156
  in Lacan's scopic drive 107–11
  liminality and the 117, 127, 173
  of objects 107, 120
  poetic power of the, in Leopardi 58
  in Proust 126, 172
  Sereni's fixation with the 102–05
  in Sereni's *Frontiera* 60, 66, 69, 75
  in Sereni's *Un posto di vacanza* 118–19
  Sereni's redefinition of the 106
Gioanola, Elio 235 n. 74
God 204, 219, 222, 232–3, 242, 252, 256–7
Gozzano, Guido 9
Greece 13, 185 n., 188 n. 6
Green, Keith 55, 156 n. 37
Grignani, Maria Antonietta 69, 75 n. 35, 97 n. 14
Gronda, Giovanna 254
Gruppo 63 36
guilt 135
  poetic 40, 82

Hainsworth, Peter 2 n. 3, 159 n. 47, 162 n., 169, 184, 258 n. 3
hallucination 74, 173, 183 n., 190, 217, 230, 261
Harrison, Robert Pogue 147, 158, 164, 243 n. 86
Heidegger, Martin 58, 265
hell 186, 215, 222, 225, 236, 242, 255
  melancholia of 210, 221, 234, 257
Hemingway, Ernest 17
Hermeticism (*ermetismo*) 9–12, 19, 37 n. 19, 137–9
  Hermetic poets 9, 11, 139
history 8, 30, 186, 230, 243, 255

history (*cont.*)
  and poetry 32, 34–6, 100 n. 18,
    159 n. 47, 162, 194–5, 205–07
  Sereni's relationship to 13, 17–20, 26,
    187–8, 217, 256, 262
  Sereni's view of 207–08

identity:
  landscape and 7–8, 24–5, 96, 131–3,
    139–40, 146
  in language 35, 38
  poetic 24–6, 31–3, 45–9, 129, 191,
    257–66
  search for 3–4, 17, 21
  poetic vs. empirical 32, 205–08, 258
  rooted in desire 105, 128, 149
ideology 9 n. 18, 11 n. 21, 19–20, 202
idyll 6, 20, 23, 234
  Leopardian 66, 74, 150 n.
  as 'luogo ideale' [ideal place] of the
    lyric 2–3
  Petrarchan 128, 131, 140–2, 162–4
  Sereni's reconfiguration of the 12, 29,
    67, 144–6, 154–5, 165–80,
    216, 260
  see also landscape, lyric
Imaginary, the, *see* psychoanalysis
imagination 105, 213 n. 51
  landscape(s) of the 141, 156–7
  poetic 2, 6, 16, 34, 56, 73–4, 102, 128,
    130, 165, 169, 208
  see also deixis at phantasma
imprisonment:
  Sereni's experience of 13, 15, 188, 213,
    216, 218 n.
intertextuality:
  dynamic form of, in Sereni 187–8,
    193, 208
  as a facet of liminality 28, 90, 263
  landscape and 6, 112–17, 138–9
  and the lyric 136, 149
  and poetic identity 92, 196–7, 199,
    251–2
  as shaping Sereni's poetic subject 25,
    166, 169–72, 175–6, 199–203,
    258
Isella, Dante 18, 21 n. 51, 56 n. 136, 137
  n. 13, 138–9, 149

Jakobson, Roman 53 n. 7
Jay, Paul 33 n. 5, 34
journey 7
  desiring 30, 91, 93, 173, 180–2
  in Dante 210–12
  in Sereni 213–15

foreclosure of, toward possession 168,
  190, 203, 222–4, 256–7
melancholy 225, 234, 248
poetic 21, 24, 130, 249–54, 266
purgatorial 15, 186, 191–2, 217
reverse, in memory 4, 26, 92, 135
toward transcendence 127, 237, 242

knowledge 1–3, 19
Kristeva, Julia:
  on Christianity 242–3
  on desire in language 30 n. 65, 40–2, 50
  on melancholia 213, 225, 231, 235,
    247–9, 253
  on the origins of the speaking
    subject 62–4, 73 n. 33
  on poetic language 46
  on the 'subject in process/on trial' 47–8

Lacan, Jacques:
  on the *corps morcelé* [fragmented body]
    177
  on desire in language 30 n. 65, 40–1,
    43–6, 127, 163–4, 243
  desire-space in 150–1, 170
  on the gaze in desire (scopic drive) 91–2,
    107–11, 123, 151
  Moebius strip in 184
  on the origins of the speaking
    subject 62–3, 77 n. 39, 81 n. 41,
    82n., 261 n. 5
  on the phantasm 152
  on the Real 235
lack:
  in deixis 59, 73, 90
  desire as 29, 102, 139, 147–8, 175,
    184, 186, 190, 235
  gaze as a function of 101, 110–11,
    127, 252
  linguistic 123, 254
  overcoming, in Dante 211, 242–3
  primordial, as motivation for poetry 24,
    26, 30, 260
  subject of 32, 42–3, 109, 115–16, 142,
    152, 218
landscape(s):
  changing lyric 4, 25, 198
  of desire 2–3, 24, 30, 105, 111, 125–8,
    149–51, 179–80, 186
  fetishized 145–6, 157 n. 39, 165
  as founded on absence 64 n. 28, 147,
    230–2, 244–6
  as fugitive 101, 171, 203
  and the gaze 66–9
  as locus of a fall 183, 204

Index

as locus of identity 49–52, 140, 266
as locus of liminality 90, 115–16, 253
as locus of memory 62, 76–7, 92, 129–33, 163, 182, 223
as locus of phantasm 29, 83 n., 135, 141, 143–4, 155, 158–60, 164, 172–3, 184
poetic 1, 22, 138–9
as shaped by deixis 27, 58–60, 259–60
as site of trauma 233–4
as space of exile (poetic) 28, 162, 167, 170, 243, 262
as space of origins 6
as threatening 7, 74–5, 96, 168
urban 15–16
see also desire-space
language:
birth of, in negation 63–4
of deixis 51–2, 54–5, 58, 89, 259
and desire 21, 25, 29, 33, 160, 175
dwelling in 266
as ec-stasis 256
exile in 28, 48, 262
failure of 174, 178, 203
frustrations of 84, 116
of hermetic poetry 10–12
and liminality 95, 100, 102
loss in 26, 42–3, 246–7
of the lyric 34
melancholy 225, 235, 244, 248–9
of memory 132–3
negativity of 75
Petrarch's 137–9, 158, 186
and the phantasm 155–6
poetic 27, 46–7, 92, 140, 252
question 38
redemption of 30, 211, 236, 242, 260
as the space of dissolution of the subject 45–6, 76, 152
subjectivity in 3, 32, 36–7, 62, 258
see also discourse, linguistics, speech
Laplanche, Jean 151, 154 n. 34, 173, 183
Leopardi, Giacomo, 22, 39, 198–9, 235 n. 74
deictic legacy of 57–60, 66, 70, 162–3
place in lyric tradition 1–2, 10, 26, 30, 135–6
Sereni's intertextual dialogue with 6, 35–7, 193, 263, 265
in *Frontiera* 66, 68, 73–4
in *Stella variabile* 150, 175–7, 179 n. 69
in *Gli strumenti umani* 83–4, 166, 173
theory of language 42, 51
Lethe 236, 243, 247, 255, 257

Liguria 20, 22, 90–2, 100, 207
Bocca di Magra, 90, 92–3, 95
in Sereni's poetry 19 n. 45, 20–1, 117–19, 127, 145 n. 21, 182, 184, 244
Sereni's writings on 99–100
limbo 6, 29–30, 48, 125, 180, 216, 253, 259
liminality:
at the border of life and death 86
definition of 93–5
and deixis 28, 33, 89, 262
and desire 93, 180–1, 263
and landscape 93, 111–16, 119–21
in Montale 92, 96–102
perceptual 102–06, 117–18
as poetic predicament, in Sereni 26, 48, 122, 142, 253
of the poetic subject 126–7, 144, 223, 259, 266
in speech 239
Linea lombarda 9
linguistics 110
linguistically articulated subject of modern poetry 26, 28, 37–8, 138
as methodology 33, 48, 158, 265
theory of the speaking subject 41–4, 46–7, 62–4
see also deixis
Logos 62, 218
Lombardi, Elena 42 n. 29, 43, 158 n. 43, 175, 239, 243, 248 n. 93
Lorenzini, Niva 52 n. 3
loss:
Dante overcoming 239–43
deixis as a way to overcome 90
desire as 99
landscape as a site of 116–17, 124, 131
in language 26, 42–3, 48, 63 n. 25, 160, 178, 249
of the 'luogo ideale' [ideal place] of lyric, in Sereni 3, 30
and (failed) mourning 147, 157, 172, 204, 212, 216, 228–9
Orphic 60, 66–7, 101, 239
poetic/in poetry 28, 38, 57, 75, 145, 149, 225, 262, 265
primordial 116, 168
Sereni's fixation on 30, 148, 186, 192, 218–19
subject at 29, 49, 72–4, 233, 252–5
unsurpassable, at root of melancholia 230–1, 235–6, 244–6, 261
see also melancholia

Luino 7–8, 22, 146, 184
  Sereni Archive in 19 n. 43, 197, 217 n. 62, 267
  in Sereni's poetry 12, 16, 60, 77, 84–5, 87, 92 n. 6, 159, 165, 175–9
Luzi, Mario 11 n. 21, 190
Lyons, John 77
Lyotard, Jean François 54
lyric:
  anti- 204
  deixis in the 51, 54–5, 89, 137, 259
  egocentrism of the 60–1, 64, 72–3
  fragmentation of the 28, 37, 181
  'I' 32–5, 40, 74, 262
  landscape of the 4–5, 30, 198
  as a 'luogo ideale' [ideal place] 1–2, 6, 29, 127–8, 137–9, 232
  lyricism 10, 186
  sequence 27
  Sereni's redefinition of the 20–1, 25–6, 36, 52, 130–1, 154, 159, 202, 258, 263–4
  Sereni's relationship to the 3, 49, 65–6, 135, 149, 174–5, 184, 199
  tradition 133, 136, 193
  transcendent 158

Mallarmé, Stéphane 10, 260
Manzi, Gianni 8
Mazzoni, Guido 190–1
Mazzotta, Giuseppe 162 n., 181
melancholia:
  Agamben's theory of 228
  in Dante 210, 236–41
  Freud's theory of 229–30
  Kristeva's theory of 213 n. 51, 234–6, 247, 253 n. 96
  melancholy desire 29–30
  melancholy speech 248–9
  melancholy subject 192, 209, 233, 261–2
  in Montale 226–8
  relationship to mourning 147, 186
  in Sereni 57, 185, 212, 214–18, 225, 231–2, 244–6, 252–7
Memmo, Francesco Paolo 32 n.
memory:
  alienation in 222
  collective/cultural 20, 176
  contamination of, in Montale 100
  cult of, in Sereni 192, 214
  dangers of 172, 181–2, 209
  in deixis 56, 156
  and desire 94, 140, 145–7, 180, 208, 212–13, 218, 236–7, 243

dissolution of 115, 252
Edenic 59, 62
of fullness 4, 48, 75
and history 207
of the idyll 140–1, 155, 170–1
infernal 224–6, 234
and landscape 2 n. 3, 77, 86, 101, 160–5
and liminality 96, 102, 262
as locus of the poetic event 61
of loss/lack 15 n. 35, 29–30, 42, 57, 191, 216
of Luino, Sereni's 7, 16
melancholy 253, 255
'memorie triste' [sad memories/memories of sin] 186, 210–11, 215, 239–40, 244–7
and perception 97–9, 103–05, 177
phantasmatic 116–17, 142–4, 174, 217, 227–9, 232, 261
poetic 6, 22, 25, 27, 32, 50, 92, 128–36, 148–50, 173, 183–5, 187–8, 199–203
and poetry 14, 71–3, 87–8, 256–7
weight of, in Sereni 169
Mengaldo, Pier Vincenzo 174, 190 n. 8, 191–2, 232
Menicanti, Daria 8
metamorphosis:
  landscape in 6, 58, 66
  poetic 24, 91, 119
Milan 8–9, 13, 15, 22–3, 129 n. 2, 267
  in Sereni's poetry 16, 84, 87, 218
mirror stage, see psychoanalysis
modernism 192–4
Moevs, Christian 255
Montale, Eugenio 9, 31, 110, 128
  liminality in 48, 93–5, 97–102, 127, 259
  melancholia in 226–9
  memory in 224–5
  place in lyric tradition 11, 135
  on Sereni 12, 20
  Sereni's intertextual dialogue with 6, 15, 22, 28, 30, 90–1, 190, 193–6, 207, 259, 263, 265
    in Diario d'Algeria 233–4
    in Frontiera 62, 68, 71
    in Stella variabile 111–16, 121, 176, 252
    in Gli strumenti umani 87–8, 166, 175
  Sereni's writings on 23, 59, 91–2, 104, 126, 258
mourning 153, 228, 235, 260
  failed 117, 147, 174, 229–30, 249
  see also melancholia

Index 287

narrative:
  contamination of the lyric 202, 204, 264
  discourse 133–4, 175
  and lyric elements as contiguous in Sereni 20, 21 n. 52, 22, 159
  poem(s) 17
  Sereni's desire for 11 n. 21
  time and 159, 162, 262
  works, by Sereni 23
narcissism, *see* psychoanalysis
negativity 28, 68, 90, 147, 181
  of desire 174, 240
  of language 75, 160, 247, 260
Neri, Laura 36
Noferi, Adelia 153 n. 33, 180 n.

Ó Ceallacháin, Eanna 97 n. 14
ontology 50, 266
Oran, *see* Algeria
Orelli, Giorgio 9 n. 17, 91 n.
original sin, of lyric discourse 2, 40
origins 4, 6, 11–12, 15, 40, 98, 116, 140, 150, 234, 266
  of desire 29–30, 39, 109, 158–60, 183 n., 215, 218–19, 225, 243
  of language (speaking subject) 42–3, 63, 75, 152, 249, 259
  of the lyric tradition 1, 25–6, 128, 265
  of poetry 24, 51, 54, 128, 142, 181, 260
Orpheus 68, 164
  Orphism 28, 60, 66–8, 101, 137, 239
Other, the 26, 33, 50–1, 61, 139, 158, 184
  loss of 172, 178
  otherness 6, 56, 64, 102, 168, 170, 184
  the self and 74–5, 94, 115, 117, 132, 144, 152, 162, 262
Ovid 141 n.

Paci, Enzo 8
Pagliarani, Elio 17, 36 n. 16
Pagnanelli, Remo 18 n. 42, 32 n., 39–40
Pampaloni, Geno 18
Papi, Fulvio 31–2, 102–03
Parronchi, Alessandro 9, 197
Pascoli, Giovanni 9, 128
Pasternak, Boris 9
Pavese, Cesare 1, 198 n. 27
Pellini, Pierluigi 187 n. 3
Perryman, Marcus 3 n., 4 n., 5 n., 10 n., 13 n. 26, 15 n. 35, 17 n. 40, 21 n. 52, 26 n., 103 n. 23, 213 n. 52, 216 n. 55, 217 n. 61, 218 n., 248 n. 91, 264 n. 11

Pertile, Lino 210, 237 n. 79
Petrarca, Francesco:
  deixis in 155–8, 162–5, 265
  desire in 29–30, 64 n. 28, 159, 181, 190, 193–4
  idyll in 141
  landscape in 146, 160, 233
  melancholia in 147, 244, 247
  phantasm in 152–4, 199
  place in lyric tradition 1–2, 10, 25–6, 37, 59, 188, 260
  poetic identity in 258
  poetic memory in 27, 100
  Sereni's intertextual dialogue with 6, 22, 83, 127–8, 134, 140, 148–9, 184–5, 261, 263
    in *Frontiera* 186
    in *Stella variabile* 144–5, 150, 175–80, 182–3
    in *Gli strumenti umani* 135, 166, 168–74
  Sereni's writings on 129–33, 136–9, 142–3
Petronio, Giuseppe 205–06
phantasm:
  deictic 69, 260
  of the desiring subject 35, 142, 144–5, 203, 259
  in/of the landscape 5 n., 29, 77, 87, 129–31, 141, 155–7, 159, 168–72
  in melancholia 191, 209, 213, 222–5, 228, 230, 232–6, 241–2
  memorial 115–16, 174, 182–3
  as a *mise en scène* of desire 143, 151–3, 158, 173, 181, 184
  of the object of desire 26, 43, 80, 99, 135, 139, 202, 261
  poetic 83, 134, 140, 162–4, 175, 178, 187, 190, 247–8, 263
  of poetry 89, 98, 127–8, 132, 148–9, 154, 160, 180, 199, 253–5
  and its relation to the uncanny 39 n. 22
  text and 205, 207
  see also deixis at phantasma, hallucination
phenomenology 47, 54 n. 10, 63, 73, 109
poetic space 21, 34, 46, 50, 260–1
  control of 74
  deixis and 55–7, 89–90
  desire in 97
  of liminality 92–4, 99–100, 103, 111, 117, 127
  revolution in 52
  in Sereni's *Frontiera* 60–2
  in Sereni's *Gli strumenti umani* 77, 84–6

Pontalis, Jean Bertrand 151, 154 n. 34, 173, 183
Pound, Ezra 9, 23, 192, 264
Pozzi, Antonia 8
Prete, Antonio 35, 58
Preti, Giulio 8
primal scene, *see* psychoanalysis
Proserpine 215
prosopopoeia 122–3, 160
Proust, Marcel 17
    Sereni's intertextual dialogue with 100–01, 126, 166, 171–2, 175, 178, 195, 263–4
psychoanalysis:
    La Chose/Das Ding in 30, 234–5, 244, 249
    drives in:
        death drive (*thanatos*) 44 n. 39, 47 n. 41, 147 n. 24, 230, 260
        scopic drive 107–11
    ego in 41, 54–6, 177 n. 66, 228–30, 241
    eros in 39–40, 230, 260
    the Imaginary in 108, 110, 127
    legacy of, for Sereni 26
    as methodology 27, 32–3, 35, 38–9, 265–6
    mirror stage in 62–3, 77, 108
    narcissism in 2, 40, 72, 209, 249
    primal scene in 7
    Real, the in 235
    semiotic in 47–8, 50
    subject in process/on trial in 46–8
    symbolic in 63, 81 n. 41, 109–10
    uncanny in 7, 39 n. 22, 86
    see also melancholia
purgatory:
    landscape of 13, 216
    as paradigm, in Sereni 186, 191–2, 202, 210–12, 217
    purgatorial memory 224–5
    purgatorialità [purgatorial quality] of the Serenian subject 15, 188, 190, 218–20, 255

Quasimodo, Salvatore 9–10

Ramat, Silvio 11, 166 n., 169, 172, 190, 193
Rebora, Roberto 9 n. 17
redemption:
    desire for, in Sereni 70
    lack of, in Sereni 186, 212, 220–1, 243–4
    of subjectivity and language, in Dante 30, 236

regression 39, 49–50, 169
    linguistic 86
    as symptom of melancholia 185–6, 209, 212–13, 215, 225, 229, 235, 253 n. 96
Riccobono, Rossella 94
Ricoeur, Paul 55, 62–3
Rimbaud, Arthur 22, 34
Risi, Nelo 9 n. 17
Robinson, Peter 3 n., 4 n., 5 n., 10 n., 13 n. 26, 15 n. 35, 17 n. 40, 21 n. 52, 26 n., 103 n. 23, 213 n. 52, 216 n. 55, 217 n. 61, 218 n., 248 n. 91, 264 n. 11
Rossani, Ottavio 13, 15 n. 38

Saba, Umberto 9, 22, 25, 198 n. 27, 263
Salinas, Pedro 198 n. 27
salvation 37 n. 18, 88 n.
    in Dante 236, 239, 243
    hope for, in Sereni 210
    lack of, in Sereni 190, 215, 246, 262
Sánchez-Pardo, Esther 147 n. 24
Saussure, Ferdinand de 54 n. 9, 81 n. 41
scopic drive, *see* psychoanalysis
Scorrano, Luigi 187, 197
Segre, Cesare 208 n. 40
semiotic, *see* psychoanalysis
Sereni, Vittorio:
    on Char 129–31
    creative crisis 17, 35, 40, 249
    on Dante 138–9, 188, 205–06
    death 4, 44
    early life 7–9, 12
    on Eliot 197–8
    experience of exile 13, 188, 213, 215–16
    on the genesis of poetry 14, 17, 24, 38, 59, 106, 264
    on Leopardi 1–2, 135–6, 198
    literary friendships 5 n., 8, 18–19, 112, 205, 217
    on Montale 11 n. 21, 59, 91–3, 97–100, 102, 104–05, 115–16, 194, 207
    on Petrarch 129–3, 135–9, 142–3, 145–6, 148, 174
    poetry:
        Diario d'Algeria 13–15, 186, 188–90, 215–23, 231–6
        Frontiera 9–12, 52, 56–7, 59–62, 65–74, 106, 136–7, 186, 213–15, 259
        Stella variabile 21, 90–1, 106–07, 111–26, 144–5, 149–50, 154–5, 176–83, 192, 199–204, 244–7, 249–57

Gli strumenti umani 16, 74–89, 134–5, 147–8, 165–75, 191
prose writings:
Gli immediati dintorni: primi e secondi 1 n. 2, 3 n., 4 n., 5 n., 8nn. 11–12, 13 n. 26, 15 n. 35, 22, 24 n. 59, 26 n., 50 n. 46, 59 n. 21, 91 n. 3, 146 n. 22, 198 n. 97, 212 n. 50, 216 n. 56, 218 n.
Letture preliminari 23, 261 n. 6
Sentieri di gloria: note e ragionamenti sulla letteratura 11 n. 21, 25 n. 91 n., 129 n. 2, 195 n. 19, 263 n. 10
La tentazione della prosa 22 n. 53, 23 n. 55, 216 n. 57
on Proust 171–2, 178
on Saba 9 n. 18, 25, 263 n. 10
on Sereni 10, 22–3, 56 n. 146, 226, 248
as translator 1 n. 2, 5 n., 17, 23, 129–32, 149, 264
shifters, see *deixis*
Sibyl, the 254
signs:
deictics as empty 53, 75
failure of, in melancholia 235, 249, 253
in the landscape 4–5, 190, 232
poetry as a field of 31, 125
retreat of, behind objects 116, 259, 265
signifying chain 43
theory of linguistic 183 n. 151
in Kristeva 46 n. 39, 47, 63 n. 25, 73 n. 33
in Lacan 41–2, 44, 81 n. 41, 110, 152
silence 20 n. 47, 167–8
creative, in Sereni 17
as an impetus to poetry 11, 45–6, 73–5, 161, 165, 183,
language bordering on or ending in 48, 67, 89, 102, 174–5, 246, 252
in melancholia 30, 235, 249
of objects 123
see also aphasia
sin 206, 233–4, 243, 255
associated with the lyric subject 2, 40
memories of [*memorie triste*] 29–30, 186, 224, 239–40, 244–6
see also damnation
Singleton, Charles 207 n. 38
Sinisgalli, Leonardo 9–10
Socialism 18, 78–9
solitude 197 n. 25, 198
poetic 1–2, 73, 145
Solmi, Sergio 23, 37, 91 n.
soul 1, 30 n. 64

in Dante 199, 208–09, 211–12, 221, 233, 236, 246, 255
in Eliot 196, 252
in Petrarch 131, 161, 165
in Sereni 19, 40, 71, 134, 218, 252, 255
Southerden, Francesca 125 n., 241 n., 251 n.
space:
of the dead 190–1, 214–15
of desire 43, 75, 140–1, 144–5, 160, 173, 211
dispossession of 77, 121–2, 125
as ground of twentieth-century lyric 262
ideal, of the lyric 1–3, 6, 20–1, 26, 58–9, 137, 184, 259
of identity 24
of language 33, 45, 76, 164, 239
melancholy 209, 228–33, 235, 249, 252–3
of memory 96, 223–5
of objects 120
of the phantasm 128, 130–1, 142, 151, 154–7, 162, 172, 182–3
psychological 15
search for 22, 25, 28
time and 48, 51, 54, 98
see also desire-space, idyll, landscape, poetic space, topography
speech:
act 52
as born from loss/lack 42
in deixis 54
and dream 74
empty/frustrated 199, 248–9, 252
full 239
and gaze 89
hybrid 246
intersubjective field of 125
of the landscape 150
as the locus of identity of the Serenian 'I' 45
vagaries of 75, 78, 80–3, 87, 118, 121, 153
in writing 45–6
see also discourse, language
Spitzer, Leo 246 n.
stasis 2, 62, 67–8, 103, 168, 185, 221, 253, 256
in melancholia 229
subjectivity:
in crisis 28, 84, 89, 118, 121, 198–9, 254–6
de-centred 41
in deixis 51–5, 61–2, 67, 73, 141

subjectivity: (*cont.*)
   and desire 4, 93, 102, 128, 145, 150–1, 155–7, 180–4 , 210–11
   displaced 15, 74–5, 77, 194, 260, 265
   inter- 122–3
   and landscape 6, 60, 129–31, 159–61, 170–4
   in language 3, 26, 33, 38, 52–3, 63–4, 258
   liminal/threshold 90–1, 94, 100–01, 105–06, 126–7, 144, 262, 264
   lyric 12, 27, 34–7, 50, 139
   melancholy 147–8, 186, 192, 209, 212–21, 228–36, 243–9, 252–3, 257, 261
   and perception 107–11, 125–6
   and phantasm 142–3, 153–4, 158, 190–1
   in process/on trial 46–8
   questing 21, 24–5
   redemption of, in Dante 236–43
   speaking subject 42–4, 258–9
   split subject 45, 82, 149, 152, 162–4
   weak subject (*soggetto debole*) 49
   writing subject 7, 32, 207, 263
suicide 45, 221, 233, 246
symbolic, *see* psychoanalysis
Symbolism 10, 33, 37
syntax 131, 138
   in deixis 27, 89
   of desire 151–2, 175
   in Sereni 81, 174, 203, 252–3
   and the speaking subject 46, 63, 73 n. 33

Tandello, Emmanuela 2 n. 4, 97 n. 14, 130 n. 6
teleology 248
temporality 51, 246, 262
   linguistic 52 n. 4, 53 n. 6, 54–5, 77 n. 38, 81, 178, 182–3
   lost time 37, 48, 116–17, 191, 198, 208, 216–17, 223, 232, 266
   melancholy 191, 233, 235, 253
   and memory 62, 100–01, 172, 247, 255
   poetic 27, 66–8, 97–8, 139–42, 159, 211, 248
   time regained 192, 255
   see also deixis, memory
Testa, Enrico 35, 38 n., 53, 61, 73, 155, 177, 265
topography:
   of death 230
   of desire 29, 159, 184, 235
   of Eden 215, 244

   and identity 17, 60, 127–9, 145, 232, 260
   of liminality 90, 99, 102, 111–12, 119, 142
   of Luino 12, 16
   of the lyric 'I' 174, 262
   and memory 30, 133, 169, 179, 251
   of the phantasm 157
   poetic 22, 24, 32, 176, 182, 208, 215, 258
   purgatorial 191
   of the subject after Freud 41–4
transcendence 131, 158, 234, 239, 243, 255
   desire for, in Sereni 91, 118, 210
   lack of, in Sereni 28, 116, 121, 127, 182, 185, 253
   transcendental ego of phenomenology 46 n. 39, 47 n. 41, 63, 73 n. 33, 207
transience 83–4, 101, 158
   of the object of desire 59, 73–4
   poetic 146, 148
   of the speaking subject 44–5
Treccani, Ernesto 8
tristitia 30 n. 64
   see also melancholia
trauma 143, 157, 172, 222
   sites of 99–100, 131, 191, 234
   writing and 38, 40
tropes 27, 60, 89–91, 96, 126, 160, 257, 259
   see also deixis, liminality

uncanny, the *see* psychoanalysis
underworld 66, 68, 164, 202, 215
Ungaretti, Giuseppe 9, 11, 14, 22
utopia 2, 29, 149, 189, 234, 255, 263, 266

Valentini, Alvaro 35
Valéry, Paul 9
Vattimo, Gianni 49
Vaucluse 22, 129–31, 149, 159, 179–80
   Luino as Sereni's 146, 165, 184
Vickers, Nancy 181
Vigorelli, Giancarlo 9, 10 n., 56 n.
Virgil:
   author 66, 112, 214
   character in Dante's *Commedia* 202, 203 n. 34, 221, 236–9
vision 6, 61–2, 66, 83 n.
   double, in deixis 53, 91
   geometral 108–11

limits of 103, 115, 122–6, 146, 148, 256
and memory 96–8, 160, 164–5, 252
oppositional structures in 120–1
and the phantasm 223, 233, 261
search for reciprocity in 104, 106–07
visionary experience 2, 140, 190
see also gaze, scopic drive
Vittorini, Elio 17, 21, 199, 202–03
voice 20 n. 47, 24, 75, 115, 161, 191, 198, 207, 256–7
  birth of the 63
  in deixis 28, 51, 156
  fading of the 99, 259, 266
  and landscape 144, 164, 246, 259
  monologism 20, 32, 40, 47, 56, 78, 80, 87, 118, 129, 134, 199
  plurivocality 149–50, 204, 208, 262–3

poetic 10–11, 21–2, 34, 54, 64, 94, 130 n. 6, 133, 264
  in Sereni's poetry 44, 48, 59, 67, 88, 122, 134, 168, 171, 254
  as a site of loss 146, 159, 181–3, 240

war 13, 16, 19, 213, 217–19
  see also Algeria, imprisonment
West, Rebecca 94
Williams, William Carlos 17, 23, 264
Wright, Elizabeth 33

Yourcenar, Marguerite 196 n. 22

Zanzotto, Andrea 7 n., 11–12, 17, 36–37, 40, 76, 130 n. 6, 132 n. 9, 154, 258 n. 1, 261–2
Zumthor, Paul 160

Index of Titles of Poems by Vittorio Sereni

A un compagno d'infanzia 266
Addio Lugano Bella 25, 51, 143–5
The African Sickness 217–23, 225
Gli amici 21 n. 49, 117 n.
Ancora sulla strada di Zenna 77, 159, 165–75
And again in a dream the tent's edge 189–90
Appointment at an Unusual Hour 78–83
Appuntamento a ora insolita 78–83
The Ashes 147–8
Autostrada della Cisa 117 n., 192, 230, 239 n. 80, 254

Bastava un niente 179–80
Beautiful Lugano Goodbye 25, 51, 143–5

Le ceneri 147–8
Città di notte 15 n. 37
City at Night 15 n. 37

Diana 56–7, 213 n. 53
The Disease of the Elm 117 n., 180–3, 244–7
A Dream 31–2

E ancora in sogno d'una tenda s'agita 189–90
Encounter 60–2, 80, 86
L'equivoco 104, 177–8

A Factory Visit 16–17
Fissità 19 n. 45, 91, 102–03, 117 n.
Fixity 19 n. 45, 91, 102–03, 117 n.
The Friends 21 n. 49, 117 n.

A Holiday Place 19–21, 28, 31, 32 n., 39 n. 22, 40, 72 n., 91–3, 110–11, 117–27, 145 n. 21, 195, 196 n. 21, 199–204, 208–09, 232, 244, 249–57

In me il tuo ricordo 70–3
Incontro 60–2, 80, 86
Interview with a Suicide 134–5, 203
Intervista a un suicida 134–5, 203
Inverno 65–71, 101
Italian in Greece 185 n., 188 n. 6
Italiano in Grecia 185 n., 188 n. 6

Lavori in corso 39 n. 22, 69 n.
The Lines 38, 45
Luino-Luvino 159, 175–9

La malattia dell'olmo 117 n., 180–3, 244–7
Il male d'Africa 217–23, 225
The Misapprehension 104, 177–8
Il muro 84–8, 104

Niccolò 19 n. 45, 28, 91, 111–17, 127
No-more-than-human spaces here 150 n.
Non sovrumani spazi qui 150 n.
A nothing sufficed 179–80

Often through tortuous alleys 231–3, 236
On the Zenna Road Again 77, 159, 165–75

Paura seconda 44–5
Un posto di vacanza 19–21, 28, 31, 32 n., 39 n. 22, 40, 72 n., 91–3, 110–11, 117–27, 145 n. 21, 195, 196 n. 21, 199–204, 208–09, 232, 244, 249–57

A Return 76–7
Un ritorno 76–7

Second Fear 44–5
Un sogno 31–2
Spesso per viottoli tortuosi 231–3, 236
Strada di Zenna 60, 165, 166 n., 167–9, 215

To a Childhood Companion 266

I versi 38, 45
Vertical Village 150
Via Scarlatti 89, 197n. 25
Villaggio verticale 150
Una visita in fabbrica 16–17

The Wall 84–8, 104
Winter 65–71, 101
Works in Progress 39 n. 22, 69 n.

Your memory in me 70–3

Zenna Road 60, 165, 166 n., 167–9, 215